# Perceptual Learning

# Perceptual Learning

Edited by **Robert L. Goldstone** and **Douglas L. Medin**

Department of Psychology
Indiana University
Bloomington, Indiana

Department of Psychology
Northwestern University
Evanston, Illinois

**Philippe G. Schyns**

University of Glasgow
Glasgow, United Kingdom

THE PSYCHOLOGY OF
LEARNING AND MOTIVATION, Volume 36

ACADEMIC PRESS
San Diego   London   Boston   New York
Sydney   Tokyo   Toronto

BF683
.P78
vol. 36

This book is printed on acid-free paper. ∞

Academic Press
*a division of Harcourt Brace & Company*
525 B Street, Suite 1900, San Diego, California 92101-4495, USA
http://www.apnet.com

Academic Press Limited
24-28 Oval Road, London NW1 7DX, UK
http://www.hbuk.co.uk/ap/

International Standard Book Number: 0-12-543336-0

PRINTED IN THE UNITED STATES OF AMERICA
97  98  99  00  01  02  BB  9  8  7  6  5  4  3  2  1

# CONTENTS

## LEARNING TO BRIDGE BETWEEN PERCEPTION AND COGNITION

*Robert L. Goldstone, Philippe G. Schyns, and Douglas L. Medin*

## THE AFFORDANCES OF PERCEPTUAL INQUIRY: PICTURES ARE LEARNED FROM THE WORLD, AND WHAT THAT FACT MIGHT MEAN ABOUT PERCEPTION QUITE GENERALLY

*Julian Hochberg*

## PERCEPTUAL LEARNING OF ALPHANUMERIC-LIKE CHARACTERS

*Richard M. Shiffrin and Nancy Lightfoot*

## EXPERTISE IN OBJECT AND FACE RECOGNITION

*James Tanaka and Isabel Gauthier*

## INFANT SPEECH PERCEPTION: PROCESSING CHARACTERISTICS, REPRESENTATIONAL UNITS, AND THE LEARNING OF WORDS

*Peter D. Eimas*

## CONSTRAINTS ON THE LEARNING OF SPATIAL TERMS: A COMPUTATIONAL INVESTIGATION

*Terry Regier*

## LEARNING TO TALK ABOUT THE PROPERTIES OF OBJECTS: A NETWORK MODEL OF THE DEVELOPMENT OF DIMENSIONS

*Linda B. Smith, Michael Gasser, and
Catherine M. Sandhofer*

# CONTRIBUTORS

Numbers in parentheses indicate the pages on which the authors' contributions begin.

**Dana H. Ballard** (309), Department of Computer Science, University of Rochester, Rochester, New York 14627

**James A. Bednar** (257), Department of Computer Sciences, The University of Texas at Austin, Austin, Texas 78712

**Yoonsuck Choe** (257), Department of Computer Sciences, The University of Texas at Austin, Austin, Texas 78712

**Virginia R. de Sa** (309), Department of Computer Science, University of Toronto, Toronto, Ontario M5S 1A4, Canada

**Shimon Edelman** (353), Department of Applied Mathematics and Computer Science, The Weizmann Institute of Science, Rehovot 76100, Israel; Center for Biological and Computer Learning, Massachusetts Institute of Technology, E25-201, Cambridge, MA 02142

**Peter D. Eimas** (127), Department of Cognitive and Linguistic Sciences, Brown University, Providence, Rhode Island 02912

**Michael Gasser** (219), Departments of Computer Science and Linguistics, Indiana University, Bloomington, Indiana 47405

**Isabel Gauthier** (85), Department of Psychology, Yale University, New Haven, Connecticut 06511

**Robert L. Goldstone** (1), Department of Psychology, Indiana University, Bloomington, Indiana 47405-1301

**Julian Hochberg** (15), Department of Psychology, Columbia University, New York, New York 10027

**Nathan Intrator** (353), School of Mathematical Sciences, Sackler Faculty of Exact Sciences, Tel Aviv University, Tel Aviv 69978, Israel

**Nancy Lightfoot** (45), Department of Psychology, Indiana University, Bloomington, Indiana 47405

**Douglas L. Medin** (1), Department of Psychology, Northwestern University, Evanston, Illinois 60208-2710

**Risto Miikulainen** (257), Department of Computer Sciences, The University of Texas at Austin, Austin, Texas 78712

**Terry Regier** (171), Department of Psychology, University of Chicago, Chicago, Illinois 60637

**Catherine M. Sandhofer** (219), Department of Psychology, Indiana University, Bloomington, Indiana 47405

**Philippe G. Schyns** (1), University of Glasgow, Glasgow G12 8QB, United Kingdom

**Richard M. Shiffrin** (45), Department of Psychology, Indiana University, Bloomington, Indiana 47405

**Joseph Sirosh** (257), Department of Computer Sciences, The University of Texas at Austin, Austin, Texas 78712

**Linda B. Smith** (219), Department of Psychology, Indiana University, Bloomington, Indiana 47405

**James Tanaka** (85), Department of Psychology, Oberlin College, Oberlin, Ohio 44074

# PREFACE

The contributions to this special volume of *The Psychology of Learning and Motivation* are concerned with perceptual learning. Over the past few years, there has been a resurgence of interest in the field. Since the last heyday of the field, culminating perhaps in Eleanor Gibson's 1969 book *Perceptual Learning,* the methods of inquiry have changed significantly. Maturing disciplines have been able to shed new light on the mechanisms underlying adaptation. Researchers in computer science have made valuable contributions to our understanding of human psychology by describing functional algorithms for adaptation in networks involving many interacting units. Neuroscience has provided concrete mechanisms of adaptation, and research on neural plasticity has recently experienced tremendous growth. In many cases, perceptual changes that have been empirically observed through studies of experts, laboratory training studies, and different cultures are given concrete accounts by computational and neural models.

Several of the chapters in this volume describe state-of-the-art computational theories of human perceptual flexibility. Other chapters discuss recent advances in developmental psychology and individual differences. Evidence from developmental psychology is important because many of the most dramatic changes to our perceptual systems occur within the first seven years of life. Analyses of expertise and cross-cultural comparisons gauge the perceptual impact of extended environmental influences. Combined with controlled studies from cognitive psychology exploring adult training and transfer, these approaches provide perspectives that support and inform one another.

Perceptual learning involves relatively long-lasting changes to an organism's perceptual system that improve its ability to respond to its environment. As people gain experience in their world, their perceptual abilities are oftentimes impressively transformed. Children organize their perceptual world differently from adults, and experts often have unique perceptual skills within their domain of expertise. In a variety of ways, the contributors to this volume argue that perceptual abilities, rather than being fixed and stable, are flexible and influenced by tasks, needs, and the environment. The chapters focus on new research techniques for exploring the mechanisms that drive perceptual learning, integrating empirical work on perceptual learning in humans and formal modeling of the resulting data. Collectively, the contributions reflect an interdisciplinary approach to the problem of perceptual learning, describing research from developmental psychology, adult perception, language acquisition, expert/novice differences, computational modeling, and neuroscience.

Through perceptual learning, an organism's initial representations of its world are adapted. Perceptual learning can exert a profound influence on behavior precisely because it occurs early during information processing and thus alters the input sent to all subsequent cognitive processes. Given this far-reaching impact, it is not surprising that researchers in several fields have taken up the challenge of ascertaining how perceptual adaptation occurs. Traditional disciplinary boundaries will have to be crossed for a complete account, and the contributions to this volume go a long way toward unifying these disciplines by describing the common mechanisms underlying perceptual learning.

*Robert L. Goldstone*
*Philippe G. Schyns*
*Douglas L. Medin*

# LEARNING TO BRIDGE BETWEEN PERCEPTION AND COGNITION

*Robert L. Goldstone*
*Philippe G. Schyns*
*Douglas L. Medin*

In building models of cognition, it is customary to commence construction on the foundations laid by perception. Perception is presumed to provide us with an initial source of information that is operated on by subsequent cognitive processes. And, as with the foundation of a house, a premium is placed on stability and solidity. Stable edifices require stable support structures. By this view, our cognitive processes are well behaved to the degree that they can depend on the stable structures established by our perceptual system.

Considered collectively, the contributions to this volume suggest an alternative metaphor for understanding the relation between perception and cognition. The architectural equivalent of perception may be a bridge rather than a foundation. The purpose of a bridge is to provide support, but they do so by adapting to the supported vehicles. Bridges, by design, sway under the weight of heavy vehicles, built on the principle that it is better to bend than break. Bridges built with rigid materials are often less resilient than their more flexible counterparts. Similarly, the chapters collected here raise the possibility that perception supports cognition by flexibly adapting to the requirements imposed by cognitive tasks. Perception may not be stable, but its departures from stability may facilitate rather than hamper its ability to support cognition. Cognitive processes involved in categorization, com-

THE PSYCHOLOGY OF LEARNING
AND MOTIVATION, VOL. 36

parison, object recognition, and language may shift perception, but perception becomes better tuned to these tasks as a result.

## I.  Insights From Perceptual Learning

One of the standard strategies of cognitive science is to establish a set of vocabulary elements, and to explain cognitive processes in terms of operations on this set of elements. The names and natures of these elements depend on the researcher's domain. In object recognition, these elements may be simple geometric solids ("geons," Biederman, 1987), textural aspects ("textons," Julesz, 1981), or primitive features (Treisman & Gelade, 1980). In speech perception, "minimal distinctive features" represent phonemes (Jakobson, Fant, & Halle, 1963). Objects to be compared or categorized are often described in terms of elementary features (Tversky, 1977). For complex scenarios, vocabularies of "conceptual primitives" (Schank, 1972) or "semantic primitives" (Wierzbicka, 1992) have been proposed. In many cases, a finite number of specific primitives are hypothesized. For example, about 36 geons, 10 minimal distinctive features, 20 conceptual primitives, and 30 semantic primitives have been proposed as sufficient to describe the basic entities in their respective domains. By combining these primitives in different arrangements, a small set of building blocks can construct a virtually infinite variety of entities.

An alternative account of cognition is that its building blocks are neither fixed nor finite, but rather adapt to the requirements of the tasks for which they are employed (Schyns & Rodet, in press). An extended development of this account is given by Schyns, Goldstone, and Thibaut (in press). Applied to perceptual learning, the claim is that perception does not provide a single breakdown of an object or event into building blocks. As notably argued by E. Gibson (1969), the perceptual interpretation of an entity depends on the observer's history, training, and acculturation. These factors, together with psychophysical constraints, mold the set of building blocks. There may be no single, privileged set of perceptual primitives because the building blocks themselves are adaptive.

Advancing from fixed to adaptive building blocks provides a new perspective on some old problems. One notorious difficulty with representations based on a limited set of elements is that it is hard to choose exactly the right set of elements that will suffice to accommodate all of the future entities that will need to be represented. On the one hand, if a small set of primitive elements is chosen, then it is likely that two entities will eventually arise that must be distinguished, but cannot with any combination of available primitives. On the other hand, if a set of primitives is sufficiently large to construct all entities that might occur, then it will likely include many elements that lie unused, waiting for their moment of need to possibly arise (Schyns et al., in press). However, by developing new elements as needed, newly important discriminations can cause the construction of building blocks that are tailored for the discrimination. If one goes for a short camping trip it is reasonable to pack cans of ready-made food. If one goes for a life-long camping trip, then one must pack tools that are useful in creating new food: fishing line, seeds, rake, and rope. By the same token, given the long and unforeseeable journeys we make, perceptual systems should be adaptive enough to develop new tools.

Evidence that people use a particular set of primitive elements is perfectly consistent with elements being developed via perceptual learning. The geons, textons, or conceptual primitives of componential theories may be the end product of a general perceptual learning strategy. Recent research in computer science has shown how sets of primitives, including oriented line segments, Gabor filters, and size detectors can be created by a system provided naturalistic scenes (e.g., Mikkulainen et al., this volume). In fact, it is more than a coincidence that computer systems often converge on primitives that bear striking similarities to those proposed by researchers advocating fixed primitives. Researchers explicitly devise their sets so as to capture important regularities in the environment—the same regularities being captured by computer systems that learn from natural inputs. The advantages of learning, rather than simply positing, elements are that (1) mechanisms are in place for acquiring slightly different primitives if the environment is modified, and (2) specialized domains within the environment can have tailored sets of primitives designed for them (Edelman & Intrator, this volume).

We believe that the acquisition of new perceptual skills is of importance not simply for researchers in perceptual learning, but for other fields as well. Perceptually minded researchers will eventually have to integrate learning into their theories. Early feature perception research indicated impressively small influences of learning and practice. In Treisman and Gelade's (1980) field-defining research on feature search, the influence of distractor letters in a conjunctive search remained essentially unchanged throughout 1664 trials, suggesting that new primitives could not be formed for conjunctions of color and shape. Although these results are generally replicable, they may have had the adverse effect of dissuading perceptual psychologists from exploring other training effects. In fact, Shiffrin and Lightfoot (this volume) report fivefold improvements in response times in a similar, conjunctive search paradigm in which the conjunctions are defined not by color and shape but by different line segments. Many studies of perception have underestimated the influence of training by the standard practice of eliminating the first few blocks of performance in a task. From a perceptual learning perspective, the common nuisance effect that performance does not stabilize until after several blocks of practice takes on notable interest. Researchers in perception cannot afford to disregard perceptual learning effects for the simple reason that they account for an impressively large proportion of variance in human performance.

In the subdiscipline of perception devoted to object recognition, perceptual learning also provides new insights. Perceptual learning can endow object recognition systems with greater testability and applicability. Perceptual vocabulary elements derived from learning systems can be compared with those assumed by object recognition theorists. To the extent that both agree, we have a potential mechanism to explain how a particular finite set of elements came into existence. Furthermore, by incorporating perceptual learning into object recognition systems, the systems can attain greater generality. For example, Biederman (1987) limits his geon theory to explaining basic level categorizations. That is, he proposes that different arrangements of geons can serve to discriminate cats from dogs, but not German Shepards from Golden Retrievers. This is a somewhat awkward limit on geon theory, for the simple reason that similar mechanisms appear to be used for basic level and more subordinate categorizations. In fact, Tanaka and Gauthier (this volume) present evidence that expertise can gradually shift whether a particular categorization is basic or not. Dog experts can categorize species of dogs as quickly as they can discriminate dogs from cats. This influence of expertise on categorization ability is predicted if perceptual learning can shift attention to discriminating features, or if it can develop entirely new features to aid discrimination. In either case, adding perceptual learning mechanisms to object recognition systems can extend their range of application, allowing them to accommodate closely related tasks.

Finally, a more general problem with treating object recognition as a separate process from learning is that no account is given for how object descriptions are initially internalized. Even under the assumption that we recognize objects by decomposing them into elements, we still need processes that learn object descriptions. One might assume that the first time an object is viewed, a description is formed and a trace is laid down for it. After this initial registration, standard object recognition routines are applied. This approach would preserve the separation of object recognition and learning, but given the strong influence of object familiarity on recognition, it is too gross a simplification. Object learning occurs simultaneously to, and interacts with, object recognition.

Perceptual learning may be relevant not just to perception researchers, but to those interested in higher-level cognition as well. Many of the chapters (Regier, this volume; Smith, Gasser, & Sandhofer, this volume) describe mutual facilitations between perceptual learning and language. Learning proper word usage often requires learning to attend established dimensions (Regier), or establishing dimensions (Smith et al., this volume).

One benefit of a perceptual learning perspective for researchers interested in concepts and categorization is to suggest an alternative to complex rule formation. Over the years, many researchers have proposed that concepts are represented by logical rules such as "white and square or circle" (Bruner, Goodnow, & Austin, 1956; Nosofsky, Palmeri, & McKinley, 1994). However, combining disparate sources of evidence into Boolean expressions may be quite unnatural. Participants in these experiments seem to adopt a laborious problem-solving strategy that seems quite different from learning about common objects such as dogs, tables, or trees. The possibility raised by perceptual learning is that concept learning involves developing new perceptual features and abilities which might reduce much of the need for complex categorization rules. These rules only seem necessary when the perceptual underpinnings of our concepts are ignored. It is worth entertaining the possibility that natural concepts harness natural perceptual learning processes.

Extending beyond psychology, perceptual learning can also play an important role in neuroscience and computer science. Interest in neural plasticity, particularly within the somatosensory cortex, is at an all-time high. Surprisingly fruitful links between neural changes and behavior have been discovered (see Tanaka & Gauthier and Miikkulainen et al.'s chapters in this volume). For computer science, sensitivity to perceptual learning can help solve problems in pattern recognition, reasoning, and induction that would otherwise be intractable. Computer scientists, like their counterparts in psychology, have tried to build systems for induction, reasoning, and creativity by composition of primitive elements according to rules. Many current systems are too constrained because their primitives are too abstract and do not develop through interactions with the environment. Conversely, these systems are often too unconstrained as well, allowing all possible logical (e.g., boolean) combinations of a set of primitive elements. A serious examination of the constraints of perceptual learning, such as those suggested by Regier's spatial templates or Hochberg's saccadic transitions, provides helpful constraints to truncate the combinatorial explosion of features assumed by many artificial intelligence systems.

## II.  Mechanisms of Perceptual Learning

Arguably, the heyday of perceptual learning was the 1960s, mainly because of the work of Eleanor and James Gibson. They generated considerable excitement for the field, and established the techniques, questions, and agenda for decades of work. One repercussion of the Gibsons' influence is that perceptual learning has become tied to the ecological psychology movement in many people's mind. The Gibsons argued for direct perception of environmental properties rather than mental computation of these properties. They argued that perceptual learning entails picking up previously unused external properties that enable organisms to be better in touch with the true external world (Gibson & Gibson, 1955). From this perspective, the major research goal is to determine what external properties are available to be picked up by people.

The chapters in this volume present a strikingly different approach to perceptual learning. In one way or another, all of the authors are interested in the internal mechanisms that drive perceptual learning. In several cases, a computational approach is taken, wherein theories of perceptual learning are formally instantiated in computer models. The computational approach to perceptual learning emphasizes internal constraints on perception. These constraints often take the form of architectural requirements for perceptual learning. Some chapters highlight the importance of architectures that allow for top-down feedback (Regier; Smith et al). Some stress the interconnectivity between different sensory modalities (De Sa and Ballard), whereas others argue for architectures that compress original object descriptions onto discriminating dimensions (Edelman & Intrator; Smith et al.). Finally, some authors propose architectures that mirror the underlying topology of the modeled set of objects at a concrete (Miikkulainen et al.) or abstract (Edelman & Intrator) level.

In all cases, the chapters propose rich internal structures in order to get perceptual learning off the ground. In doing so, they avoid the first year computer science graduate students' fallacy of "Let's just hook up a camera, give the computer years of television input, and watch it self-organize." The need for structurally sophisticated architectures to permit learning is most evident in Regier's and Eimas' chapters. Regier's layered connectionist network is a far cry from generic perceptrons. His network has many learning biases and predispositions, but these are correctly interpreted not as limiting weaknesses, but rather as testable predictions about the biases that people should, and apparently do, show. Eimas provides convincing evidence that infants come into the world with techniques for segmenting speech into parts that will later allow them to acquire the meaning-bearing units of language.

In short, it is dangerously wrong-headed to view perceptual learning as the opposite of innate disposition, or more generally, to view flexibility as the opposite of constraint. It is only by having a properly constrained architecture that perceptual learning is possible. Even if our goal is to have a single learning process that can acquire distinctly different perceptual vocabularies, we should not be surprised if the process needs to be domain specific. Domain-general learning processes can be devised, but they rarely have the power to produce genuinely novel or emergent forms.

The contributions to this volume focus on perceptual learning from a mechanistic perspective. More than half of the chapters propose particular computational, typically neural network, models; all of the chapters make concrete proposals for what changes with learning. One mechanism, *attention weighting,* involves shifts of attention to diagnostic dimensions (Eimas; Regier). A second mechanism, *detector creation,* involves creating receptors that respond selectively to one specific type of input (Miikkulainen et al. Smith et al.). These systems start with homogenous units, and gradually create specialized units. Once a functionally separated feature has been created, attention-weighting strategies can apply to it. In this way, the first two mechanisms of perceptual learning have a strong dependency relation; selective attention to a feature first requires that the feature has been isolated. A related mechanism, *dimensionalization,* creates topologically ordered sets of detectors (Edelman & Intrator; Miikkulainen et al.). The advantages of dimensionalization are that interference between dimensions is reduced and selective attention becomes possible, information from objects is compressed in efficient representations, and the topological architecture of the system can reflect the topology of the represented objects. This latter property is advantageous because it allows relations within (Miikkulainen et al.) and between (Edelman & Intrator) real-world objects to be inferred by consulting internal representations that are functionally isomorphic to the represented objects.

A fourth mechanism, *unitization,* involves the construction of single functional units that can be triggered when a complex configuration arises (Shiffrin & Lightfoot; Tanaka & Gauthier). Via unitization, a task that originally required detection of several parts can be accomplished by detecting a single unit. Unitization may seem at odds with detector creation and dimensionalization because unitization integrates parts into single wholes, whereas detector creation divides wholes into cleanly separable parts. This apparent contradiction can be transformed into a commonality at a more abstract level. Both mechanisms depend on the requirements established by tasks and stimuli. Objects will tend to be decomposed into their parts if the parts reflect independent sources of variation, or if the parts differ in their relevancy (Schyns & Murphy, 1994). Parts will tend to be unitized if the parts co-occur frequently, all parts indicating a similar response. Thus, unitization and decomposition are two sides of a process that builds appropriate-sized representations for the tasks at hand.

Another mechanism that is inherently tied to the presented stimuli is *contingency detection.* Several authors propose that perceptual learning proceeds by internalizing contingencies within a stimulus. The suggestion is that parts of a stimulus predict other parts of the stimulus. Everyday objects are not random; they exhibit strong internal relations between their parts. By extracting these relations, people can develop associations without any explicit feedback. Instructive contingencies exist at many levels: between different visual regions of a single object (Hochberg), between different sensory modalities (De Sa & Ballard), and between compared objects (Smith et al.). While the default way to implement contingency detection may be through associative learning, Hochberg argues that contingencies may drive perceptual learning by changing action procedures—by changing patterns of successive eye fixations.

### III.  Issues in Perceptual Learning

The chapters raise several issues of general importance for theories of perceptual learning. As efforts to extend perceptual learning theory continue, we expect that the following issues will become central.

### A.   CONSTRAINTS ON PERCEPTUAL LEARNING

Perceptual learning mechanisms integrate two sources of constraints. One constraint on features that are developed to represent objects is based on the manner in which objects are grouped into categories. The second constraint arises from the perceptual biases that facilitate or prevent the extraction of features from the considered objects. One issue concerns the general applicability of perceptual learning mechanisms to conceptual development. Perceptual learning is often evidenced in mature concept learners, using highly unfamiliar materials. The rationale for this approach is simply that the standard stimuli of categorization experiments tend to "wear their features on their sleeves" and could prevent the learning of new stimulus features (Schyns et al., in press). Future research may reveal that perceptual learning principles are limited to the learning of very specialized categories such as X-rays, skin diseases, and so forth. Alternatively, it may turn out that perceptual learning has a broader scope and applies to the early stages of conceptual development. Mature categorizers, who tend to know the relevant featural analysis of most objects would only evoke perceptual learning mechanisms when they learn expert categorizations that require new features. Whether perceptual learning mechanisms have broad or limited application to the understanding of early concept learning is an empirical issue for developmental psychology.

A related issue concerns the nature of the perceptual biases that might apply to the learning of new concepts at different stages of development. For example, it is well known that babies' perceptual processes filter out the fine-grain details of the visual input. More generally, biases arising from the development of the system should be specified in order to understand how the initial perceptual organization might subsequently be affected by tasks and environment. This is obviously a difficult, chicken-and-egg problem, because the perceptual organization at any point of conceptual development might arise from perceptual learning at an earlier developmental stage. However, the interplay between perceptual biases and environmental constraints can be tracked throughout the history of the organism, providing a dynamic, but componential, conception of development.

For mature categorizers who tend to know the features that distinguish between common object classes, it will be particularly important to understand how these relevant features were first determined. For example, curved (e.g., faces) and edged (e.g., chairs, appliances) objects have highly distinct geometric properties that might constrain perceptual learning. While Lowe (1987) suggested that nonaccidental properties of two-dimensional edges were sufficient to recover the three-dimensional structure of the parts of objects, Hoffman and Richards (1984) showed that other principles must apply to the segmentation of smooth objects. Generic perceptual constraints such as Hoffman and Richards' minima rule, but also symmetry and shared motion could offer grounding principles to bootstrap perceptual learning. The search for these principles, and their interactions with task constraints, is an important topic of future research in the perceptual learning that occurs when people interact with real faces, objects and scenes.

## B. Who Teaches the Learner?

One way to compare different approaches to perceptual learning is by seeing "who" (more technically, what) is the teacher for what is learned. Mirroring the distinction between supervised and unsupervised neural networks, some theories use an explicit label or categorization as teacher, whereas for others the teacher is the stimulus itself. Systems that connect percepts to words understandably take advantage of the words as guides for building the percepts (Smith et al; Regier). Even within this approach there are variations in how feedback is used. Regier shows that associations between percepts and labels can be modified not only when they are paired together, but also when one but not the other is presented. By adjusting percept-to-word associations when other words are presented (implementing a mutual exclusivity constraint), the amount of learning resulting from a single episode is dramatically increased. Smith et al. show how dimension-alization can be greatly facilitated by words that do not simply provide correct labels, but provide these labels in the context of a comparison between objects. The labels drive isolation of dimensions by highlighting particular commonalities shared by the compared objects. Both of these chapters augment the feedback provided by standard labels, and thus miti-gate the force of a major criticism of feedback-based models of language— that people do not receive enough feedback in the form of labels to drive learning. If properly implemented, labeling can be a powerful and informa-tive force for perceptual adaptation.

By a similar token, several of the other chapters point out ways in which the stimulus can itself be a surprisingly powerful source of information for learning. Instead of imagining that a label is provided externally for an object and that perception is adapted to better predict the label, one can view part of the stimulus as providing a label for other parts of the stimulus. This strategy is adopted by De Sa and Ballard, who go on to show that several modalities can simultaneously provide labels for each other, thereby pulling the system as a whole up by its own bootstraps. Similarly, regularities within and between objects can be internalized perceptually. Regularities among the shapes of presented objects can be internalized as eye fixation patterns (Hochberg). Strong interdependencies between features can be internalized by creating "chunks" that coalesce the separate features (Shif-frin & Lightfoot). By focusing on differences (sources of variation) instead of similarities within a set of objects, underlying features (Miikkulainen et al.) or dimensions (Edelman & Intrator) can be extracted for describing the set.

In short, what can be learned is a joint function of the teacher and the capabilities of the learner. The teacher's information may be externally supplied, or may be intrinsically packaged in the objects to be learned. In the computational systems described here, the capabilities of the learner are expressed in terms of architectural structures. On both fronts, the chapters hint at the sophistication that will be needed to achieve human-like adaptability, in terms of richly structured architectures and informative, naturalistic inputs.

## C.   CHALLENGES FOR PERCEPTUAL LEARNING

As the mechanisms of perceptual learning become better understood, the challenge will be to relate these mechanisms to work in other domains. Three inviting domains of application are (1) training, (2) neuroscience, and (3) high-level cognition.

Perceptual learning has promise for explaining aspects of training not just in the laboratory, but in the field as well. In addition to obvious domains of perceptual skill acquisition, such as wine tasting and baby chicken gender discrimination (Biederman & Shiffrar, 1987), recent work suggests a strong perceptual component in the development of medical expertise (Norman, Brooks, & Coblentz, 1992; Myles-Worsley, Johnston, & Simons, 1988). In these extended training situations, the relation between perceptual learning and automaticity/attention will need to be characterized. For example, in Logan's (1988) theory of automatization, the influence of training is simply to expose the would-be expert to instances within a domain. Automatic performance relies on the retrieval of specific stored instances, and performance improves as a function of the ease of retrieving relevant instances. Instance retrieval is a potential mechanism of perceptual learning, and is consistent with the finding that perceptual skills are often highly specific and restricted to the trained materials (Kolers & Smythe, 1984).

This conception links expert perceptual skills to automatic, nonstrategic processing. In fact, researchers have contrasted perceptual and strategic consequences of learning. After learning a categorization in which size is important, people may explicitly give extra weight to the size dimension in their judgments (Nosofsky, 1986) or their actual perceptual representations for size may change (Goldstone, 1994). Judgmental processes are usually assumed to be under more strategic, cognitive control than are perceptual ones. However, expert perceptual processing is frequently under impressive strategic control. Experienced tasters often have an enhanced ability to analyze a food with respect to relevant compounds, by excluding or highlighting compounds. The pulls toward greater automaticity and greater strategic control with expertise will eventually have to be reconciled.

A second challenge is to provide a better grounding for perceptual learning changes within the brain. Perceptual changes may be accompanied by brain changes at several scales, ranging from changes in the specialization of individual neurons, to changes in the patterns of local interconnectivity between neurons, to reorganizations of entire topological maps. Real progress in the cognitive neuroscience of perceptual learning will involve more than simply identifying correlations between perceptual behavior and neural structures. It will involve describing the neural processes that implement functional mechanisms of change.

A third challenge is to connect perceptual learning with higher-level cognitive processes. It seems to be difficult to alter low-level perceptual processing by high-level strategies. Genuine changes in perceptual skills probably require perceptual training. Still, as perceptual expertise increases, so does one's verbal vocabulary for the domain, and evidence from wine tasters suggests that true experts' verbal and perceptual vocabularies are closely synchronized (Melcher & Schooler, 1996).

Several of the authors in this volume argue for interactions between perceptual and cognitive processes. There are even grounds for pursuing the more radical possibility that perceptual processes may be co-opted for high-level, abstract cognition (Goldstone & Barsalou, in press). Instead of interactions between two systems, we would have two aspects of the same process. In favor of this hypothesis, many perceptual routines are also useful for general cognition. Selective visual attention processes may be borrowed for cognitive tasks requiring selective application of a criterial definition. Visual binding processes used to connect various features of an object may be useful in creating syntactically bound structured propositions. Sensory synesthesia may provide the early grounding for abstract analogies. In fact, individual differences in mental functioning provide evidence in favor of these conjectures. Schizophrenic patients often show parallel deficits with perceptual and cognitive selective attention tasks. For example, they have difficulty ignoring visual distractors perceptually, and linguistic difficulty inhibiting the incorrect interpretation of an ambiguous word. Conversely, people with autism demonstrate overly selective attentional processes perceptually and cognitively. They often attempt to shut out sensory stimulation by narrowing their perceptual focus, and their generalizations from training are often overly narrow. If this hypothesis has merit, then research on the processes of perceptual learning may tell us about general cognitive learning processes because the processes themselves may be shared.

## IV.  Conclusions

In commenting on her 1963 review of perceptual learning, Eleanor Gibson (1992) lamented, "I wound up pointing out the need for a theory and the prediction that 'more specific theories of perceptual learning are on the way.' I was wrong there—the cognitive psychologists have seldom concerned themselves with perceptual learning" (p. 322). The present volume provides evidence that Gibson's 1963 prediction was accurate. Theories of perceptual learning are available that are specific enough to be implemented on computers, and precise enough to make quantitative predictions regarding behavior. Perceptual learning may still not be one of the mainstream topics within cognitive psychology, but several laboratories seem aware of the need for adaptive perception. Researchers in cognition are interested in providing flexible support structures for higher-level processes, while researchers in perception are interested in explaining the major sources of variability in perception due to training and history. Together, these research programs hold the promise of uniting perceptual and cognitive adaptability.

## REFERENCES

Biederman, I. (1987). Recognition-by-components: A theory of human image understanding. *Psychological Review, 94,* 115-147.

Biederman, I., & Shiffrar, M. M. (1987). Sexing day-old chicks: A case study and expert systems analysis of a difficult perceptual-learning task. *Journal of Experimental Psychology: Learning, Memory, and Cognition, 13,* 640–645.

Bruner, J. S., Goodnow, J. J., & Austin, G. A. (1956). *A study of thinking.* New York: Wiley.

Gibson, E. J. (1992). *An odyssey in learning and perception.* Cambridge, MA: MIT Press.

Gibson, J. J., & Gibson, E. J. (1955). Perceptual learning: Differentiation or enrichment? *Psychological Review, 62,* 32–41.

Goldstone, R. L. (1994). influences of categorization on perceptual discrimination. *Journal of Experimental Psychology: General, 123,* 178–200.

Goldstone, R. L., & Barsalou, L. (in press). Reuniting perception and conception: The perceptual bases of similarity and rules. Invited article to a special issue of *Cognition.*

Hoffman, D. D., & Richards, W. A. (1984). Parts of recognition. *Cognition, 18,* 65–96.

Jakobson, R., Fant, G., & Halle, M. (1963). *Preliminaries to speech analysis : The distinctive features and their correlates.* Cambridge, MA: MIT Press.

Julesz, B. (1981). Textons, the elements of texture perception, and their interaction. *Nature, 290,* 91–97.

Kolers, P. A., & Smythe, W. E. (1984). Symbol manipulation: Alternatives to the computational view of mind. *Journal of Verbal Learning and Verbal Behavior, 23,* 289–314.

Logan, G. D. (1988). Toward and instance theory of automatization. *Psychological Review, 95,* 492–527.

Lowe, D. G. (1987). The viewpoint consistency constraint. *International Journal of Computer Vision, 1,* 57–72.

Melcher, J. M., & Schooler, J. W. (1996). The misremembrance of wines past: Verbal and perceptual expertise differentially mediate verbal overshadowing of taste memory. *Journal of Memory and Language, 35,* 231–245.

Myles-Worsley, M., Johnston, W. A., & Simons, M. A. (1988). The influence of expertise on X-ray image processing. *Journal of Experimental Psychology: Learning, Memory, & Cognition, 14,* 553–557.

Norman, G. R., Brooks, L. R., & Coblentz (1992). The correlation of feature identification and category judgments in diagnostic radiology. *Memory & Cognition, 20,* 344–355.

Nosofsky, R. M (1986). Attention, similarity, and the identification-categorization relationship. *Journal of Experimental Psychology: General, 115,* 39–57.

Nosofsky, R. M., Palmeri, T. J., & McKinley, S. C. (1994). Rule-plus-exception model of classification learning. *Psychological Review, 101,* 53–79.

Schank, R. (1972). Conceptual dependency : A theory of natural language understanding. *Cognitive Psychology, 3,* 552–631.

Schyns, P. G., Goldstone, R. L, & Thibaut, J. (in press). Development of features in object concepts. *Behavioral and Brain Sciences.*

Schyns, P. G., & Murphy, G. L. (1994). The ontogeny of part representation in object concepts. In D. L. Medin (Ed.), *The Psychology of Learning and Motivation* (Vol. 31, pp. 305–354). San Diego, CA: Academic Press.

Schyns, P. G., & Rodet, L. (in press). Categorization creates functional features. *Journal of Experimental Psychology: Learning, Memory, and Cognition.*

Treisman, A., & Gelade, G. (1980). A feature-integration theory of attention, *Cognitive Psychology, 12,* 97–136.

Tversky, A. (1977). Features of similarity. *Psychological Review, 84,* 327–352.

Wierzbicka, A. (1992). Semantic primitives and semantic fields. In A. Lehrer & E. F. Kittay (Eds.), *Frames, fields, and contrasts: New essays in semantic and lexical organization* (pp. 209-228). New Jersey: Erlbaum.

# THE AFFORDANCES OF PERCEPTUAL INQUIRY: PICTURES ARE LEARNED FROM THE WORLD, AND WHAT THAT FACT MIGHT MEAN ABOUT PERCEPTION QUITE GENERALLY

*Julian Hochberg*

Pictures differ so much from objects that they are often held to be learned as we learn a foreign language. In fact, for about 200 years, *all* depth and space perceptions were thought to be so learned. The fact is, however, that outline pictures have been recognized simply through experience with real objects and without any tutoring. Moreover, few cognitive theories have *any* view of the real purposive behavior by which perception proceeds, and very little to say about how the learning is supervised. I have long argued that picture perception is diagnostic of perceptual behavior more generally—that's what makes pictures pictures (Hochberg & Brooks, 1962; Hochberg, 1980,1995). This chapter outlines a general approach to visual inquiry (foveal questions asked in the context of peripheral vision) within which the recognition of least some pictures poses no problem, and that comes to terms with well-established problems that most attempts at high perceptual theory simply ignore.

Section I notes that outline drawings can be recognized with no prior training, which must tell us something about how we perceive real objects. Section II points out that even with real objects, depth information is weak or lacking in much of the visual field. Section III describes the purposive

THE PSYCHOLOGY OF LEARNING
AND MOTIVATION, VOL. 36

perceptual behavior that partitions that visual field into a large blurred peripheral context and a sequence of brief elective foveal inquiries about small selected details within that context. To understand the nature of such perceptual inquiry, we must know what is needed to guide successive glances and act as a framework for what those glances yield, and how the information provided by foveal vision is integrated with information from the periphery and from other glances.

Section IV notes (1) that visual inquiry requires guidance as to where objects are found within the visual field, not the visual world, and (2) that only the Gestalt grouping principles offer to serve this function for both objects and marks on paper. Section V argues that the Gestalt factors and the minimum principle may have multiple sources—all of which reflect resource limitations within the context of visual inquiry behavior and not the operation of a single organizational or computational process. Section VI suggests that the more specific and situational aspects of an object's identity and state are conjunctions (or schematic maps) of shape features, learned while bridging successive foveal glances within some overall parafoveally viewed undetailed grouping, and do not accord with the traditional identification of shape with figure-ground or surface-edge depth segregation. Section VII proposes that outlines and other marks on paper provide some of tbe same information about objects in the world that objects themselves do.

## I.  Pictures Don't Necessarily Need Training

Pictures do not inherently require a teacher; they certainly do not have to be learned by anything like the learning of paired associates; and that must tell us something about how the real world itself is perceived.

The pictures of interest here are marks on paper, rather than optical surrogates which present the eye with an array of light that is virtually identical to that offered by the scene being portrayed. As Ittelson (1996) has recently pointed out, it is the former that comprise the bulk of the stimuli that are used in furthering perceptual research. Although marks on paper are vastly different from objects and spatial layouts, both as distal stimuli and as proximal stimuli (see also Hochberg, 1962, 1995, 1996), they often are used as substitutes for the objects they represent. Markings do serve several different purposes simultaneously, which of course includes acting as arbitrary symbols. But if drawings and the objects they portray were as arbitrarily related as are printed words and their meaning, some supervised learning would be needed. We know that supervised learning is in fact not completely necessary.

Fig. 1.  Outline drawings recognized by a child with *no* prior pictorial training. From Hochberg and Brooks (1962).

First, line drawings are not necessarily artistic conventions, as text is. Immigrants from picture-free (Jewish Orthodox) communities, entering this picture-ridden U.S. culture at the start of the century, reported no noticeable inability to recognize pictured objects and people. There is a vast history, spanning millennia, of the use of outline drawings not substantially different from those in general use today (Cutting & Massironi, in press; Hochberg, 1995; Kennedy, 1977). Secondly, adults are not significantly worse at retrieving information from line drawings than from photographs (Biederman, 1985; Ryan & Schwartz, 1956).

Finally, although all of these permit counterarguments, there is the evidence offered in 1962 by the fact that a young child who had received no instruction in what pictures mean, and formed no associations with pictures, named outline drawings like those shown in Fig. 1 (as well as photographs) on his first contact with pictures[1] (Hochberg & Brooks, 1962). His vocabulary had been taught using only solid toys (like the doll in the drawing), the objects themselves (like the shoe, keys, truck, and car), and model scenes (composed of model houses, model animals, etc.). No TV was present, and the few billboards very infrequently visible from the car went unremarked.

This finding has far-reaching implications for understanding visual perception and cognitive psychology more generally, as noted at the time (Hochberg & Brooks, 1962). DeLoache and Burns (1994) review subsequent studies of picture recognition in early infancy, and I know of no contradictory evidence, although I should stress that experience with pictures, and with pictorial marks, does provide an education in comprehending pictures. Younger children do have more trouble using and making pictures that are intended to convey three-dimensional information (DeLoache & Burns, 1994; Hagen & Jones, 1978; Krampen, 1993), although they do respond to at least some of the pictorial depth cues at early ages (Yonas & Hagen, 1973). Moreover, in addition to dubious anthropological anecdote, there are a few studies (e.g., Hudson, 1962; 1967) concluding that pictorial representation requires the acceptance of such cues as object

[1] Drawings were shown before any photographs of the same objects, responses were taped, and were scored by judges who knew the child and his pronounciations, but not what pictures were shown.

size, interposition, and perspective as "artistic conventions," and that those pictorial conventions are not accepted in African subcultural groups that are inexperienced with Western pictures. Criticized on various grounds (Deregowski, 1968; Hagen, 1974; Hochberg, 1962; Jahoda & McGurk, 1974; Jones & Hagen, 1980; Kennedy, 1974; Kilbride & Robbins, 1968; Mundy-Castle, 1966), such studies do not contradict the conclusions reached by Hochberg and Brooks which dealt with familiar objects and not with the representation of distance.

To any theory in which spatial depth and distance are the direct starting point of all perception, pictures—because they are merely ribbons of pigment on flat planes—have nothing in common with what they represent, and training would therefore seem to be fundamentally necessary before pictorial recognition could occur.[2] As a first step toward resolving this difficulty, we dicuss why even normal seeing of a three-dimensional world is largely free of depth information.

## II.  Depth-free Seeing in World and Pictures

Pictures are flat pigmented objects, and the world consists of volumetric surfaces. How can the former represent the latter, when they are so different? In this section, as in the last, I argue that they are not that different everywhere and for every perceptual purpose.

The first important distinction here, I believe, is between pictured objects and pictured spaces. The metric static depth cues, notably linear perspective (and its related cues, like texture-density gradients) have offered difficulties to both the painter and the spectator; unless viewed from a specific canonical location, they should and often do provide the basis for perceptual distortions, and with flat picture surfaces there are irreconcilable conflicts that can only be resolved by abandoning the use of these cues (e.g., Cutting, 1986; Hochberg, 1984, 1995; Kubovy, 1986; Pirenne, 1970). But the fact that those violations, which are often deliberate (see Hochberg, 1980, 1996), do not interfere with pictorial object recognition unless the distortions are truly extreme tells us that the metric depth cues are not important to the recognition of pictured objects. The myriad violations normal when viewing moving pictures (Cutting, 1987; Hochberg, 1986; Hochberg & Brooks, 1996) argues very strongly that neither metric spatial information nor anything like a rigidity principle is essential to recognizing objects in the real world,

---

[2] Gibson originally rejected perceptual research with line drawings as being artificial and nondiagnostic, a point subsequently elaborated by Michaels and Carello (1981); but even when Gibson later discussed the "invariants" that pictures shared with the world (Gibson, 1979), he never took into account what such sharing implies about our perceptions of the world.

and is not important in what has been learned that makes such recognition possible (see also Footnote 11, in Section VI). This fact rules out those cognitive theories (e.g., Ecological Realism) that make such spatial invariants fundmental to perception: The fact that objects themselves are indeed often three-dimensional structures with relatively invariant spatial propeties is not necessarily diagnostic about the underlying cognitive properties, despite the convictions of the Ecological Realists.

In short, I argue that depth need not be signified at all in order to achieve fully recognizable, "realistic" nonarbitrary pictures of objects, and that such pictures draw in a highly diagnostic fashion on the mechanisms by which we normally perceive the world. Figure 1 contains no information about depth other than a weak form of interposition, and nothing about distance. If these pictures and their objects are in some ways equivalent, what we must explain about the perception of the world is very different from what it has usually been taken to be.

A word of caution here: I am *not* saying that object perception *cannot* be presented by means of three-dimensional defined edges (as in a dot-based stereogram, a rotating wire figure, or as a surface of moving dots). But in outline pictures the reverse can be true, and to me the question is:

> Do we have any reason to believe that the same shoe or car that is recognized without any depth information when in a picture would go unrecognized in the world were it not for its depth cues?

The fact is that there have been many proposals, especially from theorists in machine vision and neurophysiology, that objects are identifiable from two-dimensional images, and by such behavioral consequences as where a robot's hand might be able to grasp them (e.g., Biederman, 1985; Binford, 1971; Lowe, 1987; Witkin & Tenenbaum, 1983). But these are only proposals for what *might* work, not studies of how we *do* perceive.

More importantly, we should note that the real world itself often offers *only* the pictorial (two dimensional) depth cues: Beyond a few meters of distance, the cues of accommodation, binocular convergence, and small head movements can reveal only large depth distances, usually far too coarse to help contribute to object recognition (see Hochberg, 1972; Woodworth, 1938 for reviews). Cutting and Vishton (1995) have taken a strong first step toward separating the different channels of depth information by dividing the viewer's world into the ranges over which each channel is primarily effective. Furthermore, the retinal image provided by even a nearby object should differ little from that provided by a picture if the object falls in peripheral vision where low resolution prevents fine depth discrimination, and especially if it falls in only one eye's temporal field of view and therefore offers no binocular disparity.

Again, this is not to make the preposterous claim that normal perception does not include the perception of depth and distance, because it obviously does. However, I believe that the processes by which perception and recognition occur, and by which perceptual inquiry is continued or ended, are opportunistic and task dependent in important ways. For example, *depth information* is indeed needed to recognize some tool's handle in a foreshortened, head-on view, or to thread a needle. *Color* is all that is needed to distinguish an apple from an orange (or the foreshortened painted handle of a familiar pan). Most often, I must be prepared recognize a human as a particular individual, but not to recognize a particular mouse or a particular roofing nail. Perceptual learning, and the acquisition of pictorial meaning within the course of a visual inquiry, can therefore follow different routes for different tasks. Schyns (in press) makes a very similar point, in the course of outlining *diagnostic recognition,* which considers object recognition as an interaction of task constraints and potential object information. And neurological impairment reveals different ways of using space and shape in recognizing objects (Humphreys & Riddoch, 1987). So I am *not* claiming that three-dimensional information (or three-dimensional memory representation) is *never* used in recognizing objects, only that certain features or attributes that are used in learning to identify real objects in the world are offered as well by the markings on a flat picture.

The next section discusses further why the information offered by three-dimensional structures in the world are not always that different from what is offered by two-dimensional pictures on paper, while introducing the concept of the affordances of perceptual behavior.


### III.   The Interactive Behavior of Perceptual Inquiry

Most of the important characteristics of visual perception, and of the perceptual learning that shapes it, may derive from the nature of the perceptual acts by which perception proceeds, at least as much as they reflect the nature of the world (and the projective geometry and ecological optics with which so much visual psychology is concerned), about which those acts inquire.

Tolman (1948) introduced the concept of *means-end readiness* to refer to what the organism has learned in the service of purposive acts, and of *sign-gestalten* as the configurations of stimulus information that enable those acts. Gibson (1979) offered the term *affordance* which essentially bridges those two concepts by identifying the relevant stimulus information as that higher-order invariant in the optic array that "specifies" the distal structure which allows the action to be performed. Although many people find the latter term attractive, it has so far guided little research other than Warren's interesting measures of the dimensions that afford stair climbing and doorway entry (Warren, 1984; Warren & Wang,1987). Perception is looked at as a guide to behavior, and Ittelson (1996) quite rightly sees affordances as a useful term in discussing what purposes are served by marks on paper (or in other media). I do not believe that we can learn much about pictures, or about affordances, without being more explicit about the actual means-end readinesses and sign-gestalten. I think that perceptual behavior is primarily a continual process of directed inquiry, and the most important affordances are those which serve such inquiry.

Before considering some of what affordances must be learned in the course of making perceptual inquiry effective, and how they would apply to looking at outline pictures, I should list what I take to be the four most important and relevant aspects of the system that is performing the inquiry—aspects that shape the way in which perception and perceptual learning should, I think, be understood.

A. The foveal region of the retina, receiving the center of the line of sight, provides maximum resolution (e.g., 1-min separation) or sampling. The ability to see detail falls off quite rapidly from center to periphery. There are probably multiple reasons for the loss in detail: undersampling, lack of calibration (Hess & Field, 1993), refractive error in peripheral vision (Leibowitz, Johnson, & Isabelle, 1972), etc. There are also more specialized differences between top and bottom of the retina (Previc, 1990; Rubin, Nakayama, & Shapley, 1996), still being discovered and not yet reconciled, so the retina is inhomogeneous in different ways. But even beyond that, normally only the surface at which the viewer is looking will be in focus—most other things will lie at different distances, well beyond the eye's depth of field. For my present purpose, I simply note that the detail available falls off rapidly outside of the small fovea (although the acuity curve is of course not actually discontinuous), and that there is greatly lowered resolution, or *blur,* outside of central vision.

The differences between what are often called the focal and ambient systems (Schneider, 1969; Trevarthen, 1968) are so great that perception must proceed by using one system to answer questions raised by the other: a discourse or dialog between the two (or more) channels, not a simple registering of the information presented (or "specified") by the input from the world. Objects larger than, say, 4°—that is, 2.5 in. at 3 ft, 5 in. at 6 ft—do not fall within the focal vision of a single glance; within that region, details delineated by as little as 1 min of arc are available, but not the detailed shape of any larger object. For larger large divisions or features (of low spatial frequency), more peripheral vision is needed, but small divisions and details are simply not available to the extrafoveal vision that comprises 98% of the single binocular glance. To obtain information of both kinds, successive glances must be undertaken and successfully executed. The stimulus field itself can provide an enormous amount of potential informtion, which must be reduced if the organism to deal with it (see Edelman & Intrator, this volume). The amount of information actually handled by the fovea is small because the fovea is small (and, I will argue in Sections IV and VI, is filtered or preselected in ways that depend on perceptual learning), and the amount of information handled by the periphery is small because it is of very low resolution.[3]

We do not perceive the world all at once. (Except in tachistoscopic presentations, which from this viewpoint need special study.) As is true in reading text, in which only about four new letters are discernably seen within each single fixation, each inquiry we execute is elective, and has a purpose. Usually, that purpose is to provide detailed information about some small specific part of the field of view that would otherwise be left to the low resolution (or low calibration or blur) of peripheral vision.

B. The glance constitutes a purposeful cognitive act, given that an attentional shift must precede the saccadic eye movement for the latter to occur (Hoffman & Subramaniam, 1995). Note that I have not said "conscious" or "deliberate"—we are surely not conscious of most of the glances that we take; but they nevertheless have a purpose, that of obtaining information about a specific place in the field of view, corresponding to but not identical to its distal referent. Very small glances can be made within the foveal region, but they are still directed to specific places within that region.

C. Although the saccadic movements that change fixation are themselves ballistic and very rapid (e.g., 50 msec for a large glance) but cannot

---

[3] Field (1987) suggested that the lower spatial frequencies contain most of the power in stimulus arrays provided by the natural environment, thus perhaps accounting for the response properties of the corresponding cortical cells. In a wide review of the literature Hughes, Nozowa, and Kitterle (1996) make a convincing case that a variety of factors work to provide an initial (early processing) advantage to low-resolution information. As I mention here, not only distal image statistics, but the optics of accommodation on attended items, and the need to reduce drastically the information available in the light to the eye, should keep one from deploring the fact that we have low peripheral resolution. It is probably pretty much as it should be, a statement not meant in praise of evolution but as a suggestion that these constraints are diagnostic of the true nature of the perceptual process.

occur faster than four glances per second for any protracted sequence, the perception of any scene or object is not a seamless scanning but a discontinous set of guided actions.

D. Because there does not seem to be any automatic mechanism for storing the overall pattern of information across successive glances in an integrated fashion (see Haber, Haber, Levin, and Hollyfield, 1993; Hochberg, 1968; Irwin, Zacks, & Brown, 1990), the continued presence of the peripheral pattern that has been displaced within the field of view when the eye has moved provides for relative positioning of the details that have been sampled. Placing the details with respect to each other would, without such a framework, require special mnemonic procedures. And that means that the peripherally viewed pattern must be identifiable and salient if it is to guide the visual inquiry (by salient, I mean detectible from a fixation that is distant from it, and therefore itself fixatable without point-by-point search). That is, it can then serve as a *landmark* against which to anchor local detail between (or after) other acts of inquiry.

If the object in peripheral vision is not recognized by the perceptual inquiry system as having been just previously fixated, it might be refixated repeatedly. We know that infants soon stop looking at what initially seemed a very attractive stimulus, and that such cessation is a major measure of recognition and learning of object identity (Kellman, 1995; Spelke, 1985).

In terms of Hebb's (1949) conception of the learning of *phase sequences*—a proposal that I think has not received the attention it deserves—we would expect that after sufficient practice in looking successively at different features of some object the entire set of *cell assemblies* would be activated by any member of the sequence. Add to Hebb's account the fact, discussed above, that ambient views normally precede any directed glance, and we have a *supervised learning process* that teaches the system where specific information can be found if the appropriate glance is taken.

The viewer may elect not to undertake the inquiry. Or the inquiry may be made but the expectation may be disappointed, that is, the information expected will not be found, the edge anticipated from parafoveal viewing will turn out not to be in focus, etc. Or the inquiry may be made and the expected information obtained. This constitutes parafoveal recognition. Achieving such recognition should be a major motor and a supervisor in perceptual learning, and one of its main benefits may be learning to recognize the same object over different retinal locations (i.e., what used to be called "the" Gestalt problem in the days when it was believed that the same configuration elicited the same response despite any spatial transformations it underwent; we now know better.)

To return to the stimulus basis of the perceptual inquiry: what I will term a *perceptual affordance*[4] refers to how the effective two-channel retinal image (as distinct from the optic array) might serve to guide visual inquiry. attempting to make explicit the two components—the means-end readiness and sign-gestalten—that the concept subsumes. Although there has been a fair amount written about what information the world *affords* to guide and invite the organism's purposive behaviors within it, there has been virtually no concern over the affordances that guide *perceptual* actions, even though we surely execute an enormously greater number of goal-directed perceptual acts in the course of a normal day (say, $3 \cdot 60 \cdot 60 \cdot 16 =$ ca.150,000 saccades) than of any other goal-directed actions. (Note: I am *not* saying that the acts in question are necessarily cognitively penetrable, nor consciously and deliberately undertaken, but that by definition an act that is elective, ballistic, and whose end-point within the visual field has been fixed before the actual move occurs, has a behavioral purpose and physically specified goal.) Not only is perceptual inquiry the most frequent purposive behavior, but it is surely the most important, because it serves to initiate and guide those behaviors that operate on the distal environment.

The next section considers some of what affordances or "rules"the viewer might learn from these two-system visual inquiries that would help guide this highly practiced perceptual behavior, and how such learning would relate to recognizing pictures as well as the world.

## IV.  What Is Needed to Guide Visual Inquiry

It has been stated many times that perception reflects ecological probabilities, and that we perceive at any time just that state of distal affairs which would normally produce the sensory response being experienced. I have listed elsewhere my strong reservations about this truism; here I will only try to show what those reservations amount to in the present context.

Although the argument has been made that research with pictures is irrelevant to the real world, because in that world our behaviors are organized with respect to depth and distance, that argument is not true of all behavior. Pointing one's hand or head, aiming a weapon, recognizing the composition of a landscape, all refer to what has been termed the *visual*

---

[4] I mean this set of affordances to be distinct from those currently thought to allow and guide effective actions within the distal environment. The latter are properties of the distal surfaces and manipulable objects in the world; the former are properties of the proximal stimulus array.

*field* as distinguished from the *visual world* (Gibson, 1950). It is the visual world that provides the interest to most realist and/or behaviorist psychologists. But that cannot be true of what I have argued earlier to be the most important behavior of all—perceptual inquiry. Visual perceptual inquiry, at least, necessarily occurs within what is called the visual field (or within the retinal image, which Ecological Realists often term a myth). Note that when the eye changes direction in an act of perceptual inquiry (or in tracking a moving object) it is the two-dimensional retinal image that must guide that behavior if it is to be successful, and it is the two-dimensional retinal image that must be moved over the retina as the purposes of the inquiry require (Hochberg, 1972).

What needs to be learned in order to use this system of inquiry? First, in exploring the three-dimensional world saccadically, the viewer must learn how and where to direct the focal system within the two-dimensional retinal image projected by that three-dimensional world. At least since Bishop Berkeley, it has been emphasized that the perceiver must learn what walking distances, what acts of reaching and touching, and what names or categories, are associated with what patterns in the eye. In these actions, perception and perceptual learning serve nonperceptual purposes. If we want to study how perceptual learning might serve perceptual purposes, the first question must be how does the viewer know (or learn) what can be looked at in the field of view. Depth and reachability is a secondary issue.

To answer that first question requires some knowledge of where one can look that will not in fact be vitiated by the course of looking, that can comprise a framework whose parts can be successively examined because they hang together for more than one inquiring glance. That means: objects (and swarms or clumps). These are parts of the visual field that are likely move together (cf. Kellman, 1993; Hochberg, 1972; Spelke, 1985), and which will still occupy a coherent region in ambient vision to which the focal inquiry can be addressed even after an eye or head movement has caused a displacement within the field of view. Note that this definition of an object has no need for permanence of its parts, or for structural rigidity, and it does not depend on continuity of surfaces between edges (as I once wrongly thought); it depends only on the perception of its spatial and temporal coherence.

Of course, the eye asks not only what part of the field is an object, but what the object is, or what state it is in. At least sometimes, however, this is a separate question from the previous one, and I will defer discussing it until Section 6. The question, what parts of the visual field comprise sufficiently stable objects for visual inquiry, has primarily been addressed by the putative Gestalt "laws" (or rules) of organization. These are probably the closest thing to being a set of visual rules both for predicting the

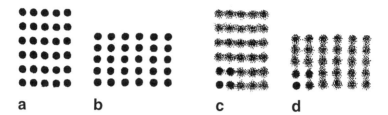

Fig. 2. Organization (proximity grouping) enhanced by the "blur" of extrafoveal vision. At (A) and (B), dots spaced so as to appear grouped (but not strongly so) in horizontal rows and vertical columns, respectively. At (C) and (D), a visualization of the effects of increasing blur around a foveal fixation at lower left (adjacent dots are differentially filtered through a Gaussian blur).

presence of objects in the field of view and for explaining the appearance of marks on paper.[5] But both Gestalt theory and its more recent descendants face severe problems when we take the course and consequences of visual inquiry into consideration, as we do in the next section.

## V.   The Gestalt Principles and the Minimum Principle: What They May Be Able to Do and What They Cannot Be or Do

The Gestalt principles were attempts to codify what patterns seem to form perceptually coherent units; they were arrived at primarily by applying a form of carefully unanalytic introspection to selected demonstrations. Fig. 2 shows the effect of the *proximity principle* on grouping, causing perceived rows or columns, respectively, to emerge from separate dots; in Fig. 3, the principle of *good continuation* causes the familiar letter "4," made visible at 3b, to be concealed in the less familiar set of uninterrupted curves at 3a. (The example is a variation of one used by Köhler, 1929, to demonstrate good continuation.) Gestalt theory explained such organizational principles only by attributing them to the properties of underlying isomorphic figural current flows, or to attractive and constraining field forces within the brain. Neither of these explanations are credible today, and the "laws" themselves are too multitudinous, too prone to conflict, too unquantified, and indeed

[5] It should be noted that they were obtained almost exclusively by contemplating marks on paper. If the major Gestalt principles did in fact apply validly both to partitioning our views of the world into objects and to grouping marks of paper into coherent regions of reference, they would account for much of picture perception. But they do not, as the next section attempts to show.

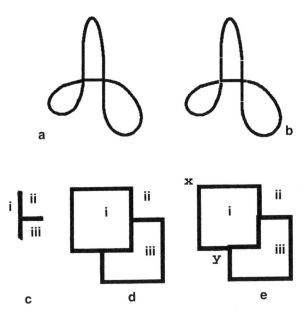

Fig. 3. Foveal information about object organization lost to the "blur" of extrafoveal vision. Fig. 3. a. A hidden number; b. the number revealed, but only to foveal vision; c. the potential depth cue of interposition (or occluded good continuation); d. simple ordinal depth; e. as in D, when X is fixated; the reverse, when Y is fixated. (See text.)

for the most part too unmeasured, to be applied and tested in most situations (Hochberg, 1974).

A single principle had been proposed, the *minimum principle* (see Koffka, 1935), by which the simplest organization of the whole pattern in question determines what object or scene one perceives. Quantitative measures of simplicity have been with us for some time (Attneave, 1954; Hochberg & McAlister, 1953; Leeuwenberg, 1971). With a suitable measure of simplicity, this would cover a great deal of perception in general, including spatial layout in depth as well as object grouping and structure (see Hochberg, 1964). Because it assumed the same laws manifest in drawings as in real objects, the problem broached in connection with Fig. 1 was not necessarily a problem for Gestalt theory or its derivatives. The line segments in Fig. 3C are not compellingly spatial,[6] but become so when they are parts of the objects of Fig. 3d. To perceive Fig. 3d as a square object *i* in front of another square object *iii*, and both in front of ground *ii*, is simpler than the alternatives (e.g., separate marks on paper, or *iii* as a nearer and reversed "L"- shaped).

[6] Actually they comprise the local depth cue of interposition, formalized since Helmholtz.

Unfortunately, the entire approach is unviable today, in my opinion (although I was one its early perpetrators), for reasons related to the nature of eye movements and the fovea/periphery differences addressed in Section III. A. Whole figures are not in fact processed as a unit, and how they are processed—indeed, what stimulus information is available—depends on how the attentive eye is directed. If you attend the thin white gaps on Fig. 3b, the "4" is clearly visible. If you keep your gaze pinned to X in Fig. 3e, it looks like much the same pair of objects as in Fig. 3d, but while you keep your gaze and attention fixed on point Y, region *iii* comes forward as the reversed "L." Although we know that the perceptual consequences are not based on all of the information in the pattern, we have no way to know how much of the pattern will be used, or what it spans. Indeed, as we will see in discussing Fig. 4, it is easy to devise both pictures *and* real objects that violate the minimum principle *to any extent desired,* depending on how and where the viewer looks.

There is therefore simply no Gestalt-type stimulus-anchored explanation for the perception of either real or pictured objects, only groupings of demonstrations. I think that it is more plausible now to approach such demonstrations as the result of a mix of different mechanisms and constraints that allow the perceptual system to predict what would very likely turn out to be an object in the course of perceptual inquiry, if it is fixated, or to predict what will turn out to move in a coherent unit within the visual field if viewer and object move relative to each other. At least some of these must depend on how the system of visual inquiry is designed, so it is important to remember that most of what we see at any moment is what is offered by extrafoveal vision, the ambient system. As we start to consider that fact, I think that a very different understanding of how we see objects and their pictures will emerge.

A.  MULTIPLE BASES FOR THE GESTALT FACTORS AS
    PERCEPTUAL AFFORDANCES

In peripheral vision, the boundaries of objects and of swarms or clumps—that is, of collections of nearby elements—are of course greatly simplified because detail is lost, especially in young infants. There are diverse contributory factors (see Section III), so "low resolution" and degree of eccentricity are therefore only part of the story. Because these differences are observable only if one knows what to measure, we need to come at them from the other end, from the perceptual consequences that different patterns provide in the outcome of the looking behavior. Perhaps comparisons between peripherally viewed test shapes that have been degraded in different ways may tell us more about what goes on in ambient vision.

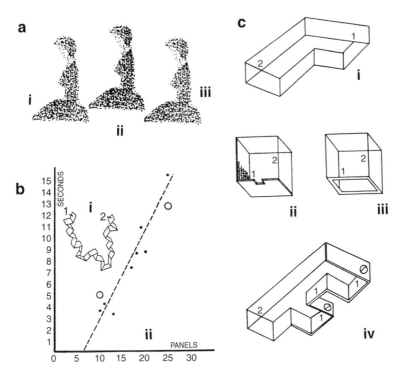

Fig. 4. The limited learning and remembering from one inquiring glance to the next. (a) in one of the three pointillist sketches, a large region of dots has been inverted; can you tell which one? (After Hochberg, 1995.); (b) in the picture at (i), are ends (1) and (2) the same or opposite sides of the ribbon's surface? An answer can be reached, but it takes time to parse the figure, as shown in the graph (ii) for different numbers of panels; the points are data for drawn figures, the open circles are data for real objects (Klopfer, 1983); (c) although all objects shown (i to iv) can be parsed to yield consistent figures, and each intersection marked (1) is fixed in orientation when focally attended, intersections marked (2) reverse relatively freely, even if the eye has just come from (or is still directed at) intersection (1). The object at (ii) was used as a real, oscillating three-dimensional object; objects (i, iii, iv) show how the number of violations of consistent and simple structure that are entailed by reversals at intersection (2) can be increased indefinitely. [Figure (i) is from Hochberg, 1970; also, Gillam, 1979; (ii) is from Hochberg & Peterson, 1987; Peterson & Hochberg, 1983; (iii, iv) are from Peterson & Hochberg, 1989].

With all of these reservations, simple "blurring" should do as a first step. Years ago, there were proposals (notably, Ginsburg, 1980) that the Gestalt laws of organization, the geometrical illusions, and much else, resulted from the contribution of low-spatial frequency channels. Palmer's higher-order analyzers (Palmer, 1982) would do even better. But I think something like Ginsburg's proposal approximately descibes the contents of the ambient system—the extrafoveal region that comprises most of the field of view at any moment, that affords guidance as to whether to look and where, and to which we must elect to fit foveally sampled detail in the pursuit of perceptual inquiry as such inquiry is made.

Thus, swarms and clumps have overall shapes and boundaries that substantially differ from those of unified objects, provided both fall outside of the central regina. Sufficiently blurred, nearby dots or patches may activate the same receptor mechanisms as would unbroken extended objects. Although the dots may be distinguishable in higher frequency channels, and are certainly so when brought to the fovea (the lower left corners, in Figs. 2c and 2d), they may go unresolved in the extensive low-resolution periphery, so that even when they are seen as separate in successive glances those details are samples selected from, and fitted within a framework of connectedness. This might be one component of what has been considered the Gestalt "law of proximity" (Figs. 2a, 2b). In addition there are many ways in which overlapping processing structures will have similar consequences extrafoveally.

If the small area of high-resolution foveal vision were the sole basis for perception, surface inhomogeneities might easily destroy the apparent unity of a single object's image. And the unity of an object is important to behavior in general and to visual inquiry in particular. There is some evidence that bounded regions near each other within the visual field are likely to be physically connected, so that the blur patterns in Figs. 2c, and 2d, by emphasizing proximity, may actually offer cues as to distal connectedness.[7] It is obviously desirable to be able to perceive objects where they exist in one's environment, so that they can be handled and dealt with as units, and discussions about visual ecology has usually centered on such distal behavioral referents (Brunswik, 1956; Brunswik & Kamiya, 1953; Gibson, 1979). But the shifts of fixation and attention that comprise visual inquiry, and that precede such distally directed behaviors as handling objects or walking through doorways, are the present concern. And it is surely desirable for the behaviors of visual inquiry to be guided by information as to where objects exist in the visual field, so that they can be directed toward the features that offer diagnostic detail when that is needed.

By moving together, the *relative* loci of features of a rigid or semirigid object usually remain relatively unchanged when the viewpoint shifts. Any cues available in peripheral vision as to what regions correspond to objects

---

[7] That is, the "illusory" connections in Fig. 2C and 2D may probabilistically be signs of real connectedness in the distal object, even though there is no physical connection on the printed page. The evidence referred to was obtained by Brunswik and Kamiya (1953) from a careful analysis of magazine photos reported, but because those pictures must have survived various levels of editorial selection, a study of ecological representativeness would be useful.

in the world, and therefore afford relatively stable targets for features, should be learned (if not prewired). Therefore, there is reason to learn the signs that something is likely to be a coherent object, and the fovea's confirmation or disconfirmation (i.e., of what details are found where) should probabilistically serve to supervise the learning of such peripherally given cues.

Proposals (of varying explicitness) have been offered (Hochberg, 1972, 1980; Kellman, 1993) regarding how diverse potential Gestalt principles, and indeed the figure-ground phenomenon itself, would be reinforced in the service of looking behavior, over the course of perceptual behavior. This assumes a very opportunistic and varied set of principles, and some of these (which we will discuss later) apply to pictures of objects as well as to the objects.

That leaves the most powerful and unified of the Gestaltist proposals, the simplicity principle (or minimum principle) that has been offered to replace the separate Gestalt "laws." As noted earlier, I think that it is not viable today, despite continued adherants. A brief survey of why it is not viable will strongly suggest, I believe, that what seemed so plausible as a minimum principle has multiple sources that are rooted in the nature of visual inquiry and not in any organizational or brain-field metaphors.

B.   LEARNING ONE GLANCE AT A TIME: MULTIPLE MINIMUM
     PRINCIPLES AND THEIR CONSEQUENCES

It is hard to reconcile the simplicity or minimum principle with what we know about the piecemeal and limited nature of visual inquiry. The minimum principle is that we perceive the simplest organization that can be fitted to the "whole configuration" with which the object confronts the eye. The problem with this is that the whole configuration often does not enter the visual system at one time, and that its separate entries are not encoded directly, automatically, or in their entirety. In fact, at least five different constraints on the course of visual cognition reduce the information that the perceptual system obtains from the field of view.

1. The extrafoveal field minimizes or simplifies the scene it transmits through omission and blurring (i.e., low-spatial frequencies predominate).
2. The foveal region simplifies by providing only such details and features as can fit its small span.
3. The "question" that is being "asked" by any glance limits what that glance addresses, partly through initial encoding constraints. Only a very few independent items can be picked up in one glance, unless

they are "chunked" in some larger recognized structure.[8] What cannot be so encoded is largely lost. As an example, note how very difficult it is to detect which of the three pointillist sketches in Fig. 4A has had a large region dots inverted near the bottom of the skirt.

4. The working memory that stores the brief foveal glance is itself highy limited in capacity, needing landmarks and an embedding mental structure with which to place the encoded glimpse. Such integration is not an automatic stitching together. One does not simply perceive, or enter into working memory, the turns and orientations of surfaces in unfamiliar objects: As the number of panels in the object at Fig. 4Bi increases, the time to decide whether or not ends *1* and *2* are of the same surface increases accordingly (the dots are response times for pictures, the circles are for real objects).[9]

5 Unless constrained by a specific task, the need to make other inquiring glances probably restricts the inquiry to one or two glances (or sometimes no inquiry beyond what the highly ambiguous periphery provides).

Information is lost and therefore simplicity in one sense of the term is gained by each of these routes, and probably others as well. But, taken together, they rule out any simplicity principle that supposedly draws on the whole configuration (and rules out any other such theory, whether "direct," isomorphic, or inferential/logical which assumes that all of the information is taken into account). The intersections marked *1* in Fig. 4ci to 4civ fix the orientation of the objects (i.e., to one in which they are viewed from below), in accordance with the good continuation and interposition cues of Fig. 3. It is also simpler to see them as three-dimensional objects in that orientation, rather than as flat collections of individual lines on paper or in the reverse orientation (Hochberg & Brooks, 1962; Kopfermann, 1930), but that explanation fails when we note that in all these cases intersection 2 reverses orientation while we look at it. It happens in the object of Fig. 4cii even when it is a *real object in rotary motion,* and not just a static picture, and it happens when the object is small enough to fit into the fovea (Hochberg & Peterson, 1987). And it is not merely that

[8] Although this point was made influentially by Miller's classic paper in 1956, and by Sperling's classic research of 1960, it seems not to have been taken seriously by the major perceptual theories. It probably applies as well to features that are detectible but surrounded by clutter in peripheral vision (see Hochberg & Gelman, 1977).

[9] Some or all of the chunking mentioned in Section V.B.4 may in fact not occur during foveal pick but rather reside in the memory structures that guided the inquiry. Terrace, Jaswal, Brannon, and Shaofu, (1996) has shown strong evidence of chunking in sequential behavior of humans and monkeys; Chase and Simon (1973) have shown that chess experts perceive board layouts in much larger chunks than novices do; and the demonstrations in Figs. 4 and 5 seem plausible entries to the study of chunking in the perception of objects.

the violation of simplicity is too small to be effective, as has sometimes been argued (e.g., by Boselie & Leeuwenberg, 1986; Hatfield & Epstein, 1985), because the reversal at 2 is still evident when as in Fig. 4civ we increase the number of intersections that contradict it, perhaps without limit. I had originally considered such resource limitations as an alternative quite early (Hochberg, 1962); recent overviews of the minimum principle can be found in Pomerantz and Kubovy (1986) and Peterson and Hochberg (1989).

Such resource limitations can of course be overcome. The viewer can perhaps compare small corresponding subsets of the dots in Fig. 4ai to 4aiii, and can parse the planes and local depth cues in the drawings and objects of Figs. 4b and 4c, devising mnemonics to help track what each detailed glance discloses. When such search and mnemotechnics are not used, however, the unencoded details and features go unperceived (except as indeterminate clutter). The demonstrations in Fig. 4 essentially tell us that perception does not follow a strong consistancy constraint: whatever consistancy is manifest in what we see reflects the consistancy presented by the world, and not some cognitive operating principle.

The fact that pictures are in many ways inconsistent with the objects they represent, as mentioned in Section 1, is therefore not necessarily important. They are clearly identified as marks on paper, locally inconsistent with a three-dimensional volumetric reading, and the viewer has no need for further visual inquiry to encode that fact. But that does not tell us in what way outline pictures like those in Fig. 1 can share the familiarity of familiar real objects. To do that, we have to ask what might be involved in encoding separate details in a familiar shape, and what the nature of perceived object shape is so that an outline drawing can possess it.

## VI. Perceived Familiar Shapes Are Sets or Strings of Features and Not Figure's Edges

Figure 5 is one version of a classroom demonstration I have been using since 1962 (Hochberg, 1964). It takes far longer to distinguish which squiggle is reversed between the upper and lower row, or to recognize which squiggle you have seen before, etc., in Fig. 5a than in Fig. 5b. The stimuli in Fig. 5a and 5b are configurationally identical, so that it is the results of perceptual learning that are unavoidably implicated here.[10] In Fig. 5a, the squiggles have to be compared detail by detail, in deliberate successive inquiries, in order to decide whether any two are reversed; in Fig. 5b, the chunking is

[10] The faces are horizontal in Fig. 5a in order to avoid providing the misleading feature strings that would result from inversion.

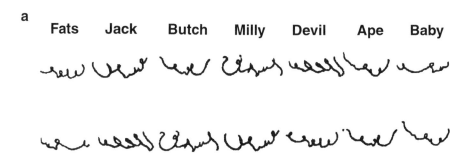

Fig. 5. Recognizing squiggles. One squiggle appears in the lower row reversed end for end from its appearance in the upper row. Compare the ease of detecting which it is in (A), the present figure, and in (B), which is printed on facing page. See text.

evident in the ease with which the lines are compared. The same lines that are meaningless independent curlicues in Fig. 5A act as though they were familiar shapes (identifiable members of the class of objects called faces) in Fig. 5b. Why do the lines in Fig. 5b act in this way?

If we can answer this question, we may have a handle on how the ability to recognize objects in Fig. 1 can be learned from seeing objects in the world.

Other than to tell us that only those regions that become figures can have perceived shape, and that ground cannot, neither the Gestalt theory of object perception nor its simplicity-based descendants can address this issue. Near object's edges have shape in one direction, whereas further surfaces or space continue behind that edge and hence are not shaped by that edge. Figure-ground segregation, which occurs with lines on paper for reasons we are not told, presumably taps the same process. The prevailing assumption was (and still is) that figure-ground segregation is determined first by configurational factors, and that only after figure's (or object's) edge is established, can we determine whether or not the object's shape is one we know.[11]

Figure 6a is an old demonstration which appears to support the assertion that what is not figure does not have a recognizable shape (Hochberg, 1964). If we accept this as true, it is hard to reconcile with the nature of visual inquiry as explored in Section III and with the piecemeal nature of object- and picture-perception as discussed in Section IV. But we will see

[11] Support for the assertion that figure-ground segregation must precede shape recognition often rests on the assertion that a region's shape must, "logically," be perceived before the viewer can learn to perceive it. I think anything like a piecemeal, a multilevel, or an RBC approach voids the premises of that paradox.

b

Fats     Jack     Butch     Milly     Devil     Ape     Baby

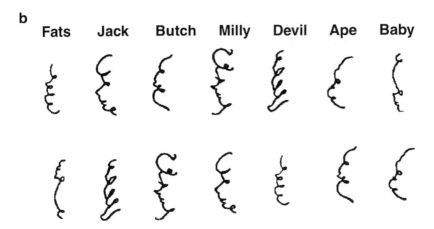

Fig 5b the squiggles of Fig 5a, rotated 90 degrees. See text.

that it is probably not true, and that it offers a misleading idea of the basis of shape perception in objects and in pictures of them.

First, I want to note that neither Gestalt theory nor its descendants had much to say about how we recognize the shape of objects. Two recent and distantly related lines of groundbreaking work, one by Biederman and his colleagues, and the other by Peterson and her colleagues, have changed how we must think of object perception quite generally.

Since 1985, Biederman and his colleagues (e.g., Biederman, 1985; Hummel & Biederman, 1992) have made a vigorous case for a theory of *recognition-by-components* (RBC), in which basic level objects (e.g., dogs, telephones, airplanes) are very rapidly recognized in terms of a relatively small set of nonaccidental features (*geons*) that are themselves as recognizable in outline drawings as they are in solid objects. "Nonaccidental" means that the characteristics that differentiate one three-dimensional form from another are not likely to be eliminated or greatly changed when viewed or pictured from another position.[12] I think that the RBC approach is a liberating one, and obviously (given Section I) I have long agreed that some of the features by which three-dimensional objects are recognized are available to the viewer in outline drawings as well as in the objects themselves. But I see no meaningful way to generalize about whether or not all recognition of three-dimensional objects relies on three-dimensional mental representa-

[12] The idea of nonaccidental features was first developed (see Kanade, 1981; Lowe, 1987) in an effort to develop procedures by which computer vision could recognize an object without first having to take into account its three-dimensional layout, i.e., its slant to the line of sight. It fits very comfortably, therefore, with the ideas presented in Section II.

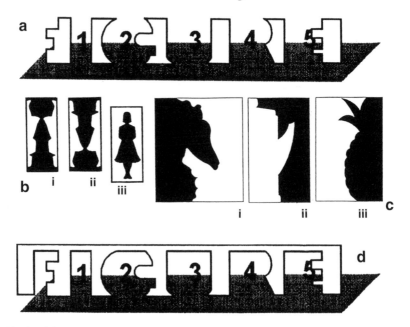

Fig. 6.   (a) A row of irregular white shapes, designed (as was Fig. 3a) to show that organizational factors can overcome familiarity (Hochberg, 1964; Metzger, 1953). (b) The white regions at bii are more readily seen as recognizable shapes than those at bi, especially after contemplating their similarities to biii. (c) Patterns high in what Peterson (1994) calls *denotivity*, like the "seahorse," "coffeepot," and "pineapple" reversible figure-ground compounds at (ci), (cii), and (ciii), are reportedly perceived earlier and longer than the alternative regions when the high-denotative shapes are in their canonical orientation. This argues that familiar shapes manifest effects of perceptual learning prior to figure-ground segregation (Peterson, 1994; Peterson & Gibson, 1993). In fact, at (d), we see that the recognizable shape is *not* inherently tied to the outward profile of figural surfaces, because the word "figure" is seen even though all of the letters are holes.

tions, and I think that there is still no evidence that viewers actually use geons, as described, in object perception (Hochberg, 1994, 1996; Schyns, in press). In any case, however, we still do not know why outlines provide shape, as they do in Figs. 1 and 5, and I am not convinced that the proposed geons, or any other *specific* set of features, provide the *necessary* basis for shape recognition of objects and their pictures: Geons certainly do not account easily for most of the object pictures discussed in this paper (Figs. 1 and 5 in particular).

Familiar and unfamiliar orientations of the same configuration, as in Fig. 5, may help with both of these issues—why outlines work, and what components of shape they communicate. Not only faces and alphanumerics, but many real objects also come with canonical orientations, and can therefore allow comparison of the familiar and unfamiliar orientations. The white regions in Fig. 6bi meet goodness criteria no worse than the same regions in Fig. 6bii, yet the latter are favored more than the former in the course of figure-ground reversal; this is especially so if the viewer recognizes them as half-views, canonically oriented, of the upright woman's black silhouette in Fig. 6biii.

Peterson and her colleagues devised and tested a large set of such silhouettes that had been separately rated as to their familiar meaning or *denotivity* (e.g., Figs. 6ci to ciii). Using a variety of experiments, they (Peterson, 1994; Peterson & Gibson, 1994; Peterson, Harvey, & Weidenbacher, 1991) argue persuasively that segregation according to Gestalt configurational principles does *not* precede the effects of familiarity. Instead, the perceptual system proceeds in both directions from the contour, using both configurational and familiarity as independent biases or constraints (Peterson, 1994; submitted). To explain the basis for the familiarity effect itself, she proposes and offers evidence that learning proceeds not by geons, but by short feature strings. Such strings need not consist of the two-dimensional projections of three-dimensional geons, and would form distinctively constrained combinations, as with printed words which are not freely assembled out of just any letters at all, but from characteristic strings (freight, through, etc.; see Wickelgren, 1969).

I believe that this, like RBC, can be a very powerful step. The idea of strings seems more applicable than geons to at least some of the shapes considered in this paper, but research is needed to differentiate the two approaches and where each would best apply. In any case, I have long doubted that full figure-ground segregation must precede learned shape recognition. Indeed, a region does not have to be a surface to have its shape recognized: think of a keyhole. Also, note that the word FIGURE is perfectly recognizable in Fig. 6D. What Figs. 3A and 6A have done, as had all of the Gottschaldt experiments, was to remove essential parts of the feature-strings normal to the shapes being concealed. I now doubt that there is a necessary or fixed relationship between the two most important of the various components that are lumped under the "figure-ground" distinction (that is, shape and surface nearness): If we consider feature strings as essentially learned, chunked template-like triggers that provide expectations about what further fixations will disclose, then the familiarity of Fig. 6cii includes a means-end readiness to look to the upper left in that pattern to see whether a pot's handle is in place. And that readiness is just my definition of what makes a picture a picture: the fact that the viewer's implicit knowledge about some object will serve to guide perceptual inquiry into the picture.

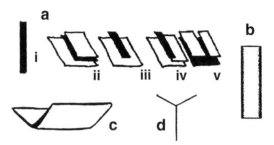

Fig. 7. Lines in the world. (a) (i) The line at (i) is a ribbon of pigment; (ii-v) different arrangements of occluding surfaces that should provide the much same image. (b) The gradients of light reflected to the eye from a uniform nonspecular cylinder (termed *modeling*); similar effects, and areas of shading or shadow, occur at corners and folds (c, d). Unlike the lines in (a), modeling and shadows have at least one diffuse edge, like the gradient in (b) or the penumbra around a shadow. (Figures 7a, c, d are from Hochberg, 1962).

As to whether *all* shape recognition depends on some identifiable set of features, which both the Biederman and Peterson proposals seem to accept, I have no opinion. Things may be more opportunistic than what is implied by a preset vocabulary, other than what is imposed by resource limits like those considered in Sections III and IV. [Schyns & Rodet (1997) report that varying the order in which subjects had to categorize unfamiliar objects changed the parts perceived in those objects.) But I do believe that whether or not the feature set is fixed, one last step helps us understand why marks can work as pictures.

## VII.  Marks as Pictures: Why Outlines on Paper Can Act as Objects' Edges

When first confronted by the findings in Fig. 1, I thought that Mach's lateral inhibition (now, higher-order analyzers) provided the outlines at object's edges in both the real world and in outline drawings (Hochberg, 1962, 1980). I still think that spatial frequency channels or Gabor functions may yet be a useful way to consider the problem, but also that the focal/ambient distinction provides us with a much simpler and immediate (but not exclusionary) answer. I propose that what amount to lines and outlines are frequent in the parafoveal view of objects, and that these often afford information about where more detailed edge information can be found if needed.

Thus, Fig. 7a shows a line or ribbon of luminance difference at (i), and four common distal arrangements by which it might arise, at (ii-v). There are also distal sources that should be more important in object perception, notably the very sharp gradient that is provided by the modeling tone on the vertical edges of the cylinder in Fig. 7b, and wherever surface orientation

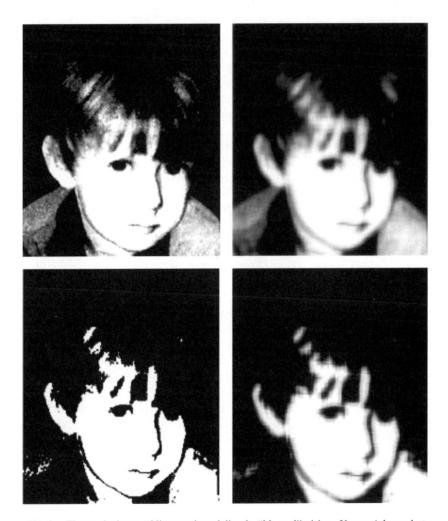

Fig. 8. The equivalence of lines and modeling in "blurred" vision. *Upper right:* a photograph; note the contour of the jaw and nose provided by modeling as in Fig. 7b; eyebrows, lips and eyes are essentially pigmented layers, like Fig. 7a. *Lower left:* a linework picture. *Upper and lower right:* blurred versions of upper and lower left, respectively; note how much more similar the right two are than the left two.

[13] Such gradients commonly arise where nonspecular surfaces change their slant to the line of sight. For a pleasurable history of their use in pictures, see Baxandall (1995).

changes (e.g., Figs. 7c and 7d).[13] When viewed as a blur, it does not differ substantially from any of the alternatives in Fig. 7a, and vice versa. There are several such gradients in the photograph at upper left of Fig. 8, whereas the picture at lower left holds only marks and lines. But when both pictures are blurred, as at right, the differences become negligible. Both pictures at left should be approximately equivalent when viewed in peripheral vision, and afford similar guidance for perceptual inquiry, even though they differ in foveal view (cf. Fig. 2c and 2d).

Such sharp gradients should therefore be major vehicles of learning to perceive objects and the features or feature strings of which they are composed. There are other likely sources of equivalent affordances for perceptual inquiry, and I assume that they would also be opportunistically and nonexclusively learned as cues that signal where the fovea can find more detailed view at object's edges, but these are enough to answer the question raised by Fig. 1.

None of this means that outline pictures are the same as objects, or can normally be confused with them. It does mean, however, that they should not be dismissed as learned artifacts, irrelevant to the general study of perception and perceptual affordances.

## IX.  Summary

The untutored recognition of objects from outline drawings poses no principled difficulties for a perceptual approach with the following testable characteristics: It takes extrafoveal vision as a large part of perception, and as the context for the process of visual inquiry; it accepts peripheral vision as relatively depth-free; it assumes that at least some of the traditional Gestalt principles arise when either objects or their pictures are viewed in (blurred) peripheral vision. Perceived objects (and their pictures) are schemas to be sampled or tested by piecemeal visual inquiry, rather than consistent detailed mental representations; an object's shape is identified by features or feature strings that can also be fitted by any similar luminance difference in the field of view, and not just by objects' edges or figures' contours; and the view of an object or its picture affords guidance as to where the fovea can find detailed informative features.

Although each foveal glance at a picture reveals that the optic array contains only marks on paper, it can also reveal that at least some of those marks conform to what would be found when looking at the object.

ACKNOWLEDGMENT

My thanks to R. L. Goldstone, M. A. Peterson, and P. G. Schyns for their helpful comments on an early version of this paper.

## REFERENCES

Attneave, F. (1954). Some informational aspects of visual perception. *Psychological Review, 61,*183–193.

Baxandall, M. (1995) *Shadows and enlightenment.* New Haven, CT: Yale University Press.

Biederman, I. (1985). Human image understanding: Recent reserch and a theory. *Computer Vision, Graphics , and Image Processing, 32,* 29–73.

Binford, T. (1971). Visual perception by computer. *Proceedings, IIEE conference on systems science and cybernetics.* Miami, Fl.

Boselie, F., & Leeuwenberg, E. (1986). A test of the minimum principle requires a perceptual coding system. *Perception, 15,* 331–354.

Brunswik, E. (1956). *Perception and the representative design of psychological experiments* (2nd ed.) Berkeley: University of California Press.

Brunswik, E., & Kamiya, J. (1953). Ecological cue-validity of "proximity" and other Gestalt factors. *American Journal of Psychology, 66,* 20–32.

Chase, W. G., & Simon, H. A (1973). Perception in chess. *Cognitive Psychology, 4,* 55–81.

Cutting, J. E. (1986). *Perception with an eye for motion.* Cambridge, MA: MIT Press.

Cutting, J. E. (1987). Rigidity in cinema seen from the front row, side aisle. *Journal of Experimental Psychology: Human Perception and Performance, 13,* 323–329.

Cutting, J. E., & Vishton, P. M. (1995). Perceiving layout and knowing distances: The interaction of relative potency, and contextual use of different information about depth. In W. Epstein & S. J. Rogers (Eds.), *Handbook of perception and cognition. Vol.5. Perception of space and motion* (pp. 69–117) San Diego, CA: Academic Press.

DeLoache, J. S., & Burns, N. M. (1994). *Cognition, 52,* 83–110.

Deregowski, J. B. (1968). Difficulties in pictorial depth perception in Africa. *British Journal of Psychology, 59,* 195–204.

Field, D. J. (1987). Relations between the statistics of natural images and the response properties of cortical cells. *Journal of the Optical Society of America, 4,* 2379–2394.

Gibson, J. J. (1950). *The visual world.* Boston: Houghton Mifflin.

Gibson, J. J. (1979). *The ecological approach to visual perception.* Boston: Houghton-Mifflin.

Gillam, B. (1979). Even a possible figure can look impossible. *Perception, 8,* 229–232.

Ginsburg, A. (1980). Specifying relevant spatial information for image evaluation and display design: An explanation of how we see objects. *Perception & Psychophysics, 21,* 219–228.

Haber, R. N., Haber, L. R., Levin, C. A., & Hollyfield, R. (1993). Properties of spatial representations: Data from sighted and blind subjects. *Perception & Psychophysics, 54,* 1–13.

Hagen, M. A. (1974). Picture perception: Toward a theoretical model. *Psychological Bulletin, 81,* 471–497.

Hagen, M. A., & Jones, R. K. (1978). Differential patterns of preference for modified linear perspective in children and in adults. *Journal of Experimental Child Psychology, 26,* 205–215.

Hatfield, G. C., & Epstein, W. (1985). The status of the minimum principle in the theoretical analysis of visual perception. *Psychological Bulletin, 97,* 155–186.

Hebb, D. (1949). *The organization of behavior.* New York: Wiley.

Hess, R. F., & Field, D. (1993). Is the increased spatial uncertainty in the normal periphery due to spatial undersampling or uncalibrated disarray? *Vision Research, 33,* 2663–2670.

Hochberg, J. (1962). The psychophysics of pictorial perception. *Audio-Visual Communications Review, 10,* 22–54.

Hochberg, J. (1964). *Perception.* Englewood Cliffs, NJ: Prentice-Hall.

Hochberg, J. (1968). In the mind's eye. In R. N. Haber (Ed.), *Contemporary theory and research in visual perception.* New York: Holt, Rinehart & Winston.

Hochberg, J. (1970). Attention, organization and consciousness. In D. I. Mostofsky (Ed.), *Attention: Contemporary theory and analysis.* New York: Appleton-Century-Crofts.

Hochberg, J. (1972). Perception I. Color and shape. II. Space and movement. In J. W. King & L. A. Riggs (Eds.), *Woodworth & Schlosberg's experimental psychology.* New York: Holt, Rinehart & Winston.

Hochberg, J. (1974). Organization and the Gestalt tradition. In E. C. Carterette & M. Friedman (Eds.), *Handbook of perception. Vol. I.* New York: Academic Press.

Hochberg, J. (1980). Pictorial function and perceptual structures. In M. A. Hagen (Ed.), *The perception of pictures* (Vol. 2, pp.47–93). New York: Academic Press.

Hochberg, J. (1984). The perception of pictorial representations. *Social Research, 51,* 841–862.

Hochberg, J. (1986). Representation of motion and space in video and cinematic displays. In K. Boff, J. Thomas, & L. Kaufman (Eds.), *Handbook of perception and human performance* (Vol. 1, pp.1–64). New York: Wiley.

Hochberg, J. (1994). Construction of pictorial meaning. In T. A. Sebeok & J. Umiker-Sebeok (Eds) *Advances in visual semiotics: The semiotic web 1992–93* (pp. 110–162). Berln: Mouton de Gruyter.

Hochberg, J. (1995). Construction of pictorial meaning. In T. A. Sebeok & J. Umiker-Sebeok (Eds.), *Advances in visual semiotics: The semiotic web 1992–93* (pp. 110–162). Berlin: Mouton de Gruyter.

Hochberg, J. (1996). The perception of pictures and pictorial art. In M. Friedman & E. Carterette (Eds.), *Handbook of perception & cognition: Cognitive ecology* (pp. 151–203). New York: Academic Press.

Hochberg, J., & Brooks, V. (1962). Pictorial recognition as an unlearned ability: A study of one child's performance. *American Journal of Psychology, 75,* 624–628.

Hochberg, J., & Brooks, V. (1996). The perception of motion pictures. In M. Friedman & E. Carterette (Eds.), *Cognitive ecology* (pp. 205–292). New York: Wiley.

Hochberg, J., & Gelman, L. (1977). The effect of landmark features on mental rotation times. *Memory and Cognition, 5,* 23–26

Hochberg, J., & McAlister, E. (1953). A quantitative approach to figural "goodness." *Journal of Experimental Psychology, 46,* 361–364.

Hochberg, J., & Peterson, M. A. (1987). Piecemeal organization and cognitive components in object perception: Perceptually coupled responses to moving objects. *Journal of Experimental Psychology: General, 116,* 370–380.

Hoffman, J. E., & Subramaniam, B. (1995). Saccadic eye movements and visual selective attention. *Perception and Psychophysics, 57,* 787–795.

Hudson, W. (1962). Pictorial depth perception in sub-cultural groups in Africa. *Journal of Social Psychology, 52,* 183–208.

Hudson, W. (1967). The study of the problem of pictorial perception among unculturated groups. *International Journal of Psychology, 2,* 89–107.

Hughes, H. C., Nozowa, G., & Kitterle, F. (1996). Global precedence, spatial frequency channels, and the statistics of natural images. *Journal of Cognitive Neuroscience, 8,* 197–230.

Hummel, J., & Biederman, I. (1992). Dynamic binding in a neural network for shape recognition. *Psychological Review, 99,* 480–517.

Humphreys, G. W., & Riddoch, M. J. (1987). *To see but not to see: A case study of visual agnosia.* Hillsdale, NJ: Erlbaum.

Irwin, D. E., Zacks, J. L., & Brown, J. H. (1990). Visual memory and the perception of a stable visual environment. *Perception & Psychophysics, 47,* 35–46.

Ittelson, W. H. (1996). Visual perception of markings. *Psychonomic Bulletin & Review, 3,* 171–187.

Jahoda, G., & McGurk, H. (1974). Pictorial depth perception in Scottish and Ghanaian children: A critique of some findings with the Hudson test. *International Journal of Psychology, 9,* 255–267.

Jones, R. K., & Hagen, M. A. (1980). A perspective on cross-cultural picture perception. In M. A. Hagen (Ed.), *The perception of pictures, II* (pp. 193–226). New York: Academic Press.

Kanade, T. (1981). Recovery of the three-dimensional shape of an object from a single view. *Artificial Intelligence, 17,* 409–460.

Kellman, P. J. (1993). Kinematic foundations of infant visual perception. In C. Granrud (Ed.), *Visual perception and cognition in infants* (pp. 121–173). Hillsdale, NJ: Erlbaum.

Kennedy, J. M. (1974). *A psychology of picture perception.* San Francisco: Jossey-Bass.

Kennedy, J. M. (1977). Ancient and modern picture-perception abilities in Africa. *Journal of Aesthetics and Art Criticism, 35,* 293–300.

Kilbride, P. L., & Robbins, M. C. (1968). Linear perspective, pictorial depth perception and education among the Baganda. *Perceptual and Motor Skills, 27,* 601–602.

Klopfer, D. S. (1983). *Parsing of complex, unfamiliar objects, and their pictorial representations.* Ph.D. Dissertation, Columbia University.

Koffka, K. (1935). *Principles of Gestalt psychology.* New York: Harcourt Brace.

Kopfermann, H. (1930). Psychologische Untersuchungen über die Wirkung Zweidimensionaler Darstellunger köperlicher Gebilde. *Psychologische Forschung, 13,* 293–364.

Krampen, M. (1993). *Children's drawings: Iconic coding of the environment.* New York: Plenum.

Kubovy, M. (1986). *The psychology of linear perspective in Renaissance art.* Cambridge, UK: Cambridge University Press.

Leeuwenberg, E. (1971). A perceptual coding language for visual and auditory paterns. *American Journal of Psychology, 84,* 307–349.

Leibowitz, H., Johnson, C., & Isabelle, E. (1972). Peripheral motion detection and refractive error. *Science, 177,* 1207–1208.

Lowe, D. (1987). Three-dimensional object recognition from single two-dimensional images. *Artificial Intelligence, 31,* 355–395.

Metzger, W. (1953). *Gesetze des Sehens.* Frankfurt-am-Main: Kramer.

Michaels, C. F., & Carello, C. (1981). *Direct perception.* Englewood Cliffs, NJ: Prentice-Hall.

Miller, G. A. (1956). The magical number seven, plus or minus two: Some limits on our capacity for processing information. *Psychological Review, 63,* 81–97.

Mundy-Castle, A. C. (1966). Pictorial depth perception in Ghanian children. *International Journal of Psychology, 1,* 288–300.

Palmer, S. E. (1982). Symmetry, transformation, and the structure of perceptual systems. In J. Beck (Ed.), Organization and representation in perception. Hillsdale, NJ: Erlbaum.

Peterson, M. A. (1994). Object recognition processes can and do operate before figure-ground organization. *Current Directions in Psychology, 3,* 105–111.

Peterson, M. A. (Submitted) The relationship between depth segregation and object recognition: Old assumptions, new findings, and a new aproach to object recognition.

Peterson, M. A., & Gibson, B. S. (1993). Shape recognition contributions to figure-ground organization in three-dimensional display. *Cognitive Psychology, 25,* 383–429.

Peterson, M. A., & Gibson, B. S. (1994). Must shape recognition follow figure-ground organization? An assumption in peril. *Psychological Science, 5,* 253–259.

Peterson, M. A., Harvey, E. M. H., & Weidenbacher, H. L. (1991). Shape recognition inputs to figure-ground organization: Which route counts? *Journal of Experimental Psychology: Human Perception and Performance, 17,* 1075–1089.

Peterson, M. A., & Hochberg, J. (1983). The opposed-set measurement procedure: The role of local cues and intention in form perception. *Journal of Experimental Psychology: Human Perception and Performance, 9*, 183–193.

Peterson, M. A., & Hochberg, J. (1989). Necessary considerations for a theory of form perception: A theoretical and empirical reply to Boselie and Leeuwenberg. *Perception, 18*, 105–119.

Pirenne, M. (1970). *Optics, painting and photography.* Cambridge, UK: Cambridge University Press.

Pomerantz, J. R., & Kubovy, M. (1986). Simplicity and liklihood principles. In K. Boff, L. Kaufman, & J. Thomas (Eds.), *Handbook of perception and human performance* (Vol. 2, Ch.36, pp. 1–46). New York: Wiley.

Previc, F. H.(1990). Functional specialization in the lower and upper visual fields in humans: Its ecological origins and neurophysiological implications. *Behavioral and Brain Sciences, 13*, 519–575.

Rubin, N., Nakayama, K., & Shapley, R. (1996). Enhanced perception of illusory contours in the lower versus upper visual hemifields. *Science, 271*, 651–653.

Ryan, T. A., & Schwartz, C. (1956). Speed of perception as a function of mode of representation. *American Journal of Psychology, 69*, 60–69.

Schneider, G. E. (1969) Two visual systems. *Science, 163*, 895–902.

Schyns, P. G. (Submitted). Diagnostic recognition: Task constraints, object information, and their interactions.

Schyns, P. G., & Rodet, L. (1997). Categorization creates functional features. *Journal of Experimental Psychology: Learning, Memory & Cognition, 23*, 1–16.

Spelke, E. S. (1985). Preferential looking methods as tools for the study of cognition in infancy. In A. Yonas (Ed.), *Perceptual development in infancy: The Minnesota Symposia on Child Psychology* (Vol. 20). Hillsdale, NJ: Erlbaum.

Sperling, G. (1960). The information available in brief visual presentations. *Psychological Monographs,74* (11, Whole No. 498).

Terrace, H. S., Jaswal, V., Brannon, E., & Shaofu, C. (1996). What is a chunk? Ask a monkey. *Abstracts of the Psychonomics Society, 1*, 35.

Tolman, E. C. (1948). Cognitive maps in rats and men. *Psychological Review, 55*, 189–208.

Trevarthen, C. (1968). Two mechanisms of vision in primates. *Psychologische Forschung, 31*, 299–337.

Warren, W. H. (1984). Perceiving affordances: Visual guidance of stair climbing. *Journal of Experimental Psychology: Human Perception and Performance, 10*, 683–703.

Warren, W. H., & Wang, S. (1987). Visual guidance of walking through apertures: Body-scaled information for affordances. *Journal of Experimental Psychology: Human Perception and Performance, 13*, 371–383.

Wicklegren, W. (1969). Context sensitive coding, associative memory, and serial order in (speech) behavior. *Psychological Review, 76*, 1–15.

Witkin, A. P., & Tenenbaum, J. M. (1983). On the role of structure in vision. In J. Beck, B. Hope, & A. Rosenfeld (Eds.), *Human and machine vision.* New York: Academic Press.

Woodworth, R. S. (1938). *Experimental psychology.* New York: Holt, Rinehart and Winston.

Yonas, A., & Hagen, M. A. (1973). Effects of static and kinetic depth information on the perception of size in children and adults. *Journal of Experimental Child Psychology, 15*, 254–265.

# PERCEPTUAL LEARNING OF ALPHANUMERIC-LIKE CHARACTERS

*Richard M. Shiffrin*
*Nancy Lightfoot*

## I. Perception vs Learning

In using vision, audition, touch, or other senses to take in information from the world around us, we may be unaware how universally that world is partitioned into objects. If it weren't for this fact the world might appear as a "blooming, buzzing confusion" of a myriad of more primitive features, such as colors, sounds of different frequencies, shapes, slants, and so forth (James, 1890). Almost all of the these objects are of course learned through experience. Consider the upper two visual displays in Fig. 1. These appear quite distinct, in meaning, complexity, and on other grounds; for example, if asked to guess, the reader would probably estimate the central pattern to contain more line segments than the upper pattern. Yet these two patterns contain exactly the same line segments, differing only in the spatial arrangement. One factor that leads to this perceptual distinction is probably learning: the fact that we interpret the upper pattern as a "house." On the other hand, we cannot too hastily assume that the differences in percept are due to object learning. Another factor is simply the perceptual coherence of the upper figure (related to the Gestalt properties investigated in the early part of this century, e.g., see Koffka, 1935), coherence that seems to occur with little or no learning. This is illustrated by the presumably unknown object at the bottom of Fig. 1, an object whose phenomenology may be closer to the house pattern than the random line pattern.

THE PSYCHOLOGY OF LEARNING
AND MOTIVATION, VOL. 36

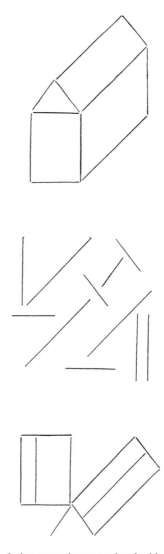

Fig. 1.   An illustration of phenomenology associated with object perception and object learning. The three figures consist of the same line segments in the same orientations, but rearranged spatially. The top figure is a learned object, but also has Gestalt properties of good form. The middle figure is neither learned nor of good form. The bottom figure has elements of good form, but is not learned.

A well-known example of the role of objects in perception, and the interrelationship of features within objects comes from the work of Garner (e.g., 1974). Fig. 2 gives one set of stimuli and a diagnostic sorting task that illustrates Garner's approach. The subject is asked to look at a series of stimuli, for example the two sets of parentheses in the row labeled "control," ((vs.)(, and sort them into two groups. In this single feature sorting task, just one parenthesis changes from trial to trial (the left one in the example): the subject can try to attend to only the left parenthesis of each pair. In a redundant feature condition, either or both of two features can be used to sort. For example, in the row labeled "redundancy," in which sorting of

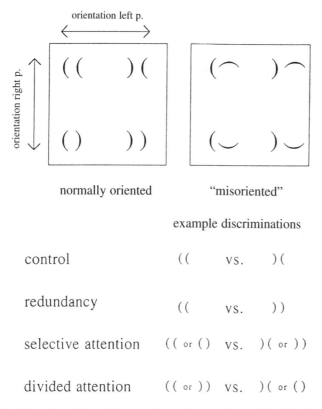

Fig. 2.   An illustration of a task that can be used to test for configurality (Pomerantz & Garner, 1973). Subjects must sort two a sequence of two stimuli into two groups. For normally oriented parentheses, the "redundancy" sort is easier than the "control" sort, suggesting that the two features are processed and used together, configurally. This does not occur for the misoriented parentheses, suggesting these features are not perceived configurally. Such effects seem to occur with little if any training.

((vs.)) is required, the right hand parenthesis changes orientation redundantly with the left. Does this redundancy help? In fact it does, suggesting that the parallel parentheses are seen as a configural group. In contrast, no redundancy gain is seen for the misorientated parentheses in the right hand square at the top of the figure (even though the logical structure of the two tasks is identical), suggesting such perpendicular parentheses do not form a configural group (see Pomerantz & Garner, 1973).

We prefer not to identify such effects with object learning, because they seem to occur with little or no training, and are probably based on very basic, primitive, and automatic processing carried out by our visual systems. There are many properties of this character, a number studied by the Gestalt psychologists, such as closure, good form, continuation, symmetry, parallelism, and so forth. These properties may be innate, or may, in some cases, be learned early in infancy (see Kellman, 1993; research by Spelke, 1990, may be interpreted as showing a type of perceptual learning in infancy: the learning of properties that characterize objects). These properties of vision are of course very important, and form the building blocks for all perceptual learning. Our interest, however, is in those aspects of perception that must be learned, and that change with training, as when we learn a visual code for a "table," or a visual code for an alphanumeric character.

## II. Perceptual Learning vs Other Types of Learning

How one might distinguish perceptual learning from other types of learning, such as associative or procedural, has never been very clear. Historically, this issue was seen in the debate between those favoring the Gibsonian view, in which perceptual learning resides in changes in our perception (i.e., changes in perceived stimulus characteristics; e.g., Gibson, 1969; Gibson & Gibson, 1955), or the associationist view, in which perceptual learning consists of the development of a complex network of internal associations, which fill in the blanks in a relatively impoverished representation of external stimuli (i.e., changes in our responses to stimulus characteristics; e.g., see Hall, 1991). In light of the recent proliferation of cognitive models, this earlier debate, often rooted in empirical studies of learning with and without reinforcement, may seem to some a bit dated (and we will not review it in this chapter). On the other hand, none of the recent advances in cognitive theory and experimentation appears to have brought us any closer to establishing a dividing line between perceptual learning and other types of learning.

It is worth taking a brief look at some of the criteria that might be used to draw such a line (or at least used to motivate research in perceptual learning). The first is phenomenology—learning that changes the subjective feel or appearance of the external world. An example of such a perceptual shift might be the change in appearance of the world that occurs when it is viewed with one eye (when binocular depth cues are missing) or two eyes (when binocular depth cues are present). Other examples of phenomenological shifts include shifts between bi-stable percepts (such as Necker cube reversals), or changes in appearance that occur with extended experience with adapting prisms (e.g., Kohler, 1962). Most such changes occur autonomously (e.g., Bi-stable perception), or without extended training (usually due to changes in the physical input, such as the case of binocular depth perception). Although there may be a few cases in which learning produces changes in phenomenology, it is doubtful that it would prove useful to limit perceptual learning to such cases: Phenomenology is probably useful as a criterion only in a few clear-cut cases. In other cases, changes in appearance may be hard to judge. For example, does a Chinese character appear different after we have learned its use and meaning? Does an English word appear different after it has been learned and assigned meaning? This being the case, most of the learning that occurs in our experience would be eliminated from consideration.

A second criterion involves "change of state." It must be admitted at the outset that change of state could occur for any type of learning, and an observation of change of state cannot really be used to draw a line between perceptual and other types of learning. Nonetheless, the large number of perceptual learning studies that involve this criterion requires its discussion. The general idea is that the learning should involve a qualitative rather than quantitative change (a criterion we try to utilize when interpreting the results of the research presented in this chapter). For example, if alphabetic characters are learned in the context of certain tasks, the improvement might involve: (1) gradual improvement in speed or accuracy of a fixed set of processes, or (2) development of a new representation, or new processes. Such a distinction is extremely difficult to verify, based as it is on a theory of the task and the processes used to perform the task. Even when a plausible account of the observed learning based on change of state can be developed, it may be most difficult to rule out an alternative account(s) based on continuous and gradual learning. Nonetheless, a number of investigators have attempted to demonstrate the learning of new perceptual categories evidenced by some sort of qualitative change of state. In a number of instances, learning itself is not studied, but research has identified perceptual categories, as in the various analyses of identification and discrimination within and across phonemic boundaries (e.g., Lieberman, Harris, Hoffman, & Griffith, 1957). The degree to which such perceptual categories are based on innate featural distinctions has been debated, but it seems clear that learning is involved in generating phonemic categories (e.g., Logan, Lively, & Pisoni, 1991; Strange & Jenkins, 1978). Whether such acquisition represents a qualitative change of state or development of a new representation, or a quantitative shift, is hard to determine. In another approach, researchers have tried to show that the requirements to make discriminations may make subjects invent new conceptual distinctions "on line," distinctions that then modulate performance in the future (e.g., Pevstow & Goldstone, 1994; Schyns & Murphy, 1994). Though these studies may be interpreted in terms of the formation of a new representation, it is hard to rule out the possibility that subjects notice a new combination of other perceptual states, in which case the distinction between learning and cognitive strategy becomes an issue. In addition, it is most difficult to rule out the possibility that training raises the salience of some already existing representation; arguments usually rely on the claim that there are too many possible representations for them all to have been developed prior to the experiment (Schyns & Murphy).

A third criterion might involve "depth" or "stage" of processing. Whether models of perception and learning involve discrete or cascaded transfer of information, and whether or not the model of processing includes feedback, it is universally the practice to postulate stages of processing, from sensory analysis at the input, to decisions and response assignments at the output. Arguments about the nature, structure, and arrangement of such stages have been a major theme of theory development, methodological measurement, and empirical research for many years, especially in such fields as attention and perception. To the extent that it is possible to locate the stage(s) at which learning occurs, it might be possible to define perceptual learning as that which occurs at an early stage. One approach is neurophysiological, by demonstrating changes associated with learning in neural structures in sensory areas (e.g., Jenkins, Merzenich, Ochs, Allard, & Guic-Robles, 1990). Even when such changes are found, however, one might be reluctant to define learning in the task as perceptual, unless a link to behavior is shown, and unless a significant proportion of the learning in the task can be traced to changes in sensory areas. A more typical approach involves developing and defending a model of task performance that carefully delineates the stages of processing. One must then generate agreement among theorists and researchers concerning how early in the resultant framework a change must be to be called perceptual, and then demonstrate that all or some of the learning that is observed can be assigned to such a stage. How difficult this might be in general can be appreciated if one imagines developing a model of word learning, and imagines trying to define the stage(s) at which meaning occurs, and whether this stage(s) is early enough to be called perceptual. Notwithstanding these difficulties, we shall also discuss and utilize this approach in the present chapter, albeit for a very simple task, when exploring what we believe is a process of visual unitization.

A fourth approach to perceptual learning involves identifying such learning with automatization. For example, most people would probably not want to ascribe to perceptual learning changes in performance that are due to choice of strategy, or that come and go with slight changes in setting, instruction, or payoffs. Thus, automatization might be accepted by some as a necessary prerequisite for perceptual learning. However, if one is willing to accept the distinction between automatic and attentive processing (e.g., Shiffrin, 1988), one would almost certainly have to accept the premise that many or all types of learning could be subject to automatization, so that automatization could not be a sufficient criterion.

Considering the various difficulties alluded to in the preceding paragraphs, it is probably impossible to draw a clear line between perceptual learning and learning in general. In this chapter, therefore, we tackle this issue through instantiation, by studying a type of learning that most investigators would be willing to call perceptual (assuming we can show that such learning exists): the processes that underlie the transformation of a set of more primitive visual features into a unitary alphanumeric character. To do this, we have studied the learning that occurs in visual search. That is, the character to be learned must be located in a visual display containing generally similar but different characters.

Because we are interested in learning, we could not utilize known characters like letters and numbers, so we invented novel characters, which are illustrated in Fig. 3. We studied the learning of these characters, obtaining a striking set of findings, whose implications would be quite strong if they prove to generalize to other sorts of perceptual learning. Whether such generalization is warranted will have to be explored in future research.

## III.   Visual Search

It is natural to suppose that an early stage in the learning of an alphanumeric character involves its transition from a collection of disparate features (e.g., lines, orientations, angles, shapes) into a holistic unit.[1] However, typical tasks in which alphanumeric characters participate, such as reading and arithmetic, involve many types of learning beyond unitization. In order to

[1] This transition is not obviously reflected in phenomenology; even strange looking, complicated, and novel characters such as Chinese ideographs appear as holistic objects when presented for the first time, and attended. The situation may be similar to that obtaining when comparing the phenomenology associated with the top and bottom patterns in Fig. 1.

Novel, Conjunctively Defined Stimuli

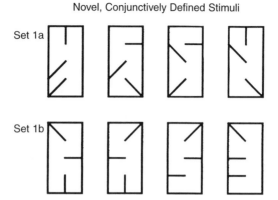

Fig. 3. Novel characters used in experiment 1 and several other studies. One visual search condition uses the characters in just one of these rows. In a given row, each feature (i.e., internal line segment) occurs in exactly two characters, and every pair of characters shares exactly one feature. This forces subjects to search for a conjunction of features—no one feature can be used to identify a target. The two sets share no features.

study unitization in isolation, we decided to utilize a visual search task. In this task, a target stimulus is presented in advance of each trial, followed by presentation of a display of generally similar items. Typically, half the displays contain targets (positive trials) and half do not (negative trials). The subject's task is to make a binary response identifying which type of display has been presented. Accuracy is high, and the response time is the critically dependent measure.

This choice of task confers a number of advantages. First, visual search is intensively used, and relatively well understood. One complication involves the possibility of automatic detection (e.g., Shiffrin & Schneider, 1977; Schneider & Shiffrin, 1977; Treisman & Schmidt, 1982): When the target on each trial is always the same, and when the target is discriminable from the other display items by a simple primitive feature (e.g., an "O" target among "X" distractors), then response time may be almost independent of display size (either at the outset of testing or after a certain amount of practice), as if the target "pops out" from the display in a parallel, unlimited process. However, in most cases, visual search is describable as a serial search process at a constant average rate per comparison, with the process terminating when a target is found in a display. In these cases the function relating response time to display size is linear, with a slope on negative trials twice that on positive trials (the target is found, on the average, halfway through the search of a positive display; a negative display must be searched exhaustively in order to ensure a correct response).

Further, for known stimuli the rate of search (i.e., the slope of the negative RT function) is about 40–60 msec.

The idea underlying our studies is quite simple: If novel characters start as a collection of features, and the task is arranged so that more than one of these features must be compared to identify the presence or absence of a target in a given display position, then the rate of search should be slowed relative to a situation in which comparison of a single feature or the entire character can occur in a single step. However, as a novel character becomes unitized, then it can be compared in a single step, and the rate of search should speed up to a level similar to that observed for alphabetic characters.

## IV.  A Study of Perceptual Learning in Visual Search

There are two sets of stimuli illustrated in the two rows of Fig. 3. One set of stimuli were used in a condition called CM (for *c*onsistent *m*apping); these trials were clearly demarcated in separate blocks. In CM, one of the stimuli is selected as a target and remains so throughout training; the other three stimuli are always used as distractors. The other set of stimuli were used in a condition called VM (for *v*aried *m*apping), also tested in separate blocks. In VM, the target is randomly selected from the set of four before each trial, and the other three stimuli serve as distractors for that trial, but the assignments keep changing across trials. In numerous studies using VM, search shows the serial terminating pattern, but in some studies using CM, automatic detection (i.e., "pop out") develops.

In order to compare the rate of learning in CM to that in VM, we gave four times as many trials per VM block as CM block, so that the amount of experience with each target item (and each target-distractor combination) was equated between the two conditions. This manipulation was motivated in particular by a model of visual search proposed by Fisher (1986). In this model, the display is searched in parallel for the presence of a particular feature; all objects containing that feature are then searched in parallel for a second feature, and so on, until a target is identified. Learning in search tasks consists of finding an optimal order in which to carry out the feature comparisons (optimality is especially important because the system capacity is assumed to drop as successive levels of comparisons continue). Finding an optimal order would almost certainly depend on experience with particular target-distractor combinations. We did not wish to study strategic order of comparisons, or allow different strategies to explain our differences between conditions, so we equated experience with particular targets, and particular target-distractor combinations, between VM and CM.

The stimuli illustrated in Fig. 1 were carefully chosen to have certain properties. Note first that the stimuli each have three internal line segments that provide the identifying information; all stimuli have a common rectangular frame. These internal segments were quite distinct spatially, and were not allowed to meet, in the hope that they would turn out to be the functional features of the stimuli, before any unitization is learned. It is of course possible that configurations of the line segments with the external frame could be features. Later we shall provide evidence against this possibility. For now the internal line segments will be termed features, on a provisional basis.

Second, no feature in the VM set appears in the CM set, and vice versa. This was done to keep the sets distinct, and nonconfusable. Even more critical, this design allowed unambiguous transfer-of-training tests to be carried out later in the study.

Third, and most important, in each set of stimuli, each feature appears in exactly two stimuli, and the three features of a given stimulus appear once each in each of the other three stimuli. Thus no one feature can be used to identify the target. Instead, a minimum of two features must be located that match the target for a display stimulus to be identified as a target. This arrangement is known as conjunction search. Our particular choice of stimuli has an important property: no one feature can identify a target, but any two features will work equally well. Because every feature comparison sequence works equally well, improvements in performance cannot be ascribed to learning of an optimal ordering of feature comparisons. Hence Fisher's (1986) theory, and others like it, provide no direct basis for expecting training to improve the rate of search. Of course, one need not be wedded to a feature comparison theory. As in the theory of Duncan and Humphreys (1989), similarity may play a critical role. Similarity might help guide search, and might change the rate of an individual comparison. Because each distractor contains a feature that overlaps the target, similarity between targets and distractors is almost certainly higher than would have been the case had some or all distractors shared no features with the target, and one might expect slowing of search. Improvements with training might then be described generally as due to some process that increases dissimilarity between targets and distractors. Unitization of the characters could be one process that increases dissimilarity, but there might be others; we shall return to this issue later.

A few procedural details are worth mentioning: See Fig. 4 for an illustration. A trial began with a central fixation mark, and the rest of the trial was initiated by a key press by the subject; upon initiation of a trial, a target was presented centrally for 1000 msec followed by a blank screen for 500 msec, followed by the display which remained until a response was

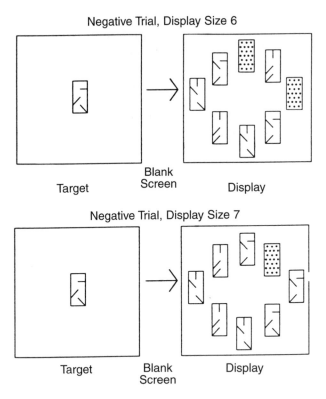

Fig. 4.   Two examples of trials used in experiment 1, in the heterogeneous condition (the distractors are not all identical). A target is presented, and after a brief delay, a display is presented; the subject identifies as quickly as possible the presence or absence of the target. *Top* A display of six characters with no target (negative trial); bottom: a display of seven characters with a target (positive trial).

made. Displays contained eight potential character positions, spaced evenly on a circle of about four degrees external diameter centered about fixation. Each character subtended about .82° vertical and about .55° horizontal. Targets occurred on half the trials. Display size was chosen randomly in the range of 1 to 8; any of the eight positions not filled with characters were filled with masks that were not confusable with characters. Typical studies used blocks of 64 trials for CM, and a typical session had 640 trials, though these numbers varied a bit from one study to the next. In Experiment 1 described below, four subjects each participated in many sessions of training and transfer.

Beyond the manipulations discussed thus far, we also varied the similarity of distractors to each other, within a given display. This manipulation was suggested by research of Duncan and Humphreys (1989) in which they claimed search rate is determined by two factors: Faster search is said to occur when there is an increase in the dissimilarity of targets to distractors (as a group), and an increase in the similarity of distractors to each other. In as yet unpublished research we examined this hypothesis for letter stimuli and discovered that almost all of the similarity effect of distractors to each other is due to the use of homogeneous displays, in which all distractors are identical. When displays did not use identical distractors, similarity among distractors appeared to make little difference. It appeared that the search system is especially sensitive to oddity in a visual display and can use the existence of such to improve search (see Yantis, 1996, and Theeuwes, 1996, for related research in which oddity in a display can attract attention to a visual location). With this in mind, we used two types of trials mixed in each block: homogeneous trials in which a single distractor was chosen randomly for that trial, and then used for every distractor in that display, or heterogeneous displays, in which the distractors were distributed among the three possibilities as uniformly as the display size would permit (but then inserted in random spatial positions in a display).

It turns out that the observed functions relating RT to display size in the heterogeneous conditions all exhibit linearity, with negative slopes twice positive slopes. An example is shown in Fig. 5, in the left panel, for sessions 35 to 50, when asymptotic performance has been reached. Such functions can be described by slope values and intercepts. We have not found the intercept values to be particularly informative or interesting, and therefore present only the slope values in this chapter.

The right panel in Fig. 5 shows that the RT functions in the homogenous trials were curvilinear, and to the extent that such functions can be assigned slope values, had lower slopes. To us, this suggested that a special search process, guided at least in part by oddity, comes into play on homogeneous trials, incorporating some sort of parallel search.

Figure 6 gives the slopes of the RT functions for heterogeneous trials, as a function of sessions of training. It is evident that subjects in the hetero- geneous trials start training with very high slopes, as high as 250 msec, much higher than those usually seen in visual search studies. Over 35 sessions of training, these slopes gradually drop to a stable asymptotic level of about 60–70 msec, similar to those often observed for known stimuli in visual search. It is tempting to propose that this slope reduction represents a process of visual unitization, a proposal to be explored further in transfer tasks and additional studies.

Before discussing other aspects of the training results, some remarks are in order concerning the large slopes seen early in training. One might be tempted to postulate that the similarity of targets to distractors early in

## Set Size Effects as Asymptote

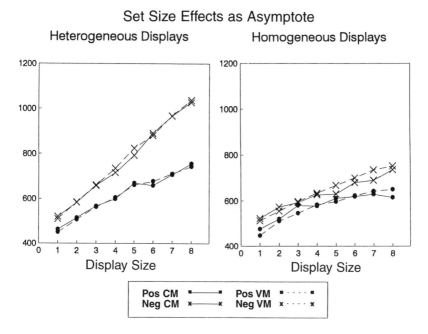

Fig. 5. Examples of response time as a function of set size, after training is complete and performance has stabilized (sessions 35–50). *Left* When the distractors are not all identical (heterogeneous), response time grows linearly and the negative slope is double the positive slope, interpreted as limited capacity terminating search. In this case the slope is interpreted as the rate of comparison per display character. *Right* When the distractors are identical (homogeneous), response time grows nonlinearly, the effect of display time is smaller, and negative and positive trials are similar; a pattern interpreted as parallel, less capacity limited search.

training leads the subjects to check all three features exhaustively, each requiring about 80 msec, in order to carry out each comparison. Why exhaustive search should be used for each comparison is less clear, especially because the search through the displays is terminating. Further, most comparisons of target to display item can be terminated relatively early, when the first mismatching feature is determined. Thus the exhaustive feature checking hypothesis is perhaps questionable. Somewhat more likely is the possibility of successive eye movements to one display item after another (although this could not be verified directly because we did not have eye movement monitoring equipment available at the time of the study). Perhaps the difficulty of comparison when operating in our conjunction search paradigm made searching too difficult while maintaining central fixation. If this account is correct, then the gradual improvement in search rate

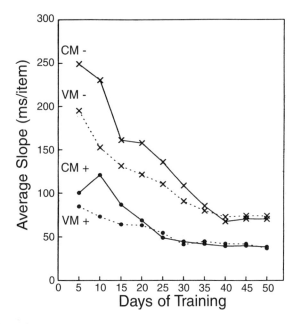

Fig. 6.   Slopes (averaged over four subjects) of the functions relating response time to display size, in the heterogeneous conditions, as a function of sessions of training, for negative (−) and positive (+) trials, for CM training with one set of four characters (the target and the distractor set remain fixed over training) and VM training with the other set of four characters (the target is chosen randomly for each trial and the other three characters become the distractor set for that trial).

that was observed might well reflect a gradual tendency to eliminate eye movements. Further, because eye movements cannot be made much faster than about 200 msec, it cannot be assumed that all of the time per character (i.e., per eye movement) is used to perform feature comparisons. Thus the precise nature of the comparison process per character early in training is difficult to assess. Of course, even if eyemovements are being used, and eliminated gradually with training, unitization of the characters might well be the factor that allows the eye movements to be eliminated.

Although not illustrated in the figure, initial slopes at the outset of training were lower by a factor of more than two to one in the homogeneous trials (the slopes started at about 100 msec), and gradually improved over 35 sessions to an asymptotic level of around 25 msec. Further, throughout the course of training, the slopes were only slightly larger for negative than positive trials. These results suggested that homogeneous displays lead to a rather different type of search process, possibly one in which search is guided by oddity to the relevant target position, and/or one in which an observation of a completely homogeneous display can be used to produce a negative response. On the other hand, the fact that training produced gains on homogeneous trials over the same 35 sessions as for heterogeneous trials suggests that the learning that is occurring helps search in both types of trials. Possibly the perception of oddity is enhanced by perceptual unitization of the characters. Although the homogeneous trials give a picture of perceptual learning that is generally consistent with the heterogeneous trials, the special nature of homogeneous search complicates the story, and we shall focus only on the heterogeneous conditions in the remainder of this chapter.

## V.  The Effects of Training

The effects of training in Experiment 1 are enormous, both in magnitude and in the duration of training over which they are expressed. From about sessions 35 to 50, CM and VM slopes have converged and remain constant, and the RT functions exhibit the linear terminating pattern typical of visual search (Fig. 5). Further, the slopes in these asymptotic sessions are generally a little slower than, but in the range of, those observed for known alphabetic characters. Because our characters are all surrounded by rectangular frames, something not true of alphanumeric characters, it would not be surprising if they are more similar to each other than are alphanumeric characters, possibly accounting for a slower rate of comparison. Nonetheless, by the end of training it appears that search for our novel characters is similar to that observed for known visual characters in numerous studies.

It is interesting that the rate of descent of the slopes to asymptote is faster for VM than CM trials, because in most studies CM training confers an advantage. However, CM training produces an advantage when it leads to automatic attention attraction to the targets (a kind of pop out; see Shiffrin & Schneider, 1977). Automatic detection did not appear to develop in our studies: Even at the end of training, search in both VM and CM appears to be attentive rather than automatic, judging by the slope values and the linear terminating pattern. Why automatic detection did not develop is a question orthogonal to our concerns in this chapter (but similar results are often found in the literature, and the result may be related to the difficulty of the comparisons required). In any event, if automatic detection did not develop, then the difference between CM and VM seen in early stages of training must be due to a different factor. This factor is almost certainly the fact that the VM conditions included four times as many trials as CM. Although this procedure equated specific experience with a given item as a target, and with specific target-distractor combinations, the total number of exposures of the characters in displays was much greater in VM than CM. Whatever is being learned, learning appears to be based in part on presentation in displays. Most likely, participation in a comparison process, even as a distractor, causes learning to proceed more rapidly for characters in the VM conditions.

What is being learned during this period of 35 sessions of training? We offer the provisional hypothesis that the subjects have learned to unitize the novel stimuli (how unitization might help will be discussed later). Evidence bearing on this hypothesis and others is found in transfer tasks and additional studies that we will discuss next. Due to space limitations, and the desire to maintain clarity, the following tasks and results will be presented in abbreviated form (and not necessarily the order in which they were carried out in practice).

## VI.   What Has Been Learned?

A.   TRANSFER TO NOVEL CHARACTER SETS

It is conceivable that a subject's experience with characters of this sort is sufficient to improve search performance to asymptotic levels, irrespective of the specific characters used in training. We need to ask, then, whether subjects given new stimuli generally similar in all respects to those encountered during training would exhibit good transfer. This was tested on one of the subjects in experiment 1, in an experiment carried out fairly late in the experimental series. The stimuli used in original training (repeated from Fig. 3) are shown with the transfer stimulus sets in Fig. 7. The transfer sets were made as dissimilar as possible to the original sets, with carryover of as few feature conjunctions as possible. Because this subject had participated in a number of other transfer tasks before this one, and in addition had not participated in any studies in the series for several months, the study began with five sessions of retraining. The slopes for the original sessions for this subject are shown to the left of the vertical line in Fig. 8, and for the five retraining sessions shown just to the right of the vertical line. Performance remained at approximately the original asymptotic level during this retraining. The points to the right of the retraining results give the slopes for the new sets of stimuli. It is clear that transfer is quite poor to new stimuli, and the rate of learning for these new sets is no faster than for the original set. Thus learning seems quite specific to the particular characters trained, and there is little gain associated with general procedural knowledge, or general familiarity with the task and the types of stimuli that are used. Such a result would be consistent with the development of

Set 1a

Set 1b

Set 2a

Set 2b

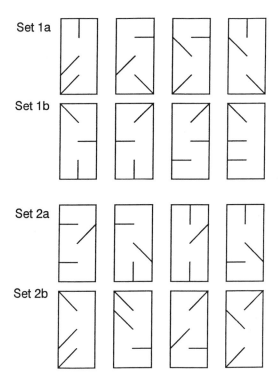

Fig. 7. Character sets used to assess task learning in experiment 2 (for one of the subjects from experiment 1). *Sets 1a* and *1b* Original training with character sets requiring conjunction search (and presumably leading to unitization). *Sets 2a* and *2b* New character sets used in transfer. The sets are dissimilar from sets 1a and 1b, with mostly new line segments, but incorporate the same logical structure, and require conjunction search.

unitization for the trained characters. More generally, one could argue that dissimilarity between targets and distractors has been increased by training, but this change is clearly specific to the characters trained, and not a matter of general expansion of some psychological space.

## B.   EFFICIENCY OF SINGLE FEATURE SEARCH

It is possible that subjects never learn units, but simply learn to search in a more efficient fashion for those features that have been trained. What efficiency means in this context is an open question. The possibility of developing a more efficient order of selection of features is pretty well ruled out by our design, because all orders are equally diagnostic. However, it is possible that feature searches are being used at the end of training, but much more quickly than at the outset of training.

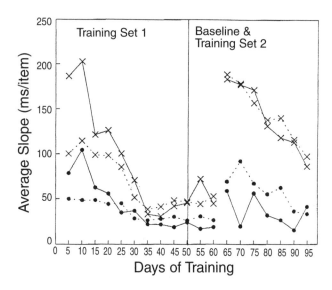

Fig. 8.   Results of experiment 2. Slopes as a function of sessions during original training, retraining on the same characters, and transfer to new characters.

As a first attempt to address this issue, we transferred our original set of subjects to what should have been a trivially easy task if search was based on features: No feature in the target was present in any distractor in the display. The first feature compared for any character will then identify that character as a target of distractor. Under these conditions, one might expect an immediate lowering of slope when the transfer task begins.

Figure 9 illustrates the transfer task: The former VM items were made the CM targets during transfer, each paired with the CM distractors from original training. This ensured that no target feature occurred in any distractor item. In addition, the original CM distractors maintained their role, and the VM items, which were originally targets on some trials were now targets on every trial, which should only improve performance. Figure 10 shows the results. Performance at the outset of transfer was essentially identical to that during training. Thus the relation of particular items to other items (which changed during transfer) seems less critical than the effect of training on the item itself. In addition, the failure to see improved performance at the start of transfer is at least mild evidence against an hypothesis of feature-based search. The results appear quite compatible with the hypothesis that subjects have unitized these stimuli, and therefore are able to use these stimuli in recombination without difficulty. (The recombination results also bear on the question: Have subjects learned

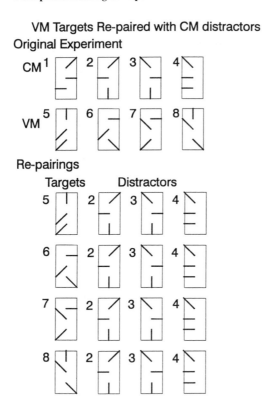

Fig. 9. Characters used for transfer following initial training (50 sessions) in experimental 1. *Top* Example of original character sets. *Bottom four rows* Sets of characters used in CM transfer. The targets were from the original VM set; the distractors in each case are the CM distractors from original training. During transfer, no target feature is present in any displayed distractor.

increasing dissimilarity between targets and distractors? This issue will be deferred until the following study.)

It is rather interesting that continued training during transfer leads (slowly) to improved performance, with slopes eventually dropping to almost one half the asymptotic value at the end of original training. There are to things to note about this result. First, the targets and distractors are quite dissimilar once transfer begins, and single features rather than conjunctions of features suffice to carry out the search. It is possible that single feature search is inherently faster than conjunction search for (recently) unitized items. More generally, search rate may be inherently faster when the dissimilarity between targets and distractors is increased (i.e., the

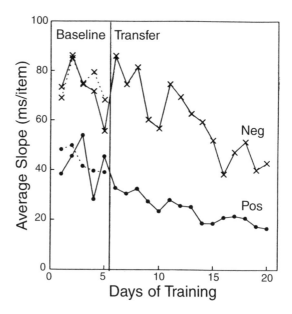

Fig. 10.   Results of transfer for the sets illustrated in Fig. 9. Slopes as a function of sessions, for five sessions immediately prior to transfer (*solid lines;* the last five sessions of original training are given in *dotted lines;* there were some largely irrelevant transfer sessions between these two phases), and sessions during transfer.

more defensible half of the hypothesis of Duncan & Humphreys, 1989). It is interesting that it takes quite a long time for these benefits to evidence themselves. Perhaps the system has a certain amount of inertia, and units continue to be used for comparison (once learned and practiced) even when simpler and better constituent features are available to govern the search.

Whatever is the explanation for the continued improvement during transfer, the existence of such improvement opens the possibility that the unchanged performance at the onset of transfer is actually the result of two offsetting factors: (1) improvements due to whatever process leads to the eventual learning during transfer, and (2) decreased performance due to re-pairing of targets and distractors. This possibility motivated us to carry out a new study with new subjects. This study also bears on the question whether what is learned is unitization or increased dissimilarity.

C.   EFFECT OF RE-PAIRING OF TARGETS AND DISTRACTORS
     DURING TRANSFER

New subjects were each given VM training on six different character sets, each structurally similar to those used in experiment 1, in terms of feature overlap; the sets are given in Fig. 11. After training, they were transferred to two tasks, now run in CM. In the conjunctive transfer task, characters were re-paired so as to maintain the conjunctive nature of the search—the feature overlap has the structure used during training. This is termed testing set 1 in the figure, and consists of one character from each of the first four training sets. In the feature transfer task, characters are re-paired so as to produce a target whose features never appear in any distractor. This is termed testing set 2 in the figure; the target (on the left of testing set 2) comes from training set 5 and the distractors come from training set 6. In this design, all characters used in transfer have been trained equivalently and are equally familiar.

The results are given in Fig. 12 and are fairly remarkable: Transfer is essentially perfect to both conjunctive sets and to feature sets. If re-pairing of stimuli were offsetting some advantage due to feature uniqueness, then the transfer would have been worse in conjunction transfer, because the advantage would have been absent. On the other hand, the perfect transfer for conjunction sets shows that re-pairing of characters after training does not lower performance. Both findings, as well as the results of the previous

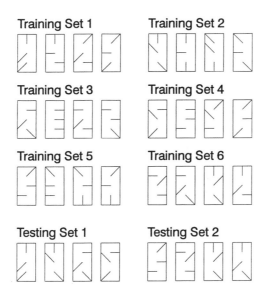

Fig. 11.   Character sets used for new subjects in experiment 3. Six training sets were used in VM, each with the same logical structure as those in experiment 1. In transfer, the characters were rearranged into new combinations, each run in CM. Testing set 1 has the same logical structure as the training sets, with overlapping features, requiring conjunction search. Testing set 2 has no features in common between the target and any distractor.

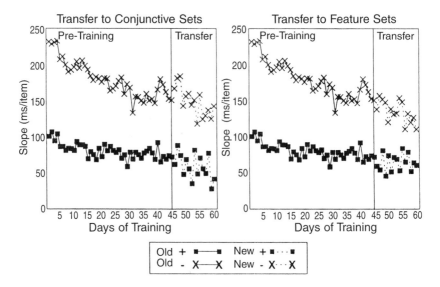

Fig. 12.   Results of experiment 3. Slopes as a function of sessions of original training (termed "pretraining"); these data are plotted in both left and right panels, for convenience. Although performance has not yet reached asymptote, a reasonable degree of unitization has probably occurred by the end of training. *Left* Slopes during transfer to sets requiring conjunction search. *Right* Transfer to sets allowing search on the basis of a single feature.

study, are consistent with the view that the characters had been unitized during training, and once unitized can participate in comparisons in a single step, without the necessity for eye movements.

These results also bear on the hypothesis that the effects of training are to increase dissimilarity between targets and distractors. One way to interpret such a statement is in terms of unitization. A somewhat different way is to suppose that training of particular characters with particular distractors produces increasing dissimilarity between those specific characters. If so, rearrangement of characters should have produced higher levels of similarity, and hence reduced performance, but this did not occur. Thus dissimilarity is apparently associated with the character itself rather than the relations between the characters being trained together. Such results seem to favor a unitization hypothesis (or a dissimilarity hypothesis that may be functionally equivalent).

## VII.   What Are the Features?

Much of the discussion thus far either implicitly or explicitly is predicated on the assumption that the primitive features available to subjects at the outset of training are the internal line segments (segments that are transformed by training, according to our hypothesis, into a single unit). This featural composition of our novel characters is addressed in the following two studies.

## A.  ARE THE INTERNAL LINE SEGMENTS THE FEATURES OF OUR NOVEL CHARACTERS?

It is conceivable that the functional features for subjects are configural arrangements of the internal line segments with the external frame, rather than the internal segments in isolation. For example, a feature might be the angle a segment makes with the rectangular frame. This problem was attacked in what seemed like the simplest possible way: The subjects who participated in experiment 1 took part in a transfer task in which all the external rectangular frames were removed. If the functional features for subjects after training required these frames, their removal should lower performance during transfer. Figure 13 shows the stimuli once the frames were removed (the characters in Fig. 13 are closer together than would have been the case in an actual display on a screen, making them seem less distinct than they appeared in practice). Figure 14 shows the results.

Amazingly, removal of frames produced no harm, whatsoever. Transfer was perfect. Apparently, subjects had learned the insides of each frame as

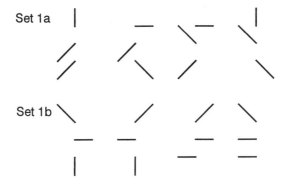

Fig. 13.   Characters used in transfer following original training in experiment 1, and also used in original training in experiment 4 (see Fig. 15). The characters are identical to those in Fig. 3, save that the external frames have been removed (the distance between characters in the figure, relative to the character size, is much less than in an actual display; in actual displays, the characters are easily perceived as separate objects).

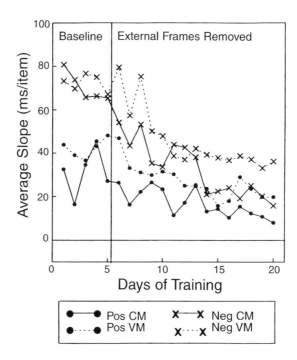

Fig. 14.   Results of transfer from framed characters used in experiment 1 to unframed characters. Slopes as a function of sessions.

the functional unit, so that removal of the frame caused no harm. If the functional features utilized by subjects included configural arrangements of the internal segments with the frames, then their removal should have harmed performance.

It may also be noted that continued training produced continued improvement, so that asymptotic performance without frames is superior to asymptotic performance with frames. Two of the possible explanations for the asymptotic superiority of unframed stimuli are: (1) The frames (being part of every character) make all the characters more similar. Decreased similarity when frames are removed may allow individual comparisons to proceed more quickly. (2) Subjects may have learned to unitize and utilize the inside fo each frame, but nonetheless some effort may be needed to parse the internal pattern from the external frame, a process that might slow comparisons.

As an attempt to address this question, we trained a new set of subjects on stimuli identical to those used in experiment 1, except that they had no frames. These are the stimulus sets illustrated in Fig. 13. In this study, training used CM conditions only. The results are shown in Fig. 15. The training results are shown on the left of the figure. Although slopes began at the same level as for framed stimuli, learning proceeded much more rapidly, and reached asymptotic levels much lower than for the framed stimuli. A plausible interpretation of the faster learning rate is the hypothesis that two types of learning had to be undertaken in the original paradigm: (1) parsing of the internal patterns from the frames, and (2) unitization of the internal pattern. In the present study only the second of these needed learning.

At this point in training, the missing frames were added back to the stimuli, with results shown in the right hand part of the figure. The results were just the opposite of that obtaining in the previous study when the frames were removed. There was no transfer whatsoever, and performance reverted to that seen at the outset of training. Apparently, these subjects had not learned to ignore the frames and at the start of the transfer task were unable to parse out the internal pattern, even though this pattern had just been learned. The framed stimuli were therefore perceived as new

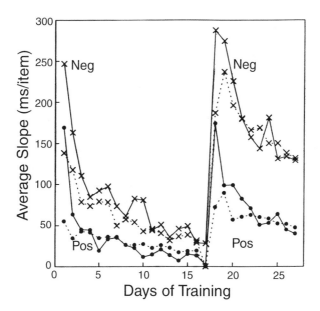

Fig. 15.  Results of experiment 4 using new subjects. Slopes as a function of sessions. Original training utilized unframed characters (see Fig. 13). *Solid lines* CM training and transfer (with one fourth as many trials per block as VM); *dashed lines* VM training and transfer Session 17 and thereafter: Transfer to character sets using identical character sets, save that the external frames have been added.

collections of features rather than as units, and performance dropped to initial levels. Continued training with the frames did produce learning, and at a faster rate than that seen for subjects who had frames at the start of training (the rates shown in Fig. 6). If these subjects learn the internal patterns as units during training, then during transfer they would only need to learn to parse these patterns from the frames. Because only one type of learning was needed, they would learn correspondingly faster.

## B. WHAT FEATURES ARE USED IF EVERY LINE SEGMENT IS FULLY DIAGNOSTIC?

What do subjects learn when trained in a task in which there is no overlap between features of the target and those of the distractors? This question bears on the issue of the featural representation for nonunits, and also on the following question: Will a character made up of several features be learned as a unit if the training task can be accomplished with use of a single feature?

The design was simple: Two new subjects were trained in a task, using CM only, in which no features overlapped between targets and distractors. The sets were in fact those used during transfer in experiment 1 (the transfer sets in Fig. 9). Four targets were trained, each with the same set of three distractors. The training results were shown in Fig. 16: The subjects started with the usual 250 msec slopes, but improved rapidly, reaching asymptote in about half the number of sessions required for conjunction search. The asymptotic slopes were lower than for the conjunction search task, but had values near the level eventually reached by subjects who started in conjunction search and then switched to single feature search (Fig. 10).

It was now possible to ask what had been learned during single feature search. Several transfer tasks were used in each of which there was only a single diagnostic feature. The diagnostic features used were the features of the target during training. An example of the transfer sets is shown in Fig. 17. In each quadrant are the transfer tasks used for a given target that had been trained in phase one. For example, the target in the upper left of the upper left quadrant is tested in turn with displays containing targets consisting of characters in one of the rows to its right. For the first row, the vertical segment is the only diagnostic feature; for the second row, the upper slanting segment is the only diagnostic feature; for the third row, the lower slanting segment is the only diagnostic feature. This design makes it possible to ascertain how much learning had occurred, if any, for each of the individual features in each target. A control transfer task was also used in which for each target every feature was completely diagnostic (as in training), but the distractors were different than those during training.

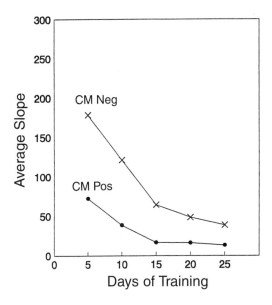

Fig. 16. Results of original training (CM) in experiment 5, using new subjects; slopes as a function of sessions. No feature overlapped between targets and distractors. The sets were those that had been used during transfer in experiment 1 (for other subjects), and are illustrated in Fig. 9 at the bottom.

The most interesting and important transfer results are given in Fig. 18 (for one of the subjects—the other subject had similar results). Each row corresponds to one of the targets tested in transfer. Within each row, the columns give from left to right the feature giving best transfer, next best transfer, and worst transfer. Also in each panel is the control performance for the case when all features are diagnostic (but the distractors are new). What is striking is that in each case, the best feature of the three gives slopes as good as these seen in the control condition, when all features are diagnostic. This result occurs despite the fact that the similarity of target to distractors is much higher in the experimental conditions (because all characters share two features).

The most straightforward interpretation of these results is quite simple: In a task in which all features are (equally) diagnostic, the subject learns the best of these (we assume), and utilizes this feature for the search. Performance is the same in the control and best of the experimental conditions because search is governed by the same feature. This seems to imply that the subject using a single feature is not much harmed by similarity of the other features in the characters being compared. A different question

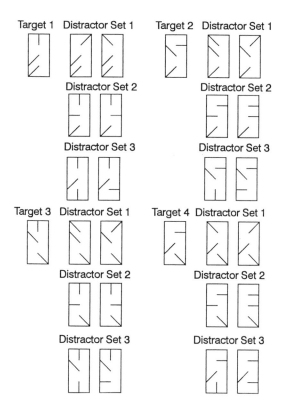

Fig. 17. Transfer sets used after original training in experiment 5 to assess the usefulness of individual features. For each target used in original training there are three transfer conditions, each represented by a set of distractors in a row of two to its right. In each row the distractors overlap with the target in two features, and differ in one. The differing feature differs in each row. Not shown is another transfer condition used as a control, in which the same targets are used, but the set of two distractors is new (untrained) and has no feature overlapping with the target.

concerns why the second and third best features are noticeably worse than the best. Perhaps these are inherently more difficult at the outset of training, and/or require more practice in order to improve (as indicated by their improvement from session one to two).

The fact that one feature seems to subserve search when one or more features are completely diagnostic does not preclude the possibility that the entire character had been unitized during training. Such learning could have occurred in parallel with the searching governed by single features. To check this possibility we simply regrouped the training stimuli, so that conjunctive search was required, just as an experiment 1 (the stimulus groups of Fig. 3 were used). The results are given in Fig. 19, and are quite

# Feature Varied

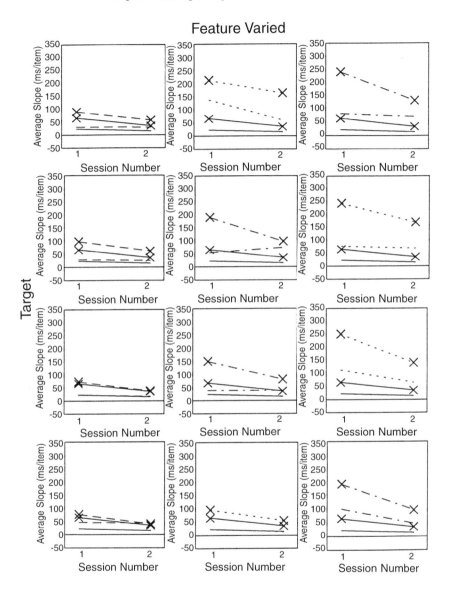

Fig. 18. Results (slopes) of two sessions of transfer in experiment 5. Data for one subject are shown; the data for the other subject were similar in pattern. The X's represent negative trials. Solid lines give the control data, which is repeated from panel to panel. For experimental transfer conditions, each row represents a given target, and transfer for the three features of each target is given in the three columns to the right. For each target, the left most panel shows performance for the feature which has the best transfer (lowest slopes), then next best, then worst.

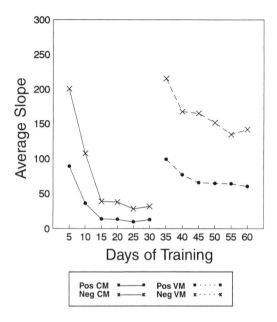

Fig. 19. Additional transfer tests in experiment 5. Transfer tests used VM, and slopes are given as a function of sessions. Data are shown for the same subject illustrated in Fig. 18 (data for the other subject were similar). To the left are results for original training in which any feature is diagnostic (targets and distractors share no features). To the right are results when stimuli are rearranged into sets identical to those in Fig. 3, which require conjunction search since targets and distractors share one feature each.

clear. There is no transfer of training. Learning proceeds slowly as transfer training continues, as if unitization is occurring.

The implication of this finding is important: Unitization may not occur unless the task requires unitization for success. When a task can be accomplished by some more simple or primitive means, the mere co-occurrence of features over thousands of trials may not produce unitization. (This finding is clearly related to studies in the animal learning literature on overshadowing; e.g., Kamin, 1969, and Mackintosh, 1975.)

## VIII.   Does the Process of Unitization Produce a
## Distinctive Percept?

At the least, the studies presented thus far paint a cohesive picture that is consistent with the idea that relevant practice produces unitization. The next study is aimed to obtain evidence concerning what is a rather speculative hypothesis—that units as a class may be perceptually distinct from nonunits. We trained eight sets of stimuli in CM. For four targets, no features overlapped between targets and distractors, so presumably these searches were carried out with single feature search, and no units were formed. For the other four sets, conjunction search was required, as in our earlier studies, so the targets were presumably unitized. In transfer, these eight targets were combined with each other into new search sets in such a way that all search tasks were conjunction searches. In one transfer condition, the targets were units and the distractors nonunits; in the other transfer condition the targets were nonunits and the distractors units. (It is worth reminding the readers that the other two combinations have already been studied: units re-paired with other units in a conjunction search exhibit perfect transfer; nonunits re-paired with other nonunits in a conjunction search show no transfer).

The results are shown in Fig. 20. Initial training for 45 sessions showed the usual pattern: Both conjunction search and single feature search improved with training, with larger training effects for the conjunction case, and higher slopes at the end of training for the conjunction conditions. The transfer results are quite remarkable: Even though nonunits in our earlier studies show no transfer, nonunits as targets show excellent transfer when paired with units as distractors. That is, the slopes are as low as for unit targets in unit distractors prior to transfer. Unit targets in nonunit distractors show even better transfer, better even than the single feature results before transfer. This improvement occurs despite the increase in similarity that results when a shift is made from single feature search (no features in common between targets and distractors) to conjunction search (one feature in common between targets and every distractor). Without further empirical study, one should not read too much into these results, but they appear to provide evidence for a perceptual distinction between units and nonunits, a distinction that can help guide or enhance search.

## IX.  Can Any Character Be Unitized?

It is worth reporting one negative result that could be meaningful in the context of the present studies. In one task we studied, the similarity among characters was made even higher than in our most similar case. Ten subjects were trained in conjunction search for 30 sessions with these highly confusable stimuli. Of these, eight subjects showed no learning (slopes stayed at 300 msec throughout), and two subjects improved only slightly, with slopes dropping from 300 to 200 msec. At this point we decided to stop training. We mention this failure only as a demonstration that at least some similarity

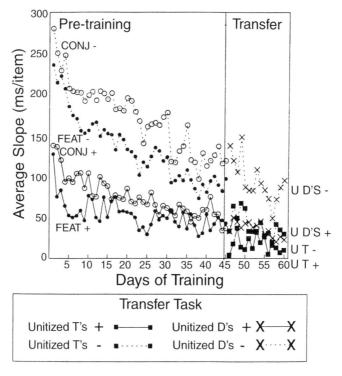

Fig. 20.    Results given as slopes over sessions of training and transfer, both using CM, for experiment 6, using new subjects. Some character sets were trained with the structure of Fig. 3 (overlapping features, requiring conjunction search, presumably producing unitization; results are denoted CONJ), and some character sets were trained in which targets and distractors had no overlapping features (so unitization presumably did not occur; results are denoted FEAT). Characters were reorganized into new sets for transfer; all transfer tests requiring conjunction searches. In one (denoted UD), the presumably unitized characters were distractors, and the target was a character presumably not unitized; in the other (denoted UT) a presumably unitized character was the target, and the distractors were characters presumably not unitized.

constraints must be satisfied for unitization to occur. Of course one could imagine a host of tests of conditions that might or might not allow unitization to occur. For example, one could vary the physical distance between features to be conjoined, introduce variability of irrelevant features, allow variation and transformation of relevant features (such as size), and examine a host of other similar questions. Such studies lie in the future.

## X.   Is Unitization Equivalent to Garner Configurality?

In the introduction, we suggested that there is an important distinction between visual properties extracted automatically by the visual system and those that require training before they can be utilized. We suggested further that a number of properties long studied by Gestalt psychologists lie in the former category. When we chose the stimuli for our studies, we attempted to combine features in such a way that the conjunctions needed to perform the task would not be extracted automatically by the visual system (separated line segments that did not touch). Our choice was guided by phenomenology and experience, and was apparently successful.

As one attempt to discover possible relations between unitization and other types of presumably more innate forms of visual processing, Mark Steyvers, a student now at Indiana, trained subjects in our typical paradigm to learn units. He then transferred the subjects to a set of Garner tasks that are used as tests for configurality. We asked whether the individual features of a trained unit would show the kind of configurality result seen, e.g., for two parallel right facing parentheses (see Fig. 2). The study is too complex to describe here in any detail, but the main result is easy to describe: The central tests for configurality were negative. Such results reinforce our hypothesis that Garner's tests primarily measure basic perceptual properties of the visual system, not derived and secondary properties like unitization.

## XI.   Unitization in Visual Search

The hypothesis that unitization underlies the improvements in visual search rate provides one simple account for the findings presented in this chapter. A model for visual search, and the way in which search changes with training, is not a goal of this chapter. Furthermore, the lack of firm evidence concerning the (probable) use of eye movements in our studies makes any proposed search model somewhat speculative. Nonetheless, a few remarks are in order. Assume first that eye movements are being made from one display character to another at the outset of training, and that these eye movements are gradually eliminated during the course of training. One can presume that the use of eye movements means that, initially, search is too difficult to be carried out even in the near periphery. A lack of unitization could contribute to this difficulty, perhaps by causing the characters to appear more similar to each other. Unitization then occurs during training as a result of some unspecified process, but one presumably related to the use of characters in a comparison process. As unitization develops, some characters in the visual field that are not currently at fixation can be compared, and the eye movements are directed to the remaining locations.

If eye movements do not occur, then unitization provides an even simpler story, in which features are compared one at a time before unitization, and then a switch occurs to comparisons based on whole characters, in one step.

In either of these views, throughout training search remains resource demanding and attentive (in the terminology of Shiffrin & Schneider, 1977, or Shiffrin, 1988) and an algorithmic process (in the sense of Logan, 1988). We suggest that one task component has been automatized: the merging of the disparate features of the unknown character into a holistic unit.[2]

## XII.  Summary

The various tests and studies described here are consistent with a rather straightforward account in which novel characters consisting of separate features are perceptually unitized through extensive practice in a task whose accomplishment required utilization of combinations of features. We would stop well short of claiming that this account is the only one consistent with our findings, but it is the simplest and most compelling that we have found.

In order to summarize the findings and their implications, it helps to separate them into two classes: (1) those having to do with the nature of the visual search process that is utilized in our experimental procedure, and (2) those having to do with perceptual learning.

### A.  VISUAL SEARCH

When displays are homogeneous (all distractors identical), a special, parallel search process is enabled, one that produces curvilinear set size functions, and relatively little effect of set size.

When displays are heterogeneous, search for our novel stimuli is attentive, not automatic, based on the relatively high slope values throughout training, and the equality of VM and CM training conditions at asymptote. (The failure to develop automatic detection, i.e., the attraction of attention to the target, may be due to the relatively high degree of similarity of targets to distractors.)

The attentive search observed is limited in capacity and self-terminating, judging by the linear set size functions, and the negative-to-positive slope ratios of $2:1$.

[2] The fact that only one component of an attentive task has undergone automatization makes it most difficult to know whether or not the rate of learning in our tasks is consistent with Logan's 1988 instance theory, or other theories prescribing a particular functional form for learning.

Before perceptual unitization occurs, the functional features are the internal line segments (based in part on the tasks in which frames are removed or added—see Figs. 13–15). In addition, comparisons are based on the best individual feature, for as long as this type of search produces excellent results and superior performance (based on the single feature transfer study; see Figs. 16–18).

## B. PERCEPTUAL LEARNING

When needed to carry out the search, a holistic, unitary representation of the stimuli develops (judging in part by the transfer tests in which conjunction training produces excellent transfer even when the trained stimuli are used in new combinations, and the failure to obtain transfer to conjunction tests when training allowed search to be carried out on the basis of individual features).

Unitization may provide a better account of the observed learning than the development of increased dissimilarly between studied targets and studied distractors, because learning is not specific to particular target-distractor combinations; new combinations of learned units do as well as old combinations.

What is learned is not a general familiarity with stimuli of the type used in the training tasks. It is something specific to an individual character, if that character had been trained in a task requiring conjunctions of features to be attended. Unitization has these properties.

The number of occurrences in displays (i.e., the number of comparisons in which a stimulus takes part), rather than the number of occurrences as targets, determines the rate of unit formation for a novel character (based on the rate of learning for VM vs CM in experiment 1).

The rate of unit formation varies with the similarity structure of the stimulus ensembles, ranging from no learning for highly confusable stimuli, to 35 sessions for our moderately confusable set (with frame), to 15 sessions for our least confusable set (without frames).

Nondiagnostic and redundant visual features tend not to become part of the learned unit (at least when they are easily segregated from the diagnostic part of the patterns, as demonstrated by the studies in which the frames are removed and transfer is high).

Nondiagnostic visual features slow learning (either because they must be parsed out before unitization occurs, or because they increase similarity, or both; the evidence comes from the studies in which frames are added and removed).

After learning, the holistic unit is an abstraction, not a vertical template of the stimulus (based on the fact that the learned units apparently do not include the frames).

There is preliminary evidence that units as a class may be perceptually distinct from nonunits as a class (the study with results reported in Fig. 20). We view these various conclusions and suggestions as starting points for additional investigations of perceptual learning. Some of these findings and hypotheses will probably prove to generalize to other paradigms and stimuli, and some will not. The present findings nonetheless provide a rich set of phenomena to guide future research in this area.

ACKNOWLEDGMENT

This research was supported by NIMH Grant 12717 to the second author. Reports of parts of this research in early stages appeared in Lightfoot and Shiffrin (1992), and Lightfoot, Czerwinski, and Shiffrin (1993). Reprint requests should be addressed to Richard M. Shiffrin, Psychology Dept., Indiana University, Bloomington, IN 47405. Communications and queries may be directed via e-mail to shiffrin @ indiana.edu.

REFERENCES

Duncan, J., & Humphreys, G. W. (1989). Visual search and stimulus similarity. *Psychological Review, 96,* 433–458.

Fisher D. L. (1986). Programmable perceptrons: Serial and parallel visual search. Paper presented at the annual meetings of the Society for Mathematical Psychology, Boston.

Garner, W. R. (1974). *The processing of information and structure.* Potomac, MD: Erlbaum.

Gibson, E. J. (1969). *Principles of perceptual learning and development.* New York: Appleton-Century-Crofts.

Gibson, J. J., & Gibson, E. J. (1955). Perceptual learning-differentiation or enrichment? *Psychological Review, 62,* 32–41.

Hall, G. (1991). *Perceptual and associate learning.* Oxford Psychology Series, No. 18. New York: Oxford University Press.

James, W. (1890). *The principles of psychology.* New York: Holt.

Jenkins, W. M., Merzenich, M. M., Ochs, M. T., Allard, T., & Guic-Robles, E. (1990). Functional reorganization of primary somatosensory cortex in adult owl monkeys after behaviorally controlled tactile stimulation. *Journal of Neurophysiology, 63,* 82–104.

Kamin, L. J. (1969). Predictability, surprise, attention, and conditioning. In B. A. Campbell & R. Church (Eds.), *Punishment and aversive behavior* (pp. 279–296). New York: Appleton-Century-Crofts.

Kellman, P. J. (1993). Kinematic foundations of infant visual perception. In C. Granrud (Ed.), *Visual perception and cognition in infancy: CMU symposium on cognition.* Hillsdale, NJ: Erlbaum.

Koffka, K. (1935). *Principles of Gestalt psychology.* New York: Harcourt, Brace & World.

Kohler, I. (1962). Experiments with goggles. *Scientific America, 206,* 62–84.

Lieberman, A. M., Harris, D. K., Hoffman, H. S., & Griffith, B. C. (1957). The discrimination of speech sounds within and across phoneme boundaries. *Journal of Experimental Pscyhology, 54,* 358–368.

Lightfoot, N., & Shiffrin, R. M. (1992). On the unitization of novel, complex visual stimuli. *Proceedings of the Fourteenth Annual Conference of the Cognitive Science Society,* 277–282.

Lightfoot, N., Czerwinski, M. P., & Shiffrin, R. M. (1993). On the automatization of visual search. In C. Izawa (Ed.), *Cognitive psychology applied* (pp. 159–185). Hillsdale, NJ: Erlbaum.

Logan, G. D. (1988). Toward an instance theory of automatization. *Psychological Review, 95,* 492–527.

Logan, J. S., Lively, S. E., & Pisoni, D. B. (1991). Training Japanese listeners to identify /r/ and /l/: A first report. *Journal of Acoustical Society of America, 89,* 874–886.

MacKintosh, N. J. (1975). A theory of attention: Variations in the associability of stimuli with reinforcement. *Psychological Review, 82,* 276–298.

Pevtzow, R., & Goldstone, R. L. (1994). Categorization and the parsing of objects. *Proceedings of the Sixteenth Annual Conference of the Cognitive Science Society* (pp. 717–722). Hillsdale, NJ: Erlbaum.

Pomerantz, J. R., & Garner, W. R. (1973). Stimulus configuration in selective tasks. *Perception & Psychophysics, 14,* 565–569.

Schneider, W., & Shiffrin, R. M. (1977). Controlled and automatic human information processing: I. Detection, search and attention. *Pscyhological Review, 84,* 1–66.

Schyns, P. G., & Murphy, G. L. (1994). The ontogeny of part representation in object concepts. In D. Medin (Ed.), *The psychology of learning and motivation, 31,* 301–354.

Shiffrin, R. M. (1988). Attention. In R. C. Atkins, R. J. Herrnstein, G. Lindzey, & R. D. Luce (Eds.), *Steven's handbook of experimental psychology: Volume 2. Learning and cognition* (pp. 739–811). New York: Wiley.

Shiffrin, R. M., & Schneider, W. (1977). Controlled and automatic human information processing: II. Perceptual learning, automatic attending, and a general theory. *Psychological Review, 84,* 127–190.

Spelke, E. S. (1990). Principles of object perception. *Cognitive Science, 14,* 29–56.

Strange, W., & Jenkins, J. J. (1978). Role of linguistic experience in the perception of speech. In R. D. Walk & H. L. Pick, Jr. (Eds.), *Perception and experience* (pp. 125–169). New York: Plenum.

Theeuwes, J. (1996). Perceptual selectivity for color and form: On the nature of the interference effect. In A. F. Kramer, M. G. H. Coles, & G. D. Logan (Eds.), *Converging operations in the study of visual selective attention* (pp. 297–314). Washington, DC: American Psychological Association.

Treisman, A. M., & Schmidt, H. (1982). Illusory conjunctions in the perception of objects. *Cognitive Psychology, 14,* 107–141.

Yantis, S. (1996). Attentional capture in vision. In A. F. Kramer, M. G. H. Coles, & G. D. Logan, (Eds.), *Converging operations in the study of visual selective attention* (pp. 45–76). Washington, DC: American Psychological Association.

# EXPERTISE IN OBJECT AND FACE RECOGNITION

*James Tanaka*
*Isabel Gauthier*

A considerable amount of psychological research has been devoted to understanding conceptual changes that occur as a result of domain-specific expertise. This research includes de Groot's (1966) early work on the memory abilities of chess experts and Chi and colleagues' experiments (1981) examining the problem-solving strategies of physics experts. Less research has focused on perceptual changes that occur as a result of expertise. If expertise influences higher cognitive functions, such as those involved in memory and problem-solving, how might it influence the more fundamental processes involved in object perception and recognition?

This chapter explores the role that experience plays in shaping the object recognition process by examining the recognition processes of object experts (i.e., people who quickly identify objects at subordinate levels of abstraction). By definition, experts have more experience with and more knowledgeable about objects in their domain of expertise than are novices. However, a provocative question is whether qualitative differences exist between the recognition processes of experts and novices.

We begin with the assumption that the name by which an object is identified can provided important insights into the mental representation mediating recognition. In his seminal paper, "How shall a thing be called?," Brown (1958) argues that the object name reflects the level at which the object referent needs to be categorized for the community's nonlinguistic purposes or, to use his term, the level of *usual utility*. As Brown points

THE PSYCHOLOGY OF LEARNING
AND MOTIVATION, VOL. 36

out, the level of usual utility changes according to the demands of the linguistic community and this is especially true for expert populations. So, for example, while it is quite acceptable for most of us to refer to the object outside our office window as a "bird," if we were among a group of bird watchers, it would be important to specify whether the object was a "white-throated" or "white-crown sparrow." Generally, experts prefer to identify objects in their domain of expertise more specifically than novices do.

Although few would argue that experts identify objects in their domain at a more specific level than novices, a separate question is whether experts initially recognize objects at this more specific level. In Section I of the chapter, we define object expertise as the ability to quickly and accurately recognize objects at specific or subordinate levels of abstraction. In this section, two kinds of object expertise are discussed: a specialized kind of expertise involving the recognition of objects from a particular object class (i.e., birds, dogs) and a ubiquitous form of expertise involving the recognition of faces. Object experts and "face" experts are similar in that both kinds of recognition involve identification at subordinate levels of abstraction. In the case of object experts, this is the level of "robin" or "beagle," and in the case of face experts, this is the level of "Bill Clinton" or "Margaret Thatcher."

However, despite the subordinate shift in recognition demonstrated by both kinds of experts, it is controversial as to whether the processes of face recognition and expert object recognition are mediated by the same or different mechanisms. As we discuss in Section II, on one side of the issue, the modularity hypothesis maintains that faces are recognized by a separate face-specific module that is biologically endowed and relatively unaffected by experience. In contrast, the expertise hypothesis claims that face recognition is not "special" in a biological or computational sense, but, like other forms of object expertise, is acquired through extensive training and experience.

One approach to the modularity/expertise question is to take a putative face-specific computation and see how it might apply to expert object recognition. It has been suggested that, unlike other objects, faces are recognized holistically (i.e., memory for a face feature is better when tested in the whole face than when tested in isolation). Is holistic recognition specific to faces or does it emerge as a consequence of expertise? In Section III, we discuss two recent empirical studies in which the holistic processes of real-world and laboratory experts were compared to the processes of novices. Our general conclusions are that, first, contrary to the predictions of a strict modularity account, holistic recognition is not unique to faces in light of evidence demonstrating the holistic recognition of other nonface objects. Second, experts differ from novices in their enhanced sensitivity to the configural properties of a stimulus. Thus, although novices and experts can recognize nonface objects holistically, only the experts seem to be acutely aware of configural properties that distinguish one object from another. Before discussing the cognitive processes of expert object and face recognition, we begin by defining what it means to be an "object expert."

## I. Object and Face Experts

A single object can be categorized at many levels of abstraction. For instance, the object *white crown sparrow* can be categorized as an "animal," "bird," "sparrow," or "white crown sparrow." Although an object may be categorized at many levels of abstraction, it is recognized at only one level of abstraction. In recognition, the initial level at which the perceived object triggers its representation in memory has been referred to as its *entry point*[1] (Jolicoeur, Gluck, & Kosslyn, 1984).

### A. ENTRY POINTS AND BASIC LEVELS

Rosch (1978) believed that entry points are not arbitrary, but are determined by the structure found in the stimulus environment. She argued that "in the perceived world, information-rich bundles of perceptual and functional attributes occur that form natural discontinuities and that basic cuts in categorization are made at these discontinuities" (p. 31). Accordingly, Rosch believed that the fundamental or *basic* level of categorization would be determined by the level at which objects showed the most increase in shape similarity.

To test this claim, Rosch, Mervis, Gray, Johnson, and Boyes-Braem (1976) calculated the amount of overlap that objects share with their category cohorts at different levels of abstraction (e.g., the amount of shape similarity for objects that are members of the category "furniture" vs "chair" vs "kitchen chair"). It was found that objects showed the largest increase in perceptual similarity at the level of "shirt," "car," "dog," or "chair," and therefore, should be considered basic. Rosch et al. tested the primacy of this level of abstraction across a variety of object recognition tasks. In a speeded naming task, they found that subjects preferred to use basic level terms to identify objects (e.g., chair, dog) rather than superordinate level terms (e.g., furniture, animal) or subordinate level terms (e.g., easy chair, beagle). In a category-verification task, subjects were faster to verify objects at the basic level than at the superordinate or at the subordi-

[1] The term entry point is equivalent to Biederman's notion of primal access.

nate category levels. In an identity priming task, subjects were faster to judge whether pictures of two simultaneously presented objects were identical or different when primed with a basic level name than with a superordinate level name whereas subordinate level names provided no additional priming over basic level names. Based on this evidence, Rosch et al. argued that the basic level of categorization is the level at which objects are first recognized[2] (i.e., the entry point in recognition).

What kind of information distinguishes objects at the basic level? Basic level objects share a greater number of part features relative to members of superordinate and subordinate categories (Rosch et al., 1976; Tversky & Hemenway, 1984). Part features are defined as divisible, local components of an object that are segmented at points of discontinuity, are perceptually salient, and are usually identified by a linguistic label. For example, attributes such as "wings," "legs," "beak," and "head" are the part features shared by members of the basic level category "bird."[3]

Given the predominance of distinguishing part features at the basic level, it is not by coincidence that current models in vision (Biederman, 1987; Hoffman & Richards, 1985) have taken a parts-based approach to entry point recognition. These models share the common processes of extracting primitive part features from the object image and comparing their part descriptions to object representations stored in memory. Most part-based models of object recognition postulate a finite alphabet of primitive parts which can be organized together to represent objects. One example of this is Biederman's Recognition-By-Components (RBC) theory which proposes that objects are represented by a small number of simplified parts (taken from a finite set of 32 "geons") and abstract relationships between them such as "on top of" or "to the right of" (Biederman & Gerhardstein, 1993). Although such models are designed to account for basic-level recognition, they are not sufficiently robust to support subordinate level identification of objects that share a common part description (e.g., different kinds of cars or birds).

Despite this shortcoming, the appeal of part-based models is that they provide a perceptual or bottom-up solution to the problem of object recognition. However, other categorization studies have suggested that it is not the identification of part information per se, but the diagnosticity of the part information that is the most important in recognition. Schyns and

[2] Other studies (Jolicoeur, Gluck & Kosslyn, 1984; Murphy & Brownell, 1984) have shown that for atypical objects (e.g., penguin, rocking chair), the subordinate level category, not the basic level category, is the entry point of recognition. However, consistent with the shape similarity position, atypical objects are structurally distinctive to typical category members.

[3] In contrast, superordinate categories tend to contain functional features (e.g., "eats," "breathes"), whereas subordinate categories tend to contain modified parts (e.g., "large beak") or surface (e.g. "red") features.

Murphy (1994) used complex three-dimensional shaded objects (Martian rocks) which could be parsed in different ways to test this hypothesis. Subjects studied objects from one of two categories of Martian rocks: Category A always included part A, category B always included part B, all other parts varied randomly. Subjects' parsing of Martian rocks including either part A or B was measured in a part delineation task before, during, and after exposure to one of the two categories. Before learning a given category, subjects almost never selected the target part, whereas they almost always did so after learning. Subjects of both groups and a new group of naive subjects were then exposed to a new group of rocks (category C) which all had parts A and B adjacent to each other. Subjects previously exposed to categories A and B delineated parts A and B as two distinct units, whereas naive subjects grouped parts A and B together as a single unit. Although parts A and B could clearly be segmented as individual units, subjects did not do so unless they had learned that those parts were diagnostic for categorization.

Murphy (1991) has also shown that nonpart information, such as size, color, and texture, can play a role in basic level categorization. In a series of experiments, he found that categories that were optimal in their distinctiveness and informativeness showed a basic-level advantage, regardless of whether distinctiveness and informativeness were based on part information. For example, objects that were the same color and texture as other category members and differed from contrast category members on the color and texture dimensions were the fastest to be categorized in a verification task. These results point out one of the potential problems associated with part-based models of entry-level recognition. In some cases, part information might not be essential to the basic level representation and thus, may play no role in entry-point recognition (Murphy, 1991). Murphy acknowledged that in the real world, basic-level objects might very well be centered about part information. His findings merely emphasized that parts are not necessary nor sufficient to the basic level.

## B. DEFINING EXPERTISE IN OBJECT AND FACE RECOGNITION

If basic-level categories in the natural world are typically distinctive with respect to their parts, object categories subordinate to the basic level are distinguishable on the basis of "modified" parts and color attributes (Tversky & Hemenway, 1984). For example, "beak" is a part feature that differentiates the basic level "bird" from its contrast categories, whereas "long beak" is a modified part feature that distinguishes the subordinate "woodpecker" from its contrast categories. There is a trade-off between informativeness and distinctiveness with regard to subordinate-level categories. On one hand, subordinate categories have the advantage of being more visually informative than basic-level categories so that, for example, more is known about the visual appearance of an object if it is categorized as a "sparrow" vs as a "bird." On the other hand, subordinate-level objects are more visually similar to their contrast categories than basic-level objects and thus, additional analysis is required to differentiate the subordinate "sparrow" from its contrasting subordinates, "wren" and "finch."

The processing cost incurred by subordinate-level categorization was demonstrated in the study by Jolicoeur, Gluck, and Kosslyn (1984). In their study, they asked subjects to categorize pictures of common objects at superordinate ("furniture," "tool," "animal,"), basic ("chair," "saw", "bird"), and subordinate ("kitchen chair," "cross-cut saw," "robin") levels of abstraction. Pictures were presented in either a long exposure (250 msec) or short exposure (75 msec) condition. Their main finding was that for basic-level categorizations, reaction times were the same in the short and long exposure conditions. Presumably, 75 msec was sufficient time for subjects to abstract the part features necessary for the basic-level categorizations. In contrast, subordinate-level categorizations were disrupted by the brief exposure duration suggesting that additional visual analysis was required for subordinate-level categorizations beyond the amount required for basic-level categorizations.

For most tasks, categorization at the generic basic level is adequate. However, for some tasks, specific, subordinate categorization is required. For instance, basic-level access is sufficient to find a chair to sit on or to run away from a lion, but subordinate-level access is necessary to find a friend in a crowd or to identify the type of fish one just caught. When forced to perform subordinate recognition of a large class of objects on a repeated basis, people can improve dramatically to the point of performing with such ease that they appear to use an entirely different mechanism. Thus, because subordinate recognition is so taxing perceptually but can be strongly influenced by experience, it is the most relevant factor in object-recognition expertise. Taking the example of bird watching, the level of interest for experts is that of differentiating between similar species birds and not that of spotting birds in the forest. Typical measures of bird expertise would be both the speed and the accuracy with which one can identify an object at the subordinate species level of "white-throated sparrow" or "yellow warbler." Although experts clearly have greater accessibility to subordinate-level representations than novices do, it is not clear whether the subordinate level plays a direct role in entry-level recognition. It is plausible, for instance, that experts, like novices, initially recognize objects at the basic level and, once the basic-level representation is activated, are simply faster to access the subordinate-level concepts. According to the basic-first hypothesis, expertise doesn't directly influence the entry point in recognition, but facilitates postentry-level categorization. Alternatively, it is possible that expertise could affect the entry point recognition such that initial recognition might occur at the more subordinate level of abstraction.

## 1. Object Expertise

As a test of the two competing hypotheses, Tanaka and Taylor (1991) investigated the entry-level recognition in two kinds of experts: dog experts and bird experts. They found that in a speeded naming task, experts identified pictures of objects from their domain of expertise using subordinate-level labels rather than basic-level labels (e.g., bird experts identified a picture of a robin with the label of "robin" rather than "bird"). However, when identifying objects outside their domain of expertise, the expert subjects used basic-level terms (e.g., bird experts identified a picture of a beagle with the label of "dog"). The role of subordinate-level representations in entry-point recognition was more directly shown in a category-verification experiment. When categorizing pictures of objects from their domain of expertise, Tanaka and Taylor found that experts were just as fast to categorize objects at the subordinate level as at the basic level. Based on the naming and verification measures, it can be inferred that the experts' subordinate-level representations were equally as accessible as their basic-level representations

This research suggests that entry-point recognition at the basic level is not mandatory. Depending on the task demands and the amount of experience of the categorizer, the entry point can shift downward to subordinate levels. In view of the finer grain of visual analysis needed for the subordinate-level categorizations relative to basic-level decisions, downward shifts in recognition demonstrate the influence that task demands and experience have on the recognition process. What are the limits of this influence? The task demands of face recognition and our experience with faces presents the ideal test case for this question.

## 2. Face Expertise

Whereas relatively few people in the population qualify as experts in the recognition of dogs and birds, it has been claimed that virtually everyone is an expert in the recognition of faces (Carey, 1992; Diamond & Carey, 1986). Like other kinds of object expertise, face expertise requires the identification of people at specific levels of abstraction. Indeed, face recognition signifies the most specific kind of *unique identity* categorization in which the category label (i.e., proper name) contains a single exemplar. Objects categorized at the level of unique identity are maximally similar to their category cohorts because structural similarity and category level are highly correlated. Therefore, categorization at the level of unique identity is the most taxing level of categorization for the visual recognition system. From a perceptual standpoint, there are good reasons to think that faces are *not* first recognized at the level of unique identity. Instead, the level at which members begin to bear a structural resemblance to one another, the level of "person" or "human" might serve as the basic level.

Following the recognition tasks used by Rosch et al. (1976), Tanaka (1994) tested the entry point of face recognition. In a speeded naming task, subjects were asked to label quickly and accurately a stack of pictures depicting common objects and familiar faces (e.g., Bill Clinton, Margaret Thatcher). The main finding was that subjects preferred to identify faces with proper name labels rather than basic-level terms (i.e., person or face), whereas they identified nonface objects with basic level labels. However, naming faces with their proper names might not necessarily reflect enhanced accessibility to the unique identity level inasmuch as showing a social bias for using proper names to identify familiar people.

The accessibility of the unique identity level was tested in category verification. In this experiment, subjects verified category membership of familiar faces at the superordinate level of "living thing," basic level of "human," and subordinate level of unique identity (e.g., Bill Clinton). Subjects were as fast to verify faces at the subordinate, unique identity level as at the basic level. Hence, the unique identity representation was as accessible as the basic level representation.[4] Similar to the bird and dog experts study, equal accessibility of basic and subordinate levels for faces suggests that the subordinate level does not replace the basic level as the entry point of recognition. Rather, it is possible that the two levels are accessed in a parallel. The issue of single or multiple entry points in recognition is discussed below.

As a final test, the underlying face representation was probed in an identity priming task. In this task, subjects were presented with a superordinate (e.g., "living thing"), basic (e.g., "human"), subordinate (e.g., Bill Clinton), or neutral word primes followed by two simultaneously shown pictures. The subjects' task was to decide whether the two pictures were visually identical or different. Facilitation was measured as the difference in reaction time between primed trials and neutral trials for the same matching picture stimuli. The priming paradigm assumed that the word prime activates the subjects' visual representation, which in turn is used to enhance the matching response (Posner & Mitchell, 1967; Rosch 1975; Rosch et al., 1976). Results revealed no difference in priming between

---

[4] Verification times to the subordinate level of gender (i.e., male, female) were no faster than unique identity judgments.

basic-level (e.g., "dog") and subordinate-level (e.g., "beagle") word primes for nonface objects, whereas for faces, subordinate-level words (e.g., Bill Clinton) produced greater priming effects than basic-level primes (e.g., "person"). Presumably, the unique identity prime elicited a highly detailed face representation that was utilized in the matching paradigm. Although the notion of multiple entry points remains an open issue, the behavioral evidence indicates that one of the entry points in face recognition at least is the level of unique identity.

Whether the level of unique identity is preferentially accessed over the basic level or whether both are accessed in parallel could be tested in a repetition-priming task. Ellis, Young, and Flude (1990) found that prior exposure to a face produced repetition priming of faces in a familiarity decision task, but not in an expression or sex judgment task. They argued that a familiar face automatically activates identity-level representations and tasks (e.g., familiarity decision tasks), which access the same identity representations should show facilitative priming effects. According to this logic, prior exposure to a face should facilitate identity level judgments (e.g., Bill Clinton), but not basic-level judgments (e.g., "human"). Alternatively, if both levels are activated by the face stimulus, identity- and basic-level responses should shown the facilitative effects of repetition priming for identity- and basic-level judgments.

Finally, it is important to emphasize the type of structural information that distinguishes faces at the level of unique identity. Obviously, all faces share a common description in terms of generic parts and their organization which is why a structural description in terms of simplified parts (as in Biederman's RBC theory) cannot differentiate faces at the level of unique identity. In principle, more precise (metric) representations of each part of a face could support face recognition. In face recognition, metric differences have been referred to as second-order relational properties (Diamond & Carey, 1986). Second-order relational properties are derived by encoding metric differences in part and configural information between a given face and the average face in the population. For example, a particular face might be differentiable from other faces on the basis of how large a nose is relative to the average nose and how narrow the set of eyes are relative to the average inter-eye distance. Therefore, second-order relational properties are vital to the successful recognition of faces at the level of unique identity.

## 3. Summary

The hallmark of expertise is the ability to recognize objects at subordinate levels of abstraction quickly and accurately. This form of expert recognition was demonstrated in a specialized domain, as in the case of bird and dog recognition, or a general domain, as in the case of face recognition. Downward shifts in recognition produced by expertise suggests that a strict structuralist approach to recognition advocated by Rosch might not be entirely accurate. Although Rosch was correct in asserting that world is rich in information about "basic cuts in categorization," research in expert recognition suggests that the fundamental divisions in object categories are modifiable as a consequence of expertise. In one sense, expert object and face recognition are similar in that both demonstrate entry-point recognition at a level that is subordinate to the basic level. However, what is not clear is whether subordinate recognition in these two domains is achieved via the same mechanisms. Although there is little doubt that expert recognition in specialized domains is obtained through years of experience and training, as discussed in the next section, there is considerable debate as to whether face recognition is the product of experience or biology.

## II.  Face Recognition as a Model of Perceptual Expertise

Recognition expertise has been discussed mainly in the context of face recognition (Carey, 1992; Cohen-Levine, Banich, & Koch-Weser, 1988; Diamond & Carey, 1986; Rhodes, Tan, Brake, & Taylor, 1989), for both practical and theoretical reasons. First, because it is usually assumed that all normal humans are experts at face recognition, face experts are the most available subjects! Second, the role of expertise in face recognition has been discussed by several authors (Cohen-Levine, 1989; Diamond & Carey, 1986) as an alternative to the idea that face processing is mediated by a specialized module (Farah, Levinson, & Klein, 1995a; Nachson, 1995; Yin, 1969). However, if face recognition turns out to be modular, its use as the conventional model for the study of expertise could be problematic. Thus, although the modularity of face recognition has been discussed by several authors (Farah et al., Nachson), we believe it is appropriate to ask what evidence supports the idea that face recognition is predetermined and what are the possible contributions of face recognition to the study of expertise. (Note that in the following discussion, face recognition will be used interchangeably with "individual face recognition".) Behavioral effects occurring when faces are categorized at other levels, such as the cross race classification advantage in which subjects classify the race of other-race faces faster than same-race faces, will both be discussed here (see Levin, in press, for a discussion of whether the cross race advantage can be accounted for by differential expertise).

### A.  THE EXPERTISE HYPOTHESIS

Although it is often taken for granted that face recognition is a universal domain of expertise, it may be important to clarify this idea. There is no doubt that individual face recognition from a perceptual standpoint is a difficult task (as discussed in Section I) and that humans perform it efficiently and almost effortlessly. In this sense, face recognition is a universal domain of expertise because we are better at it than would be predicted by our ability with other tasks of comparable difficulty. In fact, defining face recognition as a domain of expertise often is a relative statement: Humans are experts at face recognition relative to object recognition and adults are expert face perceivers compared to children. However, this view is still ambiguous in that it does not specify how adults come to perform at this level with faces and no other category. In other words, face recognition could distinguish itself during development because: (1) a face module was predetermined in the organism, or (2) the organism has had particular experience with faces.[5] Thus, the first meaning (1) of face expertise is simply an observation that there seems to be something different in the way we process faces but remains agnostic as to its cause. The second meaning (2), which we will use here, consists of a particular hypothesis about how face recognition eventually becomes different from the recognition of objects in other subordinate classes.

It may be that the modularity and the expertise hypotheses cannot be successfully tested against each other using faces as stimuli. First, adult novices are practically impossible to find for face recognition. Perhaps one case may be the identification of cross-race faces, which is typically worse than own-race face recognition and perhaps not recognized in the same holistic fashion (Rhodes et al., 1989). However, it may be argued that faces of any kind cannot really be used as control stimuli. We are so proficient at extracting several types of information from faces, be it gender, emotion, or race, that several automatic processes may interact together. For instance, while same-race faces are better identified at the subordinate level, the reverse advantage is true when faces are classified by race (Levin, in press), and how the two may interact is not yet understood. Second, changes in face processing in a child's development could be due to her experience, to maturation of predetermined systems, or to some kind of interaction between the two. In this context, comparisons between face and nonface object recognition in adults with different levels of expertise are key in determining whether the expertise hypothesis can provide a complete account of adult face recognition. Nonetheless, the study of face recognition can be pursued differently depending on whether it is conducted within

[5] We do not wish to ignore the fact that most behaviors probably are a product of an interaction between biology and environment. Even the strongest expertise claims would have to acknowledge the genetic influences on the organization of the visual system. However, in our discussion, any effect which can be obtained with various nonface object categories will not be considered a modular effect. If an effect (or a brain area) does not appear to be specific to faces, changes correlated with development must then be due either to the maturation of general recognition systems or to learning.

the expertise or the modularity framework. For this reason, we will first describe the expertise and modularity views as two different ways to approach and analyze the question of face recognition and will later discuss some relevant empirical data.

To understand how the expertise hypothesis contrasts with the modularity hypothesis, it may be useful to describe what an analysis of expertise must include. Unlike the case of modularity which has been abundantly discussed in general terms, there is no clearly defined framework for the study of expertise. Any expertise problem can be analyzed in terms of four components, the first being a description of the initial problem to be solved. As described earlier, a task description solely in terms of the stimuli (e.g., a "face task" or a "letter task") is ill-defined because objects can be categorized at different levels of abstraction. An adequate description of the problem should therefore include an analysis of the stimulus set as well as a task analysis in terms of what operations are required from the subjects. The initial problem of interest for face processing is individual recognition of faces at the level of unique identity.

The second component of an expertise analysis is a description of how the novice and the expert solutions to the problem differ. Indeed, if the study of expertise phenomena is justified over and above the general study of learning processes, it is because such phenomena at least appear to reflect more than a mere increase in performance. (We acknowledge that expertise phenomena can eventually be explained by continuous learning mechanisms. However, the most interesting expertise phenomena may be those where the novice and expert strategies appear to be qualitatively different.) In the case of face recognition, several researchers have suggested that novices (children) use a feature-based strategy and that experts (adults) use a more holistic strategy (Carey, 1992). Moreover, we have suggested earlier that expertise is accompanied by a shift in the hierarchical organization of categorization levels.

A third component consists of specifying the training conditions that are necessary and sufficient for expertise to develop. The *sufficient* training conditions of expertise for face recognition are obvious: they exist in our common everyday experience with faces, which are omnipresent stimuli in our visual environment starting in infancy. It is less clear however what are the *necessary* constraints without which we would not become as efficient as we are at individuating faces. For instance, would passive exposure to faces be sufficient? Due to the difficulty of doing experimental studies of expertise, this has been the least well-studied component in the expertise account of face recognition.

A final component in the description of an expertise phenomenon pertains to the specific conditions under which subjects can perform at an expert level (or the transfer conditions). Simply put, we are testing experts only to the extent that we are testing them in conditions in which they can use their expert abilities. Expertise is not merely a property of the subject but is defined by a match between a subject's training experience and the testing conditions. In the case of face recognition, expertise seems to be very specific to presentation conditions which resemble our everyday experience with faces. This is supported by evidence that certain test conditions, such as inversion and a number of configural transformations (Tanaka & Farah, 1993; Yin, 1969), appear to reduce differences between face and general nonface (nonexpert) object processing.

## B.   THE MODULARITY HYPOTHESIS

As already mentioned, it has been suggested that face processing is mediated by a specialized module (Farah et al., 1995b; Fodor, 1983; Nachson, 1995; Yin, 1969). According to Fodor, a module can be recognized as a mandatory, domain-specific, hardwired input system which performs innately determined operations. Nachson (1995) reviewed evidence in favor of the modularity of face recognition which includes the claim that face preference may be innate (Goren, Sarty, & Yu, 1975), that there are cortical cells responding specifically to faces (Rolls, 1992), that face recognition is disproportionately impaired by inversion (Yin, 1969), and that there is a face selective neuropsychological deficit (prosopagnosia—see Farah, 1990). As we will briefly review, none of these claims stands unchallenged. More particularly, we wish to discuss some reasons why trying to confirm a modular model is vulnerable to alternative explanations even in the face of a large amount of supporting evidence.

Unlike the expertise hypothesis, a modular hypothesis of face recognition proposes that an object's category membership rather than the particular task demands is the most important factor in engaging the face module. The importance of category-membership relative to other stimulus or task properties in the modular framework can be illustrated by the range of evidence which is cited as supporting the modularity hypothesis. The use of faces may in fact be the only common task factor underlying findings such as the existence of cells responding to the presentation of faces (Perrett, Oram, Harries, Bevan, Hietanen, Beason, & Thomas, 1991), the innate preference for facial configuration (Goren et al., 1975), and behavioral effects with face identification (Yin, 1969) or face-parts recognition (Tanaka & Farah, 1993). An assumption of the modularity framework is that all of these effects are signs of an underlying face module: Any dissociation between face and nonface stimuli can be used to support this view.

Complicating the debate on the modularity of face recognition, different authors have used the concept of modularity in different ways. Attempting to clarify this problem, Hay and Young (1982) dissociated the question of the existence of a specific part of the brain processing faces (specificity) from the question of whether or not faces are recognized in a qualitatively different way (uniqueness). Nonetheless, the use of terms such as specificity, uniqueness, and modularity remains confusing in the discussion of face recognition (Nachson, 1995). Specificity and uniqueness are theoretically independent and both have been invoked as evidence for modularity, although even obtaining evidence supporting both criteria does not logically disconfirm an expertise account. However, a strong modularist position such as the one described by Fodor (1983) cannot do without either of them. The confusion may arise from an important difference between the expertise and the modularity hypotheses. The first focuses on a changing phenomenon that improves with learning. The second considers the adult performance as a steady state in which mechanisms are relatively unaffected by experience. Both models predict that performance improves and changes during development, but they disagree on the causes of this change. Thus, although it may be difficult to resolve the question by studying the development of face recognition, a more powerful strategy may be to investigate the plasticity of the adult visual system. For example, the modularity model rejects the possibility that what happens to face recognition in development could be produced with nonface stimuli in adults, given enough experience.

One difficulty of the modularity hypothesis is that it can't be directly confirmed which is why its tests are often attempts to disconfirm a competing hypothesis, such as the expertise account. In contrast, the expertise hypothesis for any particular effect can be confirmed experimentally, in demonstrations that expertise with nonface objects can lead to results which have been claimed to be face-specific. This has been done in cases of the inversion effect (Diamond & Carey, 1986), the caricature effect (Rhodes & McLean, 1990), and the sensitivity to configural changes (Gauthier & Tarr, in press, a). As we will show in Section III, the two hypotheses are not exhaustive and it is possible that some effects cannot be entirely accounted for either by the modularity or the expertise account.

C.  TESTS OF UNIQUENESS AND THE USE OF CONTROL STIMULI

Of all the criteria for modularity, most attention has been given to domain specificity or uniqueness of face recognition (Nachson, 1995). Though a criterion such as innateness is difficult to test experimentally, it is possible to compare faces with control stimuli in order to test whether a neuropsychological deficit, a physiological response, or a behavioral effect is specific to face recognition. One drawback to this approach is that results attributed to face-specific processes might be based on experiments lacking some critical control. For instance, despite the numerous studies showing a dispro-portionate inversion effect for faces relative to various control stimuli (e.g., Yin, 1969; Scapinello & Yarmey, 1970; Yarmey, 1971; Valentine & Bruce, 1986), Diamond and Carey (1986) demonstrated that the inversion effect can be obtained from dog experts when recognizing dogs. Thus, the face inversion effect can be eliminated from the list of face-specific effects.

The difficulty in interpretation of most face-specific results resides in the many possible explanations for any given dissociation between faces and control stimuli. Face recognition falls at the extreme of many continua and such factors cannot be controlled completely in an experimental situation. One reason why this lack of evidence replicating a face effect with non-face objects may not be compelling is because the richness and complexity of face recognition renders the task of developing adequate control measures challenging. Imagine the multidimensional space composed of all the factors which can be manipulated in a visual object recognition experiment (sche-matically represented in Fig. 1). Some of these factors are stimulus-class membership, categorization level, and expertise level and they could possi-bly interact together to produce a large number of recognition situations which differ in crucial ways. A considerable amount of work has been done comparing face recognition to basic-level recognition of nonface objects (Kanwisher, McDermott, & Chun, 1996; Rumiati, Humphreys, Riddoch, & Bateman, 1994; Sergent, Otha, & MacDonald, 1992; Takahashi, Kawamura, Hirayama, Shiato, & Isono, 1995) as well as to recognition of nonface objects at the exemplar level (Farah, et al., 1995a; Tanaka & Farah, 1993; Tanaka & Sengco, in press). The general finding in such experiments is a behavioral or neurophysiological dissociation between faces and control stimuli. Note that even in the simplified framework shown in Fig. 1A, any difference between face recognition and novice basic-level object recogni-tion could be explained by one of three factors (stimulus-class membership, categorization level or expertise level). The usual approach to this problem, illustrated in Fig. 1B, is to try to equate all dimensions between a face and a nonface object task so that only stimulus-class membership could explain the results obtained. The difficulty with this approach is that, on the one hand, equating factors perfectly is always difficult and, on the other hand, we do not even know how many relevant factors there are to equate. Not only do face and nonface tasks differ in categorization level and subject expertise, but social importance, stimulus homogeneity, stimulus complex-ity, etc., could also be important dimensions. Thus, a more cautious ap-proach to investigate whether some of these dimensions could explain differences between face and nonface tasks is to manipulate them one at

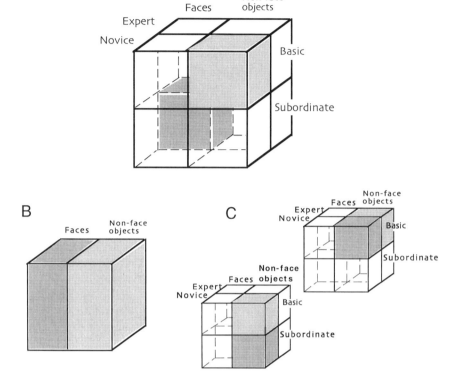

Fig. 1. Simplified representation of the multidimensional space arising from all possible combinations of factors constraining object recognition, such as stimulus-class membership, and expertise and catagorization level.

a time in the domain of nonface objects, so that if particular face effects are replicated, they cannot be explained by stimulus-category[6] (Fig. 1C).

Although subjects' expertise for control stimuli and faces is rarely matched, the few studies which have manipulated expertise have shown its importance. As described earlier, Tanaka and Taylor (1991) have found that expertise leads to a downward shift in entry-point recognition. Diamond and Carey (1986) found that dog experts' recognition of dogs was as disrupted by inversion as face recognition. Rhodes and McLean (1990) obtained a caricature advantage previously found with faces (Rhodes, Brennan, &

[6] Of course, although this approach is more cautions when testing the hypothesis that a particular effect is due to stimulus-class membership, it does not permit very strong claims that the effect is actually due to the manipulated dimension, again because an unknown number of possible confounds apply.

Carey, 1987) in bird experts identifying birds from a very homogeneous class. Using an ingenious manipulation of expertise level with face stimuli, Rhodes et al. (1989) reported that the effect of inversion was larger for faces of the subjects' own race than for different race faces. Together, such results provide evidence that expertise may be as important as stimulus-class membership to explain behavioral dissociations between objects and faces.

## D. TESTS OF NEURAL SPECIFICITY

Behavioral measures tend to show that although face recognition can be dissociated from nonface object recognition, those dissociations might be a result of the subjects' expertise in a particular object domain. Perhaps for this reason, discussion of modularity has recently shifted toward Hay and Young's second criterion (1982) of specificity at the neural substrate level (Davidoff, 1986, 1988; Nachson, 1995; Newcombe, Mehta, & DeHaan, 1994). The premise is that the face recognition system is not qualitatively different from the regular object recognition system but that it is nonetheless separate and engaged in a mandatory fashion by the presentation of faces. Evidence for this view comes mainly from two sources: findings of cells in the temporal cortex that respond selectively to faces (Perrett et al., 1991; Rolls & Baylis, 1986) and the existence of a selective deficit for face recognition called prosopagnosia (Farah, 1990, 1992). Additional support comes from intracranial recording (Allison, McCarthy, Nobre, Puce, & Belger, 1994) and functional neuroimaging (Haxby, Horwitz, Ungerleider, Maisog, Pietrini, & Grady, 1994; Kanwisher et al., 1996; Sergent et al., 1992) studies in humans, which all indicate activation of a region of the ventral temporal cortex (including the fusiform gyrus) to face stimuli. However, as discussed here, none of these lines of research has produce conclusive evidence on the face specificity question.

Logothetis, Pauls, and Poggio (1995) have conducted single-cell experiments in monkeys which suggest that the selectivity of neurons can be tuned by experience with artificial objects similar to face cell selectivity. They extensively trained monkeys to identify novel three-dimensional objects (~600,000 trials for a given object category) and found a population of IT neurons that responded selectively to novel views of previously unfamiliar objects (wire and spheroidal shapes). Moreover, the response pattern of those IT cells points to a direct role in recognition as monkeys showed no selective response for objects they failed to recognize. Logothetis et al. suggested that IT neurons may be "tunable" to accommodate changes in the recognition requirements of the animal and that neurons selective for particular views of objects in an homogeneous class may be mediating configural (holistic) representations. These results also appear to go against the idea that nonface cells show less selectivity than face cells (Bayliss, Rolls, & Leonard, 1985). Importantly, the tuning properties of cells to novel objects can hardly be explained by an innate predisposition and are more consistent with the type of plasticity postulated by the expertise hypothesis. Of course, it could still be the case that face cells are segregated from general recognition cells, but this still needs to be shown. First, face cells of various types of selectivity are found in several parts of the monkey cortex such as IT and the superior temporal sulcus. Second, selectivity to a certain class is never found for all cells tested in a given area (Logothetis et al. 1995; Perrett et al., 1991). Third, experimenters rarely test the same cells with both faces and nonface objects so that it is difficult to assess the extent of overlap between cell populations tuned to face and nonface objects.

Another way to test the idea of a segregated face-specific neural substrate is to consider the possibility that it can be selectively damaged by brain lesions. There may not be a more debated question in the neuropsychology of object recognition than the one of whether a "pure" case of impaired face recognition exists. For example, many cases of prosopagnosia have been observed to be accompanied by more general deficits in object recognition as well as perceptual deficits (Kosslyn, Hamilton, & Bernstein, 1995; Levine & Calvanio, 1989; Rentschler, Treutwein, & Landis, 1994). However, correlated deficits need not be functionally related—in at least a subset of the patient population, face processing may actually be selectively damaged (e.g., De Renzi, 1986; De Renzi, Faglioni Grossi, & Nichelli, 1991). Pure cases of prosopagnosia are rare and most prosopagnosics show some level of impairment for perceiving and/or recognizing nonface objects, especially for within-class recognition of visually similar stimuli. This observation led to the hypothesis that faces could simply be the most difficult objects to recognize and that prosopagnosia could be explained by a mild form of agnosia which would only be detectable for the most difficult recognition task (Damasio, Damasio, & Van Hoesen, 1982). Contrary to this account, there is at least one prosopagnosic, WJ, studied by McNeil and Warrington (1993) who was able to recognize sheep faces much better than human faces, even though normal subjects found the sheep faces more difficult. In another study designed to show that prosopagnosics can be disproportionally impaired at face processing, Farah et al. (1995a) tested the patient LH and normal controls for old/new recognition of faces and eye glass frames. While normal subjects achieved scores of ~85% for faces and ~70% for eye glass frames, LH did not show the same superiority for faces and scored ~65% in both conditions. It was concluded that LH's performance shows that prosopagnosia is a face-specific impairment.

However, it is not evident from accuracy measures alone whether a patient's performance is qualitatively the same or different from normal controls. A complete picture of a patient's impairment cannot be provided without signal detection measures (which control for the possibility that patients may differ from normals on bias rather than sensitivity) and response time measures (which can reveal speed-accuracy tradeoffs; see Kosslyn et al., 1995). Along these lines, Gauthier, Behrmann, Tarr, Anderson, Gore, and McClelland (1996b) tested two prosopagnosics and normal subjects with shaded images of common and novel nonface objects at different levels of categorization and recorded both accuracy and response times. They found evidence that even though prosopagnosics could produce accuracy levels in the normal range for both common and novel objects, the patients' reaction times showed a disproportionate increase with each categorization level. These results illustrate how accuracy alone cannot provide an adequate measure of the relative performance of two groups of subjects.

Techniques such as PET and fMRI may offer a more flexible alternative than lesion studies to address the question of a specific neural substrate for face recognition. Several functional neuroimaging studies have found selective activation for faces in the fusiform gyri (Haxby et al., 1994; Kanwisher et al., 1996; Puce, Allison, Gore, & McCarthy, 1996; Sergent et al., 1992). However, none of these studies has attempted to control for factors such as level of categorization or expertise. One exception is a recent study that found selective activation in the fusiform gyri during subordinate category verification of nonface familiar objects (Gauthier, Anderson, Tarr, & Gore, 1996a). While a direct comparison with faces is required, such results indicate that the level of visual categorization may account for at least part of the dissociations found between face and object tasks in the ventral pathway. Similar experiments manipulating expertise could inform us on the plasticity of the adult extrastriate cortex.

E. WHAT CAN BE LEARNED ABOUT FACE RECOGNITION USING THE EXPERTISE MODEL AND ABOUT EXPERTISE USING THE FACE MODEL?

In view of the numerous factors (among which level of categorization and expertise) confounded in face processing, one question is: Can an expertise analysis help us to understand the relative contributions of these factors. Fig. 2 presents a list of factors which may constrain the expert solution to the face recognition problem, such as the symmetry of the objects, their shared configuration and their social importance, and a list of effects and measures, such as the inversion and composite effects, which have produced dissociations between face and nonface processing. One challenge resides in understanding which combination of constraints leads to any of these face

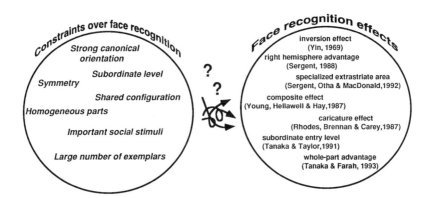

Fig. 2. Different constraints over face recognition and several effects which distinguish face recognition. Little is known about the causal relationships between them.

effects. For instance, is expertise with objects that have a strong canonical orientation sufficient to produce an inversion effect, or is a shared configuration also necessary? Similarly, it is not entirely clear which of the listed effects should be grouped together as properties of the same underlying phenomenon. For example, are the composite and the whole/part advantage really two measures of a same holistic recognition mechanism, or can they be dissociated? These issues are particularly difficult to resolve because of the impossibility of performing experimental studies of face expertise.

Developmental studies of face recognition have indicated that measures which have often been considered equivalent may in fact reflect different underlying components. For example, Carey and Diamond (1994) compared the composite and the inversion effects in adults as well as children of 6 and 10 years of age. The composite effect (Young, Hellawell, & Hay, 1987) is demonstrated by the disruption of the recognition for a part of a face (i.e., the top half) when it is aligned with a complementary part from another face (i.e., the bottom half). When presented upright, the parts seem to fuse together to produce an entirely novel face and disrupt part recognition. Carey and Diamond obtained a strong composite effect at all ages. However, when the fused faces were turned upside down, inversion was more disruptive for the older children than the younger children as measured by reaction time (but see Carey, 1981 and Flin, 1985). This suggests that there are at least two sources to the configural sensitivity in face processing: one seen throughout development and the other appearing with experience.

The expertise model offers a valuable tool to investigate the source of different face effects. Expertise studies count among the most successful methods to replicate face effects with nonface objects and such work plays a major role in bridging the gap between the face and object recognition literatures. That is, if behaviors such as configural encoding are not exclusive to faces, they may turn out to be very informative about general object recognition mechanisms. However, there is one drawback to face recognition being the prototypical expertise model. Because the study of expertise in object recognition has been set up around the face issue, all the nonface recognition tasks studied with experts are constrained to be as similar as possible to the face problem. In some sense, we have been exploring a very small part of the multidimensional space composed of all the possible combinations of constraints on visual object recognition (Fig. 1A). For instance, Diamond and Carey (1986) proposed three conditions for a face-like inversion effect to emerge: (1) the exemplars of the stimulus-class must share a configuration; (2) it must be possible to individuate the exemplars by using second-order relational features; and (3) subjects must have the expertise to exploit such features. This proposal has shaped the study of expertise in that these conditions are often assumed to be necessary for the emergence of any of the face-specific effects. However, note that while these three conditions may produce *sufficient* circumstances for the inversion effect, it is still unknown whether they are *necessary* for the inversion effect, even less so for other effects. Although Diamond and Carey imply that only expertise with a set of homogeneous objects would lead to the inversion effect, this claim is only supported by their failure to find an inversion effect for landscapes. Contrary to this claim, Tanaka and Farah (1991) found that the magnitude of the inversion effect was the same for dot patterns that differed in first-order relational properties and second-order relational properties.

Another frequent assumption seems to be that sets of objects which share a configuration of features are the most challenging for the visual recognition system (Rhodes & Tremewan, 1994). However, there are a few examples in which sets of objects composed of the same or similar features in different spatial organizations lead to very difficult recognition tasks and to performance that shows dramatic orientation sensitivity, not unlike face recognition (Edelman & Bülthoff, 1992; Rock & DiVita, 1987; Tarr & Pinker, 1989). One example is a simple set of seven stick figure objects (Tarr & Pinker, 1989; Gauthier & Tarr, 1997) all composed of a small number of the same features in different configurations. Subjects learning to associate names with four of these objects may take as long as 30 min of practice, which speaks of the difficulty of the discrimination for such a small set of fairly simple stimuli. The face literature would suggest that such a stimulus category does not possess the characteristics necessary to lead to the inversion effect with expertise, as they do not share a configuration of features. However, because expertise can produce surprising qualitative shifts in behavior, it may be presumptuous to predict expertise performance with such objects from experiments with novices. The expert recognition of such a class has not been tested but it could turn out to produce some of the face effects. Therefore, even though the understanding of face processing may profit largely from experiments using tasks matched with face recognition, it can be argued that the study of expertise in object recognition could benefit from moving beyond the particular set of constraints which are combined in the face recognition problem.

## 3. Summary

The study of expertise in visual recognition has been shaped by the problem of face recognition. Even when experiments are not conducted with face stimuli, researchers have matched the constraints of the recognition task to that of face recognition in the hope of replicating face-like effects with nonface stimuli. This approach has led to a body of evidence supporting the idea that face recognition is not unique because similar mechanisms can be engaged with nonface objects given appropriate constraints and subject expertise. Although the face recognition mechanisms may not be unique, there may nonetheless be a face-dedicated neural substrate. Converging evidence from several techniques indicate that a region of the human inferior temporal cortex plays a crucial role in face recognition. However, the same region is also implicated in subordinate-level recognition of non-face objects and the existence of a strictly face-specific cortical area is still an open research question in cognitive neuroscience.

Apart from what it can contribute to the understanding of face recognition, the experimental study of expertise could be a valuable tool to study general object recognition mechanisms. Recognition and categorization tasks can be constrained in many different ways and most current models may fall short of accounting for this diversity. As a partial solution, the expertise model attempts to identify the relevant factors that influence recognition and how experience might shape recognition processes in a particular task domain.

## III.  An Operational Test of the Expertise Hypothesis

One experimental approach to the expertise question is to identify a putative face recognition operation and test whether that same operation is involved in other forms of expert object recognition. For a long time, face recognition researchers have claimed that faces are recognized more holistically than other kinds of objects. Although this claim is not controversial, good operational tests of holistic processes were missing in the literature.

Recently, Tanaka, and Farah (1993) have operationalized the concept of holistic recognition in the following task: In the learning phase of the experiment, subjects memorized a set of normal faces and a set of contrast stimuli; scrambled faces, inverted faces, and houses. After learning, in a two-choice test of recognition, subjects identified the face parts (eyes, nose, mouth) and the house parts (small window, large window, door) presented in isolation and in the whole object. For whole-object test items, the targets and foils were constructed such that they differed only with respect to the critical feature under test. For example, if the nose feature was being tested, the other features of the target and foil faces (e.g., face outline, hair, eyes, mouth features) were identical. Therefore, the difference in subjects' performance between isolated part and the whole object test conditions should reflect the extent to which the object is represented as a whole. The central finding was that for normal faces, subjects recognized parts better in the whole face than in isolation. In contrast, subjects were no better at recognizing parts of scrambled faces, parts of inverted faces, and parts of houses when shown in the whole-object condition than when shown in isolation. Thus, whereas recognition of a part from a normal face was facilitated by presence of the whole face, recognition of parts from the contrast stimuli (i.e., inverted faces, scrambled faces, houses) was not facilitated by whole-object information. From these data, Tanaka and Farah suggested that faces are represented holistically.

Assuming that holistic processing is a specialized operation for the recognition of faces, the part/whole recognition paradigm can be used to address the following questions relevant to the expertise hypothesis:

1. Can the part/whole advantage be found for recognition of other objects besides faces?
2. Does expertise affect the magnitude of the part/whole advantage? In an effort to examine these questions, two studies were carried out. In the first study, current object experts were tested for their holistic recognition of domain-specific objects and faces. The second study was a training experiment in which novice subjects were trained in their recognition of artificial "Greeble" stimuli. After training, their holistic recognition of old and new Greebles was tested.

## A. EXPERIMENT 1: TESTING HOLISTIC RECOGNITION IN EXPERTS

Tanaka and Farah's (1993) part/whole experiment showed that whereas normal upright faces are recognized holistically, other stimuli (i.e., inverted faces, scrambled faces, and houses) are recognized on the basis of their features. Although results from this study are informative about normal face recognition processes, they do not directly test the predictions of the expertise hypothesis. Given the ubiquity of faces in the environment, subjects obviously had more exposure to normal, intact faces than to inverted faces, scrambled faces, and houses. Differential amounts of preexperimental exposure might produce changes in encoding strategies such that, for example, more familiar objects might be encoded holistically relative to less familiar objects. Therefore, a fairer test would be to assess holistic recognition of expert subjects who had extensive exposure to contrast stimuli.

Taking the expertise factor into account, Tanaka, Giles, Szechter, Lantz, Stone, Franks & Vastine (1996) recently tested holistic recognition of real-world experts who specialize in the recognition of particular classes of objects. Tanaka et al. reasoned that if holistic recognition emerges as result of extensive experience in making fine visual discriminations, then individuals who have significant experience in other object domains should show similar effects of holistic recognition for those objects. To test this prediction, they recruited expert subjects who had extensive experience in the recognition of biological cells, automobiles, or Rottweiler dogs. Cells, cars, and Rottweiler dogs were selected as the appropriate contrast stimuli for faces because these objects, like faces, had local identifiable features that were organized in a prototypical configuration.

In this study, all experts had a minimum of 5 years experience (most had more than 10 years experience) and were currently active in their field of expertise. Previous studies have shown that children as young as 5 years of age demonstrate holistic face recognition; hence, 5 years of expertise should be sufficient for holistic recognition to develop in other object domains. It is important to point out that given the vast amounts of experience that humans have with faces, it was not expected that experts would show the same levels of holistic processing for recognition of objects in their domain of expertise as faces, only that the experts show *more* holistic processing for these objects relative to novice controls.

In the training phase of the experiment, expert and novice subjects learned to associate names to six face stimuli and six nonface objects (i.e., cells, automobiles, Rottweiler dogs). Training continued until subjects could identify all 12 stimuli without error. This procedure was followed to help ensure that any differences found between the expert and novice groups in holistic processing were not attributable to general attention or memory effects. That is, it is possible that experts might demonstrate more holistic recognition for domain-specific objects simply because experts remember these objects better than novices. Therefore, once overall recognition performance between the expert and novice groups were equated, the parts and wholes task could be employed to assess the recognition strategies that govern performance.

In this study, the recognition strategies of three types of experts were examined: biology experts, car experts, and dog experts. Biology expertise was tested because biological cells are similar in morphology to faces in that cells have identifiable internal features (i.e., nucleus, nucleolus, mitochondria) that can be manipulated in the frontal plane. Also, similar to face recognition, expert biologists must differentiate individual cells on the basis of metric differences in cell parts and their configuration.

Car expertise was also considered an appropriate expertise domain because automobiles when viewed from the frontal perspective are similar to faces in that they have discernible internal features (i.e., headlights, grill, and bumper) that are arranged in a prototypical configuration (i.e., the two headlights flank the grill and these features are above the bumper). Although there are many varieties of car experts (e.g., people who specialize in repairing cars, people who specialize in racing cars, etc.), the car experts recruited for this study specialized in identifying particular makes and models of cars. These recognition experts typically are members of car clubs, frequent auto shows, and subscribe to publications that review the most current car models (e.g., *Car and Driver, Road and Track*). For these individuals, identifying cars at subordinate levels of abstraction is a critical element of their expertise.

The final group of experts were dog experts who specialized in the breeding or judging of Rottweiler dogs. Because Diamond and Carey (1986) found that dog experts demonstrate an inversion effect for the recognition of dogs, it is also possible that they might recognize dogs holistically. While Diamond and Carey tested the recognition of body profiles, recognition of dog faces was tested in the current experiment. According to the standards specified by the American Kennel Club, the facial qualities of a dog are as crucial to successful dog breeding as its body posture. Therefore, sensitivity to facial structure seems to be an important component of dog expertise.

According to the expertise position, if holistic processing is a product of experience then experts should show an increased amount of holistic recognition (i.e., larger part/whole difference) for objects in their domain relative to novice subjects. The aim of this experiment is to address whether the holistic operations implicated in face recognition are also involved in the recognition of other objects and how expertise might affect holistic processing.

## 1. Method

The biology experts were faculty members of either the departments of Biology or Neuroscience at Oberlin College. Car experts were recruited from a local advertisement or were recommended to the experimenters by other car experts. The dog experts were members of Rottweiler dog organizations in the Oberlin/Cleveland area with extensive experience in either training, showing, breeding, or judging Rottweiler dogs.

Stimuli were generated according to the procedure described by Tanaka and Farah (1993). Six composite target faces, cells, cars, and dogs were constructed with the Adobe Photoshop graphics package (see Fig. 3 for examples). For the human face stimuli, the eyes, the nose, and the mouth features were taken from yearbook pictures of different individuals. For the cell stimuli, the nucleus, nucleolus, and mitochondria features were taken from an introductory textbook in cell biology. For the car stimuli, the headlights, bumpers, and grill features were constructed from pictures of various late model automobiles (e.g., Honda Accord, Ford Taurus). For the dog stimuli, the eyes, nose, and mouth features of different Rottweiler dogs were taken from various dog books. Foil objects were generated by replacing the feature of the target object with the feature from a different target. Isolated part versions of target and foil features were made by removing the feature from the item and placing it on a white background. Stimulus items were individually mounted on white card stock.

The experiment was divided into a learning and a recognition test phase. In the learning phase, subjects were informed that their task was to associate a name to a given face or object. Subjects were introduced to the face (object) with the appropriate name. After the initial introductions, subjects were shown a face (object) and asked to identify the stimulus with the correct name. If the subject responded incorrectly, the experimenter provided the correct name. Learning continued until the subject identified each item twice without error, at which time the procedure was repeated for the other stimulus set. Once subjects identified both face and nonface sets, a final learning test was administered and learning continued until the subject was able to identify all face and nonface items without error. Because we were interested in *processing* differences between experts and novices, we thought that it was important to train each group to the same level of competency.

Fig. 3. Sample of parts and wholes test items for face, cell, car, and dog stimuli used in experiment 1.

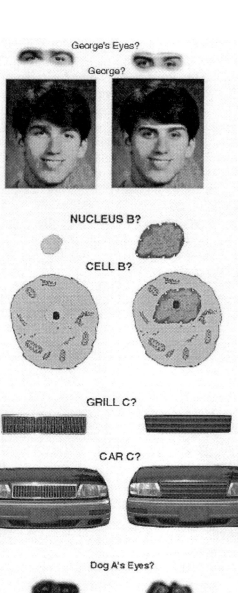

George's Eyes?

George?

NUCLEUS B?

CELL B?

GRILL C?

CAR C?

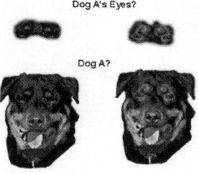

Dog A's Eyes?

Dog A?

Immediately following learning, a two-choice recognition test was administered. In the isolated feature condition, subjects saw a target and foil exemplar presented in isolation. The subjects were asked to identify the correct target exemplar (e.g., "Tom's nose," "Cell A's nucleus"). In the equivalent full object condition, subjects saw the target and foil exemplars embedded in a whole item and were asked to identify the correct target face (object). The full face (object) stimuli were constructed such that they differed only with respect to critical feature under test; the other features were held constant. The left and right positions of the correct isolated part and full target stimuli were counterbalanced across test items. Experimental trials were randomly presented with the restriction that items from the same face (object) could not be tested on consecutive trials.

## 2. Results and Discussion

a. Biology Experts vs Novices   Overall, subjects correctly recognized face parts presented in isolation and in the whole face on 67% and 91% of the trials, respectively. Cell parts were correctly recognized on the 54% of the trials when presented in isolation and 68% when presented in the context of the whole cell. While cells demonstrated a reliable part/whole difference, faces demonstrated a larger part/whole difference than cells. As shown in Fig. 4A, experts and novices did not differ in their part and whole recognition of cells and faces. Specifically, there was a greater part/whole difference for faces than cells and this pattern was essentially the same for experts and novices.

While faces demonstrated more holistic processing than cells in absolute terms, it could be argued that cell recognition demonstrated even greater holistic recognition than faces when chance performance is taken into account. Specifically, whereas recognition of cell parts improved from 4% above chance in the isolated part condition to 18% above chance in the whole cell condition (a greater than fourfold improvement), recognition of the face parts increased from 17% in isolation to 41% in the whole face condition (less than a threefold improvement). Hence, interpretation of the relative differences in holistic processing between cells and faces is somewhat clouded by the disparate baselines between cell and face parts recognition in isolation. However, an important control used in this study was that both experts and novices were trained to the same performance criterion. Once the same level of competence is achieved, it is a fair question to ask to what degree was identification based on the recognition of a single part vs recognition of the whole object. Data from the isolated test condition suggest that subjects did not remember individual cell parts (i.e., mitochondria, nucleus, nucleous) and only some of the face parts. In the whole-

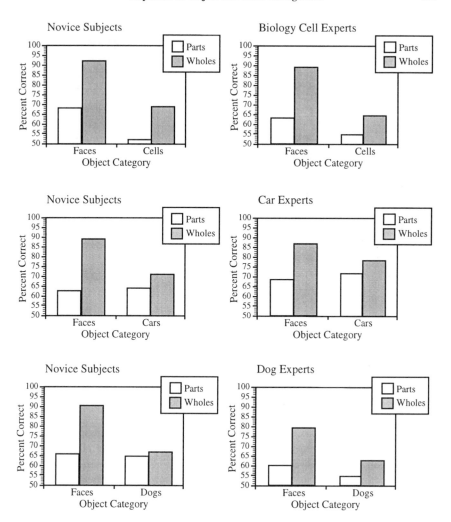

Fig. 4. Recognition of face, cell, car, and dog stimuli by experts and novices.

object condition, cell recognition improved, but not to the same degree as face recognition. Therefore, while all subjects learned to identify the cells and faces perfectly, a more holistic route was taken in face recognition than in cell recognition.

Importantly, counter to the predictions of the expertise hypothesis, experts did not demonstrate greater holistic effects for recognition of objects in their knowledge domain relative to novices. However, as mentioned in

Section II, there are numerous reasons why any experiment might fail to find an expertise effect. First, an expert biologist possesses many skills and abilities in which the recognition of cells might play only a minor role. Unlike face recognition where expertise is defined by the ability to recognize faces quickly and at specific levels of abstraction, this trait might not be a defining characteristic of biological expertise. Additionally, although biological cells, like faces, have internal features, unlike faces, these features are not found in a standard configuration (e.g., the mitochondria can be found above or below the nucleus). Objects that lack a prototypical configuration might not engender holistic recognition. Thus, failure to find an expertise effect with biology experts might be due to the inappropriate contrast population and object domain.

b. *Car Experts vs Novices*  As mentioned, car fronts might serve as a better contrast stimulus than cells because the features of a car, like the features of a face, are arranged in a prototypical configuration. Also, recognition might play a larger role in car expertise than cell expertise.

Subjects correctly recognized face parts presented in isolation and in the whole face on 67% and 87% of the trials, respectively. Car parts were correctly recognized in isolation and in the whole car on the 67% and 75% of the trials, respectively. Faces demonstrated a larger part/whole difference than the contrast stimulus set of cars. However, as shown in Fig. 4B, car experts, like the cell experts, did not show a larger part/whole difference for cars than novices.

Results with the car experts mirrored the results with the cell experts. Overall, faces were recognized more holistically than the contrast stimulus set of cars. However, unsupportive of the expertise hypothesis, car experts did not recognize domain-specific objects (cars) more holistically than novices. Therefore, increased holistic recognition must require something more than just expert identification of objects that share a prototypical configuration.

c. *Dog Experts vs Novices*  Given that cell and car expertise failed to promote holistic recognition, it is reasonable to ask what kind of expertise might be expected to encourage whole-object processing. Diamond and Carey (1986) found that dog experts were disproportionately impaired in their recognition of dog pictures when the stimuli were inverted relative to novices. Interestingly, inversion effects were restricted to the particular breed of dog in which the experts specialized. If dog expertise produced an inversion effect for recognition of dogs, dog experts might also demonstrate greater holistic recognition for their specialized breed of dog.

Subjects correctly recognized human facial features tested in isolation and in the whole face on 64% and 87% of the trials, respectively. Dog facial features were correctly recognized in isolation and in the whole dog face on 62% and 65% of the trials, respectively. Once again, whereas human faces demonstrated a larger part/whole difference, the contrast stimulus set of dog faces did not. As shown in Fig. 4C, dog experts failed to show a larger part/whole difference for Rottweiler dog faces than novices.

The dog expert results do not support the expertise hypothesis. Both dog experts and novices failed to show a part/whole difference. Because there was no evidence that dog faces were recognized holistically, holistic recognition of human faces seems not to generalize to the recognition of dog faces. This finding is consistent with earlier work showing that recognition of dog faces, unlike human faces, failed to show an inversion effect (Scapinello & Yarmey, 1970). Similarly, holistic face recognition appears to be a species-specific rather than a face-specific effect.

Two main findings emerged from Tanaka et al.'s expert study. First, there was no evidence to suggest that expertise influenced the holistic recognition of cells, cars, or dogs. Cell, car, and dog experts demonstrated the same level of holistic processing for domain-specific objects as novice subjects. Do these results argue against the expertise explanation of face recognition? Not necessarily. As pointed out in the earlier section, there are various reasons why recognition of domain-specific objects might differ from face recognition. Although cell, car, and dog experts were selected because it was believed the cognitive operations required for the recognition of these objects were similar to the operations necessary for face recognition, it appears that their skills were not tapped in the part/whole paradigm. Of course, there is always the possibility that some other, as yet untested, group of experts might demonstrate greater holistic recognition for objects in their domain of expertise than novices. However, after testing the expertise hypothesis using a representative cross-section of experts, this claim currently remains unsupported.

The second main finding was that while faces produced the largest amount of holistic processing, other contrast stimuli—cells and cars—were also recognized holistically. This result indicates that holistic processing is not exclusive to faces, but that recognition of other objects can rely on holistic representations, albeit to a lesser extent than faces. Therefore, differences in holistic processing of face and nonface objects appears to be a quantitative rather than a qualitative distinction. Consistent with this idea, Farah (1990, 1992) has argued that objects vary along a continuum to the degree that they are represented as parts and wholes. In Farah's model, faces are located at one extreme of the continuum in that they are represented more as wholes than other nonface objects. As shown in Fig. 5, faces, cells, cars, and dogs did not differ with respect to the recognition of their parts. It was only when the parts were reinserted in the context of the whole object

Combined Parts and Wholes Recognition

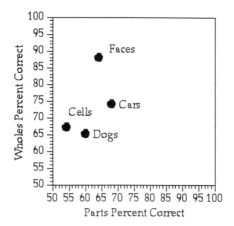

Fig. 5. Combined parts and wholes recognition for face, cell, car, and dog stimuli. Note that faces show the largest advantage in whole-object recognition.

that faces dissociated themselves from the other objects. Thus, face recognition, if not "special," is at least distinctive in its dependence on whole object representations.

### B. EXPERIMENT 2: TRAINING GREEBLE EXPERTS

The results of the foregoing study with cell, car, and dog experts failed to support the expertise hypothesis, because holistic recognition did not increase with experience. One caveat to such expertise studies is that there is limited control over the degree and quality of the expertise of the subjects. In this sense, studies using an experimental manipulation of expertise could offer more control over these variables. While it has been suggested that it takes several years to achieve the level of expertise that adults have with faces (Diamond & Carey, 1986), Gauthier and Tarr (in press) demonstrated that it is possible to create "experts" at novel object recognition in a relatively brief period (7 to 10 hr) of extensive training.

Two goals of the Gauthier and Tarr (in press) study were:

1. to test whether experts with artificial, nonface objects (Greebles) could demonstrate a part/whole effect.

2. to test whether Greeble experts could show sensitivity to configural transformations.

### 1. Method

Expertise with the novel objects ("Greebles") was attained by training subjects at three levels of categorization with a set of 30 objects not used in the test phases. During training, subjects saw examples of the two genders, the five families, and ten specific objects and learned novel names for these categories and objects (Fig. 6). They then performed repeated runs of 60 trials of a yes/no paradigm at each of these levels of categorization. On any trial, one gender, one family, or one individual name was displayed followed by a single object. The task is to verify ("yes/no") whether the object is consistent with the label. The training continued until subjects reached a pre-established criterion: subjects' recognition of Greebles (as measured by sensitivity and response time) at the level of the individual was not reliably different from recognition at the level of gender or family. This is the "categorization shift" proposed in Section I as a characteristic of expert recognition (Tanaka & Taylor, 1991). This took approximately 8 hr of practice (over many days) or close to 5500 trials.

In the test phase of the experiment, a Greeble version of the part/whole recognition paradigm was used. Expert and novice subjects learned names for six Greebles and the generic nonsense names of the individual parts of each. They were tested on part recognition in three different conditions: isolated parts, parts in a new configuration (each of the top parts reoriented 15° toward the front), and parts in the trained configuration (Fig. 7). On each trial one part of a particular target object is specified by a prompt (e.g., the equivalent of "Bob's nose"), followed by two pictures side-by-side on the screen. Subjects then selected whether the right or left image contained the specified part (2AFC design). Trials from each of the three

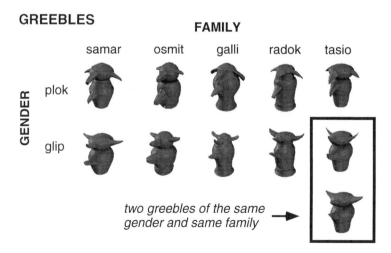

Fig. 6.   Sample objects chosen from a set of 60 control stimuli for faces. Each object can be categorized at the Greeble, family, gender, and individual levels. The Greebles were created by Scott Yu using Alias Sketch! modeling software.

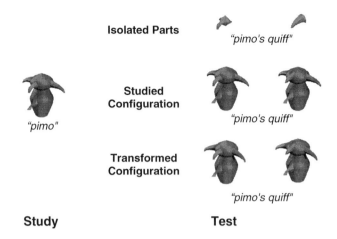

Fig. 7. Example of the forced-choice recognition paradigm used in Gauthier and Tarr (1996).

conditions were randomly intermixed. Gauthier and Tarr (in press) tested 16 experts and 16 novices (not submitted to the training procedure) with sets of upright and inverted untrained Greebles.

## 2. Results and Discussion

The results demonstrated that experts were overall reliably faster, $F(1,30) = 8.21$, $p < .01$, and marginally more accurate, $F(1,30) = 3.65$, $p = .06$, than novices. This confirms that the part recognition task tapped into the type of experience for these particular experts, even though they were only trained at whole object recognition. Moreover, the part/whole advantage was obtained with Greeble stimuli. Greeble parts were better recognized in the context of intact Greebles relative to the recognition of the same parts in isolation. Although this advantage was only reliable (Scheffé's test, $p < .05$) for experts with upright Greebles, it was no different for experts as compared to novices for inverted Greebles (although the effect was smaller in magnitude, see Table 1). Moreover, there was no reliable interaction between Expertise (novice/expert) and Condition (studied/isolated). This led Gauthier and Tarr (1996) to argue that the visual properties of the objects and/or the task, rather than the level of expertise, may have been responsible for the part/whole advantage. This is consistent with results of the Tanaka et al. (1996) expertise study in suggesting that the part-whole advantage is *not* face-specific, but does *not* appear to depend on expertise since it can be found for novices.

## TABLE I

RESPONSE TIMES (MS) AND PERCENT CORRECT FOR PART RECOGNITION OF
UPRIGHT AND INVERTED GREEBLES BY NOVICES AND EXPERTS

|  | Upright Greebles | Inverted Greebles |
|---|---|---|
| NOVICES |  |  |
| Transformed | 3560/80 | 2919/76 |
| Studied | 3853/76 | 3129/80 |
| Isolated parts | 2923/70 | 2234/78 |
| EXPERTS |  |  |
| Transformed | 2695/86 | 2204/85 |
| Studied | 2306/87 | 2382/83 |
| Isolated parts | 1991/76 | 1717/79 |

Gauthier and Tarr (in press) also found that experts recognized Greeble parts faster in the studied configuration as compared to Greeble parts in the transformed configuration. The Studied-Transformed comparison showed a significant effect of expertise $F(1.30) = 10.8$, $p < .005$, and a near-reliable interaction with expertise $F(1.30) = 3.85, p = .059$. Consistent with a recent study by Tanaka and Sengco (in press) with faces, the Studied-Transformed difference was found across the three types of Greeble parts even though only the top parts were moved. This strongly suggests that Greeble experts were no longer representing Greeble parts independently of each other. Unlike the part/whole advantage, the sensitivity to configural changes appears to measure a shift in recognition behavior produced by the expertise training. As discussed in the next section, perhaps the part/whole advantage and the sensitivity to configural changes are indicative of different types of holistic processing, one which appears with expertise and one may be seen as well in novices (just as Carey, 1992, has proposed for the inversion and composite effects). Further support for this conclusion could be gathered by testing other types of experts as well as children's face recognition abilities to see whether the part/whole advantage indeed occurs earlier than sensitivity to configural changes.

Several conclusions can be made from considering the expertise studies just described together with previous findings about the part/whole advantage in face recognition. First, all evidence indicates that the part/whole advantage and sensitivity to configural changes are not face-specific as was originally proposed. Second, the second of these two effects only appeared with expertise but the first showed no difference between novices and experts. We are still far from understanding the stimulus characteristics which lead to these effects. At this point, there does not seem to be a simple factor which distinguishes the type of stimuli for which the part/ whole advantage has been obtained (upright faces, cells, cars, and Greebles) from those stimuli which fail to produce it (scrambled and inverted faces, houses, and dog faces). Third, although both novices and experts showed a part/whole effect, experts nonetheless showed a larger effect (11% difference) than novices (6%) with upright Greebles. Thus, the possibility that the whole/part advantage may be potentiated by expertise remains open.

It may be wise not to generalize the results obtained with a single measure to all tasks measuring configural processing. As described earlier, several authors have recently suggested that tasks which were once thought to be measuring a single "configural processing" factor may in fact be independent (Carey & Diamond, 1994; Rhodes & Tremewan, 1994). This is supported in the Greeble study by the finding of a cross-over interaction with expertise for the test measuring sensitivity to a configural change. Finally, although replicating a face effect with nonface objects may provide a test of the face-modularity hypothesis, it cannot be taken as direct evidence for the expertise alternative. In the case of the part/whole advantage, experiments with different types of control stimuli indicate that neither class-stimulus membership nor expertise holds a complete answer.

## IV.  Conclusions

In this chapter, we began by defining object expertise as the ability to recognize objects at the subordinate level of abstraction. Following this criterion, object experts, such as bird and dog experts, demonstrated a downward shift in recognition when identifying objects from their domain of expertise and normal adults when identifying faces. However, the functional equivalence of expert object recognition and face recognition does not imply that they are mediated by a similar mechanism. Indeed, there has been considerable debate in the literature as to whether face recognition is a form of expert object recognition or whether it is a special (i.e., distinct) kind of recognition.

In this chapter, we have adopted a computational approach to the *specialness* question. Face recognition researchers have suggested that faces, unlike other objects, are recognized holistically—a process that can be operationalized as difference in recognition of part when presented in isolation and in the whole object. Thus, we asked whether holistic recognition is a face-specific computation or whether it is a general form of expert object recognition. The following discussion, addresses the separate questions of uniqueness and expertise as they relate to our studies with real-world and laboratory experts.

1. Is holistic recognition unique to faces? Because some nonface objects were recognized holistically in these studies, we cannot conclude that holistic recognition is the exclusive domain of face processes. Specifically, we found that real-world experts and novices recognized real, nonface objects (i.e., cells, cars) holistically as did Greeble experts and novices when recognizing Greebles. While the strong version of holistic recognition as face-specific was not supported by these results, faces, nevertheless, demonstrated the greatest degree of holistic processing relative to cell, car, and dog stimuli. These findings suggest that the distinction between featural processing vs holistic processing is a continuum rather than a dichotomy. On one end of the continuum are objects that are recognized exclusively with respect to their parts and, on the other end, are objects that are recognized exclusively on the basis of their wholes. Given that faces are recognized more holistically than other tested contrast stimuli, it would appear that they lie on the extreme end of the featural/holistic processing continuum. Thus, although face recognition may not be unique in its reliance on holistic representation, faces might be exceptional with respect to the *degree* that they are processed holistically.

2. Does expertise require holistic processing? The test of real-world experts revealed that cell, car, and dog experts demonstrated no more holistic processing than novices as measured by the parts and wholes test. Similarly, Greeble novices and Greeble experts recognized Greeble parts better when tested in the original Greeble than when tested in isolation. These findings demonstrate that both novices and experts recognize objects holistically, but that experts did not demonstrate greater holistic processing than novices. However, in a test of configural sensitivity, it was found that Greeble experts, unlike Greeble novices, recognized parts reliably faster when those same parts were shown in an original configuration than when viewed in a new configuration. Moreover, changing the spatial position of one Greeble part disrupted the recognition of the other parts whose spatial positions were unchanged. These findings are consistent with the results of Tanaka and Sengco (in press) in which they found that changing the inter-eye distance in a face disrupted recognition of the nose and mouth features. Thus, for people who are expert in the recognition of faces or Greebles, the distinction between featural and configural information is blurred in the sense that changing one type of information (i.e., configural) affects recognition of the other type (i.e., featural).

Our work with experts and novices indicates that there are multiple routes to object recognition along the featural/holistic continuum. As shown

| Representation | Configural Information | Stimuli | Novice and Expert Population |
|---|---|---|---|
| featural | none | dog faces | dog novices & experts |
| holistic - relative | categorical (1st order relational) | cars, cells | Greeble novices, car & cell novices (?), car & cell experts (?) |
| holistic - integral | metric (2nd order relational) | faces, Greebles | normals w/ faces, Greeble experts |

Fig. 8.   The type of information found in featural and holistic representations as demonstrated by the studies with real-word experts and Greeble experts.

in Fig. 8, there are objects, such as houses, scrambled faces, and inverted faces, that are represented solely on the basis of their features, independent of the whole object context (Tanaka & Farah, 1993, Tanaka & Sengco, in press). Given that recognition of a dog part (i.e., eye, nose, mouth) was no better when tested in isolation than when tested in the whole object, dog novices and experts seemed to have adopted a featural approach to recognition.

If holistic processing is defined as the difference in part/whole recognition, our expertise studies indicate that it may be important to distinguish between two types of holistic representation. In the first kind of holistic representation, which we will refer to as a *relative* holistic representation, recognition of a part benefits from the presence of general or first-order configural properties of the object. Greeble novices, for example, demonstrated better performance when the part was tested in the whole object than in isolation. However, there was *no* difference in performance between the transformed configuration and the studied configuration conditions. This latter result indicates that Greeble novices were sensitive to the first-order relational properties of the Greeble (e.g., the quiff was located between the boges), but not the more subtle second-order relational properties (e.g., the angle of the boges).

In contrast, face recognition and expert Greeble recognition seems to rely on the encoding of second-order relational properties. We found that face recognition and expert Greeble recognition is reliably better if the parts are tested in the studied configuration than if tested in a different configuration. Moreover, recognition of *all* object features is disrupted if second-order relational information is altered. For this reason, we refer to this kind of holistic processing as *integral* (Garner, 1974) given that changes in configural information produces changes in featural information. While Greeble experts form integral, holistic representations of Greebles, it is an open question whether the holistic representations of cell and car novices and experts are relative or integral.

In summary, there seem to be many routes to visual expertise. Real-world experts do not necessarily generate holistic representations to identify domain-specific objects and in fact, recognition of diagnostic features may be what distinguishes an expert from a novice. However, in other cases where there is a high degree of homogeneity between object features, individuation of an exemplar must be based on several features and their configuration rather than on a single distinctive feature. Greebles and faces are good examples of homogenous object categories and therefore, learning to identify these kinds of objects would be expected to promote holistic processing. Because featural and configural distinctions between exemplars in a homogenous object class are subtle, it is reasonable to assume an extensive amount of experience and perceptual learning is necessary in order to be proficient in recognizing these kinds of objects. Hence, integral, holistic processes are recruited under the conditions where people have extensive experience identifying objects from a homogeneous shape class at subordinate levels of abstraction. This particular combination of stimulus factors and task demands is relatively rare in the natural world and might only occur when people recognize faces. However, our findings suggest that it is possible to simulate these conditions in the laboratory when subjects are trained to recognize Greebles. In this sense, we can say that the processes underlying face recognition may be ecologically special, but not computationally unique.

### ACKNOWLEDGMENTS

We are grateful to Philippe Schyns, Risto Miikkulainen, and Doug Medin for their comments and suggestions on a previous draft of this manuscript. This research was supported by a Hughes Research Grant, Keck Foundation Faculty Research Award and NIH grant R15 HD30433. Correspondence concerning this manuscript should be addressed to James Tanaka, Department of Psychology, Severance Lab, Oberlin College, Oberlin, OH, 44074.

### REFERENCES

Allison, T., McCarthy, G., Nobre, A., Puce, A., & Belger, A. (1994). Human extrastriate visual cortex and the perception of faces, words, numbers, and colors. *Cerebral Cortex, 4,* 544–554.

Bayliss, G. C., Rolls, E. T., & Leonard, C. M. (1985). Selectivity between faces in the responses of a population of neurons in the cortex of the superior temporal sulcus of the macaque monkey. *Brain Research, 342,* 91–102.

Biederman, I. (1987). Recognition-by-components: A theory of human image understanding. *Psychological Review, 94,* 115–147.

Biederman, I., & Gerhardstein, P. C. (1993). Recognizing depth-rotated objects: Evidence and conditions for three-dimensional viewpoint invariance. *Journal of Experimental Psychology: Human Perception & Performance, 19,* 1162–1182.

Brown, R. (1958). How shall a thing be called? *Psychological Review, 65,* 14–21.

Carey, S. (1981). The development of face perception. In G. Davies, H. Ellis, & J. Shepherd (Eds.), *Perceiving and remembering faces* (pp. 9–38). New York: Academic Press.

Carey, S. (1992). Becoming a face expert. *Philosophical Transactions of the Royal Society of London, B335,* 95–103.

Carey, S., & Diamond, R. (1994). Are faces perceived as configurations more by adults than by children? *Visual Cognition, 1,* 253–274.

Chi, M. T. H., Feltovich, P. J., & Glaser, R. (1981). Categorization and representation of physics problems by experts and novices. *Cognitive Science, 5,* 121–152.

Cohen-Levine, S. (1989). The question of faces: Special is in the brain of the beholder. In A. W. Young & H. D. Ellis (Eds.), *Handbook of research on face processing* (pp. 37–48). Amsterdam: North-Holland.

Cohen-Levine, S., Banich, M. T., & Koch-Weser, M. P. (1988). Face recognition: A general or specific right hemisphere capacity? *Brain and Cognition, 8,* 303–325.

Damasio, A. R., Damasio, H., & Van Hoesen, G. W. (1982). Prosopagnosia: Anatomic basic and behavioral mechanisms. *Neurology, 32,* 331–341.

Davidoff, J. B. (1986). The specificity of face perception: Evidence from psychological investigations. In R. Bruyer (Ed.), *The neuropsychology of face perception and facial expression* (pp. 147–166). Hillsdale, NJ: Erlbaum.

Davidoff, J. B. (1988). Prosopagnosia: A disorder of rapid spatial integration. In G. Denes, C. Semenza, & P. Bisiachi (Eds.), *Perspectives on cognitive neuropsychology* (pp. 297–309). Hillsdale, NJ: Erlbaum.

de Groot, A. D. (1966). Perception and memory versus thought. In B. Kleinmuntz (Ed.), *Problem solving research, methods and theory* (pp. 19–50). New York: Wiley.

De Renzi, E. (1986). Current issues in prosopagnosia. In H. D. Ellis, M. A. Jeeves, F. G. Newcombe, & A. Young (Eds.), *Aspects of face processing* (pp. 243–252). Dordrecht, Netherlands: Martinus Nijhoff.

De Renzi, E., Faglioni, P., Grossi, D., & Nichelli, P. (1991). Appreciative and associative forms of prosopagnosia. *Cortex, 27,* 213–221.

Diamond, R., & Carey, S. (1986). Why faces are and are not special: An effect of expertise. *Journal of Experimental Psychology: General, 115,* 107–117.

Edelman, S., & Bülthoff, H. H. (1992). Orientation dependence in the recognition of familiar and novel views of three-dimensional objects. *Vision, 32,* 2385–2400.

Ellis, A. W., Young, A. W., & Flude, B. M. (1990). Repetition priming and face processing: Priming occurs within the system that responds to the identity of a face, *Quarter Journal of Experimental Psychology, 42A,* 495–512.

Farah, M. J. (1990). *Visual agnosia: Disorders of object recognition and what they tell us about normal vision.* Cambridge, MA: MIT Press.

Farah, M. J. (1992). Is an object an object an object? Cognitive and neuropsychological investigations of domain-specificity in visual object recognition. *Current Directions in Psychological Science, 1,* 164–169.

Farah, M. J., Levison, K. L., & Klein, K. L. (1995a). Face perception and within-category discrimination in prosopagnosia. *Neuropsychologia, 33,* 661–674.

Farah, M. J., Wilson, K. D., Drain, H. M., & Tanaka, J. W. (1995b). The inverted face inversion effect in prosopagnosia: Evidence for mandatory, face-specific perceptual mechanisms. *Vision Research, 35,* 2089–2093.

Flin, R. H. (1985). Development of face recognition: An encoding switch? *British Journal of Psychology, 76,* 123–134.

Fodor, J. (1983). *The modularity of mind.* Cambridge, MA: MIT Press.

Garner, W. R. (1974). *The processing of information and structure.* New York: Erlbaum.

Gauthier, I., & Tarr, M. J. (1997). Becoming a Greeble expert: Exploring mechanisms for face recognition. *Vision Research.*

Gauthier, I., & Tarr, M. J. (1997). Orientation Priming of novel shapes in the context of viewpoint-dependent recognition. *Perception, 26,* 51–73

Gauthier, I., Anderson, A. W., Tarr, M. J., & Gore, J. C. (1996a). Level of categorization in visual recognition studied with function MRI. Presented at the *Annual Meeting of the Cognitive Neuroscience Society,* San Francisco, CA.

Gauthier, I., Behrmann, M., Tarr, M. J., Anderson, A. W., Gore, J., & McClelland, J. (1996b). Subordinate-level categorization in human inferior temporal cortex: Converging evidence from neuropsychology and brain imaging. *Neuroscience Abstracts, 1,* 10–11.

Goren, C. C. Sarty, M., & Yu, P. W. K. (1975). Visual following and pattern discrimination of face-like stimuli by newborn infants. *Pediatrics, 56,* 544–549.

Haxby, J. V., Horwitz, B., Ungerleider, J. M., Maisog, Pietrini, P., & Grady, C. L. (1994). The functional organization of human extrastriate cortex: A PET-rCBF study of selective attention to faces and locations. *The Journal of Neuroscience, 14,* 6336–6353.

Hay, D. C., & Young, A. W. (1982). The human face. In A. W. Ellis (Ed.), *Normality and pathology in cognitive function* (pp. 173–202). New York: Academic Press.

Hoffman, D. D., & Richards, W. (1985). Parts in recognition, *Cognition, 18,* 65–96.

Jolicoeur, P., Gluck, M. A., & Kosslyn, S. M. (1984), Pictures and names: Making the connection. *Cognitive Psychology, 16,* 243–275.

Kanwisher, N., McDermott, J., & Chun, M. M. (1996). A module for the visual representation of faces. *NeuroImage, 3,* S361.

Kosslyn, S. M., Hamilton, S. E., & Bernstein, J. H. (1995). The perception of curvature can be selectively disrupted in prosopagnosia. *Brain & Cognition, 27,* 36–58.

Levin, D. T. (in press). Classifying faces by race: The structure of face categories. *Journal of Experimental Psychology: Learning, Memory, & Cognition.*

Levine, D. N., & Calvanio, R. (1989). Prosopagnosia: A defect in visual configural processing. *Brain & Cognition, 10,* 149–170.

Logothetis, N. K., Pauls, J. & Poggio, T. (1995). Shape representation in the inferior temporal cortex of monkeys. *Current Biology, 5,* 552–563.

Logothetis, N. K., Pauls, J., Bülthoff, H. H., & Poggio, T. (1994). View-dependent object recognition by monkeys. *Current Biology, 4,* 401–414.

McNeil, J. E., & Warrington, E. K. (1993). Prosopagnosia, a face-specific disorder. *The Quarterly Journal of Experimental Psychology, 46A,* 1–10.

Murphy, G. L. (1991). Parts in object concepts: Experiments with artificial categories. *Memory and Cognition, 19,* 423–438.

Nachson, I. (1995). On the modularity of face recognition: The riddle of domain specificity. *Journal of Clinical and Experimental Neuropsychology, 17,* 256–275.

Newcombe, F., Mehta, Z., & DeHaan, E. D. F. (1994). Category specificity in visual recognition. In M. J. Farah & G. Ratcliff (Eds.), *The neuropsychology of high-level vision* (pp. 103–132). Hillsdale, NJ: Erlbaum.

Perrett, D. I., & Oram, M. W., Harries, M. H., Bevan, R., Hietanen, I. K., Beason, P. J., & Thomas, S. (1991). Viewer-centered and object-centered coding of heads in the Macaque temporal cortex. *Experimental Brain Research, 86,* 150–175.

Poggio, T., & Edelman, S. (1990). A network that learns to recognize three- dimensional objects. *Nature, 343,* 263–266.

Posner, M. I., & Mitchell, R. F. (1967). Chronometric analysis of classification. *Psychological Review, 74,* 392–409.

Puce, A., Allison, T., Gore, J. C., & McCarthy, G. (1995). Face-sensitive regions in human extrastriate cortex studied by functional MRI. *Journal of Neurophysiology, 74,* 1192–1199.

Rentschler, I., Treutwein, B., & Landis, T. (1994). Dissociation of local and global processing in visual agnosia. *Vision Research, 34,* 963–971.

Rhodes, G., Brennan, S., & Carey, S. (1987). Identification and ratings of caricatures: Implications for mental representations of faces. *Cognitive Psychology, 19,* 473–497.

Rhodes, G., & McLean, I. G. (1990). Distinctiveness and expertise effects with homogeneous stimuli: Towards a model of configural coding. *Perception, 19,* 773–794.

Rhodes, G., Tan, S., Brake, S., & Taylor, K. (1989). Expertise and configural coding in face recognition. *British Journal of Psychology, 80,* 313–331.

Rhodes, G., & Tremewan, T. (1994). Understanding face recognition: Caricature effects, inversion and the homogeneity problem. *Visual Cognition, 1,* 2/3, 275–311.

Rock, I., & DiVita, J. (1987). A case of viewer-centered object perception. *Cognitive Psychology, 19,* 280–293.

Rolls, E. (1992). The processing of face information in the primate temporal lobe. In V. Bruce & M. Burton (Eds.), *Processing images of faces* (pp. 41–68). Norwood, NJ: Ablex.

Rolls, E., & Bayliss, C. G. (1986). Size and contrast have only small effects on the responses to faces of neurons in the cortex of the superior temporal sulcus of the macaque monkey, *Experimental Brain Research, 65,* 38–48.

Rosch. E. (1975). The nature of mental codes for color categories. *Journal of Experimental Psychology: Human Perception and Performance, 1,* 303–322.

Rosch, E. (1978). Principles of categorization. In E. Rosch & B. B. Lloyd (Eds.) *Cognition and categorization* (pp. 27–48). Hillsdale, NJ: Erlbaum.

Rosch, E., Mervis, C. B., Gray, W. D., Johnson, D. M., & Boyes-Braem, P. (1976). Basic objects in natural categories. *Cognitive Psychology, 8,* 382–439.

Rumiati, R. I., Humphreys, G. H., Riddoch, M. J., & Bateman, A. (1994). Visual object agnosia without prosopagnosia or alexia: Evidence for hierarchical theories of visual recognition. *Visual Cognition, 1,* 181–225.

Scapinello, K. F., & Yarmey, A. D. (1970). The role of familiarity and orientation in immediate and delayed recognition of pictorial stimuli. *Psychonomic Science, 21,* 329–331.

Schyns, P. G., & Murphy, G. L. (1994). The ontogeny of part representation in object concepts. In D. Medin (Ed.), *The psychology of learning and motivation* (Vol. 31, pp. 305–354). San Diego, CA: Academic Press.

Sergent, J. (1988). Face perception and the right hemisphere. In L. Weiskrantz (Ed.), Thought without language (pp. 108–131). New York: Oxford University Press.

Sergent, J., Ohta, S., & MacDonald, B. (1992). Functional neuroanatomy of face and object processing. *Brain, 115,* 15–36.

Takahashi, N., Kawamura, M., Hirayama, K., Shiota, J., & Isono, O. (1995). Prosopagnosia, a clinical and anatomical study of four patients. *Cortex, 31,* 317–329.

Tanaka, J. W. (1994). The basic level of face recognition. Poster presented at the 35th Annual Meeting of the Psychonomic Society, St. Louis, Missouri.

Tanaka, J. W., & Farah, M. J. (1991). Second-order relational properties and the inversion effect: Testing a theory of face perception. *Perception & Psychophysics, 50,* 367–372.

Tanaka, J. W., & Farah, M. J. (1993). Parts and wholes in face recognition. *Quarterly Journal of Experimental Psychology, 46A,* 225–245.

Tanaka, J. W., Giles, M., Szechter, L., Lantz, J. A., Stone, A., Franks L., & Vastine, K. (1996). Measuring parts and wholes recognition of cell, car, and dog experts: A test of the expertise hypothesis. Unpublished manuscript, Oberlin College, Oberlin, OH.

Tanaka, J. W., & Sengco, J. A. (in press). Features and their configuration in face recognition. *Memory & Cognition.*

Tanaka, J. W., & Taylor, M. (1991). Object categories and expertise: Is the basic level in the eye of the beholder? *Cognitive Psychology, 23,* 457–482.

Tanaka, K. (1996). Inferotemporal cortex and object vision. *Annual Review of Neuroscience, 19,* 109–139.

Tarr, M. J., & Pinker, S. (1989). Mental rotation and orientation dependence in shape recognition. *Cognitive Psychology, 21,* 233–282.

Tversky, B., & Hemenway, K. (1984). Objects, parts, and categories. *Journal of Experimental Psychology: General, 113,* 169–193.

Valentine, T., & Bruce, V. (1986). The effect of race inversion and encoding activity upon face recognition. *Acta Psychologica, 61,* 259–273.

Yarmey, A. D. (1971). Recognition memory for familiar "public" faces: Effects of orientation and delay. *Psychonomic Science, 24,* 286–288.

Yin, R. K. (1969). Looking at upside-down faces. *Journal of Experimental Psychology, 81,* 141–145.

Young, A. W., Hellawell, D., & Hay, D. C. (1987). Configural information in face perception. *Perception, 10,* 747–759.

# INFANT SPEECH PERCEPTION: PROCESSING CHARACTERISTICS, REPRESENTATIONAL UNITS, AND THE LEARNING OF WORDS

*Peter D. Eimas*

## I. Introduction

This chapter describes three different but related aspects of the processing of speech. The first is to provide a relatively brief review of the abilities for speech perception that are available to the human infant during the early months of life along with a consideration of their modification by the parental language and the resulting perceptual consequences. The second is to present recent evidence from infants and adults supporting the idea that the prelexical processing and representational units of speech in mature listeners in many languages derive from the same, but perhaps more rudimentary syllabic units that are available to infants as young as neonates. The continued presence and use of syllabic representations is argued to be a consequence of their presence and use in the parental language. In languages that use other forms of prelexical units, experience with the parental language is viewed as determining the specific form of a listener's prelexical units. These representations presumably define the format of the initially acquired and later learned words of a language and thereby ultimately permit their access later in life when listening to coherent speech. Somewhat greater emphasis is given to this section on the units of segmentation and representation, primarily because of recent converging findings from adults and infants that are relatively infrequently discussed together, whereas the

THE PSYCHOLOGY OF LEARNING
AND MOTIVATION, VOL. 36

basic processing procedures of infants have been reviewed often and recently (e.g., Aslin, Pisoni, & Jusczyk, 1983; Eimas, 1996; Jusczyk, 1996, 1997; Kuhl, 1987). The focus of attention in the third and final section is directed to the growing, but still relatively small body of findings concerned with the acquisition of the very early, perhaps earliest word-like structures and words in infants less than a year of age and the properties of languages that may make this acquisition possible. It is here that the influence of the parental language on the perception and representation of what I take to be biologically determined sensitivities to a number of linguistically important acoustic properties is again clearly in evidence. Finally, it should be noted that there is virtually no discussion of theoretical positions describing the development of speech processing abilities and lexical acquisition, although consideration is given to the possible special nature of the system underlying the perception of speech. Limitations of space require constraints on topics that could be covered. And inasmuch as theoretical discussions of this nature are at present necessarily speculative and open to change in the very near future, they are perhaps more appropriately a major concern of future discussions of the processing of speech by young infants. However, the interested reader can consult the writings of Best (1994, 1995), Jusczyk (1993, 1997), Kuhl (1993), or Werker (1993), for example, for recent theoretical discussions that vary considerably and interestingly in their frames of reference and emphases.

## II.  Basic Processing Characteristics of Young Infants

The comprehension of speech ultimately requires extracting the speaker's intended meaning from the acoustic signal and our goal as researchers in this domain of language is to understand and describe the processes that underlie comprehension. In the many years devoted to this task, a major endeavor has been to understand the means by which the spoken signal makes contact with the mental lexicon. This effort itself has taken on many facets, from understanding how the speech signal is transformed by processing systems such that it attains a form appropriate to access the lexicon to how the meaning elements of lexical units are elicited and selected so as to permit abstraction of the speaker's intended meaning from an utterance. This initial section is devoted to describing the processes of speech perception at the very lowest levels of comprehension that are available to the young infant. Thus, those concerned with these aspects of infant speech perception have devoted their efforts to delineating the available mechanisms of perception and their consequences especially as they might relate to the acquisition of a lexicon. Moreover, we have been concerned with the nature of speech perception at these levels, in particular with the extent to which the infant's perception of speech is categorical. We have also been interested in the extent to which these categorical percepts, when found, are influenced by factors that affect the perception of speech by mature listeners, such as the interaction or trading relations that exist among the many sources of information that are sufficient to signal phonetic contrasts and context in the form of rate of speech. Research at this level is likewise concerned with whether the infant's perception of speech is organized and the possibility that the structural format of the initial precepts is universal. In the past decade, consideration has turned to when and how the parental language impresses itself on the processes and consequent products of infant speech perception. And, for some of us, considerable effort has been devoted to the attempt to determine whether it is at this level of processing that the special processes of speech perception that are evident at higher levels of language comprehension and production first make their appearance. It is thus toward describing the basic aspects of the beginnings of speech perception with respect to both age and levels that this initial section is devoted.

What is necessary for communication (and perception in other sensory modalities as well) is that the perception of speech be marked by constancy. That is, it is necessary to know when the same intended words and hence meanings were produced despite the marked differences in their acoustic signals. These variations in the signal result from differences in the articulatory mechanisms of different speakers, differences arising from the instance-to-instance changes in movements of the articulatory mechanism of a single speaker, the emotional state of the speaker, alterations in the speech act such as the rate of speech, and of course the phonetic environment of any segment—the famous effects of coarticulation that operate most strongly across segments, but are still present across syllables and words.

The study of perceptual constancy involves understanding the mechanisms of speech perception and the manner in which they extract what must be a (nearly) phenomenally identical percept from physically differing signals. To be complete it also requires understanding when these mechanisms become functional and how they change, if indeed they do, during the course of development. However, in that the concern here is with the processing characteristics of young infants, it is obvious that our units of analysis cannot involve words in the conventional sense (i.e., meaningful linguistic units) and that experimental investigations into the phenomenal experiences of infants are simply not possible. What is possible with infant listeners, however, is to measure the extent to which two acoustically different speech signals, typically consonant-vowel (CV) sequences that are phenomenally the same (or very nearly so) for adult listeners yield equivalent responses. This is in effect to study the extent to which signals are perceived as members of the same linguistic category, which, although not a direct indicant of perceptual constancy, is certainly a necessary condition for perceptual constancy.

The methods for such studies are quite varied. They typically involve a variant of familiarization/ release-from-familiarization procedures that rely on unlearned responses and hence can be used with very young infants, including neonates. In these procedures, the infant is familiarized with a stimulus for a varying number of trials and then presented with a novel second stimulus for typically two to four trials. Discrimination of the two stimuli is evidenced if there is an increase in the response (e.g., sucking or looking to produce the sound) over the last familiarization trial(s) and over the response of control infants who received the familiar stimulus again during final test trials. These methods also include conditioned head-turning procedures that rely on attention and learned responses and are thus more suitable to older infants, infants from about 5 or 6 months of age to 12 or 14 months of age. In this procedure a background stimulus is continuously administered except for brief test periods when the background stimulus is interrupted by a different stimulus or stimuli. Discrimination is inferred by a greater number of head turns when the novel stimulus(i) is presented than when it is not presented in comparable periods of time—the control trials. Finally, simple preference procedures have been used with older infants to determine when they come to prefer various characteristics (e.g., the prosodic structure) of the native language. The results of these studies will be described in the final section. With the first two procedures, measures of response equivalence or differentiation are directly available. The studies with younger infants, using the familiarization/release-from-familiarization procedure and commonly referred to as studies of categorical perception, have typically been concerned with the acoustic variables that are sufficient to signal phonetic contrasts. Unfortunately the results of these studies on categorical perception do not permit differentiation among the nature of the perceptual representations, that is, whether featural, segmental, or syllabic. Investigations with older infants using a conditioned head-turning procedure that permits the study of the availability of response equivalence classes, typically investigate the equivalence of variation in the speech signal produced by differences in speaker, intonation, and at times the phonetic environment. Although studies of this nature can in principle differentiate among the possible forms of equivalence, almost all have not been designed to do so.

There is at this writing considerable evidence that infants as young as 1 month of age represent speech categorically; which is to say that acoustically different members of the same phonetic category, different presumably as a consequence of instance-to-instance changes in articulatory processes, are responded to in an equivalent manner. The categorical nature of the infant's perception of CV sequences is very similar to that which is evidenced in adult listeners (see, e.g., Eimas, Miller, & Jusczyk, 1987, and Repp, 1983, among others, for reviews). There are differences in the location of category boundaries and undoubtedly differences in the acuteness with which categories can be differentiated. However, the basic phenomenon of categorical perception is the same. What is interesting about categorical perception is that as a consequence of this perceptual mapping, two exemplars of speech that differ equivalently in acoustic terms are either difficult or easy to discriminate. If two acoustically different exemplars of speech are mapped onto the same categorical representation, discrimination is typically difficult. However, if two exemplars distinguished by the same acoustic difference are mapped onto different internal structures, discrimination is easy. The ease of discriminability may be viewed as a consequence of listeners finding it difficult to attend to the acoustic differences among exemplars mapped onto the same category and easy to attend to acoustic differences that are sufficient to signal different categories.

Eimas, Siqueland, Jusczyk, and Vigorito (1971), for example, found that 1- and 4-month-old infants failed to discrimination small (20 msec) differences in voice onset time (VOT) that marked different exemplars drawn from within either of the two voicing categories in syllable-initial position of English (and many other languages). However, when the same acoustic difference in VOT provided information sufficient to distinguish two syllable-initial stop consonants from different voicing categories—[b] and [p] in this instance—the two speech sounds were reliably discriminated. Similar findings have been obtained for voicing information with infants about the same age being raised in other language communities (e.g., Spanish: Lasky, Syrdal-Lasky, & Klein, 1975; Kikuyu: Streeter, 1976). Indeed, what appears to be true is that there are initial universal voicing categories with common boundaries. Thus, young infants appear to process speech varying in VOT such that a boundary region falls between +20 and +60 msec and between -20 and -60 msec, the former corresponds to the voiced-voiceless distinction in syllable-initial position in English and other languages, whereas the latter corresponds to the syllable-initial prevoiced-voiced distinction found in a considerable number of other languages. As will be discussed below, it is not the boundaries per se that yield or make categories possible, or so I believe. Rather it is the assignment of speech to categories by the very nature of the mechanisms of speech perception that yield by necessity the boundaries between categories. These mechanisms, presumably, make their assignments on the basis of the fit between the sounds of speech and the initial biologically given processing structures that are organized to yield categorical representations of speech. Whether this representation is represented by exemplars or a summary representation, perhaps a computed prototype that forms the center of this space, or both remains a matter of theoretical contention.

The discrimination and categorization of speech by young infants is by no means confined to the information for voicing. Information in the form of formant transitions that signal phonetic contrasts based on place of articulation, that is, the point of greatest constriction during articulation, has also been found by Morse (1972) and Moffitt (1971) to be discriminable in 2- to 5-month-old infants in syllable-initial position, by Jusczyk (1977) in syllable-final position, and for utterance-medial position by Jusczyk and Thompson (1978). Moreover, Bertoncini, Bijelac-Babic, Blumstein, and Mehler (1987) have shown that neonates are able to discriminate the relevant information for place of articulation in syllable initial position even with very short stimuli (from 34 to 44 msec) consisting of only the initial burst and formant transitions. In addition, Eimas (1974) has shown the information for place of articulation to be categorically perceived by 2- to 4-month olds: Stimulus distinctions based on identical acoustic differences in the starting frequency and slope of the formant transitions were discriminated at points along the continuum that matched adult boundaries and not at others. Infants below the age of 4 months are also able to distinguish among the contrasts between stops and glides, specifically between [b] vs [w] and to do so in a categorical manner (Eimas & Miller, 1980a), as is also true for the distinction between stop and nasal consonants (Eimas & Miller, 1980b). Distinctions among fricatives are also available to young infants (e.g., Levitt, Jusczyk, Murray, & Carden, 1988) as are a number of vowel distinctions (e.g., Trehub, 1973; Swoboda, Kass, Morse, & Leavitt, 1978). Moreover, perception of the vowels was found to be more nearly categorical when the vowels were brief, that is, 60 msec steady-state formants (Swoboda et al.) and thus more like naturally produced vowels as well as the temporal dimension of the consonantal information described above, further demonstrating the categorical perception of the information sufficient for phonetic contrasts.

Finally, it is worth emphasizing that there are considerable data indicating that infants younger than 6 months of age are sensitive to phonetic distinctions that are not found in the parental language (e.g., Aslin et al., 1981; Best, McRoberts, & Sithole, 1988; Eimas, 1975a; Lasky et al., 1975; Polka & Werker, 1994; Streeter, 1976; Trehub, 1976; Werker & Tees, 1984)—a finding that supports the idea that infants come to the world with a set of universal categories and the biologically given means to assign stimuli to these natural, which is to say, default, categories. In this manner, infants are well adapted to the task of acquiring the sound system of any human language (Eimas, 1975a,b). For example, the [r]-[l] distinction, which is phonemic in English but not in Japanese, has been found to be discriminable by young infants being raised in English-speaking environments and additionally their perception of this contrast was shown to be categorical (Eimas, 1975a). Of interest is the fact that the perception of the [r]-[l] distinction is exceedingly poor in native Japanese-speaking adults for whom the distinction does not exist. This was true whether listeners were asked to identify randomly presented tokens of [r] and [l] or simply to discriminate any two exemplars of these sounds, whether from the same or different categories (Miyawaki, Strange, Verbrugge, Liberman, Jenkins, & Fujimura, 1975). However, Japanese infants were able to discriminate this distinction, but only when they were younger than 10 months of age (Tsushima, Takizawa, Sasaki, Siraki, Nishi, Kohno, Menyuk, & Best, 1994). Of further interest is the fact that the loss of the [r]-[l] distinction in adults may not be a consequence of a permanent loss in sensitivity to the relevant acoustic information, but rather a failure to attend to the information in a linguistic context (Miyawaki et al.). In support of this idea, recent training studies with native Japanese-speaking adults have shown an enhancement in their ability to make the [r]-[l] distinction (e.g., Pisoni, Lively, & Logan, 1994), but whether this enhancement in ability extends to connected discourse remains to be determined.

As was true for the [r]-[l] distinction, with increasing experience with the sounds of their native language, infants come to lose their ability to make phonetic distinctions that are not part of the parental language (see especially Werker & Tees, 1984; but see Best et al., 1988). Development of a given mature sound system would thus seem to be environmentally induced, as expected, but importantly by a selective rather than an instructional process that operates on a constrained set of biologically given phonetic categories (cf. Changeux, 1985; Edelman, 1987; Mehler, 1974). Worth noting is that the effects of experience with the native language would appear to occur earlier for vowels (Kuhl, Williams, Lacerda, Stevens, & Lindblom, 1992; Polka & Werker, 1994) than for consonants (Tsushima et al., 1994; Werker & Tees, 1984).

The categorization process for speech in effect maps a potentially indefinite number of signals onto a single representation that is considered by some researchers to be phonetic (i.e., linguistic) in nature, (e.g, Eimas & Miller, 1991, 1992). However, it is not the case, or so I would suggest, that infants detect phonetic distinctions on the basis of particularly situated boundaries that separate these categories, whether auditory or linguistic in nature. Rather, as has been described, biologically determined mechanisms designed to process speech do so in a manner that assigns stimuli to a universally given, but ultimately modifiable set of categories corresponding to the consequences of articulation during perception. As a consequence, the locus of the boundaries between particular categories—such as those noted above for voicing distinctions—that may or may not correspond to the boundary locations in various languages are actually epiphenomenal. This is simply to say that if there are categories along a continuum, then by necessity there must be boundary locations. In other words, categorization does not occur because of the presence of certain natural occurring boundary locations as some argue (e.g., Pastore, 1987). Thus, it is actually the characteristics of the processing system as a whole, mechanisms together with a default set of categories, and not the apparent presence of boundaries that determine the relative discriminability of stimuli—stimuli falling within a category are difficult to discriminate, whereas stimuli falling in different categories are relatively easy to discriminate.

A major consideration for this belief is the important fact that the many-to-one mapping of stimuli to categories is itself not invariant, both for adult listeners and young infants. There are many boundary locations determined by a number of factors including those of phonetic context, rate of speech, and trading relations between the many cues for a phonetic contrast, as the evidence clearly indicates. Thus, to claim that categorization is a conse-quence of certain natural boundary locations requires assuming, unreason-ably in my view, an indefinite number of such locations along a number of dimensions for each phonetic contrast. A more realistic approach is to describe categorization as a consequence of processing characteristics that in turn yield by necessity boundaries or boundary regions—a view that is supported by the research described immediately below.

A number of studies with young infants, based on experiments performed originally with adult listeners, have shown that the boundary between cate-gories can be altered by systematically varying contextual factors. For exam-ple, Miller and Liberman (1979) who tested adult listeners revealed that one acoustic correlate of rate of articulation, syllable duration, can alter the boundary between [b] and [w] along a temporally based continuum—the duration of the formant transitions. When the exemplars to be identified represented rapidly articulated speech, the category boundary separating [b] from [w] was located at a smaller value of transition duration than when the exemplars represented slowly articulated speech. The same shift in the boundary has been found with 3- and 4-month-old infants (Eimas & Miller, 1980a; Miller & Eimas, 1983). Further evidence of a contextual effect has been presented by Carden, Levitt, Jusczyk, and Walley (1981). They found that the phonetic context can determine whether differences in the spectral properties of the formant transitions in CV sequences are discriminated by adults. Particular transitions were discriminated, but only when they were preceded by a neutral (noninformative) fricative noise and heard by adults as [fa] and [Θ a]. When the noise was absent, both sounds were heard as [ba] and were not discriminated. Levitt et al. (1988), obtained the same results with regard to discrimination (but of course without measures of identification) in infants 6 to 12 weeks of age (and see Eimas & Miller, 1991, for a similar effect of context; in this case, the duration of silence preceding formant transitions in medial syllabic position).

In a similar vein, research with adults, and more recently with infants, has shown that the multiple acoustic properties that are sufficient to signal phonetic contrasts enter into perceptual trading relations. Which is simply to say that the many properties that typically signal the same phonetic contrast have been shown to influence one another. More specifically, the value of one of these properties affects the range of stimuli varying along a second property that maps onto the phonetic categories in question. Evidence for this mutual influence has been obtained, for example, by Fitch, Halwes, Erikson, and Liberman (1980) with adults and by Miller and Eimas (1983) with infants 3 and 4 months of age. Moreover, the multiple cues for speech derive their perceptual effectiveness to a large extent from the manner in which they specify categorical, presumably phonetic representations, and not simply from their acoustic properties both in adults (Fitch et al.) and infants (Eimas, 1985)—evidence in accord with the view that there exists a module or processes dedicated to the perception of speech (e.g., Liberman & Mattingly, 1985, 1989), a topic to which I return shortly .

Further evidence for categorization in the perception of speech by infants is found in the work of Kuhl (e.g., 1979, 1983) using a conditioned head-turning procedure with infants about 6 to 7 months of age. She has demonstrated that infants form equivalence classes (i.e., categorical representations) for a number of consonantal and vocalic categories whose exemplars were selected so as to vary considerably in their acoustic properties and be readily discriminable. [That the stimuli from the same category were readily discriminable is in contrast to the within-category stimuli in the studies of categorical perception, although it should be noted that these stimuli are discriminable by adults using an appropriate procedure (e.g., Carney, Widin, & Viemeister, 1977) and at times by infants using a standard familiarization/release-from-familiarization procedure (Miller & Eimas, 1983)]. Thus, for example, 6-month-old infants showed the ability to perceive different instances of the vowels [a] and [i] as belonging to separate categories, despite substantial acoustic differences among the exemplars of each category resulting from differences in speakers and intonation patterns. Moreover, given that categorization occurred on the first exposure to novel category exemplars, categorization would appear to be a biologically driven, natural consequence of the perception of speech by infants rather than a consequence of the experimental procedure. This conclusion is further strengthened by the demonstration by Hillenbrand (1983) that infants formed equivalence classes for CV sequences that were based on manner of articulation (stop vs nasal consonants) that varied in place of articulation and speaker, but did not categorize the same segmental units when they were randomly assigned to categories—that is, when the categorical designations were arbitrary and not linguistically based. What is also important about the Hillenbrand experiment is that it is possible to infer that the basis for categorization was featural. The other studies of Kuhl do not inform us, like the studies of categorical perception as noted earlier, whether the stimuli were represented by features, segments, or syllables.

Two additional phenomena regarding the perception of speech by young infants are worth consideration: the organized nature and internal structure of the percepts. With regard to the former, it is apparent that the acquisition of higher level linguistic knowledge requires that percepts, be they represented at the level of features, segments, or syllables, must be organized entities, reflecting the organization in the signal that instantiates the consequences of articulation with the speaker's intended meaning. In other words, the representations of speech must at some point in development take the form of coherent structures and not exist simply as unstructured collections of features or higher units, such as unordered lists of segments.

Recently, Eimas and Miller (1992) showed that consonant-vowel syllables were perceived as organized entities by 3- and 4-month-old infants—a beginning into what is required for potentially meaningful linguistic representations of connected speech (and see Eimas & Miller, 1981; Miller & Eimas, 1979) . Using a methodology for the study of duplex perception, they presented synthetic speech patterns dichotically such that one ear received an isolated third-formant transition, appropriate for perceiving the syllables as [da] or [ga]. The other ear received the remaining acoustic information necessary for perception of the two syllables—the base—which was identical for both syllables. When these stimuli are presented dichotically to adults, they perceive a nonspeech-like chirp at the ear receiving the transition and the coherent (perceptually organized) syllable [da] or [ga] located at the ear receiving the base. Which syllable is heard depends on which third-formant transition is presented. Infants discriminated the two patterns, and most importantly, did so even when the third-formant transitions were attenuated in intensity to the extent that infant listeners could not discriminate them when presented in isolation. Thus, discrimination could not be based solely on the isolated transitions. Presumably the two distinct sounds, the base and transition, with their apparently different sources of production ( speech and nonspeech) and their differently perceived locations of production (left and right with respect to the speaker), were integrated into a single organized syllabic percept that made discrimination possible. In a more recent unpublished study by the authors (cited in Eimas, 1996), this integration did not occur when the intensity of two different third-formant transitions were attenuated and the base consisted only of the remaining portion of the third formant—evidence again favoring the view that the organization that occurred in the original experiment provided a percept that was linguistic in nature. Exactly what is the nature of the representation of this organized percept cannot be assessed on the basis of the results obtained by Eimas and Miller. We do not know whether undifferentiated syllables or sequentially ordered phonetic segments or even sequentially ordered lists of features from the organized percept were represented. However, we do know that the percept is organized, as we believe the evidence from our earlier studies also indicates (Eimas & Miller; Miller & Eimas). Worthy of note is that this evidence includes the organization of segmental and suprasegmental information (Eimas & Miller).

With regard to the internal structure of the representations of speech, there is at this writing considerable evidence that the categorical representations of speech in infants do in fact possess an internal structure (Miller & Eimas, 1996; Grieser & Kuhl, 1989; Kuhl, 1991, 1993; Kuhl et al., 1992). Kuhl and her colleagues found that 6- and 7-month-old infants were better able to discriminate a change in the background stimulus when the background stimulus was a poor exemplar of the vowel [i] than when it was a good exemplar as rated by adult listeners. In other words, infants who experienced the good exemplar as the background stimulus generalized more to the surrounding exemplars of the category than did infants who had experienced a poor exemplar. Kuhl has interpreted these findings as evidence for the existence of a prototype structure that acts as a "perceptual magnet," functionally attracting surrounding stimuli in psychological space. [Of course, the actual structure need not consist of a single prototype representation, but could in fact be represented by a number of individual exemplars that well typify the category (e.g., Medin & Barsalou, 1987; Nosofsky, 1991)]. What is of particular interest for the issue of the special nature of the mechanisms of lower-level speech processing to be discussed below is that Kuhl (1991) found this perceptual magnet effect for infants and adults but not for monkeys.

Miller and Eimas (1996), using a variant of Kuhl's experimental procedure, found evidence for the internal structure of voicing categories in infants, but now only 3- to 4-months of age. They showed that the ability to discriminate two stimuli, one a prototype stimulus and the other a nonprototype stimulus, was greater when the nonprototype stimulus was the familiar stimulus and the prototype exemplar was the novel stimulus than when the stimuli were reversed. This finding is analogous to the perceived asymmetry in similarity of two stimuli that depends on which of the two stimuli, the prototype or nonprototype exemplar, serves as the standard or reference for similarity judgments (e.g., Rosch, 1975). Moreover, the fact that this evidence for internal structure was obtained prior to the time when the parental language influences the repertoire of consonantal distinctions in young infants suggests that these internal structures, these prototypes, may not be a result of experience, but rather may be part of a set of biologically determined categories that we bring as infants to the perception of speech. Whether this is also true for the structure of vocalic categories remains to be determined.

The fact that the categorical representations of speech have an internal prototype structure (perhaps based on exemplars) is interesting in its own right and, on the surface at least, in conflict with findings that we also register and represent many suprasegmental aspects of the speech signal that affect processing, for example, speaker and the rate of speech, whether we are adults (e.g., Goldinger, Pisoni, & Logan, 1991) or infants (Jusczyk, 1997; Jusczyk, Pisoni, & Mullinnix, 1992). Such evidence seriously calls into question models of speech perception that assume that such sources of variation undergo normalization prior to contact with canonical (that is, prototype) representations of the speech signal, whether at the featural, segmental, syllabic, or word levels. A reasonable resolution to this apparent conflict is found in the recent work by Miller and her associates (e.g., Miller & Volaitis, 1989; Volaitis & Miller, 1992). They have argued for the existence of structured (i.e., prototype) categorical representations that are conditioned on contextual factors, such as rate of speech—a view analogous to theories of object recognition that posit multiple views rather than a single canonical representation independent of viewing orientation (e.g., Bülthoff & Edelman, 1992; Tarr, 1995). Interesting questions arise regarding the extent of this contextually determined individuation of the representations of speech and its role with fluent speech in lexical acquisition and access.

The final concern of this section is the highly contentious issue of the nature of the mechanisms of speech perception, that is, whether they are part of a species-specific system devoted to the understanding and production of language (e.g., Liberman, Cooper, Shankweiler, & Studdert-Kennedy, 1967; Liberman & Mattingly, 1985, 1989), or whether they form part of a general auditory system (e.g, Stevens & Blumstein, 1981; Kluender, Diehl, & Killeen, 1987; Kuhl, 1986). In one respect at least, the view that there are species-specific processes and neural structures dedicated to the comprehension and production of language is without debate. Language as we presently understand it is very much a uniquely human achievement and as such must involve processes and mechanisms uniquely devoted to its comprehension and production. The controversial nature of this view enters when hypotheses are offered as to where in the processing of speech, that is, at what level of processing, are these species-specific specializations first functional.

At one extreme is the view offered by Liberman and his associates (e.g., Liberman & Mattingly, 1985, 1989; Whalen & Liberman, 1987), who argue strongly for species-specific perceptual processes and that the relevant data, especially those from studies of duplex perception ". . . implies the existence of a phonetic mode of perception that takes precedence over auditory modes" (Whalen & Liberman, p. 169). My own view is that there are language-specific constraints on the processing of speech at lower levels of processing and representation, but that the argument that the species-specific processing mechanisms for speech actually take precedence, and hence must be evident at or almost at the earliest possible moment of processing may be too extreme. After all, there are data in opposition to the precedence of speech processing (Vorperian, Ochs, & Grantham, 1995; and see Bailey & Herrmann, 1993). In addition, there are data from animals (e.g., Kuhl, 1986) showing that some processing characteristics of speech, e.g., categorical perception, are available to the auditory systems of monkeys and even chinchillas and thus presumably to our auditory systems prior to species-specific processing. Of course, as Kuhl notes, caution must be exercised when interpreting the speech processing data of animals. That species with very different evolutionary histories are able to process speech at times in ways like that of human listeners in no way necessarily demands that the processes, both functional and neurological, are the same, inasmuch as we know that the processing of communicative signals is different even among species that are quite closely related (Zoloth, Petersen, Beecher, Green, Marler, Moody, & Stebbins, 1979). In addition, other processing characteristics, such as normalizing for rate of articulation, occur with nonspeech signals as well in adults ( Pisoni, Carrell, & Gans, 1983) and infants ( Jusczyk, Pisoni, Reed, Fernald, & Myers, 1983).

There are data, however, that support specialized mechanisms, albeit perhaps after greater depth of processing than the level at which categorical perception or normalization for rate occurs. First, as mentioned, Kuhl (1991) has shown that the perceptual magnet effect occurs in human listeners, whether infants or adults, but does not occur in monkeys. Moreover, Eimas and Miller (1991) have shown that the discrimination of two durations of silence, 20 or 100 msec, occurred only in the case of the latter, that is, when the duration of silence was appropriate for the production of a medial stop consonant—a finding that in the absence of any apparent effect of masking was attributed to a species-specific system dedicated to the derivation of phonetic messages. In addition, as noted, Eimas and Miller

(1992) have shown that the organization of information to signal a phonetic contrast based on place of articulation occurred only in conditions where the information was embedded in a context that signaled coherent (i.e., organized) speech percepts for adult listeners. Thus, while these data and those of Eimas and Miller (1991) are well accommodated by a hypothesis of special processing system for speech, I have no illusions that the data will remain unchallenged for long in that the history of this controversy has been one continually marked by an ever-changing set of presumably critical data that appeared at the time to be beyond challenge.

Regardless of how well the interpretation of these data fares over time, it is important to note that at some point in processing what are presumably the results of auditory processing, and hence auditory (i.e., nonlinguistic) representations, must become linguistic in nature. After all, it is linguistic representations to which the rules of language (or the distributional charac-teristics for those less inclined to rely on innate rules) apply and outside of positing that there are low-level processing mechanisms devoted to the perception of speech and hence to the near-immediate creation of low-level linguistic representations, I am not aware of any adequate descriptions of how this transformation occurs. Jusczyk (1993, 1997) has suggested that it is the weights of the auditory cues for the universal phonetic contrasts that are altered by the infant's experience with the parental language in order to create the sounds of the parental language. However, if the infant's initial representations of speech are undifferentiated with respect to which are speech and which nonspeech, as Jusczyk (1993, 1997) would seem to assume, one wonders how the alterations in weights are directed and con-fined solely to the representations of speech, unless separate representations of speech already exist.

In summary, the abilities to perceive speech by young infants are highly sophisticated and would appear to have a strong biological determination. Nevertheless, these processing abilities and their perceptual consequences are modifiable by the linguistic environment provided by the parental lan-guage. Indeed, the development of speech perception would appear to be a clear example of an innately guided learning process (Jusczyk & Bertoncini, 1988).

## III.   The Processing and Representational Units of Speech

A characteristic of spoken language is its very nearly continuous nature. Moreover, when discontinuities occur in the form of short periods of silence and abrupt changes in the nature of the acoustic energy, these discontinu-ities tend to bear no relation to our percepts, be they words or prelexical units. Moreover, there would appear to be no other acoustic cues, each of which reliably provides information about word junctures (but see, e.g., Gow & Gordon, 1995; Nakatani & Dukes, 1977; Nakatani & Schaffer, 1978, for evidence that segmental and prosodic sources of information for word boundaries exist under some circumstances). In addition, the speech signal is marked by a lack of invariant spectral and temporal information for the identification of specific phonetic contrasts (Liberman et al., 1967; but see Stevens & Blumstein, 1981) and to a lesser extent their syllabic combinations, thereby again making the process of word recognition by means of its phonetic or syllabic components difficult to describe.

Nevertheless, conventional wisdom holds that a direct mapping between the acoustics of speech and words—that is, lexical access in the absence of prelexical units (see, e.g., Klatt 1979, 1989)—is impractical at best. Presumably, the variation in production of words both between and within speakers would create an indefinite mapping between the signal and the mental instantiation of words. Consequently, processing hypotheses, despite the nearly continuous nature of speech and the absence of invariant cues for sublexical segmentations, have centered on the constraint that the speech stream is nonetheless initially segmented into smaller, prelexical representational units that serve as the basis for lexical access (e.g., Pisoni & Luce, 1987).

Phonemes and syllables are the most frequently proposed units.[1] Phonemes provide the smaller inventory of units, and given the relatively small number of phonemes in any language a phoneme-by-phoneme comparison of the input with members of the mental lexicon would be relatively efficient. However, the effects of coarticulation, among other contextual effects, makes the physical realization of the phoneme highly variable (Liberman et al., 1967) and consequently not easily segmented and identified. The repertoire of syllables in any language is considerably larger, especially in languages with complex syllabic structures such as English. Nevertheless, coarticulatory effects would be less a problem—the coarticulatory effects across segments within syllables are (or can be) informative and a part of the matching and word identification processes and not simply variation that must be overcome. Of course, coarticulatory effects across syllables remain a problem. In addition, it is also true that if lexical searches begin at any identified phoneme or any identified syllable, greater cognitive economy will be achieved if the search begins with syllabic structures as

[1] There is little argument that such structures exist postlexically (e.g., Treiman, & and Danis, 1988; Cutler, Mehler, Norris, & Seguí, 1987; Eimas, Hornstein, & Payton, 1990) or serve as input representations and instructions to processes governing the production of speech (e.g., Cutler, 1995; Fowler, 1995). The issue is whether they serve as structures that directly access the lexicon during the online processing of speech.

the ratio of successful to unsuccessful searches will be considerable higher with syllabic-initiated searches.

Research of the past several decades has focused on the role of phonemes vs syllables as possible prelexical units—units that provide the forms by which members of the lexicon are encoded and directly accessed. Which of these units (or both) provide the basis for word recognition is, I also believe, highly relevant to the search for the initial representational units of speech by young infant listeners. It is the view taken here that the processing characteristics necessary for lexical access derive from the inherent processing properties and representational units of speech in very young infants that are later tempered by experience with the parental language. Given this, the nature of these representational structures in infants will be initially described, after which I examine the recent evidence for prelexical units in adult listeners.

## IV.  The Representation and Segmentation of
## Speech by Infants

The first study to directly investigate a possible role of syllables as processing units in speech perception was performed by Bertoncini and Mehler (1981). They showed that 4-day-old infants were aided in their ability to discriminate synthetically produced sound patterns by the presence of legitimate syllabic structures in the stimulus materials. Discrimination of the reversal of an initial and final consonant was found to occur when the consonants were the syllable-initial and syllable-final consonants of a CVC syllable and not when the same consonants began and ended a CCC utterance, a structure that is not a legitimate syllable. Moreover, reversal of the first and third consonants in a VCCCV structure, which has a permissible bisyllabic configuration, were likewise discriminated. The authors concluded that "We interpret our results as favoring a view according to which the syllable is the natural unit of segmentation and processing" (p. 247)—a view that Mehler has been instrumental in developing since the early 1980s (Mehler, Dommergues, Frauenfelder, & Seguí, 1981; Mehler, 1981; Mehler, Seguí, & Frauenfelder, 1981; Bertoncini, Floccia, Nazzi, & Mehler, 1995).

Bijeljac-Babic, Bertoncini, and Mehler (1993) have recently provided further evidence that the syllable is the unit of processing (although it is possible that the unit is just the vocalic nucleus, which is actually in and of itself a syllabic structure) and serves as the basis of representation. They showed that 4-day-old infants, born into French-speaking homes can distinguish a list composed of bisyllabic utterances from one composed of trisyllabic utterances. This occurred even when the natural difference in duration between utterances of two as opposed to three syllables was reduced by means of algorithms that compress and expand natural speech, while maintaining their intelligibility. Moreover, infants from the same population did not discriminate two-syllable utterances that had either four or six phonemes, despite the fact that the difference in duration between these utterances was nearly the same as that between the two- and three-syllable utterances. Finally, Bertoncini et al. (1995) have shown that neonates, again with French-speaking parents, were able to discriminate bisyllabic from trisyllabic utterances, but did not differentiate words with two as opposed to three morae, the prelexical structures of Japanese, just as infants earlier did not differentiate utterances with a constant number of syllables but differing numbers of segments. Moreover, as shall be seen below, British English, at least, appears to use segmental units during the online processing of speech by adults and Japanese speakers appear to use the moraic units for the same purpose. These findings suggest that major changes in representational units occur during an early period of the language acquisition process at least for infants raised in some language environments, namely those that do not use syllables as the basic units of processing and representation.

A number of experiments by Jusczyk and his colleagues (Bertoncini, Bijeljac Jusczyk, Kennedy, & Mehler, 1988; Jusczyk & Derrah, 1987; Jusczyk, Kennedy, & Jusczyk, 1995; Jusczyk, Bertoncini, Bijeljac-Babic, Kennedy, & Mehler, 1990) have likewise produced evidence that supports a syllabic form of representation of speech by young infants, either 4 days or 2 months of age, although the data are perhaps more convincing for the older infants. In addition, the findings indicate that by 2 months of age the encoding of a number of syllables (CV structures in this case) to which the infant has been familiarized is highly detailed.

In a typical experiment (Bertoncini et al., 1988; Jusczyk & Derrah, 1987), an infant is familiarized with a series of monosyllabic stimuli that had a common phonetic segment, either the consonant [b] with varying vowels ([bi] as in bee, [bo] as in bowl, [b γ] as in berg, and [ba] as in body) or the vowel [i] with varying consonants ([bi], [si], [li], and [mi]). Based on studies of categorization in the visual domain (see Quinn & Eimas, 1986; 1996, for reviews), the expectation is that if categorization occurred at the level of the segment, then evidence of discrimination would only be available if a novel CV test stimulus differed with respect to the initial common consonant in the former case and with respect to the final common vowel in the latter case. Differences in the previously variable segment, whether the vowel or consonant, would be unnoticed or not attended to sufficiently to dishabituate the infants. Infants would presumably treat a familiar consonant paired with a new vowel ([bu]) or a familiar vowel paired with a novel consonant ([di]) as members of familiar consonantal and vocalic categories. This was not the case with the 2-month-old infants. After familiarization with the series of [bV] syllables, infants discriminated about equally the syllable [bu] which had a novel vowel but the common consonant, the syllable [da] which was marked by a novel consonant and a familiar vowel, and the syllable [du] which had a novel consonant and a novel vowel. After familiarization with syllables with a common vowel and differing initial consonants, discrimination occurred to all test stimuli whether they differed from the familiar stimuli in the consonant alone ([di]) or the vowel alone ([ma]) as well as in both the consonant and vowel ([da] and [dI]). Categorization, as defined, had not occurred in either case, but rather it would appear that each CV had been represented and that any segmental change was sufficient to cause dishabituation.

After familiarization with the common consonant, the 4-day-old infants, like the 2-month-olds, showed discrimination of a novel vowel, whether paired with a familiar or novel consonant, [bu] or [du], respectively. However, they did not discriminate [da] which had a novel consonant, but importantly did not have a novel vowel. In addition, all of the test stimuli were discriminated after familiarization with stimuli having the common vowel [i], except [di], the stimulus with only a novel consonant, although similar consonantal differences have been discriminated by neonates in a different paradigm, as noted above. The findings with stimuli with a common vowel are in accord with a categorical representation based on vocalic segments (cf. Mehler, Dupoux, Nazzi, & Deheane-Lambertz, 1996), that is, with a conclusion that categorization has occurred. However, this view is not supported by the findings with a common consonant and by other studies, soon to be described. For the neonates, the data were taken by the authors to more strongly support the notion of syllabic representations in which the consonants were represented with sparse, if any, detail. With regard to the older infants, each familiar CV syllabic sequence appeared to be represented and thus any new sequence, whether novel with respect to the vowel, consonant, or both, would be detected, as was the case (see also Jusczyk et al., 1995).

In an ongoing series of unpublished studies, Eimas has obtained corroborating evidence from 3- to 4-month old infants who likewise represented series of CV syllables, with a common consonant or vowel, as a set of distinct CV syllabic-like utterances. Infants were familiarized with either four or six stimuli that have a common consonant ([b] or [d]) and a variable vowel or a common vowel ([i] or [a]) and a variable consonant. I modified the test procedure of Bertoncini et al. (1988) and Jusczyk and Derrah (1987) in order to make awareness of the familiar stimuli a function of memory and thereby presumably enhance the likelihood of finding categorical or summary representations at the segmental level. On each of six test trials I presented one of two test stimuli. In one case it was a novel stimulus with respect to both the consonant and vowel. In the other, the common consonantal or vocalic segment was retained, while the previously variable vowel or consonant, respectively, was made novel. Thus, for example, after familiarization with a series of CV syllables with the same initial consonant [b] and different vowels, the infant heard two test stimuli, one beginning with [b] and the other with [d] and each was paired with a novel vowel, [u], for example. Both of these test stimuli were discriminated equally, as was typically the case for the analogous test stimuli following familiarization with CV syllables with a common vowel. Both sets of findings occurred when there were either four or six familiar stimuli—the latter presumably having been more likely to yield a categorical representation based on segmental information. In addition, there was no evidence of categorization at the segmental level when the familiarization criterion was made weaker, which I reasoned should reduce learning about individual syllables. As was true for the earlier work of Bertoncini et al. (1988) and Jusczyk and Derrah (1987) the data comport well with a representation based on wholistic syllabic structures, albeit with considerable detail, in which the segmental units are undifferentiated and their common quality unrecognized. Of course, it is possible that both integrated syllabic and individuated segmental representations are present, but that estimates of novelty based on similarity are determined by the quite possibly more salient syllabic representations ( J. L. Miller, personal communication, 1996; cf. Foss & Swinney, 1973). Determining the validity of this possibility will be difficult, given the procedures that are available for the testing of infants.

In another series of experiments, Jusczyk et al. (1990) showed that attention influenced the specificity of the syllables that were represented in neonates. When the familiar series was a set of CV stimuli with a common consonant and relatively similar vowels that presumably underwent detailed processing in order to differentiate the vowels, neonates tended to notice a vocalic change quite similar to one of the familiar vowels. However, when the set of familiar stimuli were marked by the same common consonant and relatively dissimilar vowels, and thus might undergo only coarse processing, an equivalent vocalic change went unnoticed. Interestingly, neonates familiarized with CV sequences with variable consonants of differing similarity and a common vowel did detect the addition of a consonantal change paired with a common vowel whether the familiar stimuli were presumably processed in detail or not—indicating that there was a fairly detailed representation of both the consonant and vowel in contrast to the conclusions of Bertoncini et al. (1988). Two-month-old infants discriminated the novel stimuli in all of the conditions noted above—in other words, syllabic representations are readily inferred and there was no effect of the similarity of the familiar stimuli, vowels or consonants, indicating that there may have been less detailed processing by neonates but only of the larger vocalic differences. Finally, Jusczyk et al. (1995) showed that by 2 to 3 months of age, infants represented and remembered over a 2-min period the fine grain of a series of three CV syllables that lacked either a common vowel or consonant. This is a rather remarkable finding, but one that as Jusczyk et al. noted can be highly advantageous for infants attempting to acquire the sounds of the parental language, especially their phonotactic (sequential) constraints and a set of initial lexical items; one needs to learn what sound can be paired with what other sound. It is these latter studies that argue most strongly and correctly, in my view, that the syllabic representation of speech by infants consists of more than just the vowel nucleus (Mehler et al., 1996). In addition, the specification across syllables is considerable, but most probably not always complete at first, although there is as yet no evidence for segmental representations (see especially Bertoncini et al., 1988; Jusczyk et al., 1990).

In summary, how we are to account for the possibly different findings of Bertoncini et al. (1988) with neonates remains unresolved. However, it seems improbable that categorical representations at the segmental level are available to neonates (but only for vowels) and not to infants a few months older. The more likely explanation, offered by Bertoncini et al., is that the consonantal information in the syllabic representations was relatively lacking in detail in the neonates and that any differences in the presumably more salient vocalic information between the familiar and test stimuli typically (but not always) underlay the discriminability or lack of discriminability of the test stimuli by neonates after familiarization with a CV series with a common consonant or a common vowel.

Given these data demonstrating a failure by young infants to categorize at the segmental level, it might be argued that infants below 6 months of age are unable to form equivalence classes, although a form of equivalence classes exists in infants this age as defined by categorical perception (see the discussion above). That this is not the case is attested to by the findings of Jusczyk, Jusczyk, Kennedy, Schomberg, and Koenig (1995) that likewise add strong support for a syllabic unit of representation in infancy. In their first experiment, 2- to 3--month-old infants were familiarized with four bisyllabic utterances that had a common stressed first syllable, [ba]: [ba.lo], [ba. zi], [ba.mIt], and [ba.dɛs]. (The period marks the syllabic boundary in these and other examples to be presented later.) On attaining the criterion for familiarization, a syllable was added that differed (1) in the final un- stressed syllable as did all the test stimuli, but had the same initial consonant ([ba.n^l]), (2) in a single feature in the initial consonant of the first syllable ([pa.m˄l]), (3) by two features in the initial consonant of the first syllable ([ka.f˄l] or [na.b˄l] but with the latter stimulus interestingly containing both of the familiar segments from the first syllable, although no longer as a complete syllable or part of a single syllable (see also experiment 3), and (4) in the vowel of the familiar first syllable ([bae.vern]). Infants detected the presence of the novel stimulus in all situations except condition (a) where the initial syllable was familiar—evidence in accord with the view that a categorical representation was formed based on a detailed representation of the initial CV syllable, and not the vowel alone [see particularly test condition (b)]. Moreover, this representation must have encoded the presence of the second syllable, but merely as being present without featural, segmental or wholistic syllabic details. Otherwise, the test stimulus [ba.n˄l] in condition (a) would have been considered novel. Further evidence that a categorical representation was formed that reduced the information to be retained was found in their second experiment. In this study, infants were unable to detect the presence of a novel stimulus unless the familiar stimuli contained a common initial syllable. The presence of four familiar stimuli with eight different syllables (that is, four bisyllables without any common syllables) would appear to have in effect overloaded the processing system, reducing what was remembered to perhaps simply a series of bisyllabic sounds unspecified with respect to spectral and prosodic information. In this manner new sounds even only roughly equivalent (e.g., having the same number of syllables) to the familiarizing sounds were heard as familiar and not novel sounds, and hence attention was not redirected to them.

It should be emphasized that it was not simply the presence of the common consonant and vowel as separate entities, that comprised the initial syllable and that aided the detection of new utterances. Rather, it was only when these two sounds were temporally and rhythmically connected to form a syllable did they aid detection of novel speech information. In the third experiment, it was again found that if the same consonant and vowel segments were present in each of the familiar bisyllabic sequences, but were situated so as to cross the syllabic boundary, they did not form a categorical representation and their presence did not aid detection of new information. Moreover, it should be emphasized that the data of Jusczyk et al. (1995) likewise indicated that the representation of the familiar syllable was not built around a strong vowel alone (cf. Mehler et al., 1996).

Given these latter findings, I believe there is strong support for the contention of Mehler and Bertoncini (1981) that the syllable is the natural unit of speech processing in the infant (and see Bertoncini et al., 1995) by 2 months of age and probably by a few days of age as well. Moreover, a syllabic representation of speech could serve the processing of speech and lexical access by adults in many languages. This form of representation could also serve as part of the means to find a more efficient representation or representations of speech in those languages where syllabic representations as a means of segmentation and representation are inefficient. Indeed, if the CV-like representations of infants included information about vowel duration and intensity and existed at the start of language processing (cf. Mehler et al., 1996), sufficient information would be available for infants to discriminate between languages with different rhythmicities, whether the language is familiar or not (Nazzi, 1996), and permit discovering an efficient means for segmenting and representing speech.[2]

### V.  The Representation and Segmentation of Speech by Adults: Studies of Syllable Monitoring

The results of earlier research of the 1960s and 1970s concerned with discovering the basic prelexical processing unit were contradictory and marked by a number of potentially confounding factors (for discussion see Eimas et al., 1987; Mehler et al., 1981; Culter & Norris, 1988). However, in 1981, Mehler et al. introduced a simple but powerful procedure that showed quite convincingly that listeners, native French speakers in this case, responded faster to targets that corresponded exactly to initial syllables than to initial targets that were either *longer or shorter* than the initial syllable. Thus, listeners were faster to report the presence of the phonemic sequence | pa | in the word pa.lace than in the word pal.mier and were faster to report the presence of / pal/ in pal.mier than in pa.lace. This occurred despite the fact that the target sequences occurred as the first two or three phonemes in each pair of target words. It would thus seem that the long sought prelexical unit during the online processing of speech by adults had been discovered and that it was the syllable. Phonemes, while psychologically real, were presumably derived from the initial syllabic representations or from postlexical representations or both (cf. Cutler & Norris, 1979).

However, extension of this paradigm to other languages revealed that there was not in fact a single, simple answer to the form of prelexical representations; it was language dependent. Cutler, Mehler, Norris, and

---

[2] Another view on the initial representation of speech is that no single default or natural segmentation unit exists. Instead, infants possess early in life the ability to recognize and discriminate various representational strategies and that the one (or ones) which is acquired occurs during the earliest periods of language acquisition and depends on the information in the native language as to which segmentation strategy is the most efficient for the acquisition of an initial lexicon in the parental language. However, the data, especially, those showing evidence of counting syllables, but not morae or segmental units, by neonates argue against this position.

Segui (1986) in their adaptation of the Mehler et al. (1981) methodology to native speakers of British English found no interaction between target and word. The form of the target bearing words, whether CVCV . . . (e.g., balance with a CV initial syllable) or CVCC . . . (e.g., balcony with a CVC initial syllable) did not influence the differential detectability of CV or CVC targets, a pattern of results in accord with a prelexical segmental representation.[3] Interestingly, however, native speaking French listeners showed the expected interaction with the British English materials, whereas native speakers of British English again showed no evidence of prelexical syllabic structures with the French materials. However, with English materials French listeners showed reliably faster times to detect CVC as opposed to CV targets in CVCC . . . words, whereas the facilitation for CV targets compared to CVC targets in CVCV . . . words was small and did not attain the conventional level of statistical reliability (but see Finney, Protopapas, & Eimas, 1996). The latter finding suggested to Cutler et al. (1986) that these CVCV . . . words were found by French speakers to be difficult to syllabify, perhaps due to the consequences of the ambisyllabicity of their intervocalic segments in producing unclear or ambiguous syllabic boundaries (see below). The same argument was used to explain the failure of British English speakers to syllabify the British English materials. It would appear that French and English listeners were employing different processing strategies, syllabic and segmental, respectively— processing strategies that presumably had been acquired or strengthened early during learning their respective native languages, but whose use, at least in the case of French speakers, could be tempered by the clarity of the syllabic information. Moreover, Cutler et al. (1986) noted that French listeners might well have employed two processing strategies in parallel when listening to British English, namely a syllabic segmentation strategy and a segmental analysis, with the former being more efficient for CVCC . . . words and the latter, more efficient for ambisyllabic CVCV . . . words.

A major issue is, of course, the origins of these processing strategies. A reasonable initial hypothesis was proffered by Cutler et al.:

"We assume that this difference reflects the phonological differences between French and English. . . . Furthermore, we assume that the effects are not specific to French and English, but that speakers of any language with clearly bounded regular syllables should show syllabification effects, while speakers of any language with irregular, hard-to-segment syllables should not" (1986, p. 307)

[3] This, as Cutler et al. (1986; and see Footnote 1) among others have noted, is not to say that listeners of British English do not possess structures that include information about syllables and their hierarchical nature (e.g., Treiman, 1986; Treiman & Danis, 1988), but only that these structures are unavailable prior to lexical access.

French in being a syllable-timed language with syllabic stress always falling on the final syllable has clearly marked syllable boundaries and as a result a syllabic segmentation strategy is presumed efficient and learned early in life (Cutler et al., 1986; Cutler, Mehler, Norris, & Seguí, 1992). The French words ba.lance and bal.con are both clearly syllabified, whereas ba[l]ance in English, in contrast, is marked by ambisyllabicity. Intervocalic segments between a stressed vowel and an unstressed vowel, for example, /l/ in the word balance, can belong to both the initial and final syllables. Syllabification of the physical signal in such situations is thus unclear or ambiguous (and see Selkirk, 1982, for a different explanation of how syllable boundaries in English become ambiguous). Consequently, a syllabic segmentation strategy in English could be inefficient at times with the consequence that across development a syllabic segmentation strategy has become inhibited even for words that are not ambisyllabic, e.g., bal.cony.[4]

That early experience with phonologically different languages and the resulting acoustic-phonetic differences in the speech signal underlie the different processing strategies of adult listeners is further attested to by a study with bilingual French and British English speakers (Cutler et al., 1992). Listeners whose dominant language was French showed clear evidence of syllabification, but now only for French materials and not for British English materials—a marked difference from monolingual French speakers. Listeners whose dominant language was British English showed no evidence of syllabification for English or French materials, as was true for monolingual speakers of British English. To accommodate these results, Cutler et al. hypothesized that the different segmentation strategies fall into two classes: restricted because they depend on language-specific phonological processes (and their acoustic-phonetic consequences) for development and unrestricted because they are available to all language users, most likely even after having acquired a restricted strategy (see Cutler et

---

[4] A presumably more efficient segmentation strategy for English has been offered by Cutler and her colleagues—the Metrical Segmentation Strategy (MSS) wherein segmentation is cued by the presence of strong syllables (i.e., the presence of strong vowels) and occurs at the beginning of these syllables. Lexical access is thus triggered by the presence of these segmented strong syllables that might also include one or more unsegmented weak syllables prior to the next strong syllable (Cutler, 1990; Cutler & Butterfield, 1992; Cutler & Carter, 1987; Cutler & Norris, 1988; Grosjean & Gee, 1987). These strong syllables are not assumed to be represented as such and are thus not used as the actual form that accesses the lexicon. Rather, it is simply the presence of these strong syllables along with segmental information, particularly at the onset of the syllable that is the basis for lexical searches. It is apparent that the MSS needs a processing procedure to locate the segmental onsets of strong syllables and perhaps it is the segmental information from this essentially phoneme identification procedure that permits English listeners to respond without regard to syllable structure in the syllable monitoring experiments of Cutler et al. (1986, 1992), which used words having trochaic (strong-weak) syllabic stress patterns.

al., 1986). They argued that a syllabic segmentation procedure is restricted, whereas the segmentally based strategy employed by English listeners, monolingual French listeners when processing CVCV . . . English words, and French-dominant listeners when processing both CVCC . . . and CVCV . . . words of British English is general and universally available, which is to say simply that it is part of the biology of language. Moreover, Cutler et al. have argued that the acquired restricted syllabic segmentation procedure is optional. It can be "switched off" when its use may prove to be inefficient. This is what presumably occurred for the French-dominant bilinguals when they were processing British English materials: after long exposure to British English they learned that a syllabic segmentation is with sufficient frequency inefficient. Monolingual French speakers, in not having the long exposure to English, have not learned to inhibit a syllabic segmentation strategy with English words and thus attempt to syllabify English, and do so efficiently, at least with words having a CVCC . . . structure. A second restricted strategy requiring experience is evidenced by native Japanese speakers, whose language has a periodicity based on morae, the subsyllabic prelexical structures of Japanese (Otake, Hatano, Cutler, & Mehler, 1993).

Although this view of general and restricted strategies is consistent with the data described above, other findings exist from adult listeners that are not as easily reconciled with this view. Rather they are compatible with the evidence from infant listeners showing that what can be taken to be the early default (natural) representational system is based on syllables (e.g., Mehler, 1981). The evidence from adult listeners comes from a series of studies revealing syllabification strategies in several languages, including two dialects of English [Australian (Bradley, Sánchez-Casas, & Garćia-Albea, 1993) and North American English (Allopenna, 1996)] and Dutch (Zwitserlood, Schriefers, Lahiri, & von Donselaar, 1993) that are all marked by ambisyllabicity. It is noteworthy that with speakers of Australian and North American English who listened to words with a strong-weak syllabic structure, as did the English-speaking listeners in the studies of Cutler et al. (1986), the interaction between word structure and target was not obtained. Rather, CVC targets were responded to faster than CV targets for both types of target words, CVCV . . . and CVCC . . . , suggesting that the initial syllables of the ambisyllabic CVCV . . . words were processed as CVC syllables [but see Bradley et al. (1993) for a different interpretation of their results and Allopenna (1996) for counter arguments to Bradley et al.].[5] It should be noted moreover that Allopenna obtained the same

---

[5] This particular finding of Allopenna can be interpreted as supporting the MSS of Cutler and Norris (1988), in that segmentation is occurring immediately before a strong syllable. However, it must also be the case that both syllables must be treated in some way as separable, but related entities.

results when the target words were embedded in coherent sentences and in addition, he found that speakers of North American English did in fact show an interaction between target type and word type with weak-strong stress words, matching the findings of French listeners with French materials. However, it is important to note that the difference between CV and CVC targets was considerably attenuated with CVCV . . . words (cf. Cutler et al., 1986). In sum, a syllabic segmentation procedure can be demonstrated with English materials, albeit perhaps not those of British English,[6] but its nature is conditioned by patterns of stress. The latter is not unique, however. Sebastían-Gallés, Dupoux, Seguí, and Mehler (1992) found evidence for a syllabic segmentation procedure with Catalan words, which are not ambisyllabic, but only with words having unstressed initial syllables. Moreover, although native Spanish speakers employed a syllabic segmentation procedure with Spanish materials, which like the words of Catalan are not ambisyllabic, they did so only when processing was slowed (and see Bradley et al., 1993). Sebastían-Gallés et al. attributed the variability in their results with Catalan and Spanish materials to "acoustic transparency," which when present permits decisions about segments prior to decisions about syllables, that is, it permits the use of the unrestricted segmental strategy of Cutler et al. (1986). Whether they will ultimately be able to extend this idea to accommodate the differences between segmentation strategies in the syllable monitoring procedure among dialects of English and presumably other languages remains to be determined. What is necessary for this to occur is to be able to describe just which acoustic-phonetic properties foster a syllabic segmentation strategy and which properties foster a strategy based on the identification of individual segments or other units. What at the very least does appear to be true is that a syllabic segmentation strategy is widely, but not universally evidenced at maturity, and its presence and form are conditioned by the acoustic-phonetic realization of phonological processes.

Granted that there are general and restricted strategies (Cutler et al., 1986, 1992), I suggest on the basis of the data just reviewed that the segmental identification procedure is not the unrestricted strategy, but is, in contrast to Cutler et al., the restricted strategy and that the syllabic segmentation strategy is the unrestricted strategy, that is, the general or biologically given

---

[6] It is even possible that one form of a syllabic segmentation strategy is used by listeners of British English (Kearns, 1994). She obtained evidence comparable to, but not as consistent as, that found by Allopenna (1996) and Bradley et al. (1993) for listeners of American and Australian English, respectively. In any event, the results of Allopenna, Bradley et al., and Kearns raise the possibility that the original and later findings of Cutler et al. (1986, 1992) with English monolinguals and English-dominant bilinguals may have been influenced by the small set of words that was used, which was not true of the other experiments.

default strategy.[7] This view, which is compatible with the results of studies with infants and which will be discussed in greater detail below, finds further support in recent research by Pallier, Sebastían-Gallés, Felguera, Christophe, and Mehler (1993) and by Finney et al. (1996) using a very different experimental procedure.

## VI.  Studies of Attentional Allocation to Syllabic Structures in Adult Listeners

A possible criticism of the syllable monitoring procedure is that the use of syllabic targets may induce listeners to impose a syllabic segmentation strategy. Although this criticism loses much of its force in that Cutler et al. (1986) were unable to obtain evidence for a syllabic segmentation strategy in native speakers of British English and others have found that a complete syllabic segmentation strategy is not revealed with all forms of materials (e.g., Allopenna, 1996; Sebastían-Gallés et al., 1992), it is not entirely impossible. The phoneme monitoring methodology introduced by Pitt and Samuel (1990) precludes this form of criticism and has been exploited by Pallier et al. (1993) and later by Finney et al. (1996) to test for the online use of syllabic units during prelexical processing. This procedure is based on the assumption that the psychological reality of a processing unit is evidenced if listeners are able to allocate attention to that unit or components of that unit (Posner & Synder, 1975). Pitt and Samuel altered the expected location of a phoneme target by embedding experimental words in extended lists in which the majority of words had phonemic targets in a given serial position. Their results showed that for listeners of American English, phoneme detection was facilitated for a given serial position when attention had been directed to that position, providing what they took to be evidence for phonemes as the units of prelexical processing.

However, Pallier et al. (1993) correctly noted that the materials used by Pitt and Samuel (1990) confounded phonemic position with the position of subsyllabic components. Thus, for example, the third phoneme was

---

[7] In fairness, it should be noted that not all of the evidence is easily brought into line with the notion that the unrestricted segmentation strategy is syllabic in nature. There is evidence from Bradley et al. that Australian listeners who (may well have) used a syllabic strategy during phoneme monitoring did not transfer this strategy to Spanish materials, a result Bradley et al. (1993) took for a bias-like effect. In counter to this finding, it is interesting to note that Allopenna (1996) found that American English speakers did obtain a significant interaction between syllable target (CV or CVC) and word type (CVCV . . . and CVCC . . .) with French materials. Needless to say, the data do not as yet form a completely coherent pattern and will undoubtedly only do so when the relevant knowledge of the acoustic structures underlying the segmentation strategies in different languages becomes known.

always the coda of the first syllable, whereas the fourth phoneme was always the onset of the second syllable. Pallier et al. selected words in which a given phonemic target position was always either the third or fourth phoneme in a word. However, in one condition the target would be the onset of the second syllable and the coda of the first syllable in the other condition, thereby breaking the confounding between phonemic position and subsyllabic structure. This is exemplified for the phoneme target /p/ in the French words ca.price and cap.tif where the phoneme target is the onset of the second syllable and the coda of the initial syllable, respectively. Using both native French- and Spanish-speaking listeners, Pallier et al. found strong evidence for the use of prelexical syllables in the online processing of words: attention could be allocated to syllabic codas or onsets by the use a high proportion of nonexperimental targets in coda or onset positions, respectively. As a consequence detection of phoneme targets in attended to syllabic substructures was facilitated. That the use of syllabic knowledge occurred prior to lexical access was supported by the same pattern of facilitation when pseudowords were used.

Finney et al. (1996) have replicated the results of Pallier et al. (1993) with speakers of American English—a group of listeners who on the basis of the findings of Cutler et al. (1986) would not have been predicted to be able to allocate attention to syllabic components. Moreover, control experiments eliminated the possibility that the differences were a consequence of expectations built on the presence of temporal factors or the presence or absence of clusters in the onset targets, and like Pallier et al., Finney et al. obtained the same pattern of effects with pseudowords. It is important to note that Finney et al. only obtained these effects with second-syllable stress words. Words with first-syllable stress patterns [strong-weak stress patterns, which are far more numerous in English (Cutler, 1990; Cutler & Carter, 1987)], revealed no such interaction between target and induction condition. This failure occurred at least in part, we believe, because words with strong-weak stress patterns and short vowels, for example, desert, which constituted half of the stimulus materials for the onset induction condition, have target segments that are ambisyllabic (Kahn, 1980), being both the coda of the first syllable and the onset of the second syllable. Thus, in words like "go[b]let" which are considered to ambisyllabic by Kahn, among others, the phoneme /b/ may create the coda of the initial CVC syllable (gob), as well as serve as the onset of the second CCVC syllable (blet), or the syllable boundary itself may simply be unclear. Attention thus could not be clearly directed toward onset targets in specific subsyllabic positions with inductor and test materials of this nature (see also Pallier, 1994).

Given this pattern of findings, namely, an absence of attentional allocation with first-syllable stress words and attentional allocation with second-
syllable stress words, it is possible that listeners were employing the Metrical
Segmentation Strategy (MSS) of Cutler and Norris (1988) and not a syllabic
segmentation strategy (see Footnote 4). According to the MSS proposal,
segmentation should occur only before strong syllables (i.e., syllables with
unreduced vowels such as stressed syllables; Cutler & Norris, 1988). Segmentation is assumed not to occur before weak syllables, that is, syllables
with reduced vowels. Of course, the obtained pattern of results with second-
syllable stress vowels could only have occurred if the MSS also involved a
processing procedure that located the beginnings and endings of syllables
by means of a segmental processing strategy as well as possessed knowledge
of the phonology of the language that included the hierarchically ordered
internal structure of syllables both prior to and following the point of
segmentation.

We are in the process of further testing whether listeners may have used
the MSS. In a series of studies in progress, we found that words with strong-
weak stress pattern and long initial vowels preceding onset targets (e.g.,
re.play) and short vowels preceding coda targets (e.g., rep.tile) yielded
results consistent with a syllabic segmentation strategy. However, it is apparent that target position and the nature of the preceding vowel were confounded. Consequently, listeners may have responded more quickly to the
targets following an expected vowel length as opposed to an unexpected
vowel length (established by inductors with long or short vowels) rather
than to expected vs unexpected subsyllabic structures. Unfortunately this
confound is a result of the nature of English: words with short vowels
require a coda (Kahn, 1980) and thus potential onset targets such as /p/
in re[p]licate are ambisyllabic—they belong to both the first and second
syllables. In order to break this confounding, one strategy is to construct
pseudowords to be used as target items such that both onset and coda
targets will be preceded by only long vowels. This experiment, which was
dictated by the constraints of English phonology in that initial syllables
cannot end with a short vowel, and other control experiments for expectations to vowel length are in progress. Preliminary results indicate that vowel
length was not the sole determinant of our initial effects using words having
a strong-weak stress pattern.

It would seem then that American-English and Australian-English listeners, despite marked ambisyllabicity, are able to use at least a type of syllabic
segmentation strategy during the online processing of speech (and see
Zwitserlood et al. 1993, who worked with ambisyllabic Dutch materials).
This syllabic segmentation strategy with English, however, differs from that
used by French listeners at least with the syllable monitoring procedure.

What is apparent from studies of American English is that stress pattern plays a notable role in syllabification and thus in the nature of the segmentation strategy employed by listeners. Unfortunately, we do not as yet have a clear picture of the specific acoustic-phonetic consequences of the phonology that permit listeners to segment successive syllables in any language, let alone the various dialects of English. And indeed we do not as yet know what are the phonological principles and corresponding acoustic-phonetic consequences that (might) preclude on-line syllabic segmentation in native speakers of British English.

A question of importance is what these findings from adult listeners on segmentation strategies inform us about the initial prelexical representation of speech in very young infants. An answer based solely on the adult literature is, with one major difference, noted above, much like that of Cutler et al. (1986, 1992). The adult processing strategy is acquired by early experience with the native language and with bilingual experience, listeners may acquire more than a single strategy which can function in parallel. The data also argue for a single unrestricted (which is to say again a default or biologically determined) strategy initially available to all users of human languages. Where I differ from Cutler et al. (e.g., 1986, 1992), but agree with Mehler et al. (1981, for example) is in assuming that the unrestricted segmentation strategy is one based on syllables and quite possibly on CV structures (e.g., Eimas et al., 1987) for which there are at least claims of universality. Whether more complex syllable structures are likewise initially available in very young infants remains an open question. This unrestricted syllable segmentation strategy is, if reinforced by the native language, maintained and becomes the functional strategy at maturity. However, it need not be the sole strategy in use given, for example, a second language where such a strategy is inefficient (for example, French-dominant bilinguals processing English). In other words, the unrestricted strategy, if used with the native language, need not necessarily be used with all languages. Moreover this basic, default strategy can be replaced entirely by a restricted strategy which is apparently the case for native speakers of Japanese and possibly of British English.

These earliest unrestricted units, syllables in the present argument that are, I believe, provided by the infant's speech processing system described earlier, then become the means by which the rhythmical structure of the parental language can be evaluated and acquired (cf. Mehler et al., 1996). These early syllabic representations, with reinforcement by the parental language, are retained as the basis for the representation and segmentation of speech during the initial stages of word learning and the later online processing of speech by mature listeners. On the other hand, given a native language such as Japanese, the unrestricted representational units can be (and most likely are) rapidly replaced to permit the use of morae, or the restricted strategies can be added to the use of syllables to permit combinations of strategies, including perhaps the MSS, as might be the case with speakers of American English. Moreover, the findings with infants support such a view—one that posits (possibly) simple syllabic structures as the basis for the initial attempt at segmenting and representing speech— even if it leaves for now unspecified just how detailed a representation is initially in place early in life.

Having reviewed considerable evidence favoring a syllabic representation of speech in early infancy and in adult listeners of many different languages, I turn now to the final section of this discussion to examine properties of the speech signal about which infants gain knowledge during the second 6 months of life—properties that naturally have a high degree of salience for infants and that provide some of the means for the initial acquisition of a lexicon also described below—as well as to examine word-learning abilities per se.

## VII. The Beginnings of a Lexicon

The acquisition of a lexicon by infants is a very different task from that of lexical access by (relatively) mature users of a language, although both would appear to employ many of the same processes and properties of speech. The infant begins the task with a number of processing abilities, as has been documented above, including the means for representing speech. However, the infant is at first without knowledge of words, whether in terms of their possible acoustic/linguistic structures or in terms of the specific segmental and prosodic units that comprise specific words, and perhaps without the metaknowledge that words exist and serve as the basic means for conveying meaning, which needs to be learned. What is offered here (and see Jusczyk, 1997; Morgan, 1996) is that the acquisition of words is very much a process controlled by perceptual mechanisms of infants and the properties of the speech signal in the language environment where the infant lives. What infants must do with their biologically given processing abilities, modified by experience with the native language, is to abstract the appropriate regularities of the native language—regularities that in-clude the prosodic and acoustic-phonetic information that define the words of a language. The initial task is to detect and eventually use the regularities found in fluent speech that signal to varying degrees the boundaries that can mark the presence of acoustic sequences that will come at some point to be meaningful words and to represent the information between these boundaries in, as I have argued, syllabic form. On this general view, the acquisition of meaning for these initial representations would seem a later component of word learning and perhaps very much later in some cases. Moreover, as noted, word learning must be done without the existence of lexical entries to provide a context against which new words can be segmented and their meanings determined. We have seen that the infant very likely has the means to segment isolated utterances of speech into syllables and to represent these syllables for at least short periods of time (e.g., Jusczyk et al., 1995). But these capacities alone will not yield a lexicon. What is needed in addition are segmentation procedures for fluent speech that can help the infant locate word boundaries, per se, such that the linguistic information between boundaries can be represented and associated with categorical representations of the world that form the initial meanings (see Quinn & Eimas, 1986, 1996, for reviews of these representations of the nonlinguistic world).

Consider first the growing evidence that there exists functional information, as yet not fully specified as to its undoubtedly multiplicity of forms, that marks word boundaries (e.g., Gow & Gordon, 1995; Nakatani & Dukes, 1987; Nakatani & Schaffer, 1978) and perhaps even differentiates word from syllable boundaries (cf. Bertoncini & Mehler 1981). Cristophe, Dupoux, Bertoncini, and Mehler (1994) tested whether there was information that could signal the difference between syllable and word boundaries and whether it was available to infants. They found that neonates were able to distinguish identical segmental sequences when the second CV sequence of two CV sequences occurred after a syllable as opposed to a word boundary. Another potential source of boundary information is the phonotactic properties of the native language. Segmentation of the sequence "deadbird" according to the phonotactics of English requires in this case a word break between |d| and |b| but not between |e| and |d| as that would leave |db| as initial syllabic sounds which are not permitted in English. Jusczyk, Friederici, Wessels, Svenkund, and Jusczyk (1993) showed that 9-, but not 6-month-old infants raised in English-speaking homes preferred to listen to English words as opposed to Dutch words that contained segmental units and sequences not present in English. In a second study, in which the words varied only in permissible segmental sequences, essentially the same results were found, only now Dutch as well as American babies preferred to listen to the permissible sound sequences of their respective native language (see also Friederici & Wessels, 1993; Jusczyk, 1997).

There are also allophonic differences that can provide important cues to word boundaries. For example, the acoustic-phonetic properties of the first phoneme (/p/) in "pot is" not the same as the second phoneme in "spot" or the last phoneme in "top." Moreover, the differences in each case are systematic and can be exploited by native speakers to provide information about word boundaries. What is interesting is that by the age of 2 months infants were found by Hohne and Jusczyk (1994) to be sensitive to differences in allophonic variation. Finally, stress patterns can also provide information about sequences of syllables that form words. Cutler and Carter (1987) have shown that a large proportion of the content words of English begin with strong syllables (see Footnote 4) and thus the presence of strong syllables may provide a rich source of information for segmenting words. Again, 9-month-old but not 6-month-old infants raised in American English-speaking homes were found to be sensitive to this formation, preferring to listen to words with trochaic (strong-weak) as opposed to iambic (weak-strong) stress patterns (Jusczyk, Cutler, & Redanz, 1993). That infants are sensitive to prosodic information is further attested to by the preference of neonates to the mother's voice (Mehler, Bertoncini, Barriere, & Jassik-Gerschenfeld,1978; DeCasper & Fifer, 1980) and native language (Mehler et al., 1988; Moon, Cooper, & Fifer, 1993). In the latter case, the preference also occurred when the signal was low pass filtered so that only prosodic information was clearly available. Whether any or all of these sources of information are actually used by infants in the first year of life to mark word boundaries remains to be determined, but it is important to models of lexical acquisition that sensitivity to this information exists at approximately the time of word acquisition, and even well before this time with some forms of information in the speech signal (e.g., Mehler et al.).

In a series of investigations, Morgan (1994, 1996; Morgan & Saffran, 1995) has studied the role of rhythmical and segmental information in the representation of cohesive bisyllabic utterances in 6- and 9-month-old infants. The results of these studies have shown that the younger infants from English-speaking homes form coherent bisyllabic representations primarily and perhaps exclusively by use of consistent prosodic information whether in the form of trochaic or iambic stress patterns. Nine-month-old infants, on the other hand, use the consistency of both the segmental and prosodic information. Moreover under some conditions, namely, when segmental novelty is introduced in the patterns, there is a bias toward the use of trochaic information by the older infants—a finding in line with the results of Jusczyk et al. (1993) and the MSS of Cutler and Norris (1988) and one which Morgan argues comes from experience with the distributional properties of English—a conclusion that is both reasonable and seemingly well founded.

That infants are able to form such representations using multiple sources of information by 9 months would argue that processes for the acquisition of sound patterns that are words or word-like structures are functional before comprehension is well advanced and certainly before there is any evidence of the systematic production of words or near words from the parental language (see Jusczyk, 1997; Morgan, 1996). If this is indeed the case then a reasonable hypothesis is that infants before 1 year of age may be able to detect and represent the consistent information marking words that is present in fluent speech. Jusczyk and Aslin (1995) tested this idea and the results were positive. Infants 7 and one-half months of age, but not 6 months of age, presented with stressed, monosyllabic words in isolation or in fluent speech, remembered these items and later preferred to listen to them on test trials. Thus, for example, infants presented a number of instances of the words "feet" and "cup" in fluent speech listened longer to these words than the words "bike" and "dog," which they had not previously heard, when the familiar and novel words were presented in isolation. Reversing the procedure, presenting the words in isolation during familiarization and testing for their representation when they were embedded in fluent speech produced the same preference for the familiar words [see also Mandel, Jusczyk, & Pisoni (1995) for evidence that infants at the age of 4 and one-half months recognize their names]. There were two additional findings of interest. First, there was no indication that the infant's degree of previous familiarity with the words influenced listening times on the test trials. Second and above all the representation of the words was very detailed. With respect to the latter finding, alteration of the familiar words by a single phonetic feature in the initial consonants on test trials eliminated the preference for these items (cf. Jusczyk et al., 1995). Infants are obviously ready to acquire words well before their first birthday and the representation of these words is quite, and perhaps even perfectly detailed.

Whether this is also true for bisyllabic structures was the concern of a second series of investigations by Jusczyk and his colleagues (see Jusczyk, 1997, for a summary). The purpose of the initial studies of this series was to determine whether bisyllabic words (actually meaningless sound sequences for such young infants) would be easier to detect and encode if they began with a strong (stressed) as opposed to a weak (unstressed) syllable as predicted by the MSS. Using the methodology of Jusczyk and Aslin (1995), they found that American infants 7 and one-half months of age did indeed segment and encode both syllables when the words were trochaic in nature, but that only the strong syllable of words with an iambic stress pattern was encoded. This is evidence strongly favoring use of the MSS and well in accord with the results of Jusczyk et al. (1993), as was the interesting finding that when the weak (unstressed) syllable following the strong syllabic of iambically structure words was made consistent, it too was encoded. It would seem that by 7 to 8 months of age infants use processes predicted by the MSS for the segmentation of words, which of course is based in part on syllabic segmentation. However, use of the MSS alone is insufficient for the construction of a lexicon even for English. There are the weakly stressed function words alone or in sequence that must be acquired as well as the considerable proportion of words that have an iambic structure. In line with this view, Jusczyk (1997) found evidence in further studies that by 10 and one-half months of age American infants listened longer to fluent speech with short additional pauses between words than between syllables and, most importantly, these infants were just as likely to perceive pauses between words with a strong-weak stress patterns as with a weak-strong stress pattern. This is another instance of where language development is marked or appears to be marked by the untutored use of an increasing number of sources of available information in the signal—perhaps in this case phonotactic constraints and allophonic information to which infants are sensitive. It is of interest to compare the use of multiple cues here with that found by Morgan and Saffran (1995) as well as to see how Morgan, Shi, and Allopenna (1996) have described the use and power of multiple cues in a connectionist model in acquiring grammatical categories, even when each cue by itself was not highly predictive of these categories—a form of modeling that has already been applied to word segmentation in infants (Aslin, Woodward, LaMendola, & Bever, 1996).

## VIII.   Conclusions

In summary, the very young human infant is marked by a large number of sophisticated processing abilities for speech, given at birth and modified by linguistic experience during the first year of life. These abilities range from biologically determined processing procedures concerned with detecting, categorizing, and representing speech to newly developing sensitivities during the first year to many of the multiple sources of information in the speech signal that serve the acquisition of words. Of course, the infant must be highly tuned by biological factors in order to come with time to selectively attend to and exploit the relevant properties of speech to which attention must seemingly be allocated if word learning is to occur beginning in the second semester of life—as noted earlier, a clear case of biologically determined perceptual learning ( Jusczyk & Bertoncini, 1988). According to the view taken here, a major aspect of the infant's processing of speech is the ability to represent speech in a syllabic-like form and it is these representations that serve first in many, but by no means all, languages as the building blocks for the acquisition of words and later as the means to segment fluent speech and access the mental lexicon in more mature language users.

How these processes and the infant's sensitivity to certain distributional properties of language, together with processes and sensitivities yet to be determined, actually produce a functional lexicon awaits full explication. However, given the infant's sensitivity to the distributional properties of his or her native language, it is not unreasonable to believe that to a considerable degree the acquisition of words is driven by quite sophisticated learning processes—processes that are constrained from birth and earlier and whose modification is likewise constrained by biologically given forces. Thus, a full understanding of the acquisition during the first year of life will require an integration of knowledge of biologically given processing abilities and their modification by linguistic experience together with knowledge of the information and its distribution in the language environment of infants. As we ultimately learn more about both the processes of speech perception and the properties of the speech signal, detailed quantitative models of the earliest stages of the acquisition of language should become available. The task then will be to move our understanding of how the earliest stages of language acquisition make possible the full range of competence in mature users of human languages.

ACKNOWLEDGMENTS

Preparation of this discussion and the author's research described herein was supported by Grant HD-03551 from the National Institute of Child Health and Human Development. I thank Joanne L. Miller for her comments on an earlier version of this chapter.

REFERENCES

Allopenna, P. (1996). *A re-examination of the syllable's role in the on-line segmentation of English.* Unpublished doctoral dissertation, Brown University.
Aslin, R. N., Pisoni, D. R., & Jusczyk, P. W. (1983). Auditory development and speech perception in infancy. In M. M. Haith & J. J. Campos (Eds.), *Infancy and the biology of development. Vol. 2. Mussen's handbook of child psychology.* (4th ed., pp. 573–687). New York: Wiley.
Aslin, R. N., Pisoni, D. B., Hennessy, B. L., & Perey, A. J. (1981). Discrimination of voice onset time by human infants: New findings and implications for the effects of early experience. *Child Development, 52,* 1135–1145.
Aslin, R. N., Woodward, J. Z., LaMendola, N. P., & Bever, T. G. (1996). Models of word segmentation in fluent maternal speech to infants. In J. L. Morgan & K. Demuth (Eds.), *Signal to syntax: Bootstrapping from speech to grammar in early acquisition.* (pp. 117–134). Mahwah, NJ: Erlbaum.
Bailey, P. J., & Herrmann, P. (1993). A reexamination of duplex perception evoked by intensity differences. *Perception & Psychophysics, 54,* 20–32.
Bertoncini, J., & Mehler, J. (1981). Syllables as units in infant speech perception. *Infant Behavior & Development, 4,* 24–260.
Bertoncini, J., Bijeljac-Babic, R., Jusczyk, P. W., Kennedy, L. J., & Mehler, J. (1988). An investigation of young infants' perceptual representations of speech sounds. *Journal of Experimental Psychology: General, 117,* 21–33.

Bertoncini, J., Bijeljac-Babic, R., Blumstein, S. E., & Mehler, J. (1987). Discrimination in neonates of very short CVs. *Journal of the Acoustic Society of America, 82,* 31–37.

Bertoncini, J., Floccia, C., Nazzi, T., & Mehler, J. (1995). Morae and syllables: Rhythmical basis of speech perception representations in neonates. *Language and Speech. 38,* 311–330.

Best, C. T. (1994). The emergence of native-language phonological influences in infants: A perceptual assimilation model. In J. Goodman & H. Nusbaum (Eds.), *The transition from speech sounds to spoken words: The development of speech perception.* (pp. 167–224). Cambridge, MA: MIT Press.

Best, C. T. (1995). Learning to perceive sound patterns in English. In C. Rovee-Collier & L. P. Lipsitt (Eds.), *Advances in Infancy Research,* (Vol. 9, pp. 217–304), Norwood, NJ: Ablex.

Best, C. T., McRoberts, G. W., & Sithole, N. M. (1988). Examination of perceptual reorganization for nonnative speech contrasts: Zulu click discrimination by English-speaking adults and infants. *Journal of Experimental Psychology: Human Perception and Performance, 14,* 345–360.

Bijeljac-Babic, R., Bertoncini, J., & Mehler, J. (1993). How do 4-day-old infants categorize multisyllabic utterances? *Developmental Psychology, 29,* 711–721.

Bradley, D. C., Sánchez-Casas, R. M., & García-Albea, J. E. (1993). The status of the syllable in the perception of Spanish and English. *Language and Cognitive Processes, 8,* 197–233.

Bülthoff, H., & Edelman, S. (1992). Psychophysical support for a two-dimensional view interpolation of object recognition. *Proceedings of the National Academy of Sciences, 89,* 60–64.

Carden, G., Levitt, A., Jusczyk, P. W., & Walley, A. (1981). Evidence for phonetic processing of cues to place of articulation: Perceived manner affects perceived place. *Perception & Psychophysics, 29,* 26–36.

Carney, A. E., Widin, G. P., & Viemeister, N. F. (1977). Noncategorical perception of stop consonants differing in VOT. *Journal of the Acoustical Society of America, 62,* 961–970.

Changeux, J.-P. (1985). *Neuronal man.* New York: Pantheon Books.

Cristophe, A., Dupoux, E., Bertoncini, J., & Mehler, J. (1994). Do infants perceive word boundaries? An empirical study of the bootstrapping of lexical acquisition. *Journal of the Acoustical Society of America, 95,* 1570–1580.

Cutler, A. (1990). Exploiting prosodic probabilities in speech segmentation. In G. T. M. Altmann (Ed.), *Cognitive models of speech processing* (pp. 105–121). Cambridge, MA: MIT Press.

Cutler, A., & Butterfield, S. (1992). Rhythmic cues to speech segmentation: Evidence from juncture misperception. *Journal of Memory and Language, 31,* 218–236.

Cutler, A., & Carter, D. M. (1987). The predominance of strong initial syllables in the English vocabulary. *Computer Speech and Language, 2,* 133–142.

Cutler, A., & Mehler, J. (1993). The periodicity bias. *Journal of Phonetics, 21,* 103–108.

Cutler, A., & Norris, D. (1979). Monitoring sentence comprehension. In W. E. Cooper & E. C. T. Walker (Eds.), *Sentence processing: Psycholinguistic studies presented to Merrill Garrett* (pp. 113–134). Hillsdale, NJ: Erlbaum.

Cutler, A., & Norris, D. (1988). The role of strong syllables in segmentation for lexical access. *Journal of Experimental Psychology: Human Perception and Performance, 14,* 113–121.

Cutler, A., Mehler, J., Norris, D., & Segui, J. (1986). The syllable's differing role in the segmentation of French and English. *Journal of Memory and Language, 25,* 385–400.

Cutler, A., Mehler, J., Norris, D., & Segui, J. (1987). Phoneme identification and the lexicon. *Cognitive Psychology, 19,* 141–177.

Cutler, A., Mehler, J., Norris, D., & Segui, J. (1992). The monolingual nature of speech segmentation by bilinguals. *Cognitive Psychology, 24,* 381–410.

DeCasper, A. J., & Fifer, W. P. (1980). Of human bonding: Newborns prefer their mothers' voices. *Science, 208,* 1174–1176.

Edelman, G. M. (1987). *Neural Darwinism.* New York: Basic Books.

Eimas, P. D. (1974). Auditory and linguistic processing of cues for place of articulation by infants. *Perception & Psychophysics, 16,* 513–521.

Eimas, P. D. (1975a). Auditory and phonetic coding of the cues for speech: Discrimination of the [r-l] distinction by young infants. *Perception & Psychophysics, 18,* 341–347.

Eimas, P. D. (1975b). Speech perception in early infancy. In L. B. Cohen and P. Salapatek (Eds.), *Infant perception: From sensation to cognition,* (Vol. 2 (pp. 193–231). New York: Academic Press.

Eimas, P. D. (1985). The equivalence of cues in the perception of speech by infants. *Infant Behavior & Development, 8,* 125–138.

Eimas, P. D. (1996). The perception and representation of speech by infants. In J. L. Morgan & K. Demuth (Eds.), *Signal to syntax: Bootstrapping from speech to grammar in early acquisition* (pp. 25–39). Mahwah, NJ: Erlbaum.

Eimas, P. D., & Miller, J. L. (1980a). Contextual effects in infant speech perception. *Science, 209,* 1140–1141.

Eimas, P. D., & Miller, J. L. (1980b). Discrimination of the information for manner of articulation. *Infant Behavior & Development, 3,* 367–375.

Eimas, P. D., & Miller, J. L. (1981). Organization in the perception of segmental and supraseg-mental information by infants. *Infant Behavior & Development, 4,* 395–399.

Eimas, P. D., & Miller, J. L. (1991). A constraint on the perception of speech by young infants. *Language and Speech, 34,* 251–263.

Eimas, P. D., & Miller, J. L. (1992). Organization in the perception of speech by young infants. *Psychological Science, 3,* 340–345.

Eimas, P. D., Hornstein, S. B. M., & Payton, P. (1990). Attention and the role of dual codes in phoneme monitoring. *Journal of Memory and Language, 29,* 160–180.

Eimas, P. D., Miller, J. L., & Jusczyk, P. W. (1987). On infant speech perception and the acquisition of language. In S. Harnad (Ed.), *Categorical perception: The groundwork of cognition* (pp. 161–195). New York: Cambridge University Press.

Eimas, P. D., Siqueland, E. R., Jusczyk, P., & Vigorito, J. (1971). Speech perception in infants. *Science, 171,* 303–306.

Finney, S., Protopapas, A., & Eimas, P. D. (1996). Attentional allocation to syllables in American English. *Journal of Memory and Language, 35,* 893–909.

Fitch, H. L., Halwes, T., Erickson, D. M., & Liberman, A. M. (1980). Perceptual equivalence of two acoustic cues for stop-consonant manner. *Perception & Psychophysics, 27,* 343–350.

Foss, D., & Swinney, D. A. (1973). On the psychological reality of the phoneme: Perception, identification, and consciousness. *Journal of Verbal Learning and Verbal Behavior, 12,* 246–257.

Fowler, C. A. (1995). Speech production. In J. L., Miller, & P. D. Eimas, (Eds.), *Handbook of perception and cognition, Vol. 11: Speech, language, and communication* (2nd ed., pp. 29–61). San Diego, CA: Academic Press.

Friederici, A. D., & Wessels, J. M. I. (1993). Phonotactic knowledge of word boundaries and its use in infant speech perception. *Perception & Psychophysics, 54,* 287–295.

Goldinger, S. D., Pisoni, D. B., & Logan, J. S. (1991). On the locus of talker variability effects on the recall of spoken word lists. *Journal of Experimental Psychology: Learning, Memory, & Cognition, 17,* 152–162.

Gow, D. W., Jr., & Gordon, P. C. (1995). Lexical and prelexical influences on word segmenta-tion: Evidence from priming. *Journal of Experimental Psychology: Human Perception and Performance, 21,* 344–359.

Grieser, D., & Kuhl, P. L. (1989). Categorization of speech by infants: Support for speech-sound prototypes. *Developmental Psychology, 25,* 577–588.

Grosjean, F., & Gee J. P. (1987). Prosodic structure and spoken word recognition. In L. K. Tyler & U. H. Fraenfelder (Eds), Special Issue: Spoken Word Perception. *Cognition, 25,* 135–155.

Hillenbrand, J. (1983). Perceptual organization of speech sounds by infants. *Journal of Speech and Hearing Research, 26,* 268–282.

Hohne, A. E., & Jusczyk, P. W. (1994). Two month-old infants' sensitivity to allophonic differences. *Perception & Psychophysics, 56,* 613–623.

Jusczyk, P. W. (1977). Perception of syllable-final stops by two-month-old infants. *Perception & Psychophysics, 21,* 450–454.

Jusczyk, P. W. (1993). From general language-specific capacities: The WRAPSA Model of how speech perception develops. *Journal of Phonetics, 21,* 3–28.

Jusczyk, P. W. (1996). Language acquisition: Speech sounds and the beginning of phonology. In J. L. Miller & P. D. Eimas (Eds.), *Handbook of perception and cognition, Vol. 11: Speech, language, and communication* (2nd ed., pp. 263–301). San Diego, CA: Academic Press.

Jusczyk, P. W. (1997). *The discovery of spoken language.* Cambridge, MA: MIT Press.

Jusczyk, P. W., & Aslin, R. N. (1995). Infants' detection of the sound patterns of words in fluent speech. *Cognitive Psychology, 29,* 1–23.

Jusczyk, P. W., & Bertoncini, J. (1988). Viewing the development of speech as an innately guided learning process. *Language and Speech, 31,* 217–238.

Jusczyk, P. W., & Derrah, C. (1987). Representation of speech sounds by young infants. *Developmental Psychology, 23,* 648–654.

Jusczyk, P. W., & Thompson, E. J. (1978). Perception of a phonetic contrast in multisyllabic utterances by 2-month-old infants. *Perception & Psychophysics, 23,* 105–109.

Jusczyk, P. W., Cutler, A., & Redanz, N. (1993). Infants preference for predominant stress patterns of English words. *Child Development, 64,* 675–687.

Jusczyk, P. W., Kennedy, L. J., & Jusczyk, A. M. (1995). Young infants retention of information about syllables. *Infant Behavior & Development, 18,* 27–42.

Jusczyk, P. W., Pisoni, D. B., & Mullinix, J. (1992). Some consequences of stimulus variability on speech processing by 2-month-old infants. *Cognition, 43,* 253–291.

Jusczyk, P. W., Bertoncini, J., Bijeljac-Babic, Kennedy, L. J., & Mehler, J. (1990). The role of attention in speech perception by young infants. *Cognitive Development, 5,* 265–286.

Jusczyk, P. W., Friederici, A. D., Wessels, J., Svenkerud, V. Y., & Jusczyk, A. M. (1993). Infants' sensitivity to the sound patterns of native language words. *Journal of Memory and Language, 32,* 402–420.

Jusczyk, P. W., Jusczyk, A. M., Kennedy, L. J., Schomberg, T., & Koenig, N. (1995). Young infants' retention of information about bisyllabic utterances. *Journal of Experimental Psychology: Human Perception and Performance, 21,* 822–836.

Jusczyk, P. W., Pisoni, D. B., Reed, M., Fernald, A., & Myers, M. (1983). Infants' discrimination of the duration of a rapid spectrum change in nonspeech signals. *Science, 222,* 175–177.

Kahn, D. (1980). *Syllable-based generalizations in English phonology.* New York: Garland.

Kearns, R. K. (1994). *Prelexical speech processing by mono- and bilinguals.* Unpublished doctoral dissertation, University of Cambridge.

Klatt, D. H. (1979). Speech perception: A model of acoustic-phonetic analysis and lexical access. *Journal of Phonetics, 7,* 279–312.

Klatt, D. H. (1989). Review of selected models of speech perception. In W. Marslen-Wilson (Ed.), *Lexical representation and process* (pp. 169–226). Cambridge, MA: MIT Press.

Kluender, K. R., Diehl, R. L., & Killeen, P. R. (1987). Japanese quail can learn phonetic categories. *Science, 237,* 1195–1197.

Kuhl, P. K. (1979). Speech perception in early infancy: Perceptual constancy for spectrally dissimilar vowel categories. *Journal of the Acoustical Society of America, 66,* 1668–1679.

Kuhl, P. K. (1983). Perception of auditory equivalence classes for speech in early infancy. *Infant Behavior & Development, 6,* 263–285.

Kuhl, P. K. (1986). Theoretical contributions of tests on animals to the special-mechanisms debate. *Experimental Biology, 45,* 233–265.

Kuhl, P. K. (1987). Perception of speech and sound in early infancy. In P. Salapatek & L. Cohen (Eds.), *Handbook of infant perception. Vol. 2. From perception to cognition* (pp. 275–382). New York: Academic Press.

Kuhl, P. K. (1991). Human adults and human infants show a "perceptual magnet effect" for the prototypes of speech categories, monkeys do not. *Perception & Psychophysics, 50,* 93–107.

Kuhl, P. K. (1993). Innate predispositions and the effects of experience in speech perception. The native language magnet theory. In B. de Boysson-Bardies, S. de Schonen, P. W. Jusczyk, P. MacNeilage, & J. Morton (Eds.), *Developmental neurocognition: Speech and face processing in the first year of life* (pp. 259–274). Dordrecht: Kluwer.

Kuhl, P. W., Williams, K. A., Lacerda, F., Stevens, K. N., & Lindblom, B. (1992), Linguistic experience alters phonetic perception in infants by 6 months of age. *Science, 255,* 606–608.

Lasky, R. E., Syrdal-Lasky, A., & Klein, R. E. (1975). VOT discrimination by four to six and a half month old infants from Spanish environments. *Journal of Experimental Child Psychology, 20,* 215–225.

Levitt, A., Jusczyk, P. W., Murray, J., & Carden, G. (1988). Context effects in two-month-old infants' perception of labiodental/interdental fricative contrasts. *Journal of Experimental Psychology: Human Perception and Performance, 14,* 361–368.

Liberman, A. M., Cooper, F. S., Shankweiler, D. P., & Studdert-Kennedy, M. (1967). Perception of the speech code. *Psychological Review, 74,* 431–461.

Liberman, A. M., & Mattingly, I. G. (1985). The motor theory of speech perception revised. *Cognition, 21,* 1–36.

Liberman, A. M., & Mattingly, I. G. (1989). A specialization for speech perception. *Science, 243,* 489–494.

Mandel, D. R., Jusczyk, P. W., & Pisoni, D. B. (1995). Infants recognition of the sound patterns of their own names. *Psychological Science, 6,* 314–317.

Medin, D. L., & Barsalou, L. W. (1987). Categorization processes and categorical perception. In S. Harnad (Ed.), *Categorical perception: The groundwork of cognition* (pp. 455–490). New York: Cambridge University Press.

Mehler, J. (1974). Connaitre par desapprentissage. In E. Morin & M. Piattelli-Palmarini (Eds.), *L'unite de l'homme* (pp. 187–219). Paris: Le Seuil.

Mehler, J. (1981). The role of syllables in speech processing: Infant and adult data. *Philosophical Transactions of the Royal Society, B 295,* 333–352.

Mehler, L., Dupoux, E., & Segui, J. (1990). Constraining models of lexical access: The onset of word recognition. In G. T. M. Altmann (Ed.), *Cognitive models of speech processing* (pp. 236–262). Cambridge, MA: MIT Press.

Mehler, J., Seguí, J., & Frauenfelder, U. (1981). The role of the syllable in language acquisition and perception. In T. F. Myers, J. Laver, & J. Anderson (Eds.), *The cognitive representation of speech* (pp. 295–305) Amsterdam: North Holland.

Mehler, J., Bertoncini, J., Barriere, M., & Jassik-Gerschenfeld, D. (1978). Infant recognition of mother's voice. *Perception, 7,* 491–497.

Mehler, J., Dommergues, J. Y., Frauenfelder, U., & Segui, J. (1981). The syllable's role in speech segmentation. *Journal of Verbal Learning and Verbal Behavior, 20,* 298–305.

Mehler, J., Dupoux, E., Nazzi, T., & Deheane-Lambertz, G. (1996). Coping with linguistic diversity: The infant's viewpoint. In J. L. Morgan & K. Demuth (Eds.), *Signal to syntax: Bootstrapping from speech to grammar in early acquisition* (pp. 101–116). Mahwah, NJ: Erlbaum.

Mehler, J., Jusczyk, P., Lambertz, G., Halsted, N., Bertoncini, J., & Amiel-Tison, C., (1988). A precursor of language acquisition in young infants. *Cognition, 29,* 143–178.

Miller, J. L., & Eimas, P. D. (1979). Organization in infant speech perception. *Canadian Journal of Psychology, 33,* 353–367.

Miller, J. L., & Eimas, P. D. (1983). Studies on the categorization of speech by infants. *Cognition, 13,* 135–165.

Miller, J. L., & Eimas, P. D. (1996). Internal structure of voicing categories in early infancy. *Perception & Psychophysics, 58,* 1157–1167.

Miller, J. L., & Liberman, A. M. (1979). Some effects of later-occurring information on the perception of stop consonant and semivowel. *Perception & Psychophysics, 25,* 457–465.

Miller, J. L., & Volaitis, L. E. (1989). Effect of speaking rate on the perceptual structure of a phonetic category. *Perception & Psychophysics, 46,* 505–512.

Miyawaki, K., Strange, W., Verbrugge, R., Liberman, A. M., Jenkins, J. J., & Fujimura, O. (1975). An effect of linguistic experience: The discrimination of /r/ and /l/ by native speakers of Japanese and English. *Perception & Psychophysics, 18,* 331–340.

Moffitt, A. R. (1971). Consonant cue perception by twenty- to twenty-four-week old infants. *Child Development, 42,* 717–731.

Moon, C., Cooper, R. P., & Fifer, W. P. (1993). Two-day-old infants prefer their native language. *Infant Behavior and Development, 16,* 495–500.

Morgan, J. L. (1994). Converging measures of speech segmentation in preverbal infants. *Infant Behavior & Development, 17,* 389–403.

Morgan, J. L. (1996). A Rhythmic bias in preverbal speech segmentation. *Journal of Memory and Language, 35,* 666–688.

Morgan, J. L., & Saffran, J. R. (1995). Emerging integration of sequential and suprasegmental information in preverbal speech segmentation. *Child Development, 66,* 911–936.

Morgan, J. L., Shi, R., & Allopenna, P. (1996). Perceptual bases of rudimentary grammatical categories: Toward a broader conceptualization of bootstrapping. In J. L. Morgan & K. Demuth (Eds.), *Signal to syntax: Bootstrapping from speech to grammar in early acquisition* (pp. 263–283). Mahwah, NJ: Erlbaum.

Morse, P. A. (1972). The discrimination of speech and nonspeech stimuli in early infancy. *Journal of Experimental Child Psychology, 13,* 477–492.

Nakatani, L. H., & Dukes, K. D. (1977). Locus of segmental cues for word juncture. *Journal of the Acoustical Society of America, 62,* 714–719.

Nakatani, L. H., & Schaffer, J. A.(1978). Hearing "words" without words: Prosodic cues for word perception. *Journal of the Acoustical Society of America, 63,* 234–245.

Nazzi, T. (1996). *Pole of prosody in the discrimination of foreign languages by newborns.* Poster presented at the XXVIIIth Stanford Child Language Research Forum, Stanford University, April 1996.

Nosofsky, R. M. (1991). Tests of an exemplar model for relating perceptual classification and recognition memory. *Journal of Experimental Psychology: Human Perception and Performance, 17,* 3–27.

Otake, T., Hatano, G., Cutler, A., & Mehler, J. (1993). Mora or syllable? Speech segmentation in Japanese. *Journal of Memory and Language, 32,* 258–278.

Pallier, C. (1994). *Role de la syllable dans la perception de la parole. Etude attentionnelles.* Unpublished doctoral dissertation. Ecole des Hautes Etudes en Sciences Sociales, Paris.

Pallier, C., Sebastían-Gallés, N., Felguera, T., Christophe, A., & Mehler, J. (1993). Attentional allocation within the syllabic structure of spoken words. *Journal of Memory and Language, 32,* 373–389.

Pastore, R. E. (1987). Categorical perception: some psychophysical models. In S. Harnad (Ed.), *Categorical perception: The groundwork of cognition* (pp. 1–25). New York: Cambridge University Press.

Pisoni, D. B., & Luce, P. A. (1987) Acoustic-phonetic representations in word recognition. In L. K. Tyler & U H. Frauenfelder (Eds.), *Special Issue: Spoken Word Perception. Cognition, 25,* 21–52.

Pisoni, D. B., Carrell, T. D., & Gans, S. J. (1983). Perception of the duration of rapid spectrum changes: Evidence for context effects with speech and nonspeech signals. *Perception & Psychophysics, 34,* 314–322.

Pisoni, D. B., Lively, S. E., & Logan, J. S. (1994). Perceptual learning of nonnative speech contrasts: implications for theories of speech perception. In J. Goodman & H. Nusbaum (Eds.), *The development of speech perception: The transition from recognizing speech sounds to spoken words* (pp. 121–166). Cambridge, MA: MIT Press.

Pitt, M. A., & Samuel, A. G. (1990). Attentional allocation during speech perception: How fine is the focus? *Journal of Memory and Language, 29,* 611–632.

Polka, L., & Werker, J. F. (1994). Developmental changes in perception of nonnative vowel contrasts. *Journal of Experimental Psychology: Human Perception and Performance, 20,* 421–435.

Posner, M. I., & Synder, C. R. R. (1975). Facilitation and inhibition in the processing of signals. In P. M. A. Rabbitt & S. Dornic (Eds.), *Attention and performance* (Vol. 5, pp. 669–682). New York: Academic Press.

Quinn, P. C., & Eimas, P. D. (1986). On categorization in early infancy. *Merrill-Palmer Quarterly, 32,* 331–363.

Quinn, P. C., & Eimas, P. D. (1996). Perceptual organization and categorization in young infants. In C. Rovee Collier & L. P. Lipsitt (Eds.), *Advances in infancy research* (Vol. 10, pp. 1–36) Norwood, NJ: Ablex.

Repp, R. (1983). Categorical perception: Issues, methods, findings. In N. J. Lass (Ed.), *Speech and Language: Advances in basic research and practice* (Vol. 10, pp. 243–335) New York: Academic Press.

Rosch, E. (1975). Cognitive reference points. *Cognitive Psychology, 7,* 532–547.

Sebastían-Gallés, N., Dupoux, E., Seguí, J., & Mehler, J. (1992). Contrasting syllabic effects in Catalan and Spanish. *Journal of Memory and Language, 31,* 18–32.

Selkirk, E. O. (1982). The syllable. In H. van der Hulst & N. Smith (Eds.), *The structure of phonological representations* (pp. 337–383). Dordrecht: Foris.

Streeter, L. A. (1976). Language perception of 2-month-old infants shows effects of both innate mechanisms and experience. *Nature, 259,* 38–41.

Stevens, K. K., & Blumstein, S. (1981). The search for invariant acoustic correlates of phonetic features. In P. D. Eimas & J. L. Miller (Eds.), *Perspectives on the study of speech* (pp. 1–38). Hillsdale, NJ: Erlbaum.

Swoboda, P. J., Kass, J., Morse, P. A., & Leavitt, L. A. (1978). Memory factors in vowel discrimination of normal and at-risk infants. *Child Development, 49,* 332–339.

Tarr, M. J. (1995). Rotating objects to recognize them: A case study on the role of viewpoint dependency in the recognition of three-dimensional objects. *Psychonomic Bulletin & Review, 2,* 55–82.

Trehub, S. E. (1973). Infants' sensitivity to vowel and tonal contrasts. *Developmental Psychology, 9,* 91–96.

Trehub, S. E. (1976). The discrimination of foreign speech contrasts by infants and adults. *Child Development, 47,* 466–472.

Treiman, R. (1986). The division between onsets and rimes in English syllables. *Journal of Memory and Language, 25,* 476–491.

Treiman, R., & Danis, C. (1988). Syllabification of intervocalic consonants. *Journal of Memory and Language, 27,* 87–104.

Tsushima, T., Takizawa, O., Sasaki, M., Siraki, S., Nishi, K., Kohno, M., Menyuk, P., & Best, C. (1994). Discrimination of English /r-l/ and /w-y/ by Japanese infants at 6–12 months: Language specific developmental changes in speech perception abilities. Paper presented at the *International Conference on Spoken Language Processing, 4* (pp. 1695–1698). Yokohama, Japan: The Acoustical Society of Japan.

Volaitis, L. E., & Miller, J. L. (1992). Phonetic prototypes: Influence of place of articulation and speaking rate on the internal structure of voicing categories. *Journal of the Acoustical Society of America, 92,* 723–735.

Vorperian, H. K., Ochs, M. T., & Grantham, D. W. (1995). Stimulus intensity and fundamental frequency effects on duplex perception. *Journal of the Acoustical Society of America, 98,* 734–744.

Werker, J. F. (1993). Developmental changes in cross-language speech perception: Implications for cognitive models of speech processing. In G. T. M. Altmann & R. Shillcock (Eds.), *Cognitive models of speech processing* (pp. 57–78). Hillsdale, NJ: Erlbaum.

Werker, J. F., & Tees, R. C., (1984). Cross-language speech perception: Evidence for perceptual reorganization during the first year of life. *Infant Behavior and Development, 7,* 49–63.

Whalen, D. H., & Liberman, A. M. (1987). Speech perception takes precedence over nonspeech perception. *Science, 237,* 169–171.

Zoloth, S. R., Petersen, M. R., Beecher, M. D., Green, S., Marler, P., Moody, D. B., & Stebbins, W. (1979). Species-specific perceptual processing of vocal sounds by monkeys. *Science, 204,* 870–873.

Zwitserlood, P., Schriefers, H., Lahiri, A., & von Donselaar, W. (1993). The role of syllables in the perception of spoken Dutch. *Journal of Experimental Psychology: Learning, Memory, and Cognition, 19,* 260–271.

# CONSTRAINTS ON THE LEARNING OF SPATIAL TERMS: A COMPUTATIONAL INVESTIGATION

*Terry Regier*

## I. Introduction

The language-learning child begins to speak about spatial locations and events quite early on, as the vocabulary is just starting to develop. Hank, for example, a child whose speech was tracked by Bates, Bretherton, and Snyder (1988), used the expressions "here" and "in there" at 20 months. Apart from these spatial references, the transcript shows his conversational contributions to be limited to the remarks "uh," "um," "huh," "more," "ok," "boy," "mom," "see," "baby," "yeah," "bye," and "see ya." The appearance of spatial terms at such a preliminary stage of linguistic development testifies to the child's early entry into the process of learning which words express which spatial notions.

This process is not as simple as it might seem. Despite the apparent naturalness of the English spatial categories "in," "on," "above," and so forth, they are not universally shared by all languages. Instead, there is considerable cross-linguistic variation in the ways different languages structure space. This means that the child must learn to determine which aspects of the spatial world are semantically relevant for his or her native language, and must then construct spatial categories on that basis. For example, while English uses the single spatial preposition "on" to express support, German draws a distinction between support on a horizontal surface (e.g., a cup *on* a table: "auf") and support from the side (e.g., a picture *on* a wall: "an").

THE PSYCHOLOGY OF LEARNING
AND MOTIVATION, VOL. 36

In Korean, some spatial actions are categorized by *tightness of fit* (Choi & Bowerman, 1992): placing a cassette *in* its case and placing the top of a pen *on* the pen would both be expressible by one verb ("kkita"), while placing the same objects either into or onto objects with which they mesh less tightly would call for the use of another verb ("nehta"). And the Mexican Indian language Mixtec is sensitive to whether objects are vertically or horizontally extended (Brugman, 1983): a bird above or on top of a tree would be said to be at the tree's "head" (šini), while one fluttering above or perched on a log would be said to be at the log's "animal back" (siki). The central point then is that each language picks up on some spatial features and ignores others—and different languages pick up on different features. So the child learning to speak about space must determine which features are relevant to the home language's semantic system. In this sense, each language requires its own sort of "perceiving-for-speaking." Let us say a child sees a ball being placed in a toy box and hears the English word "in." Does that mean that "in" refers to the resulting containment of the ball in the box? Or to the looseness of fit of the ball in the box? Or to the horizontal elongation of the toy box? Or to something else?

The answer of course is that the child cannot know yet, but that on repeated exposures to events of different sorts, all labeled "in," the child will form an abstraction encompassing these events. But this leads the child to another problem: how to generalize to previously unseen situations. This problem is made acute by the fact that the child cannot rely on a consistent supply of clear negative evidence. If the child is never told that a particular situation is a poor example of, say, "in," how does he or she learn not to use "in" for such a situation, while still extending the usage of "in" to other (appropriate) situations that have also not yet been experienced? In other words, how does the child know not to undergeneralize or overgeneralize from the examples seen, if nothing has been explicitly ruled out?

The challenges of this inductive task can be met if the child is armed with an appropriate set of heuristic constraints, biasing him or her to look for certain things, and not others. Thus, if the "blooming buzzing confusion" that the child encounters is viewed through a lens that indicates where the answers are likely to be, the task of learning to speak about space is much less daunting. The importance of placing constraints on the sorts of hypotheses that are entertained during induction has been noted in fields ranging from child language acquisition (Markman, 1989; Mervis, Golinkoff, & Bertrand 1994; Pinker, 1989) to connectionism and machine learning (Geman, Bienenstock, & Doursat, 1992; LeCun, 1989; Mitchell, 1980; Shavlik & Dietterich, 1990).

In this chapter I consider three such constraints on the acquisition of spatial terms, in the context of a computational model that embodies all three. In doing this, I shall build on earlier computational work (Regier,

1995, 1996) by demonstrating the empirical adequacy of some of the constraints proposed there. The first constraint concerns the shape of locative categories such as "above." I hypothesize that the appropriateness of using "above" in a given situation can be modeled as a linear combination of a set of simple orientational features, and demonstrate that a computational model embodying this hypothesis provides a very close fit to empirically collected adult "above" judgments. Thus, the end product of human learning is shown to be consistent with the hypothesis. This identifies a possible perceptual constraint on spatial term acquisition—the orientational features focused on in the modeling may underlie the acquisition process. The second constraint is a well-known one in the developmental community: mutual exclusivity (Markman, 1989). This constraint posits that children are reluctant to accept more than one name for an object, that names are "mutually exclusive" of one another. I hypothesize that children assume spatial terms to be mutually exclusive, and demonstrate the viability of this idea computationally. I also show that although mutual exclusivity encounters problems when faced with overlapping or nested concepts (e.g., "next to" and "outside"), these problems are surmountable given a particular implementation of the idea of mutual exclusivity as a probabilistic or soft constraint (Merriman & Bowman, 1989). I suggest that these simulations offer a rationale for the empirically observed tendency for mutual exclusivity to be weak in young children, and then to gradually gain in strength: as the simulations indicate, initial learning is most effective with a weak bias. I also demonstrate that the notion of mutual exclusivity as a soft constraint can account for an interesting case of overgeneralization in spatial term usage among children learning Dutch (Bowerman, 1996). The third and final constraint is based on a proposed perceptual asymmetry: the greater salience of endpoints of actions than their beginnings. While this constraint was originally suggested by computational work, there is some empirical evidence supporting this idea. I demonstrate that a computational model embodying this constraint and the first two as well is capable of learning spatial terms from a range of languages. I also demonstrate that this constraint gives rise to predictions concerning the developmental sequence of spatial term learning, and concerning the sorts of semantic systems we may expect to encounter in the world's languages.

## II.  What Does "Above" Mean?

Let us start by examining "above," by any account one of the simplest of spatial terms.[1] I am operating on the assumption that once we have deter-

---

[1] Somewhat counterintuitively, it is also one of the rarest. There are only 21 occurrences of "above" in mothers' speech in the entire Childes database (MacWhinney & Snow, 1990), as compared with 18,987 occurrences of "in," and 16,244 of "on."

mined which computational structures are descriptively adequate for capturing "above" judgments, we will know something not just about "above" itself, but perhaps also about the perceptual mechanism through which we perceive one object being above another. We may then expect these structures to play a role in other spatial terms as well, including terms from other languages. In this section, we shall see a concrete proposal for modeling "above" jdugments fit to empirical data, and shall see this idea generalized to the terms "below," "left," and "right." Later in the chapter we shall see the same principle enabling the learning of spatial terms from other languages as well.

I shall be referring to the located object as the trajector (TR), and the object relative to which it is located as the landmark (LM; Langacker, 1987). Thus, when we say "The circle is above the square," the circle is the trajector and the square is the landmark.

It is conceivable that "above" judgments might stem from a general perceptual ability to predict whether, if the trajector were to fall under the influence of gravity, it would strike the landmark. Such prediction of possible future events is a capability we clearly have, and one which is equally clearly useful. And it seems likely that language would encode notions, such as this one, that are functionally critical to predicting and manipulating the world. One possible source for "above" judgments then is an explicit mental simulation (Ullman, 1984; Siskind, 1992; Barsalou & Prinz, 1997; Glenberg, in press) of such a falling event, followed by a determination of whether the two objects collide in the simulation—and there is some empirical support for the idea that humans represent potential motion in static scenes (Freyd, Pantzer, & Cheng, 1988). But this is probably not the mechanism at work here. Note that in its most natural form the mental simulation theory predicts that reaction time for "above" judgments will increase with the distance between the landmark and trajector: if these judgments are based on our (unconsciously) mentally simulating the fall of the trajector onto the landmark in real time, the simulation should take longest when the trajector is far above the landmark. Logan and Compton (1996) tested for this and found no distance effects on reaction time in the apprehension of spatial relations such as "above." This militates against the real-time simulation theory.

A.  SPATIAL TEMPLATES

How are "above" judgments made then, if they are not the result of real-time simulation? Logan and Sadler (1996) present an alternative account of the apprehension of spatial relations, one that is consistent with the lack of a distance effect. They posit that each speaker of English possesses a mental and perceptual construct they call a "spatial template" for "above," and similar templates for other spatial terms. A spatial template is a two-dimensional visual array with an anchor point at its center. The value of the array at positon $(i, j)$ is the explicitly encoded acceptability of using "above" to describe the relationship between a trajector at that position and a landmark at the center of the array. The array can be anchored on a given perceived object by mentally shifting the array as a whole so that its anchor point is at that object; the values in the cells of the array then yield the acceptability of using "above" to locate trajectors relative to the landmark on which we have anchored. To retrieve an "above" judgment for the current trajector, we simply index into the array using the trajector's spatial position. This indexing is the only processing step involved—regardless of the distance between landmark and trajector. Thus, the time required for "above" judgments should not depend on the distance between the two objects.

In order to determine the contents of English speakers' spatial templates, Logan and Sadler (1996) presented subjects with a series of visual stimuli showing an O (the landmark) in the middle of a $7 \times 7$ grid, and an X (the trajector) in one of the remaining 48 grid positions, as shown in Fig. 1A. The subjects were asked to rate how well the sentence "The X is above the O" described each such stimulus. The position of the X changed across stimuli, but the position of the O did not. The grid was not visible to the subjects. By averaging ratings across subjects, Logan and Sadler obtained a spatial template for the English spatial term "above"; this is shown in Fig. 1B. The floor-plane of this graph indicates trajector position, while the height of the graph shows acceptability judgments for "above" as a function of trajector position, relative to the landmark at the center of the grid.

The spatial template idea is consistent with the finding that there is no effect of distance on reaction time, and this is a point in its favor. One drawback of the account, however, is that it does not specify how the values in the cells of the spatial template array are determined. What is the source of these acceptability judgments, tucked into spatial template cells? What is the mechanism that gives rise to these numbers and not other ones?

B.  GENERATING SPATIAL TEMPLATES

I shall demonstrate that spatial templates of the sort obtained by Logan and Sadler (1996) can be *generated* using a simple linear combination of directional features. This reduces the descriptive size of such templates, and provides a principle underlying observed acceptability judgments for spatial terms such as "above." It also raises the hope that the structures involved in this characterization may be consistent with other spatial terms

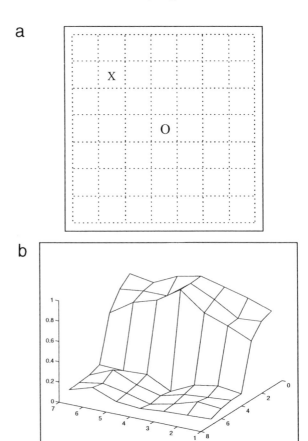

Fig. 1.   "Above" judgments, reported by Logan and Sadler (1996). (A) Stimulus for eliciting "above" judgments from subjects. (B) The resulting spatial template for "above." See text for details.

in English, as well as terms from other languages—and that these perceptual structures may constrain the child's acquisition of such terms.

   Two features that seem to play a role in spatial term appropriateness judgments are the *proximal orientation* and *center-of-mass orientation* of a scene (Regier, 1996). These features both specify the location of the trajector with respect to the landmark, but in different ways. The proximal orientation is the orientation of the imaginary directed line segment connecting the landmark to the trajector where the two objects are closest. The center of mass orientation on the other hand is the orientation of

center-of-mass orientation

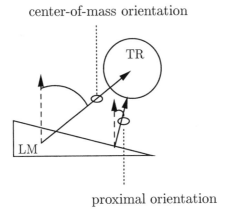

proximal orientation

Fig. 2.   Proximal and center-of-mass orientations being compared with upright vertical.

the imaginary directed line segment connecting the center of mass of the landmark to that of the trajector. Figure 2 illustrates both the proximal and center-of-mass orientations in a single scene, each being compared with upright vertical. In general, I shall distinguish between *relational* and *reference* orientations. Relational orientations, such as the proximal and center-of-mass orientations, indicate where the trajector is in relation to the landmark, whereas reference orientations, such as upright vertical, are canonical orientations with which relational orientations may or may not align.

What motivation is there for the center-of-mass and proximal orientations? Consider the three scenes of Fig. 3, showing a circle above a rectangle. The scene in Fig. 3A is an excellent instance of "above," and, in this example, the center-of-mass orientation is perfectly aligned with upright vertical. The scene in Fig. 3B is a slightly weaker example of "above," and

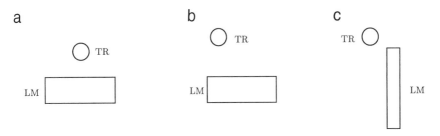

Fig. 3.   Excellent, good, and fair instances of a circle *above* a rectangle.

here the center-of-mass orientation is not as well aligned with upright vertical as in Fig. 3A—this helps to motivate our consideration of the center-of-mass orientation. These observations are supported by the fact that when Logan and Sadler (1996) asked subjects to draw an X above a square, almost all subjects drew the X directly above the center of mass of the square. The center-of-mass orientation cannot be all there is to the story, however, because in Fig. 3C the center-of-mass orientation is the same as in Fig. 3B, but Fig. 3C is clearly inferior to Fig. 3B as an instance of "above." The proximal orientation is not the same in the two scenes, however, and may account for the difference. Systematically collected "above" judgments, relative to vertically and horizontally elongated landmarks of the sort shown here, support the informal observation that "above" acceptability regions are narrower above tall, narrow landmarks than above wide, flat ones (Laura Carlson-Radvansky, personal communication). It is possible that the proximal orientation is behind the phenomenon: imagine the tall landmark in Fig. 3C rotated about its center of mass so that it is now extended horizontally rather than vertically—the resulting configuration will be a stronger example of "above," and the center-of-mass orientation will not have changed. The proximal orientation however will be much closer to upright vertical than it currently is, and may account for the difference. There is evidence that the human visual system represents the center of mass (Hirsch & Mjolsness, 1992; Huttenlocher, Hedges & Duncan, 1991), and this is clearly a useful feature for object manipulation, so it is reasonable to expect it to play a role in the spatial lexicon. Similarly, it makes sense for an organism to keep track of the closest point on an object for obstacle-avoidance purposes.

I hypothesize that "above" judgments are well modeled as a simple linear combination of the degree to which the proximal and center-of-mass orientations align with reference orientations such as upright vertical. To make the hypothesis more precise, let us define the degree of alignment between two orientations to be a Gaussian of the sines and cosines of the two orientations:

$$f_\theta(r, \sigma) = exp \left[ - \frac{(sin(\theta) - sin(r))^2 + (cos(\theta) - cos(r))^2}{\sigma^2} \right] \quad (1)$$

Here, $r$ is the relational orientation, and $\theta$ is the reference orientation to which it is being compared. This function will return its maximal value of 1.0 when $r$ is perfectly aligned with the reference orientation $\theta$, and will drop off as $r$ deviates from $\theta$. The overall shape of the function can be seen

a                                        b

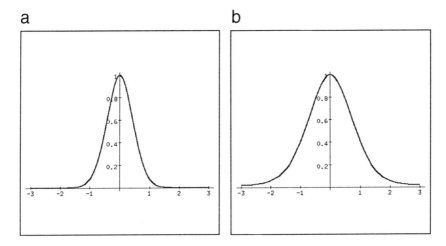

Fig. 4.    Gaussians for determining orientational alignment: (A) $\sigma = 0.6$. (B) $\sigma = 1.0$. Reprinted from Regier 1996 with permission.

in Fig. 4. The $\sigma$ parameter controls the width of the Gaussian: Fig. 4A shows the shape of the function with $\sigma = 0.6$, and Fig. 4B shows the shape of the same function with $\sigma = 1.0$. A smaller value for $\sigma$ yields a more tightly peaked response. This means that by adjusting this parameter we can control how closely the two orientations must align in order to yield a response of appreciable strength. There is some motivation for this formulation: there are orientation-sensitive cells with response profiles qualitatively similar to those of $f_\theta$ nodes in visual cortex (Hubel & Wiesel, 1959, 1962), and in other areas of the brain as well, responding to the directions of arm movements (Kalaska, Caminiti, & Georgopoulos, 1983; Georgopoulos, Schwartz, & Kettner, 1986), eye movements (Henn & Cohen, 1976), and head position (Suzuki, Timerick, & Wilson, 1985). This indicates that the mechanism is very general and widely used, and seems to underlie several aspects of human perception and action. There is also evidence for the upright vertical as a reference orientation, even in prelinguistic children as young as 2–3 months of age (Bomba, 1984).

If we let *prox* be the proximal orientation in a given scene, and *com* be the center-of-mass orientation, the simplest version of this hypothesis is that "above" judgments can be captured by:

$$above = p \times f_\uparrow(prox, \sigma_p) + c \times f_\uparrow(com, \sigma_c) + b \qquad (2)$$

Here $f_\uparrow()$ is a Gaussian responding maximally to upright vertical. The widths of the two Gaussians $\sigma_p$ and $\sigma_c$, and the weights $p$, $c$, and $b$, are the free parameters of the model. This overall function can be realized in the connectionist network shown in Fig. 5; once this is done, the free parameters just identified can be adjusted to fit empirically obtained data through the back-propagation training procedure (Rumelhart, Hinton, & Williams, 1986). In fact, if it were not for the $\sigma$ terms controlling Gaussian width, we would be able to fit the model to data using linear regression. But because we have to adjust not just the weights but also those parameters $(\sigma_p, \sigma_c)$ that affect what the values are that will be weighted, standard linear regression will not suffice. Back-propagation explicitly takes into account the dependence of parameters on one another; this makes it an appropriate choice for the task.

The inputs to the network are the center-of-mass and proximal orientations for a given scene, and the output is an "above" judgment. If such a network can be trained to produce "above" judgments that match those of human subjects, that will substantiate the hypothesis outlined above, particularly if the parameter values obtained also provide good fits to "above" judgments on datasets other than that on which the network was trained. It should be pointed out that this is a somewhat atypical use of connectionist networks in cognitive modeling. Often, relatively unstructured networks are trained on data that is assumed to be available to the child, and the question is whether such a network can generalize appropriately—if so, this demonstrates that no innate structure need be posited to account for the child's learning ability (Rumelhart & McClelland, 1986; Plunkett & Marchman, 1988). Here, in contrast, the network is structured (Feldman, Fanty, & Goddard, 1988), and the question is whether or not

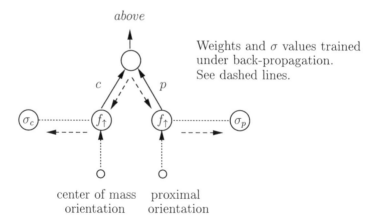

Fig. 5.   Network for computing "above" judgments.

the empirical data are consistent with the posited structures—whether or not the structure can provide a compact description of the data. We may conclude that they do only if the network is able to match the data closely. The spatial template data for "above" from Logan and Sadler (1996) was linearly scaled to the 0 to 1 range, and formed the training set for the network.[2] For each of the 48 positions of the trajector with respect to the landmark, the proximal and center-of-mass orientations were determined and given as input to the network, and the desired output was the empirically obtained appropriateness rating. The network was trained under back-propagation with a learning rate of 0.07 for 4000 epochs, at which point the summed squared error over all 48 patterns was 0.32. Figure 6A illustrates the spatial template generated by the model, while Fig. 6B shows the original empirical data. (In Fig. 6A the central point on the grid was assigned the value 0.0 by hand, as the network was not trained to respond at that position. All other positions reflect network output). The fit between the generated and actual data can also be seen in Fig. 7, which plots the model's quantitative "above" judgments against the corresponding values collected by Logan and Sadler. The fit is quite close: $r^2$ in this instance is 0.9466, and other runs of the same model yielded similar values. Once the model's parameters were set through training on the Logan and Sadler data, an experiment was conducted to see how well these parameters would fit data collected in similar fashion by Hayward and Tarr (1995). The two datasets resemble one another closely, so the fit between the model and the new data is quite good ($r^2 = 0.9221$). In a further experiment, an expanded version of the model in which the proximal and center-of-mass orientations were compared with all four cardinal directions (up, down, left and right) provided an even closer fit to the data ($r^2 = 0.9769$), again with good generalization to the Hayward and Tarr data ($r^2 = 0.9280$). Figure 8A shows this expanded model's generated spatial template for "above," whereas Fig. 8B shows the empirical data on which the model was trained. The two are nearly identical.

The networks' ability to fit the data seems to support the hypothesis that "above" judgments can be modeled as a linear combination of directional alignment features. But how strong a statement is this? What does it exclude? Perhaps these connectionist networks, like some others, are largely unconstrained in curve-fitting ability (Cybenko, 1989; Massaro, 1988). If this is so, the networks' success on this task is not particularly enlightening—it is primarily testament to the computational flexibility of the mechanisms, and tells us little about the psychological issue we are pursuing. This is not

[2] The data were originally scaled to enable modeling using another network, with nodes that have sigmoidal activation functions ranging from 0 to 1. The linear and sigmoidal networks yielded very similar results, so attention was focused on the simpler linear formulation.

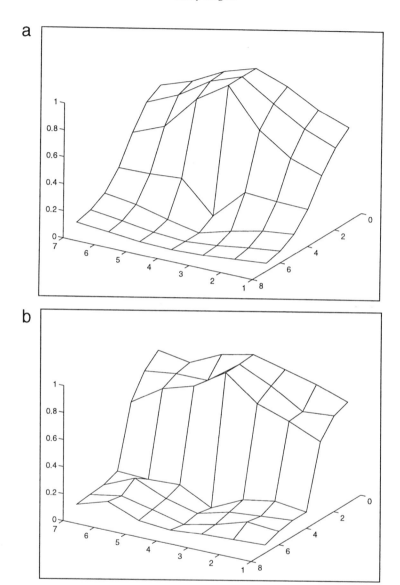

Fig. 6.   Spatial templates for "above": (A) generated by model. (B) empirically obtained, reported by Logan and Sadler (1996).

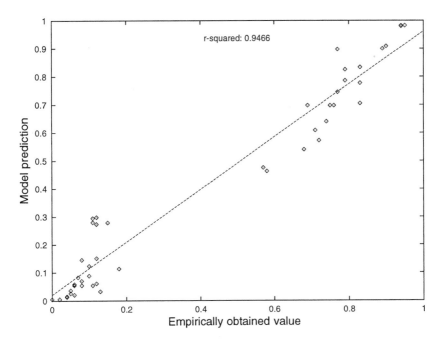

Fig. 7.   Fit of model's "above" judgments to Logan and Sadler's (1996) empirical data.

the case, however. A series of further experiments demonstrated that the networks are not capable of adapting themselves to arbitrary datasets; rather, they are constrained to match only certain sorts of data. The networks were trained on randomly generated data, rather than Logan and Sadler's empirical data, and the fits were quite poor: $r^2 = 0.1164$ for the original model, and $r^2 = 0.1818$ for the expanded model. These results reassure use that the earlier success of the networks in matching the empirically obtained "above" appropriateness data was not due to excessive flexibility on the networks' part, but rather reflects a consonance between the structures of the networks and the nature of the empirical data itself.

These results are of interest for two reasons. On the one hand, they expand on Logan and Sadler's (1996) spatial templates account by indicating how such templates might be generated, where they might come from—and this gives us a considerable reduction in descriptive size. The other point of interest concerns learning: if the child is in fact employing structures such as those in the networks in its learning of spatial terms, that would constrain the child's hypothesis space considerably. This then would be an example of a perceptual structural constraint on the set of hypotheses entertained by the child. While I have as yet no evidence that the process

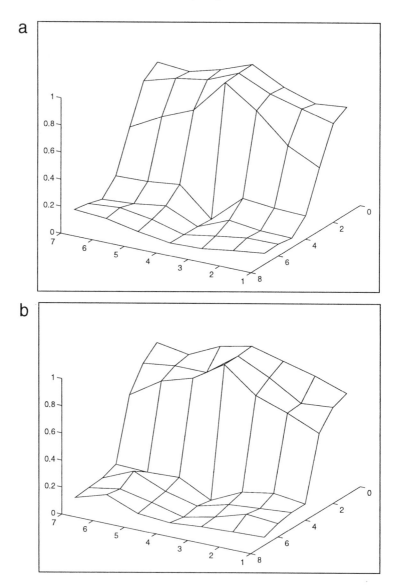

Fig. 8.   Spatial templates for "above": (A) generated by the expanded model. (B) empirically obtained, reported by Logan and Sadler (1996).

of acquisition is hemmed in by structures of exactly this sort, this section has at least demonstrated that the end product of human spatial term learning—namely, adult appropriateness judgments for spatial terms—is consistent with the model, and that the model is constrained enough that its structures could serve as helpful inductive biases for the child. Further research will be required to determine whether or not children actually explore the constrained hypothesis space implicit in the model, either prelinguistically, when learning to manipulate objects, or during the process of learning to speak about space.

## III. Negative Evidence

Children are rarely told how not to speak—they receive little explicit evidence steering them away from inappropriate utterances. This fact raises an interesting inductive question. If children learn language without being told that certain usages are infelicitous, how do they learn to avoid such usages? Clearly, they must generalize from what they have actually heard, or they would not be able to use the language productively. But equally clearly, this generalization must somehow be held in check, so that children eventually come to honor the categories of their native language. Negative evidence would serve quite well in this role, but children do not receive such evidence on a regular basis, and somehow learn language without it. The central puzzle then, given this lack of negative evidence, is how the child learns to generalize from the usages actually encountered without *overgeneralizing* to include inappropriate usages.

This "no-negative-evidence" problem is a central one in the acquisition of grammar (Bowerman, 1983; Pinker, 1984, 1989), as the absence of negative evidence concerning sentence structure is nearly absolute. In the case of vocabulary acquisition, such as the acquisition of spatial terms, the picture may be somewhat less stark (Markman, 1989) but positive evidence still seems to be overwhelmingly more common than negative evidence, and this again raises the question of how the child acquires the appropriate generalizations (Barrett, 1978). To illustrate, in the Brown (1973) corpus in the Childes database (MacWhinney & Snow, 1990), covering three children over 4 years, there are 2835 instances of a mother using the world "in," and only 46 instances of a mother using the phrase "not in," either alone or embedded in a larger sentence. This latter phrase is what one might expect to find in corrective sentences conveying negative evidence concerning the meaning of spatial terms, such as "No, it's behind the box, not in it." Similarly, there are 2484 recorded instances of a mother saying "on," but only 40 of a mother saying "not on." Another possible form that negative evidence might take is admonishments of the form "Don't . . . in . . . ," as in the sentence "Don't put it in the box," followed by an expression of either satisfaction or annoyance depending on the child's compliance. There are 55 instances of a mother using this form, and 71 instances of a mother using the analogous form for "on." While the mothers may be conveying negative evidence to the children through other means, these two constructs are quite natural ones for the purpose, and the numbers are rather low. Moreover, it is unclear how many of the instances detected were clearly interpretable by the child as negative evidence for the meanings of spatial terms. For example, the phrase "not on your leg—on the paper" (Brown, 1973) does not help to delineate the boundaries of acceptability for the English preposition "on."

However, the child comes to learn the correct generalizations despite this relative paucity of negative evidence. How does this happen? It is the role of this section to provide an initial answer to this question. I shall demonstrate computationally that even if one were to adopt the most conservative stance possible, and assume that the child has access to *no* explicit negative evidence whatsoever, the acquisition of accurate spatial term meanings would still be possible, through a simple adaptation of a learning heuristic proposed in the child language literature. Thus, the primary theoretical import of this section is that it computationally illustrates the viability of this heuristic, and helps explain the child's success in learning the correct generalizations, given the modest amount of negative evidence that is actually encountered. For if semantic acquisition can occur in the complete absence of negative evdience, as it does in the simulations, it can only be easier for the child, who receives in addition the occasional piece of explicit negative evidence. As we shall see, the simulations also suggest reinterpretations of some of the empirical data.

A.   MUTUAL EXCLUSIVITY

Markman (1989) has proposed that children take object names to be mutually exclusive. Thus, if they already know one name for an object, they should resist adopting another name for it. Similar ideas appear elsewhere in the child language literature (Clark, 1987; Pinker, 1989). This bias can serve as a source of *implicit negative evidence:* if a child hears an object referred to as a positive instance of a "dog," it is implicitly not a "cat," nor a "horse," nor a "pig," nor a positive instance of any of a number of other labels of which the child may be aware, but whose extension has not yet been completely determined. Clearly, mutual exclusivity is only useful if viewed as a learning heuristic, rather than as a hard-and-fast rule: a single object may in fact have several names ("Fido," "dog," "animal"), and the child will have to learn these. Nonetheless, as we shall see, mutual exclusivity is demonstrably capable of bringing about accurate learning in the absence of negative evidence.

While the exact nature of a mutual exclusivity assumption on the child's part is still a matter of some dispute (Merriman & Bowman, 1989; Woodward & Markman, 1991), there is empirical evidence that supports the existence of such an inductive bias. For example, when young children hear a novel label in the presence of two objects, one of which has a label that is already known to the child, and the other of which does not, they tend to associate the new label with the previously unnamed object (Golinkoff, Hirsh-Pasek, Lavallee, & Baduini, 1985; Hutchinson, 1986; Markman & Wachtel, 1988). This is what mutual exclusivity would predict, as a consequence of the child's unwillingness to entertain two names for a single object. Evidence can also be found using single objects: When 3 to 4-year-olds are presented with a new term in the presence of only one object, for which they already know a name, they tend to not take the new term as a second name for the object. Rather, they interpret it as a name for a part of the object, or for the substance of which the object is made (Markman & Wachtel, 1988). Children presented with unfamiliar objects, on the other hand, are more likely to assign the name to the object as a whole.

There is, however, a tension in the empirical literature on mutual exclusivity, concerning just when the bias becomes active, and how strong the effect is at different ages. Based on a review of existing work, and some subsequent work of their own, Merriman and Bowman (1989) reached the conclusion that the child does indeed use mutual exclusivity—but only after the age of $2\frac{1}{2}$. They failed to find support for the bias in children under this age. While Woodward and Markman (1991) suspected that methodological flaws may have led to this result, there is other evidence suggesting that mutual exclusivity is at least weaker in 2-year-olds than it is in 3- to 4-year-olds. Mervis et al. (1994) found that when 2-year-olds heard a novel word in the presence of an object for which they already knew a name, they interpreted the word as a second name for the object, rather than as a name for a part of the object or the substance of which it was made. This result is interesting because it constitutes a violation of mutual exclusivity, and because it contrasts with the results of Markman and Wachtel (1988), who observed the opposite preference in slightly older children on the same task. Finally, Liittschwager and Markman (1994) taught 2-year-olds novel labels for objects which they either could or could not already name, and found that the children learned new labels equally well in the two cases, contrary to the prediction of mutual exclusivity. But interestingly, the mutual exclusivity bias was not entirely absent: They also found that when 2-year-olds were given two new words to learn, rather than just one, the results were as mutual exclusivity would predcit—the children had trouble learning second labels for objects with known labels, but no trouble learning first labels for as-yet-unnamed objects. Liittschwager and Markman attributed the discrepancy between their two studies to the ease of learning just a single word—they suggested that 2-year-olds may override mutual exclusivity when their processing capacity is not excessively burdened. Because 16-month-olds can reasonably be assumed to have more restricted processing capabilities than 2-year-olds, Liittschwager and Markman reasoned that 16-month-olds might encounter difficulty with second labels (but not first labels) even when just a single novel label was being learned—and in fact they found just that. In sum, it appears to be the case (1) that mutual exclusivity is present as a learning bias from the age of 16 months onwards, (2) that it is weak at the age of 2 years, and (3) that it grows in strength in subsequent years.

This state of affairs presents a riddle: what is the utility of an inductive bias that is weakest in children 2 years of age, who are just beginning to develop their vocabularies? Isn't that precisely when it should be at its strongest, in order to help them acquire accurate meanings for words? And for that matter, why should the bias strengthen with age? Merriman and Bowman (1989) suggest that having a weak bias early on may be reasonable, as children may not need to rely on mutual exclusivity in order to learn words—other forces, such as conservative generalization and occasional parental correction, may suffice. They also argue that the bias may help older children integrate and systematize names. I shall be presenting a different account here. There is in fact a very good reason for the bias to be weak in the early stages of learning and to later grow in strength. As the simulations in this section demonstrate, the mutual exclusivity bias enables learning most effectively when it begins as a weak tendency and then later becomes stronger.

B.  The Application to Spatial Terms

I shall be adapting the concept of mutual exclusivity to the domain of spatial relations naming. This is an application that has been proposed in the literature (Merriman & Bowman, 1989) but not actively pursued. It is reassuring to note however that there is some evidence that such a bias may be at work in the acquisition of spatial terms: Johnston and Slobin (1979) found that in a study of children learning spatial locatives in English, Italian, Serbo-Croatian, and Turkish, terms were learned more quickly when there was little or no synonymy among terms, as one might expect if children were biased against learning more than one label for a given spatial relation. (In fact, Johnston and Slobin interpret this as support for a one-to-one meaning-to-morpheme mapping bias; this is similar to, but not quite the same as, the notion of mutual exclusivity. The difference lies in whether it is the referent or the meaning that is only allowed one label. Mutual exclusivity holds that it is the referent, while the one-to-one meaning-to-morphene mapping holds that it is the meaning. Johnston and Slobin's empirical observations are consistent with both constraints.)

If we assume that each spatial relation may have only one name, this means that when we are presented with a *positive* instance of one spatial term, we may take that spatial configuration as an *implicit negative* instance of all other spatial terms. For example, if we hear that a given spatial relationship is labeled "above," we may assume that that relationship is also a poor instance of "below," "left," "right," "in," and so on. Figure 9 shows an outline of the computational model we shall be using to examine this issue, and also illustrates how mutual exclusivity can be used to generate implicit negative instances.

The model has eight output nodes, corresponding to the eight English spatial terms "above," "below," "left," "right," "in," "outside," "on," and "off." On each training presentation, the model is exposed to an input scene that has both trajector and landmark labeled, and with a spatial term describing the scene. It is to learn to associate spatial configurations with words, such that once training is complete, presentation of a new scene will bring about activation of all output nodes that could appropriately

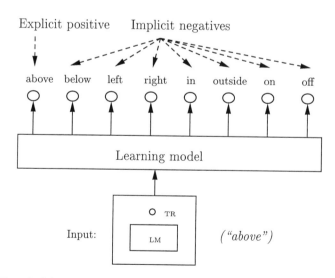

Fig. 9.   The principle of mutual exclusivity applied to spatial terms. Reprinted from Regier 1996 with permission.

describe the scene. For example, given the input scene shown in the figure, the nodes for "above" and "outside" should be activated.

How does mutual exclusivity enter the picture? The figure shows the model in the midst of a training presentation. At the bottom of the figure we see the spatial configuration and label with which the learning model is presented. Because the label is "above," the current spatial configuration is taken as a positive instance of "above" for training. And it is also taken as an implicit negative instance of all other spatial terms being learned, as indicated at the top of the figure. This method of training then can introduce implicit negative instances, which will help constrain generalization.

This generation of implicit negatives for an entire contrast set in parallel is not the customary conception of how mutual exclusivity operates. Instead, it is often viewed as helping to disambiguate referents in learning situations, as in the empirical studies cited above. But the same abstract principle is at work here: if a referent is labeled one way, it must not be labeled another way. Thus, the simulation captures the general principle of mutual exclusivity, if not the actual learning situation in which it is most often investigated in children. Critically for our purposes, the strength or weakness of this general bias can easily be investigated in this computational context, and the abstract notion of bias strength related back to the empirical literature.

If implicit negative instances are produced in this manner, however, one of the central problems with mutual exclusivity immediately becomes apparent. Once training is complete, a scene such as the one shown in the figure should elicit strong responses for both "above" and "outside," as the scene is a good example of both "above" and "outside." But during the training process that is meant to lead us to this state, the mutual exclusivity heuristic causes the model to treat this scene as a *negative* example of "outside," because it has been labeled "above" by the teacher and because spatial terms are assumed to be mutually exclusive.

The problem of course is that spatial terms are not actually mutually exclusive, so there is a mismatch between the mutual exclusivity heuristic and the linguistic reality. The heuristic is often but not always correct. A trajector cannot be both "above" and "in" a landmark, but a trajector can be both "above" and "outside" a landmark, as we have just seen. In essence, the mutual exclusivity assumption introduces *noise* into the training data: many of the implicit negatives that are generated are *false* implicit negatives—that is, they are implicit negative examples that in actuality should be positive examples. This is a general problem that will arise anytime mutual exclusivity is used in the learning of overlapping or nested categories.

One spatial term that is particularly plagued by the problem of false implicit negative evidence is the term "outside." Of the spatial terms listed above, all will supply false negative evidence for "outside," with two exceptions: "in" and "outside" itself. To see how serious the problem is, consider Fig. 10, which presents two training sets for the spatial term "outside": one idealized, and one arrived at through mutual exclusivity. In both cases, the tall rectangle is the landmark, and the circles and Xs are punctate trajectors located relative to the landmark. If a trajector is marked as a small circle, that indicates that a point at that location has been labeled as a positive instance of being "outside" the landmark. If a trajector is marked as an X, that denotes a negative instance. The positive instances are the same in both cases, and were supplied by a teacher. It is only the negative instances that differentiate the two training sets. In Fig. 10A, the negative instances were placed by a teacher just as the positive ones were, and they help to clearly delineate the region outside the landmark. But this sort of explicit negative evidence is precisely what we are assuming the child has limited access to—it is in this sense that the training set is idealized. In Fig. 10B, the negative instances were derived through the principle of mutual exclusivity from positive instances of the remaining spatial terms: "above," "below," "left," "right," "in," "on," and "off." This then is the sort of training data that can result from the use of mutual exclusivity—clearly, there are numerous false implicit negative instances. There are also several locations that have been labeled as both positive and negative instances of "outside."

Mutual exclusivity is a mixed blessing. It solves the problem of how to constrain meanings, but it does so at the considerable price of noisy training data. This is a problem that researchers in child language acquisition are

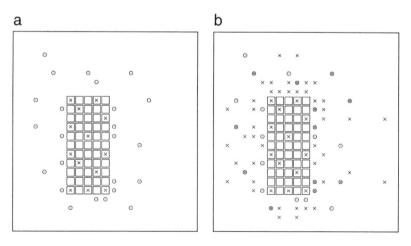

Fig. 10.    Idealized and realistic training sets for *outside*. Reprinted from Regier 1996 with permission.

quite cognizant of, and their response has been to characterize mutual exclusivity as a default assumption, a soft or probabilistic bias that can be violated should the circumstances call for it (Merriman & Bowman, 1989; Woodward & Markman, 1991). In the computational work presented below, I discuss a particularization of this general notion of mutual exclusivity as soft constraint, and demonstrate that it enables semantic acquisition in the absence of explicit negative evidence, despite the problem of false implicit negatives. I also show that learning is most effective when the constraint begins at low strength, and then eventually increases in power.

C.   A SOFT CONSTRAINT

The use of mutual exclusivity in the manner described above introduces an asymmetry in the training data. Implicit negative instances are of questionable reliability, as they are arrived at through the application of a fallible heuristic. Positive instances, on the other hand, can be assumed to be correct, as they come directly from the teacher. Thus, it seems intuitively reasonable to take negative evidence less seriously than positive evidence. That is the approach adopted here: negative evidence is deliberately weakened. When this is done, it can be shown that the false implicit negative instances do not seriously impede learning, and the remaining negative instances can still serve to constrain the generalizations made.

The connectionist model used in the simulations reported here is a simple extension of the networks we considered in the last section, with the added capability of detecting contact and inclusion. We need not consider its architecture in detail, however, as our primary interest is in the effect of the mutual exclusivity bias rather than in structural constraints. In fact, there are only two general aspects of the model's operation that are critical. The first is that it accepts input in the form of point trajectors located relative to landmarks, as seen above. And the second is that it is trained under back-propagation in the manner shown in Fig. 9—that is, using the mutual exclusivity heuristic to generate implicit negative instances from explicit positives. In back-propagation, learning occurs through incremental weight changes in the network, and weight changes occur as a function of the *error* detected at each output node; that is, the extent to which the activation of each output node departs from its desired value. For positive instances, the desired value is 1, and for negative instances, it is 0. The standard formula for the error at output node $i$ on input pattern $p$ is:

$$E_{i,p} = \frac{1}{2} (t_{i,p} - o_{i,p})^2. \tag{3}$$

Here, $t_{i,p}$ is the desired value for the output node, and $o_{i,p}$ is the activation value actually observed at that node. $E_{i,p}$ then is simply a measure of the discrepancy between the desired and observed values. In the case of positive instances, this is the equation that was used for error calculation. A slightly modified one was used for negative instances.

Back-propagation lends itself easily to the deliberate weakening of implicit negative evidence. Because weight changes are a function of the error, we can weaken the evidence from implicit negatives by simply attenuating the error caused by implicit negative evidence. We let $\beta$ be a "seriousness" parameter with value less than 1.0, indicating how the error signal from implicit negatives is to be weighted, and incorporate it into the error calculation:

$$E_{i,p}^- = \frac{1}{2}((t_{i,p} - 0_{i,p}) \times \beta)^2 \tag{4}$$

For implicit negative instances, error was calculated using this equation, meaning that the evidence from implicit negatives was deliberately weakened.

## D. Results

The model was trained on the the eight English spatial terms "above," "below," "left," "right," "in," "outside," "on," and "off." Training sets containing positive instances only were constructed for each of these terms: in each case, point trajectors were placed relative to horizontally and vertically extended landmarks. Implicit negative instances were obtained from these positive instances through mutual exclusivity.

The model was trained on all eight spatial terms in parallel, with a learning rate of 1.0, and a $\beta$ value of 0.03—meaning that implicit negative evidence was treated with 0.03 the "seriousness" of positive evidence.[3] A cross-validation set was constructed as well, containing positive and negative instances of the eight spatial terms. The model was trained on the instances in the training set until the error on the cross-validation set descended to an average of 0.0015 error per instance. Error was attenuated for negative instances in the training set only, and not in the cross-validation set. The close fit to the positives and negatives in the cross-validation set indicates that the model eventually came to neither substantially overgeneralize nor undergeneralize. Thus, the model was able to learn the proper generalizations for these spatial terms quite well, despite the false implicit negatives introduced by the use of mutual exclusivity. The theoretical significance of this simulation as a whole is that it illustrates how differential weighting

[3] $\beta$ values between 0.005 and 0.035 yielded acceptable results. See Regier (1996) for details.

of evidence sources can circumvent the problem of false implicit negatives introduced by mutual exclusivity—therefore, it demonstrates the efficacy of mutual exclusivity as an inductive bias, despite its most obvious flaw. This gives us a possible solution to the question of how children learn these terms given only modest amounts of explicit negative evidence.

The idea of giving implicit negative instances less weight than explicit positives is intuitively appealing, because of the less than complete reliability of the negative evidence. But is this deliberate weakening of evidence actually necessary? Figure 11 shows that it is indispensable. This figure presents the results of learning the spatial term "outside" under three different conditions. In all cases, the size of the black circles indicates the appropriateness, as judged by the model, of using the term "outside" to describe the relationship between a point at the circle's location and the landmark shown. Strong appropriateness is indicated by large black circles,

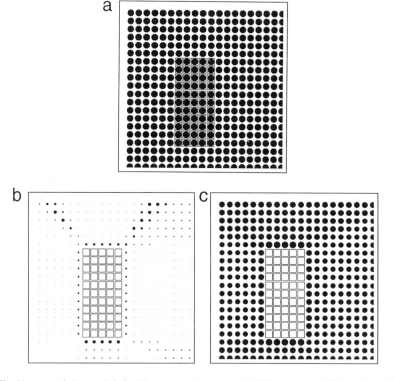

Fig. 11. *outside* learned. (A) without negatives, and with (B) strong and (C) weak implicit negatives. Reprinted from Regier 1996 with permission.

while inappropriateness is indicated by no circle at all. In Fig. 11A we see the results obtained when the model is trained without any negative evidence at all, either implicit or explicit: only positive evidence was used. With no force holding the generalization in check, the model overgeneralizes, accepting both the interior and the exterior of the landmark as regions "outside" it. In Fig. 11B we see the results obtained when the model is trained using mutual exclusivity, but with strong negative evidence—that is, with negative evidence given the same weight as positive evidence. In this case, the term is inaccurately learned. In general, when mutual exclusivity is used with negative evidence kept at full strength, the results are not always precisely as shown here, but they are of the same overall quality—quite poor. Finally, Fig. 11C shows the results obtained from the experiment just described, using mutual exclusivity with weakened implicit negatives. Clearly, the results are superior to those in either Fig. 11A or Fig. 11B, demonstrating that the weakening of implicit negative evidence is a critical aspect of the application of the mutual exclusivity bias.

This suggests why it might be beneficial to children to have a relatively weak mutual exclusivity bias in the early stages of word learning, as has been observed empirically: a weak bias enables fairly accurate learning, while a stronger bias does not, because of the problem of false implicit negatives. While children will sometimes be able to determine from context which implicit negatives are false and which are not (i.e., which should be disregarded and which should be taken seriously), they will almost certainly not be able to do this in all situations—meaning that some noise will be introduced into their training sets, as has happened here in the simulation. The deliberately weakened mutual exclusivity heuristic is an effective means of learning in this situation. Other computational work in language acquisition has identified advantages to beginning learning with limited resources (Elman, 1993; Goldowsky & Newport, 1993). In a similar spirit, this work identifies an advantage to beginning learning with a heuristic of limited strength.

Why then should the strength of the bias increase over time? Notice that the learning of "outside" in Figure 11C is not perfect—some of the circles outside the landmark are not of maximum size, as can be seen by comparing them with the circles in the overgeneralized region in Fig. 11A. This is the result of the false implicit negatives: their effect can be largely but not completely overcome by weakening the negative evidence. Once learning has progressed to this point, however, the learning can be completed by sharpening and strengthening the use of the mutual exclusivity bias. Up until now, the bias has been weak and diffuse: weak in the sense we have already discussed, and diffuse in the sense that all concepts provided equally weak negative evidence to all other concepts. This can change once the learner has an initial grasp of the concepts. The learner is now in a position to determine which concepts overlap with each other, and thus which should *not* provide negative evidence to each other. Once these extensional overlaps have been detected, they may be avoided when using mutual exclusivity, such that no implicit negative evidence is derived from concepts that have been found to overlap. This leaves the learner free to use a strong version of mutual exclusivity among the remaining—nonoverlapping— pairs of concepts. Specifically, once initial learning has taken place using weak negative evidence, the single uniform $\beta$ value may be replaced by separate $\beta$ values, one value for each concept pair. For example, $\beta_{outside,above}$ would control how seriously positive examples of "outside" should be taken as negative examples of "above," and there would be analogous values $\beta_{outside,in}, \beta_{on,above}$, and so on for other concept pairs. The strength of each of these interconcept "seriousness" parameters would be a function of the degree of overlap in extension of the concepts, in their initially learned form. Thus, $\beta_{outside,in}$ would be 1.0 (full strength) because there is essentially no extensional overlap in the initially learned versions of the concepts "outside" and "in." In contrast $\beta_{outside,above}$ would assume the value 0.0, reflecting the overlap between the two concepts, and the consequent unde- sirability of taking positive examples of "outside" as implicit negative exam- ples of "above." Thus, provided the bias is removed for those concept pairs that overlap, it may be allowed to strengthen for all other concept pairs. And the initial weak bias permits learning that is incomplete, but sufficient to determine extensional overlap. The significance of this account as a whole then is that it provides a rationale for the empirically observed tendency of children to employ a weak bias in early stages of learning, and to later shift to a stronger one (Merriman & Bowman, 1989).

E.  A CASE STUDY: DUTCH "UIT"

Bowerman (1996) has noted an intriguing difference between the general- ization patterns of children learning English and those of children learning Dutch. In English, a simple spatial distinction is made between removal from a surface ("off") and removal from containment ("out"), and young children learning English honor this distinction just as adult English speak- ers do. In Dutch, the same distinction is made, with cognate words: "af" for removal from a surface, and "uit" for removal from containment. But Dutch children do not honor this distinction. Unlike English-speaking chil- dren of the same age (2;0 to 2;5 years), they overextend "uit" to denote removal generally. Thus, taking a cassette out of its case, a top off a pen, and one's shoes off are all labeled "uit" by young Dutch children. For some reason, Dutch children overgeneralize "uit" while English-speaking children do not generalize "out," the corresponding word in English.

Why is this? As it happens, "out" and "uit" are nearly but not quite perfect translations of each other. While "uit" is used in Dutch to denote removal from containment, and "af" is used to denote removal from a surface, Bowerman points out that there is an exception to this general rule: the removal of enveloping clothing. English uses "off" to express the removal of shoes, pants, coats, and the like (e.g., "take your shoes *off*), but Dutch expresses this notion through "uit," the near-equivalent of "out." Thus in Dutch, to tell one's child to take his or her shoes off, one would say "take your shoes out." But apart from this particular usage, "uit" is used just as "out" is in English. In this light, the Dutch children's overgeneralization of "uit" makes more sense, for they are faced with a word that is used to express both the removal of clothing and removal from containment. Bowerman argues that in the attempt to find an abstraction that encompasses these two meanings, Dutch children arrive at the simple notion of removal itself, and assume that this must be the meaning of "uit."

This observation is interesting for two reasons. On the one hand, as Bowerman indicates, it suggests that children are actively generalizing, seeking abstractions to cover the usages they have heard. And this illustrates the need for negative evidence. For if children were not generalizing in this manner, but rather tended to use words only in the contexts in which they had originally heard them, negative evidence would not be required: The child's own semantic conservatism could act as the constraining force on category extension. One point of significance of this evidence from Dutch then is that it highlights the abstraction-finding game that children enter into, and by consequence also highlights the need for some means to hem in these abstractions—such as contrast with other words being learned.

On the other hand, the same evidence also poses a challenge to mutual exclusivity. Bowerman suggests that the unusual clothing-removal use of "uit" may be quite salient to the child, and that this may account for the child's failure to pick up on the general distinction between removal from surfaces and removal from containers. It seems reasonable to assume that the removal of clothing plays an important role in the life of a 2-year-old. But the removal of *nonclothing* from surfaces is regularly expressed by "af" in adult Dutch, and in fact makes its way into the Dutch of 2-year-olds as well. Consider Hein, a Dutch child of 2;4.8 whose early speech is recorded in the Dutch section of the Childes database (Elbers, 1985). Hein frequently uses "af" to express removal [e.g., "doe die af"; literally "do those off," meaning "remove those" (Hans Heineken, personal communication; Renier, 1995)]—yet Hein is at the same age as Bowerman's subjects who overgeneralized "uit" to denote generic removal. So the question is: if the child hears "af" paired with certain sorts of removal, and in fact even uses "af" him- or herself, shouldn't that keep the child from overgener-

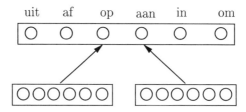

Initial configuration   Final configuration

Fig. 12.   Network for learning a set of Dutch locatives, using mutual exclusivity.

alizing "uit" to express removal generally? Certainly this is what mutual exclusivity would lead one to expect, at least at first blush. And yet the children do overgeneralize, despite input that should discourage them from doing so.

I shall demonstrate computationally that the observed overgeneralization pattern is consistent with the use of mutual exclusivity, provided it is applied in the weak and diffuse manner described in this chapter—and as we have seen, 2-year-olds do seem to have a weaker bias than older children. The child's overgeneralization of "uit" to types of removal ordinarily expressed by "af" in Dutch need not be interpreted as a failure to notice caretakers using "af" in these senses. Instead, it may be interpreted in the context of the *fallibility* of mutual exclusivity, and the accompanying idea that children may not have complete faith in the implicit negative evidence arrived at through the application of this inductive bias. In short, they may be downplaying the exclusivity of the terms they are learning, rather than failing to detect some of their linguistic input.

Figure 12 presents a simple network that was constructed in order to test the soundness of this idea. The output nodes of the network take a weighted sum of their inputs, and place this sum through the customary sigmoidal squashing function.[4] The network was trained on the six Dutch spatial prepositions "uit" (out), "af" (off), "op" (firmly on), "aan" (suspended from), "in" (in), and "om" (around). Because some of the prepositions describe events rather than static configurations, the input consisted of two six-unit feature vectors—one for the spatial configuration obtaining at the beginning of the event and one for end-event. In the case of a nonevent, such as simply being in, expressed by "in," the initial and final

[4] The use of this activation function means that concepts are implicitly assumed to be linearly separable. Linear separability is not a universal constraint on human concept learning (Medin & Schwanenflugel, 1981), although it does appear to hold in some cases (Waldmann, Holyoak, & Fratianne, 1995). In these simulations, no theoretical importance is attached to linear separation per se.

configuration vectors were identical. The six units in each feature vector stood for: (a) TR in contact with LM, (b) TR on top of LM, (c) TR suspended from LM, (d) TR in LM, (e) TR surrounds LM, (f) TR is clothing. These features were chosen because they allowed expression of the basic uses of the prepositions being learned. For example, "uit" in the clothing-removal sense was represented by the two six-bit vectors 100011 and 000001: contact, surround, and clothing are true at the beginning of the event, while only clothing is true at the end of the event. Although this representation is extremely semantically impoverished, it does permit investigation of the central issue: whether mutual exclusivity with deliberately weakened negative evidence will give rise to the generalization patterns that have been observed in young Dutch children.

The network was trained under the delta rule (Hertz, Krogh, & Palmer, 1991). The training set contained one pattern for each of the semantic contents expressible given the features presented above, and an additional pattern repeating the removal of clothing from a state of envelopment, in line with Bowerman's suggestion that this is a frequently labeled action in the child's experience. Each such input pattern had a single designated desired output label. In a reflection of adult Dutch usage, the training set labeled two sorts of removal as "uit": removal from containment and removal of clothing from a state of envelopment. The removal of nonclothing from envelopment was labeled "af," again as in adult Dutch. The question of interest was whether the network would overgeneralize in the manner exhibited by children: using "uit" to express not just the two adult senses on which it was trained, but also the removal of *non*clothing from envelopment.

Negative instances were obtained through the mutual exclusivity heuristic from the positive instances. The network was trained for 10,000 epochs, with a learning rate of 3.0, under three conditions: with no negative evidence, with deliberately weakened implicit negative evidence ($\beta = 0.03$), and with implicit negative evidence taken at full strength ($\beta = 1.0$). Figure 13 shows the acceptability, as judged by the network over time, of using the Dutch preposition "uit" to describe the removal of nonclothing from a state of surrounding or enveloping. This is shown for each of the three training conditions. In the case of no negative evidence (the solid line in the figure), the model overgeneralizes immediately, and continues to do so—this is what one would expect given that there is no force keeping the generalization in check. But in the case of weak implicit negative evidence derived through mutual exclustivity (the line of dashes and dots), the network overgeneralizes at first, and then abandons the broader meaning it had originally attached to "uit," such that the "uit" response given this (inappropriate) semantic input declines. This curve as a whole then corre-

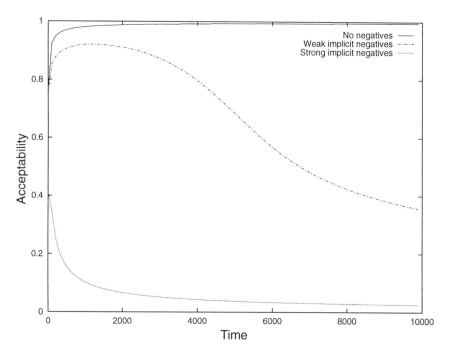

Fig. 13.   Acceptability of using Dutch "uit" to express removal of nonclothing, as judged by the model: no negative evidence, weak implicit negatives, and strong implicit negatives.

sponds to the pattern observed in Dutch children. Why does the curve appear as it does? The removal of nonclothing from envelopment is appropriately expressed by "af," and is thus a negative rather than a positive example of "uit." But there is a meaning which is very similar to this one, and which is a positive example of "uit": the removal of *clothing* from envelopment. The representations of these two spatial meanings were identical in 10 of 12 bits, as they differ only on the clothing/nonclothing feature. This similarity means that on these 10 dimensions, a weight adjustment that tends to make the removal of clothing a better example of "uit" will also make the removal of nonclothing a better example of "uit." Meanwhile, the nonclothing-removal of "af" is also taken as an implicit negative example of "uit," and this pulls in the other direction—but since implicit negative evidence is deliberately weakened, it counteracts the positive force only rather ineffectively at first. Eventually, however, the network must learn that this meaning is not appropriately expressed by "uit," because it is capable of discriminating between clothing and nonclothing, and because the negative evidence, however weak, will slowly push it to make that distinction. A comparison with the case of strong implicit negatives (dotted line) is helpful. In this case training was done with implicit negative evidence given equal strength with positive evidence. No overgeneralization pattern appears here, as the network is quickly pushed by the strong negative evidence to make whatever distinctions are implicit in the training data, including the clothing/nonclothing distinction.

What happens in the case of English? A similar network was constructed, with output nodes corresponding to the five prepositions "out," "off," "on," "in," and "around." The training set used was identical to the Dutch one except for the output labels, which were set to match English usage. Figure 14 shows the acceptability over time of using "out" to describe the removal of nonclothing from a state of surrounding or envelopment, in the same three training conditions. The curves corresponding to no negatives and strong implicit negatives are much as they were for the Dutch training set. However, there is no overgeneralization in the case of weakened mutual exclusivity, despite the fact that negative evidence is weakened here just as it was in the Dutch case. The difference between the two is that in the

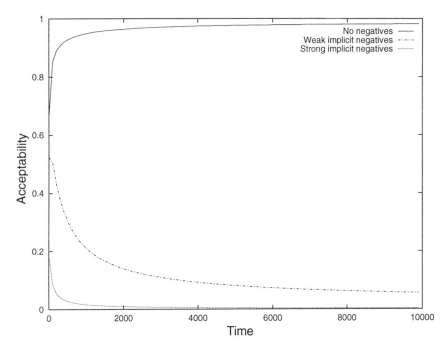

Fig. 14.    Acceptability of using English "out" to express removal of nonclothing, as judged by the model: no negative evidence, weak implicit negatives, and strong implicit negatives.

English training set, there is no semantic content labeled "out" that is very similar to the representation of removal of nonclothing from envelopment. Thus, there is no force pulling the network to overgeneralize. The significant point here is that the model shows the empirically observed tendency to overgeneralize for Dutch "uit" but not for English "out"—but it only shows this tendency in the case of attenuated implicit negative evidence.

These simulations suggest that the overgeneralization patterns observed in Dutch children may be attributable to their weakening of implicit negative evidence, arrived at through mutual exclusivity. This would explain their overgeneralization of "uit" to encompass all forms of removal in the face of input indicating that certain sorts of removal are more appropriately expressed by "af." Earlier simulations indicated the importance of weighting positive and negative evidence differently in the early stages of learning, and this set of experiments examines the ramifications of such a disparity. One result of this approach to induction is overgeneralization of the Dutch spatial term "uit," just as is found empirically—and a lack of overgeneralization of the English term "out," again in accord with empirical observation.

## IV. Motion and Result Emphasis

Consider the action of placing a ball in a toy box. I would like to propose that not all aspects of this event are equally perceptually salient. In particular, I propose that for brief perfective actions such as this one, the *result* of the action is more salient to the child than is the starting configuration from which it proceeded. Thus, in this example, the ball's resultant state of containment in the box would be more vivid in the child's consciousness than would the details of just how the ball was spatially configured relative to other objects prior to the action. As we shall see, this posited asymmetry in salience has interesting implications for the acquisition of spatial terms such as "in," and for semantic systematicity within individual languages.

An intuitive argument for such an asymmetry can be easily imagined: the child has more of a chance to absorb the result of the event than its starting configuration. By the time the child's attention has been captured by the motion, the starting configuration is no longer perceptually available—only the motion itself is, followed by the resultant end-state.

This idea, and the developmental and linguistic predictions that flow from it, were first suggested by a connectionist model of semantic acquisition that incorporated the constraints we have considered so far in this chapter, along with some others (Regier, 1996). Ultimately, the goal was to construct a model with substantive constraints on its operation which was nonetheless capable of adapting itself to the spatial system of any natural language.

As we have seen, the spatial semantic systems of different languages are sometimes quite different; thus the model's success in learning spatial terms from a number of different languages indicates that the model's constraints are consistent with the spatial structuring of each of these languages. This suggests that the model's constraints may be part of a universal human spatial semantic endowment—they may structure the way in which the language-learning child comes to adapt his or her spatial semantic system to reflect that of the language being learned.

In this section, I briefly describe this model in overview, focusing in particular on the privileged status the model assigns to event endpoints, and what considerations gave rise to that feature of the model. I then present the developmental and language-level predictions suggested by this feature of the model, and discuss supporting empirical data. Finally, I close with a brief demonstration of the model's ability to learn spatial terms from languages with markedly different spatial semantic systems.

## A. The Model

The model accepts as input movies of simple two-dimensional objects moving relative to another, and learns to categorize these movies according to the spatial system of a particular natural language. For example, Fig. 15 presents such a movie, a positive instance of the Russian preposition "iz-pod," which translates to "out from underneath." Here, the rectangle is the landmark, and the circle is the trajector. The dashed lines connect successive positions of the trajector, and the frames of the movie (five, in this case, although not limited in principle) are shown superimposed one on top of another. The final frame of the movie is marked by a small circle inside the trajector. The model takes a set of such movies, each labeled as

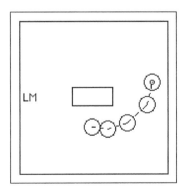

Fig. 15. A movie: Russian "iz-pod." Reprinted from Regier 1996 with permission.

a positive instance of a spatial term from a given language, and learns to associate the movies with those spatial terms that appropriately describe them.

Figure 16 presents an overview of the model. My purpose here is to highlight how the model builds on the constraints we have already seen in categorizing motion events, and the role that endpoint emphasis plays in the model.

Input frames are viewed one at a time. As each frame is viewed, the model filters the image through an adaptive perceptual core. This core is a set of structures that learns to extract static features from the current frame, producing a semantic representation of the current frame in the

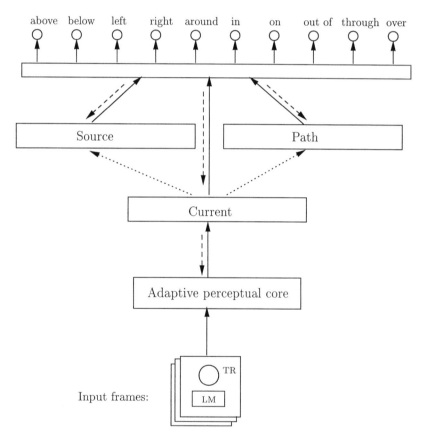

Fig. 16.    The model's architecture. Error is back-propagated along the dashed lines. Dotted lines denote node-to-node copy operations.

buffer marked "Current." For example, the adaptive orientational alignment network we saw in the first section of this chapter is a part of this core. The core as a whole is a collection of perceptual structures containing free parameters that may be adjusted by back-propagation. Thus, the critical points for our purposes are that at each time step, the Current buffer contains a representation of the current input frame, and that this representation is learned, as back-propagation adjusts the parameters of the perceptual core. For different languages, different parameter settings will be learned in the perceptual core. For example, some languages are sensitive to contact between trajector and landmark (e.g., English), whereas others appear not to be (e.g., Mixtec)—therefore, when trained on English, the core would come to pick up on contact, whereas when trained on Mixtec, it would not. The representation in the Current buffer then is a condensation of everything in the current input scene that the network has come to consider *semantically significant* in the langauge being learned. This notion of learning to pick up on relevant dimensions also appears in Smith, Gasser, and Sandhofer's (this volume) account of the acquisition of dimensional adjectives such as "big" or "red."

What happens in the case of motion? How is spatial information integrated over time? A number of researchers have noted that the linguistic categorization of motion events seems to involve a three-way decomposition of the event, into the starting point or *source* of the motion, the endpoint or *destination,* and the *path* from the source to the destination ( Jackendoff, 1983, 1990; Lakoff, 1987; Miller & Johnson-Laird, 1976). I have adopted this idea here. At the first step of the movie, the contents of the Current buffer are copied node-for-node to the buffer labeled "Source," and they remain there for the remainder of the event. Thus, there is a memory of the beginning of the event. The path representation, in the buffer labeled "Path," consists of the minimum, maximum, and average values attained by each of the nodes in the Current buffer. And the representation of the final time step, the destination, is in the Current buffer itself, at the last time step of the movie. Connections lead from the Current, Source, and Path buffers to the higher portions of the network, and these links are all adjustable by back-propagation, such that the network can learn terms that involve all or any of these. Other methods of integrating information over time, including adaptations of simple recurrent networks (Elman, 1990; Maskara & Noetzel, 1992), did not meet with the same success as this approach (Regier, 1996).

The model is only trained on the *final time step* of the movie, and it is from this that the model's endpoint emphasis ultimately derives. Why train only at the end? The linguistic training data indicate how to categorize the event as a whole, so the model must see the entire event before offering up a final categorization. For example, positive examples of "into" and "through" may look identical at the beginning of the event, but they fall in distinct categories because of what happens later in the event. Because of this need to base categorizations on the movie in its entirety, it is at the last time step that the model's outputs are compared with desired outputs, and it is at the last time step that error is computed and back-propagated. It is important to stress that this endpoint training falls naturally out of the nature of the data, because it is the source of an interesting constraint on the model's learning abilities.

When the model is trained, the connections leading up out of the Source and Path buffers can be adjusted, as can the connections leading up out of the Current buffer. And via back-propagation through the Current buffer back into the perceptual core, the perceptual discriminations made at each time step can be changed. But critically, error can travel back to the perceptual core only via the link from the topmost hidden layer down to the Current buffer—there is no back-propagation along the dotted copy links leading from the Current buffer to the Source and Path buffers. This is a nonarbitrary feature of the model. For when training occurs on the final time step, the data in the Source and Path buffers will have stemmed from Current buffer representations that have already come and gone—thus, there is no dependence of the values in the Source and Path buffers on those *presently* in the Current buffer. And because back-propagation adjusts weights between variables that depend on one another, a lack of immediate dependence makes back-propagation along these copy links meaningless— thus, no back-propagation occurs here. But the values in the topmost hidden layer at this point in time do depend on those in the Current buffer, and by extension on those in the adaptive core—so error may be back-propagated along these links. This leads to an interesting constraint on the model's operation: the perceptual core will learn to make its spatial distinctions based only on the final frame of the movie. This occurs because no error is back-propagated from the Source and Path buffers, and because training occurs on the final time step, when both the Current buffer and the perceptual core hold representations of the final frame. In short, the model will only learn to detect those static spatial features that appear at end-event. But importantly, once the perceptual core has learned to detect these features, the model as a whole may learn to correctly categorize events that involve such features at the beginning of the event or in mid-event, as the representations in the Source and Path buffers will come to contain these features.

To illustrate: the model would not be able to learn "out of" in isolation, because the critical feature of containment is not present in the final frame, but rather at the beginning. However, when "out of" is learned together with "in," this changes: the fact that the model is learning "in," that is, motion into containment, forces it to pick up on the feature of containment—and that feature can be learned, because it is present at end-event for "in." Once this happens, containment can also be used in "out of" categorizations, to distinguish "out of" from "off," for example.

More generally, the model suggests that developmentally, the acquisition of a word for motion *into* a particular spatial configuration will precede and assist the learning of a word for motion *out of* that configuration—and not vice versa. There is also a language-level prediction that is made by the same line of argumentation: languages that have spatial terms for motion out of a given configuration should tend to also have words for motion into that configuration, or static location in it. But languages that have words for motion into a given configuration need not have words expressing motion out of that configuration. This asymmetry is suggested because the acquisition of a word denoting motion out of a configuration is dependent, in the model, on the acquisition of a word denoting motion into it, or static location in it—but there is no dependency in the other direction.

To illustrate, consider the English spatial expression *out*, shown in the upper left of Fig. 17. We see here a small square trajector moving out of

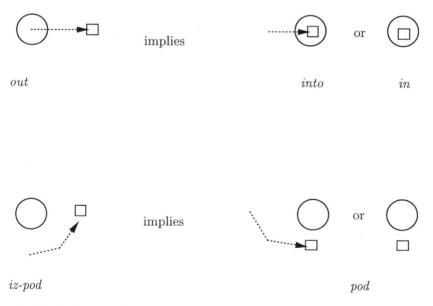

Fig. 17. Endpoint prediction. Any language that has a spatial term denoting motion *out of* some configuration will also have a spatial term denoting either motion *into* that configuration or static location in it.

a circular landmark object—moving out of a state of containment. The fact that English has this term leads us to predict that English will also have a term for motion into containment ("into") or for containment itself ("in"). The lower example is from Russian, which has a single spatial term, "iz-pod," that denotes motion of a trajector out from underneath a landmark. The fact that Russian has such a term leads us to expect, by this reasoning, that Russian will also have a spatial term denoting either motion into the region underneath the landmark, or static location under the landmark. As it happens, the Russian word "pod" can be used in either of these two senses.

This linguistic prediction is supported by inspection of the spatial semantic systems of English, German, Russian, and Arabic. In these languages, words for motion out of spatial configurations are accompanied by words for motion into those configurations. And Korean, which has words denoting motion out of tight fit and out of loose fit, also has words denoting motion into those configurations. There does seem to be a genuine asymmetry, rather than simple pairing of words: English, for example, has words for "behind" and "under" but no single words for "out from behind" or "out from underneath." There may be some exceptions to the rule however. The verbal suffix "-hiy -ik ·" in the California Indian language Atsugewi denotes "out of a snug enclosure, a socket; detached from moorings"—it can be used for example to express the action of poking someone's eye out (Talmy, 1972). Talmy claims there is no parallel form in the language expressing motion into snug enclosure or firm attachment (Len Talmy, personal communication). If so, it is true that this constitutes a counterexample to the prediction. Further empirical study of the spatial systems of the world's languages is required to determine how prevalent the predicted pattern is.

There is evidence compatible with the developmental prediction as well: children learning English, Dutch, Korean, and Tzotzil Mayan all tend to overgeneralize words for *separation* more widely than words for *joining* (Bowerman, de León, & Choi, 1995; Bowerman, 1996). This is just what one would predict given the posited asymmetry. If the child has learned the correct semantics for "onto" and "into" (words of joining), that indicates that the distinction between surface support and containment is already semantically significant for the child. But if, in line with the model, the child has not yet come to use this distinction in forms denoting separation, such as "off," one would expect overgeneralization on these forms—as is found. The overgeneralization of the separation terms then, on this interpretation, is a reflection of the child's not yet realizing that those semantic distinctions that have already been mastered at end-event may also be relevant at event beginnings.

The model presented here has been trained successfully on spatial terms from English, German, Japanese, Russian, and Mixtec (Regier, 1996). I briefly present two examples that illustrate the model's ability to learn disparate spatial semantic systems—semantic systems that are nonetheless consistent with the constraints embodied in the model's architecture and training regimen. Figure 18 presents the model's acceptability judgments, after training, on a test set for the Russian spatial term "iz-pod" ("out from underneath"). Here the small number at the bottom of each movie indicates the appropriateness, as judged by the trained model, of using "iz-pod" to describe the scene shown. Clearly, the generalization to the test set is quite good. The second example is from Mixtec. Mixtec is insensitive to the presence or absence of contact between the trajector and the land-mark, but is sensitive to the horizontal or vertical *elongation* of the landmark object (Claudia Brugman, personal communication). Thus, a bird either hovering above or perched on top of a tree could be said to be located at the tree's "head" (šini), by analogy with the head of an erect biped, while a bird hovering above or perched on a log would be said to be at the log's "animal-back" (siki), by analogy with the dorsum of a quadruped. In general, then, Mixtec, "šini" and "siki" cross-cut English "on" and "above": one language is sensitive to contact, and the other to the orientation of elongation of the landmark object. While it may at first seem unusual for a language to obligatorily mark the orientation of elongation of an object, in fact we have the same phenomenon in English, in a different part of our spatial system. The distinction between "along" and "across" in English is precisely one of orientation of elongation of the landmark object: com-pare, for example, "He walked along the corridor" with "He walked across the corridor." Because of the importance of this spatial feature, it is included as a reference orientation in the network. Figure 19 shows the model's acceptability judgments for "siki," after having been trained on both "siki" and "šini." The "siki" judgments are shown on a set of positive examples of English "above" and "on," and this helps both to highlight the differences between the two spatial systems and to demonstrate that the model is capable of adapting itself to the Mixtec system. All movies here are a single frame in length; that is, they are static scenes. The scenes in Fig. 19A are positive examples of English "above," but with landmarks that vary in their orientations of elongation. As can be seen, the model has learned to respond strongly only to those cases in which the trajector is above a horizontally extended landmark. The scenes in Fig. 19B are positive examples of English "on," and the difference between the two languages is in evidence here as well. In Mixtec classification, the fact that the trajector is in contact with the landmark is of no relevance; thus, many of the positive "on" instances yield strong responses for "siki." But again, the orientation of elongation

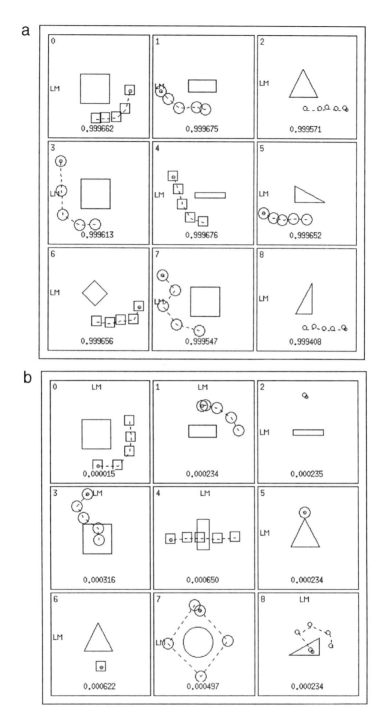

Fig. 18. Russian "iz-pod": positive and negative test sets. Reprinted from Regier 1996 with permission.

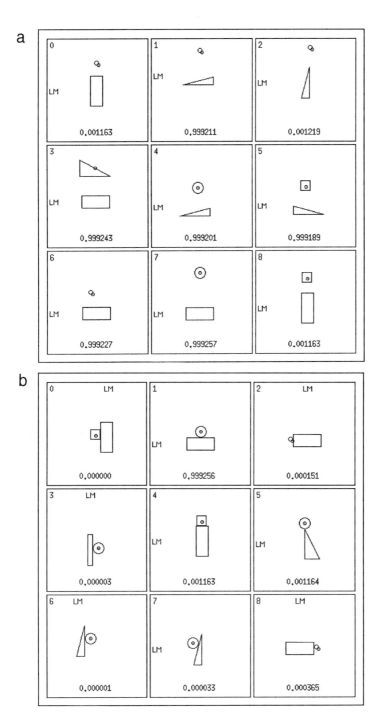

Fig. 19. Mixtec "siki" tested on positive examples of English "above" and "on." Reprinted from Regier 1996 with permission.

is critical: only those scenes that have horizontally extended landmarks are considered good examples of "siki."

This model, and the predictions to which it gives rise, highlight an interesting role that computational modeling may play relative to empirical inquiry. The model design process here gave rise to an unexpected hypothesis—it served, in essence, as a generator of ideas. While a different model may have been possible, the design considerations outlined above led naturally to a model that suggested the idea of endpoint emphasis. The testing of this hypothesis however must ultimately be a matter for empirical rather than computational inquiry.

Ultimately, the significance of this work is that it derives both developmental and language-level predictions from constraints that arose in the construction of a computational model of spatial term acquisition. While there is already some support for these predictions, their adequacy is a matter to be definitively resolved by further empirical inquiry. However, because the model makes predictions concerning both *how* spatial terms are acquired, and *what sorts* of spatial terms are acquired, future empirical investigation can proceed at both the psychological and linguistic levels.

## V.  Conclusions

This chapter has explored three possible constraints on the learning of spatial terms. It has built on earlier computational work (Regier, 1995, 1996), by demonstrating that the constraints proposed there can account for empirically obtained data concerning the perception of spatial relations, and the learning of spatial terms from English, Dutch, Russian, and Mixtec.

This chapter has shown that acceptability judgments for directional spatial terms such as "above" may be well modeled as a simple linear combination of Gaussian orientational alignment features. The simulations in the first section of the chapter show that this formulation provides a close fit to empirically collected "above" acceptability judgments, but does not fit other, artificially created, datasets. This suggests that the model's original success was not due to any excessive flexibility of the mechanism, but rather to the appropriateness of the structures proposed.

This chapter has also shown that the mutual exclusivity constraint, when adopted as an initially weak bias, can effectuate the learning of spatial terms. The weakness of the constraint can also account for the fact that overgeneralization is observed in Dutch children's usage of their spatial term "uit," but not in English-speaking children's usage of the corresponding English word, "out." Perhaps most significantly, the chapter provides a rationale for the empirically observed tendency for mutual exclusivity to be weak in 2-year-olds, and then to grow in strength with age. The simulations indicate that a weak bias is more effective in the early stages of learning, as it helps to circumvent the problem of false implicit negatives introduced by mutual exclusivity. Once the child has to a large extent determined which concepts overlap, however, the false negatives may be expunged, and the heuristic strengthened.

Finally, the work presented in this chapter has suggested that the child's categorizations made at end-event may come to inform those made at start-event. This dependency may account for semantic systematicity in terms for motion-into and motion-out in the world's languages. While the eventual fate of this idea remains to be determined by further empirical inquiry, there is some initial empirical support for it.

These three constraints are all embodied in a single computational model. Their investigation using that model, however, underlines different sorts of contributions that modeling may offer. In this chapter we have seen computational modeling operating both in the context of discovery (that is, in the generation of hypotheses to be tested), and in the context of justification (that is, in the testing and substantiation of already-suggested hypotheses). For example, the model's relation to the notion of endpoint emphasis lies in the context of discovery. The modeling process simply suggested the idea of endpoint emphasis, and the justification or refutation of the hypothesis must be decided empirically. In contrast, the demonstration that weakened mutual exclusivity can effectuate learning without negative evidence, despite the problem of false implicit negatives, occurred in the context of justification. In this case, the modeling served to demonstrate the effectiveness of a hypothesis that had already been proposed.

All in all, this constrained approach to the learning of spatial terms occupies a position intermediate between two extremes. At one extreme, the hypothesis space is so tightly constrained as to render the learning task trivial, while at the other the space is virtually unconstrained, and the task is consequently much more difficult. Let us begin at the tight-and-easy end of this continuum. Some have noted that prelinguistic experience with object manipulation and exploration of the environment will already have given the child an array of spatial concepts such as containment (Sitskoorn & Smitsman, 1995), support (Needham & Baillargeon, 1993), and the like. The acquisition of words for spatial relations should then be fairly straightforward, as the child now simply needs to learn the language's labels for these pre-existing notions—in English, this would be "in" for containment, and "on" for support. Mandler (1992, 1996; see also Clark, 1973) argues along these lines, and predicts delayed acquisition for spatial terms that do not match these pre-linguistically acquired concepts. On this view then, the child's hypothesis space is tightly constrained by the large-scale conceptual partitions that pre-linguistic spatial experience has induced.

Bowerman (1996) presents evidence that is troublesome for this position, nudging us away from the tight-and-easy stance. In particular, she notes that although Korean and English have cross-cutting spatial categories, Korean-learning and English-learning children acquire their early spatial terms in ways that reflect the native language, rather than any underlying prelinguistic concepts—and do so at the same early age. Thus, rather than simply attach labels to large pre-individuated spatial concepts such as containment or support, children seem to actually *build* their spatial categories in response to linguistic input. This evidence suggests that the child's hypothesis space is not constrained by the large conceptual partitions that Mandler proposes. And in an argument against another possible constraint on semantic acquisition, Bowerman notes that open-class forms such as verbs are less semantically constrained than closed-class forms such as prepositions: but Korean children learn their spatial verbs as accurately and quickly as English-speaking children learn their spatial prepositions. In these two examples, it is true that there is no evidence that the putative constrainedness of the space affects acquisition. But critically for our purposes, these are arguments only against the specific constraints considered, not against the more general idea of a constrained search space—which is to say that they do not force a jump to the other end of our spectrum. Children almost certainly do operate in a space that is constrained in some respects, as Bowerman herself notes while arguing against these specific constraints. There may be other constraints, stemming from other sources.

I have argued in this chapter for a set of such other constraints. The constraints investigated here stem neither from preverbal label-ready spatial concepts of containment and support nor from the open or closed class nature of the word being learned—a feature of the word that the child may not have privileged access to in any event. They stem rather from the child's general perceptual tendencies, and in the case of mutual exclusivity, from a word-learning heuristic with considerable empirical backing. In investigating the learning of spatial terms, then, the critical issue may not be whether or not the hypothesis space is constrained, but rather how it is constrained, how strong the constraints are, and how they vary in strength over time. Clearly, further empirical inquiry will help to answer these questions. I hope that this chapter has exemplified at least in some measure the role that computational modeling may play in the interpretation of such empirical data, as a part of this larger enterprise.

## REFERENCES

Barrett M. D. (1978). Lexical development and overextension in child language. *Journal of Child Language, 5,* 205–219.

Barsalou, L. W., & Prinz, J. J., (1997). Mundane creativity in perceptual symbol systems. In T. B. Ward, S. M. Smith, & J. Vaid (Eds). *Creative thought: An investigation of conceptual structures and processes* (pp. 267–307) Washington, DC: American Psychological Association.

Bates, E., Bretherton, I., & Snyder, L. (1988). *From first words to grammar: Individual differences and dissociable mechanisms.* New York: Cambridge University Press.

Bomba, P. C. (1984). The development of orientation categories between 2 and 4 months of age. *Journal of Experimental Child Psychology, 37*(3), 609–636.

Bowerman, M. (1983). How do children avoid constructing an overly general grammar in the absence of feedback about what is not a sentence? Papers and Reports on Child Language Development, 22, Stanford University.

Bowerman, M. (1996). Learning how to structure space for language: A crosslinguistic perspective. In P. Bloom, M. Peterson, M. Garrett, & L. Nadel (Eds), *Language and Space.* Cambridge, MA: MIT Press.

Bowerman, M., de León, L., & Choi, S. (1995). Verbs, particles, and spatial semantics: Learning to talk about spatial actions in typologically different languages. Paper presented at the 1995 Annual Child Language Research Forum, Stanford.

Brown, R. (1973). *A First Language: The Early Stages,* Cambridge, MA: Harvard University Press.

Brugman, C. (1983). The use of body-part terms as locatives in Chalcatongo Mixtec. In Report No. 4 of the Survey of California and other Indian Languages, 235–290. University of California, Berkeley.

Choi, S., & Bowerman, M. (1992). Learning to express motion events in English and Korean: The influence of language-specific lexicalization patterns. In B. Levin, & S. Pinker (Eds.), *Lexical and conceptual semantics.* Cambridge, MA: Blackwell.

Clark, E. (1987). The principle of contrast: A constraint on language acquisition. In MacWhinney (Ed.), *Mechanisms of language acquisition.* Hillsdale, NJ: Erlbaum.

Clark, H. (1973). Space, time, semantics, and the child. In T. Moore (Ed.), *Cognitive development and the acquisition of language,* (pp. 27–63). New York: Academic Press.

Cybenko, G. (1989). Approximations by superpositions of a sigmoidal function. *Mathematics of Control, Signals, and Systems,* 2:303–314. Also available as report number 856, Center for Supercomputing Research and Development. University of Illinois at Urbana-Champaign, 1989.

Elbers, L. (1985). A tip-of-the-tongue experience at age two? *Journal of Child Language, 12,* 353–365.

Elman, J. L. (1990). Finding structure in time. *Cognitive Science, 14,* 179–211.

Elman, J. L. (1993). Learning and development in neural networks: The importance of starting small. *Cognition, 48,* 71–99.

Feldman, J., Fanty, M., & Goddard, N. (1988). Computing with structured neural networks. *IEEE Computer, 21*(3), 91–104.

Freyd, J., Pantzer, T., & Cheng, J. (1988). Representing statics as forces in equilibrium. *Journal of Experimental Psychology: General, 117*(4), 395–407.

Geman, S., Bienenstock, E., & Doursat, R. (1992). Neural networks and the bias/variance dilemma. *Neural Computation, 4,* 1–58.

Georgopoulos, A. P., Schwartz, A. B., & Kettner, R. E. (1986). Neuronal population coding of movement direction. *Science, 233,* 1416–1419.

Glenberg, A. (in press). What memory is for. *Behavioral and Brain Sciences.*

Goldowsky, B. N., & Newport, E. L. (1993). Modeling the effects of processing limitations on the acquisition of morphology: The less is more hypothesis. In J. Mead, (Ed.), *Proceedings of the 11th West Coast Conference on Formal Linguistics.* Center for the Study of Language and Information, Stanford, CA.

Golinkoff, R., Hirsh-Pasek, K., Lavallee, A., & Baduini, C. (1985). What's in a word?: The young child's predisposition to use lexical contrast. Paper presented at the Boston University Conference on Child Language, Boston.

Hayward, W., & Tarr, M. (1995). Spatial language and spatial representation. *Cognition, 55,* 39–84.

Henn, V., & Cohen, B. (1976). Coding of information about rapid eye movements in the pontine reticular formation of alert monkeys. *Brain Research,* 108, 307–325.

Hertz, J., Krogh, A., & Palmer, R. G. (1991). *Introduction to the theory of neural computation.* Redwood City, CA: Addison Wesley.

Hirsch, J., & Mjolsness, E. (1992). A center-of-mass computation describes the precision of random dot displacement discrimination. *Vision Research, 32*(2), 335–346.

Hubel, D., & Wiesel, T. (1959). Receptive fields of single neurones in the cat's visual cortex. *Journal of Physiology, 148,* 574–591.

Hubel, D., & Wiesel, T. (1962). Receptive fields, binocular interaction and functional architecture in the cat's visual cortex. *Journal of Physiology,* 160, 106–154.

Hutchinson, J. (1986). Children's sensitivity to the contrastive use of object category terms. Paper presented at the 1986 Annual Child Language Research Forum, Stanford, CA.

Huttenlocher, J., Hedges, L., and Duncan, S. (1991). Categories and particulars: Prototype effects in estimating spatial location. *Psychological Review, 98*(3), 352–376.

Jackendoff, R. (1983). *Semantics and cognition.* Cambridge, MA: MIT Press.

Jackendoff, R. (1990). *Semantic structures.* Cambridge, MA: MIT Press.

Johnston, J., & Slobin, D. (1979). The development of locative expressions in English, Italian, Serbo-Croatian and Turkish. *Journal of Child Language, 6,* 529–545.

Kalaska, J., Caminiti, R., & Georgopoulos, A. (1983). Cortical mechanisms related to the direction of two-dimensional arm movements: Relations in parietal area 5 and comparison with motor cortex. *Experimental Brain Research, 51,* 247–260.

Lakoff, G. (1987). *Women, fire, and dangerous things: What categories reveal about the mind.* Chicago: University of Chicago Press.

Langacker, R. (1987). *Foundations of cognitive grammar I: Theoretical prerequisites.* Stanford, CA: Stanford University Press.

LeCun, Y. (1989). Generalization and network design strategies. Technical Report CRG-TR-89-4, Connectionist Research Group, University of Toronto.

Liittschwager, J., & Markman, E. (1994). Sixteen and 24-month-olds' use of mutual exclusivity as a default assumption in second label learning. *Developmental Psychology, 30,* 955–968.

Logan, G., & Compton, B. (1996). Distance and distraction effects in the apprehension of spatial relations. *Journal of Experimental Psychology: Human Perception and Performance, 22*(1), 159–172.

Logan, G., & Sadler, D. (1996). A computational analysis of the apprehension of spatial relations. In P. Bloom, M. Peterson, M. Garrett, & L. Nadel (Eds.), *Language and space.* Cambridge, MA: MIT Press.

MacWhinney, B., & Snow, C. (1990). The child language data exchange system: An update. *Journal of Child Language, 17,* 457–472.

Mandler, J. (1992). How to build a baby: II. Conceptual primitives. *Psychological Review, 99*(4), 587–604.

Mandler, J. (1996). Preverbal representation and language. In P. Bloom, M. Peterson, M. Garrett, & L. Nadel (Eds.), *Language and space.* Cambridge, MA: MIT Press.

Markman, E. (1989). *Categorization and naming in children: Problems of induction.* Cambridge, MA: MIT Press.

Markman, E., Wachtel, G. (1988). Children's use of mutual exclusivity to constrain the meanings of words. *Cognitive Psychology, 20,* 121–157.

Maskara, A., & Noetzel, A. (1992). Forced simple recurrent neural networks and grammatical inference. In *Proceedings of the 14th Annual Conference of the Cognitive Science Society.*

Massaro, D. (1988). Some criticisms of connectionist models of human performance. *Journal of Memory and Language, 27,* 213–234.

Medin, D., & Schwanenflugel, P. (1981). Linear separability in classification learning. *Journal of Experimental Psychology: Human Learning and Memory, 7*(5), 355–368.

Merriman, W., & Bowman, L. (1989). The mutual exclusivity bias in children's word learning. *Monographs of the Society for Research in Child Development, 54*(3–4).

Mervis, C. B., Golinkoff, R. M., & Bertrand, J. (1994). Two-year-olds readily learn multiple labels for the same basic-level category. *Child Development, 65,* 1163–1177.

Miller, G., & Johnson-Laird, P. (1976). *Language and perception.* Cambridge, MA: Belknap Press.

Mitchell, T. M. (1980). The need for biases in learning generalizations. Technical Report CBM-TR-117, Computer-Science Department, Rutgers University.

Needham, A., & Baillargeon, R. (1993). Intuitions about support in 4.5-month-old infants. *Cognition, 47,* 121–148.

Pinker, S. (1984). *Language learnability and language development.* Cambridge, MA: Harvard University Press.

Pinker, S. (1989). *Learnability and cognition: The acquisition of argument structure.* Cambridge, MA: MIT Press.

Plunkett, K., & Marchman, V. (1988). U-shaped learning and frequency effects in a multi-layered perceptron: Implications for child language acquisition. *Cognition, 28,* 73–193.

Regier, T. (1995). A model of the human capacity for categorizing spatial relations. *Cognitive Linguistics, 6*(1), 63–88.

Regier, T. (1996). *The Human semantic potential: Spatial language and constrained connectionism.* Cambridge, MA: MIT Press.

Renier, F. G. (1995). *Dutch dictionary: Dutch-English and English-Dutch.* London: Routledge.

Rumelhart, D., Hinton, G., & Williams, R. (1986). Learning internal representations by error propagation. In D. Rumelhart, J. McClelland, and the PDP Research Group (Eds.), *Parallel distributed processing: Explorations in the microstructure of cognition.* (Vol. 1, pp. 318–362). Cambridge, MA: MIT Press.

Rumelhart, D., McClelland, J. (1986). On learning the past tenses of English verbs. In J. McClelland, D. Rumelhart, & the PDP Research Group (Eds.). *Parallel distributed processing: Explorations in the microstructure of cognition* (Vol. 2, pp. 216–271). Cambridge, MA: MIT Press.

Shavlik, J., & Dietterich, T. (1990). *Readings in machine learning.* Morgan Kaufmann. San Mateo, CA.

Siskind, J. (1992). *Naive physics, event perception, lexical semantics and language acquisition.* PhD thesis, Massachusetts Institute of Technology.

Sitskoorn, M. M., & Smithsman, A. W. (1995). Infants' perception of dynamic relations between objects: Passing through or support? *Developmental Psychology, 31*(3), 437–447.

Smith, L. B., Gasser, M., & Sandhofer, C. M. (1997). Learning to talk about the properties of objects: A network model for the development of dimensions. In D. Medin, P. Schyns, & R. Goldstone (Eds.), *Psychology of learning and motivation: Mechanisms of perceptual learning this volume.*

Suzuki, I., Timerick, S. J. B., & Wilson, V. J. (1985). Body position with respect to the head or body position in space is coded by lumbar interneurons. *Journal of Neurophysiology, 54*(1), 123–133.

Talmy, L. (1972). *Semantic structures in English and Atsugewi.* PhD thesis, University of California, Berkeley.

Ullman, S. (1984). Visual routines. *Cognition, 18,* 97–159.

Waldmann, M., Holyoak, K., & Fratianne, A. (1995). Causal models and the acquisition of category structure. *Journal of Experimental Psychology: General, 124*(2), 181–206.

Woodward, A., & Markman, E. (1991). Constraints on learning as default assumptions: Comments on Merriman and Bowman's "The mutual exclusivity bias in children's word learning." *Developmental Review, 11,* 137–163.

# LEARNING TO TALK ABOUT THE PROPERTIES OF OBJECTS: A NETWORK MODEL OF THE DEVELOPMENT OF DIMENSIONS

*Linda B. Smith*
*Michael Gasser*
*Catherine M. Sandhofer*

". . . the undeniable fact being that *any number of sensory sources, falling simultaneously on a mind* WHICH HAS NOT EXPERIENCED THEM SEPARATELY, *will fuse into a single undivided object for that mind.* William James, 1890, pg. 488, italics and capitalization as in the original).

A classic question in philosophy and psychology asks whether the object or its properties are more fundamental (see, e.g., Carnap, 1967; Locke, 1964; James, 1890; Boring, 1942). Clearly we perceive both—a dog is apprehended as an integral whole *and* as being big and brown and furry. But which perception is prior? This question is often interpreted in terms of the logical priority of parts and whole. And the contemporary concensus is that parts are logically and computationally prior; complex percepts and concepts are built from simpler primitives. More than 100 years ago, however, William James concluded that whole objects are experientially prior, that constituent properties are a secondary product of perceptual learning. This chapter provides support for James' conclusion.

Our starting point is the protracted course of children's acquisition of dimensional language, a lengthy process that includes the acquisition of dimensional terms and the development of selective attention. We explain

THE PSYCHOLOGY OF LEARNING
AND MOTIVATION, VOL. 36

this developmental course by simulating it in a connectionist network. Our results suggest that dimensions are created, that they are the product of learning dimensional language.

## I. The Developmental Data

Both Gentner and Rattermann (1991) and Smith (1989, 1993) provide extensive reviews of the development of dimensions. We highlight the main findings here.

### A. Dimensional Terms Are Hard to Learn

Young children are rapid word learners, learning as many as nine words, per day (Carey, 1978). They are not, however, rapid learners of the words that refer to the perceptible properties of objects. Instead, the dimensional adjectives—words like *wet* and *soft* and *big* and *red*—are remarkably hard for young children to learn.

One line of evidence for this conclusion is the composition of early productive vocabularies; in these vocabularies, dimensional adjectives are rare or nonexistent. For example, in Stern and Stern's (1924) diary study of the acquisition of English, 78% of the words produced at 20 months were common nouns, the rest were verblike; *none* were adjectives. Similarly, in Nelson's (1973) study of 18 children learning English, fewer than 7% of the first 50 words were adjectives (see Bates, Benigni, Bretherton, Camaioni, & Volterra, 1979). Dimensional adjectives are late for children learning other languages as well. In Dromi's (1987) study of one child learning Hebrew, only 4 of the first 337 words were adjectives. In a longitudinal study of the acquisition of Spanish by 328 children. Jackson-Maldonado, Thal, Marchman, and Bates (1993) found only one adjective among the 88 most common words. The finding that adjectives are infrequent in early vocabularies is notable given the frequency of common dimensional adjectives in adult language.

A second line of evidence consists of studies that attempt to teach children new words. Children as young as 18 months are one-trial learners of nouns (Woodward, Markman, & Fitzsimmons, 1994) and perhaps also verbs (Tomasello & Kruger, 1992). In contrast, studies attempting to teach young children adjective terms typically fail—even after as many as 2000 trials (Rice, 1980).

A final line of evidence showing the difficulty of learning dimension terms concerns children's errors. Long after children begin to use dimensional words, when they are as old as 3, 4, or even 5 years, their interpretations of dimensional terms are still errorful. This literature provides many examples of both within- and between-dimension errors, interpreting "big" to mean "tall" (Keil & Carroll, 1980), "little" to mean "big" (Donaldson & Wales, 1970), "big" to mean "bright" (Carey, 1982), "dark" to mean "loud" (Mark, Hammeal, Bornstein, 1987; Smith & Sera, 1992), and "red" to mean "green" (Binet, 1890).

In sum, children learn the names for object properties slowly and errorfully. We ask: Why is this learning so hard?

## B.  THE DEVELOPMENT OF SELECTIVE ATTENTION

The slow course of children's extraction of dimensions is evident in nonlanguage tasks as well. The evidence on children's difficulties are so substantial that the trend from wholistic to dimensionally differentiated perception has been offered as a principle of development (Gibson, 1966; Werner, 1957; Wohlwill, 1962). This large and well-documented literature shows that young children have difficulty in any task that requires them to attend selectively to one dimension. In these tasks, selective attention is measured by asking how much judgments along one dimension are disrupted when additional variation is added on another dimension. For example, a child is said to fail to attend selectively if when the child is asked to put red objects in one pile and blue objects in another, she makes more errors (or performs more slowly) when the red and blue things also vary in size and shape. Preschool children commonly fail to attend selectively in such tasks; indeed, they commonly fail to do them at all when irrelevant variation is added. In total, the evidence from discrimination learning tasks, classification tasks, matching-to-sample tasks, and same-different judgment tasks all show that young children perform poorly whenever they must attend to only one dimension of variation and ignore others (see Aslin & Smith, 1988; Smith, 1989; Gentner & Rattermann, 1991, for reviews). These results fit the idea that object properties fuse into an undivided whole in the minds of young children. Is this, then, why young children have difficulty learning dimensional terms?

## C.  LANGUAGE THEN SELECTIVE ATTENTION

Children's difficulties in attending selectively might seem to suggest an explanation of children's difficulties in learning dimension words. If children cannot perceptually isolate properties from the object as a whole, then they cannot map dimensional adjectives onto object properties. But what drives the development of selective attention to dimension? The evidence suggests that learning dimensional language plays a key role.

Learning dimensional words and selective attention to dimensions are closely related achievements in children (Gentner & Rattermann, 1991; Smith, 1989). But overall, the evidence suggests that learning dimension words comes first. Although children learn attribute terms such as *big* and *wet* and *red* with difficulty, they often do so *years* before they can make judgments in nonlanguage tasks about one dimension *unaffected* by variation on other dimensions. Indeed, knowing the relevant dimensions words seem a prerequisite for successful selective attention in many tasks (Kendler, 1979; Ehri, 1976; Smith & Sera, 1992; see also Gentner & Rattermann, 1991, for a review). Other studies have shown that supplying children with words to describe properties and dimensions facilitates selective attention (Kotovsky & Gentner, 1996; Kendler, 1979). In sum, it appears that children first learn the names for attributes and *then* they become able to selectively attend to those properties (Sandhofer & Smith, 1996). In light of this evidence, Kotovsky and Gentner (1996) and Smith (1993) proposed that children's abstraction of perceptual dimensions is a consequence of learning dimension words. This chapter provides a demonstration of how learning dimensional language might lead to selective attention.

## II.  Toward a Model

To this end, our specific goal is a network that learns dimension words and through this learning develops the ability to selectively attend to dimensions. Three further issues influenced the architecture of the network and the learning tasks we presented to it.

### A.  DIFFERENT DIMENSIONS AT DIFFERENT LEVELS

Figure 1 presents the classic view of dimensions: Different kinds of physical energy activate distinct sensory channels. These distinct sensory channels constitute the dimensions we can selectively attend to, perceive, and talk about. In brief, in the figure there are the same dimensions all the way down—from the dimensions we talk about to those we perceive to those that are given in the sensory system. By this view, the reason we *perceive* the dimensions we do is because these are the perceptual primitives our sensory system gives us.

The assumptions depicted in Fig. 1 are latent in much research in cognitive psychology: the search for primitive features (Treisman & Gelade, 1980), studies of dimensional crosstalk (Melara & Mounts, 1994), theories of category learning (Krushke, 1992) and in studies of infant perception and cognition (Husaim & Cohen, 1981; Coldren & Colombo, 1994).

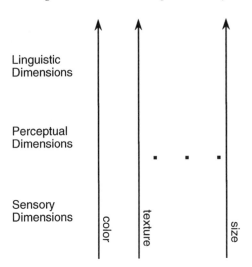

Fig. 1.   A representation of the idea that sensory, perceptual, and linguistic, representations are organized by the same dimensions.

There are reasons to question this view, however. The first reason is the difficulty young children have in learning dimension words and in selectively attending to dimensions. The second reason is the fact that many of the dimensions that people talk about and use in their everyday lives to compare objects—the dimensions of size, shape, color, texture, wetness—do not correspond in a 1:1 fashion (and sometimes not all) to the features and dimensions identified at preperceptual or sensory levels of analyses (Treisman & Gelade, 1980; see also Hurvich & Jameson, 1957; Halff, Ortony, & Anderson, 1976). The third reason is the growing evidence that adults construct new features and dimensions as a consequence of learning categories (Freyd, 1983; Schyns, Goldstone, & Thibault, in press; Goldstone, 1995; Sanocki, 1991, 1992).

And, finally, is the evidence on the variability of the world's languages. The world's languages differ dramatically in how they lexicalize object properties. While all languages (apparently) have nouns and verbs as syntactic categories, some languages (Mandarin Chinese, Quechua) do not have a separate syntactic category of adjective. Rather, property words behave more like verbs. Thus there seems to be something less fundamental about how languages organize property terms. Second, languages slice up the sensory space in very different ways. For example, English "thick" brings together viscosity and width: Japanese "koi" brings together viscosity and concentration (see Schachter, 1985). Differences among languages strongly suggest that dimensional words are not simple refections of fixed sensory attributes.

In light of this evidence of noncorresponding and changing dimensions at different levels in the cognitive system, we distinguish three senses of dimensions: (1) Sensory dimensions that structure the input to the cognitive system; (2) perceived dimensions that can be perceptually isolated, that is, attended to selectively; and (3) lexical dimensions that structure the relationships among words. Critically, our network will make no assumption that these three levels must correspond. Specifically, sensory dimensions will be hardwired into the network and linguistic dimensions will be given to the network in training. In simulations 1 and 2, linguistic and sensory dimensions will correspond and in simulation 3, they will not. In all cases, perceived dimensions must be constructed.

## 1.  Three Kinds of Mappings

In learning dimension words, children learn three kinds of mappings. One mapping is between dimension words and object properties. For example, in learning the word "red" children associate "red" with red cups, red cars, red gum, red dresses, and so forth. These mappings are characteristically what one thinks of when one thinks of learning dimensional terms, and such mappings could be sufficient for the child to abstract the common property referred to by a single word. However, these word–property maps are not the only associations learned in the course of learning dimension words.

Children also learn word–word maps. The words "What color is it?" are associated with the words "red," "blue," and "green" but not "big." The word "size" is associated with the words "big" and "little"; "wet" is associated with "dry." There is evidence that children learn these associations and moreover that they sometimes do so before they learn the specific properties to which individual words refer (Cruse, 1977; Backsheider & Shatz, 1993; Clark, 1973; Carey, 1982). For example, Backsheider and Shatz showed that children who cannot correctly map a single color word to the right property often know to answer the question "What color is it?" only with color words.

Finally, *in the context of dimension words,* children also make property–property maps (Sandhofer & Smith, 1996). People put pairs and sets of objects before children and say such things as "These are both red," "They are the same color," and "These are the big ones." This learning context affords not just the mapping of words to properties but the mapping of properties to properties. Such simultaneous presentation of two objects with the linguistic specification of how they alike may encourage their comparison and the discovery of their common property. Gentner & Rattermann (1991); see also Kotovsky & Gentner, 1996) have suggested that such explicitly presented comparisons are crucial to the discovery of relations and kinds of similarity.

Accordingly, our network was designed to simultaneously learn word–property maps, word–word maps, and (word-)property–property maps. In simulation 1, we specifically examine the role of word–property maps and word–word maps in the creation of perceptually isolatable dimensions. In simulations 2 and 3, we examine the role of explicitly comparing objects on a linguistically specified dimension, that is the role of property–property maps.

## 2. SUPERVISED LEARNING

Children learn dimension words through explicit teaching; adults provide both positive and negative evidence as to the properties to which dimension words refer (Callahan, 1990; Mervis, 1987; Snow, 1977; Wood, 1980). Adults as part of their regular interaction with young children ask such things as "What color is that?" "Is that big?" "Is kitty soft?". And, adults provide appropriate feedback. When a child labels a red object as *green* or a big one as *little,* parents tell them what the correct labels are. Thus back-propagation is a suitable learning algorithm because children's learning of dimensional terms is "supervised."

However, supervision as typically realized in connectionist networks is not perfectly appropriate as a model of children's word learning (see also Gasser & Smith, 1996). In traditional back-propogation, the connection weights on each learning trial are changed to increase the correct response and to decrease *all* other potential responses. This is like the parent saying to the child "This is red, not blue, not big, not wet, not soft, not bumpy. . . . Parents do not do this but instead explicitly reinforce correct answers ("yes, that's a red one") and provide negative feedback only when the child explicitly provides the wrong answer ("that's not red, its blue").

Traditional back-propagation is also inappropriate in the present case because the task of learning to label the multiple attributes of individual objects means that possible responses are not simply right or wrong. There are kinds and degrees of wrongness. Consider a big, black wet dog and the question "What color is it?" The answers *big* and *red* are both wrong. However, it seems unlikely that parents would respond to these errors in the same way. A toddler who answers the question "What color is it?" by correctly noting that the dog is *big* seems likely to hear a parental response of "yes, its a big dog, a big black dog." A toddler who answers the same question by saying *red* is likely to hear, instead, a parental response "its not red, its black."

Accordingly, we modified the back-propagation algorithm to fit these assumptions about the kinds of feedback provided by parents. The next section provides a detailed description of the network and the learning rule.

## III.  Network for Learning Dimensional Language

The architecture for our network instantiates three overlapping sets of mapping: property–word, word–word, and property–property. Figure 2 shows the network. Following convention each layer of units is represented as a box and the arrows between each layer represents complete connectivity between the layers of one unit and the next. There are three types of layers: (1) *Input layers*—these correspond to the sensory specification of an object and the linguistic context in which an object is perceived; (2) *Output layer* which corresponds to labels for attributes, words like *big, red, wet,* and *soft;* and (3) *Internal hidden layers.* We conceptualize the activity on these hidden layers as corresponding to representations at the level of conscious experience. We propose that the patterns of activations on these internal levels come, with the learning of language, to represent isolated attributes such that if the network selectively attends to the color

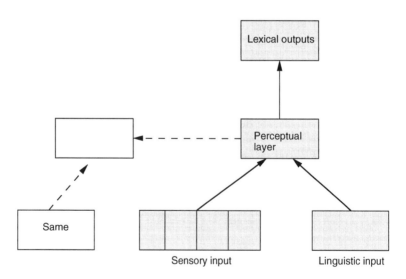

Fig. 2.   The network trained to label attributes and to make comparisons. The shaded portion is the portion used to train attribute categories.

of a big black dog, blackness is isolated in the pattern of activity on the hidden layer.

We trained the network in two tasks common in children's learning of dimensional terms: (1) learning to label the attribute of a single object and (2) comparing objects. We describe the network in more detail by describing the layers and training procedure for each of these tasks separately.

A. LEARNING ATTRIBUTE NAMES: OBJECT–WORD AND
   WORD–WORD MAPS

The canonical test of a child's knowledge of dimensions terms—the one principally used by experimenters, parents, and educators—consists of presenting the child with an object and asking them a question about it: "What color is that?" "Is it big or little?" "What shape is it?" The child is thus presented with a single object along with linguistic input that specifies the relevant dimension and the child is asked to output the relevant dimensional term. Learning, to do this require mapping object properties to words, for example, the redness of the object to the word *red*. It also requires mapping dimensions words in the input to dimensions words in the output, for example, *what color* to *red*. One training task which we present to the network is based on this canonical test of dimension-word knowledge.

Four layers are involved; these are the shaded layers in Fig. 2. The sensory input and the linguistic-dimension input connect to a hidden layer which we call the perception layer. The activation of the perception layer in turn activates the units in the output layer. These output units represent words that name the properties of single objects along several dimensions. This portion of the network and its operation is the same as the network used by Gasser and Smith (1996) to model young children's faster learning of concrete nouns than dimensional adjectives.

*1. Sensory Input*

The object to be labeled is specified on independent sensory dimensions. In the present simulations, objects are specified on four (or in experiment 3 on five) sensory dimensions. The values of each sensory dimensions are represented using "thermometer" encoding (Harnad, Hanson, & Lubin, 1991). In this form of representation, units are activated in a series; the nth unit in the series is not activated until the activation on the n-1 unit is 1. Each dimension consists of 11 units, so two of the values along one 11-unit dimension are [1,1,1,1,1,1,.8,0,0,] or [1,1,1,.3,0,0,0,0,0,0,0].

*2. Linguistic Input*

The linguistic *input* signals the dimension specified in the question asked of the network. Each possibly relevant dimension is represented by a single unit in this layer. Each of these units is thus associated with a class of possible answers—for example, activation of the linguistic input *color* is associated with the outputs *red, blue, green; size* is associated with the outputs *big, medium,* and *little.* Note, that there is no prior requirement that these linguistic dimensions match the sensory dimensions. In the first two simulations, there were three linguistic dimensions and thus three units in this layer.

Critically, from the perspective of the network, there is no distinction between the input activation that corresponds to the input object and that which corresponds to the linguistically specified dimension. From the network's point of view, there is just one input vector of 47 numbers jointly specifying an event in the world.

## 3.  Perceptual Layer

Activations on the hidden perceptual layer represent the transient contents of immediate awareness. Thus these patterns of activation should change systematically with changes in the sensory and linguistic input such that the pattern of activation when labeling a big red dog as *red* will differ from that when labeling the same object as *big.* The patterns of activation that emerge on this layer in the context of different questions about different dimensions will thus constitute our definition of *perceived dimensions.* Importantly, the perceptual layer compresses the sensory dimensions so that the sensory dimensions are not directly recoverable in the patterns of activation on the perceptual layer. Rather, prior to learning, patterns on the perceptual layer are distributed, wholistic, representations of the input object. In this way, we embody James' claim in the opening quote that prior to learning, separate sensory sources "fuse into a single undivided object."

## 4.  The Output Layer

The output layer consists of a single unit for each word, that is, each units corresponds to a dimensional adjective such as *red, green, big, little, rough,* and *smooth.* A +1 activation on the output unit represents the network's labeling of the input object with the corresponding word. A −1 activation represents the network's decision that the corresponding word is inappropriate for the input object, and a 0 activation represents an intermediate response, one that might be made if an object is described by a word that is not an appropriate answer to the question asked. For example, if asked "what color?" and given a large smooth red object, the output *red* would be represent by +1, the output *smooth* by 0, and the output *green* by −1. In this way we model parents likely nonresponse to true but not requested descriptors of the input object.

B.  MAKING COMPARISONS: PROPERTY–PROPERTY MAPS

In the course of learning dimension words, children are often presented with *sets* of objects and *told* how objects within the set are alike, for example, that two objects are "the same color" or "both soft." The portion of the network that learns attribute labels cannot learn from this sort of experience because it has no way of simultaneously representing more than one object and no way of comparing objects (see Smith, 1993). Our goal was to add to the network such that it could make internal comparisons of objects, the internal comparisons that would be triggered by being told that two objects are alike in some lexically specific way. To do this, we added two layers to the network used in learning attribute names: a Perceptual buffer had a "Same" unit (see Fig. 2). This "Same" unit simply turns on the comparison process which works in three steps:

1. Step 1. An object and a linguistic input specifying the relevant dimension are input to the network, activation is passed to the perceptual layer, and then the pattern on this layer is stored in the perceptual buffer.
2. Step 2. A second object is input along with the same linguistic input. This second object always has the same value as the first object on the linguistically specified dimension. Thus, at the end of this step, we have input two objects that are alike in some way and we have linguistically specified the dimension on which they are alike.
3. Step 3. The two patterns of activation on the perceptual buffer and the perceptual layer are compared: The pattern on the perceptual buffer is treated as a target for the pattern on the perceptual layer. The error is the difference between the two patterns. This error is back-propagated from the perceptual layer to the sensory and linguistic input layer. In this way the network is trained to make the internal representations for two objects which are the same on a linguistically specified dimension to be more similar to each other. In other words, the network is trained to find out what is alike about two objects "said" to be alike in some way.

C.  MAJOR THEORETICAL CLAIMS

In summary, the network and training tasks instantiate four theoretical claims about how children learn to perceptually isolate and represent dimensions:

1. Prior to learning, perception is wholistic; separate sources of sensory information are combined into one unitary pattern.

2. Sensory, perceptual, and linguistic dimensions are distinct. Sensory dimensions are given in the biology and linguistic dimensions are in the language input; they need not correspond.
3. Perceptual dimensions are the product of learning dimensional language and thus may be constrained by both the sensory dimensions and the linguistic dimensions.
4. Two tasks are critical to the development of perceived dimensions: Learning to label the properties of objects which includes learning property–word maps and word–word maps and comparing objects on linguistically specified dimensions which creates property–property maps.

In the following simulation experiments, we demonstrate the plausibility of these ideas and show how they account for aspects of the developmental trend in children, yielding new insights and new predictions about the development of dimensions and selective attention.

Simulation 1 examines how learning to label attributes on linguistic dimensions that conform to sensory dimensions might lead to the perceptual isolation and representation of individual attributes. Simulation 2 examines the joint effects of learning to label attributes and of comparing objects on linguistically specified dimensions that conform to the sensory dimensions. Simulation 3 examines how this learning might create new perceived dimensions when linguistic dimensions do not conform to sensory dimensions.

## IV.  Simulation 1: Learning Property Names

The central question behind this simulation is what one knows about dimensions when one has learned to call red things *red,* blue things *blue,* and big things *big.* Does labeling an attribute require the conscious isolation of that attribute from the other aspects of an object? This is an important developmental question because young children use dimensional terms *before* they can make other decisions about one dimension unaffected by variation on other dimensions, that is, before they can effectively selectively attend in nonlanguage tasks.

We addressed this question by asking the network to learn to label attributes on independent sensory dimensions. We then examined the character of the network's internal representations via what we call the Selective Attention Test. In addition, we assessed whether the network formed word–word maps on its way to acquiring attribute terms. This simulation involves only learning to label the properties of objects presented one at a time and thus only the shaded layers in Fig. 2.

A. METHOD

*1. Training*

The network was taught to answer three questions—each a request for the name of an attribute on one sensory dimension. In total, the network was taught nine attribute categories. Each adjective category was organized by a range of values on one sensory dimension; specifically, each attribute label referred to .33 of the maximum possible range on *one* sensory dimension. Three attribute categories each were defined for three of the four sensory dimensions. There were no terms that corresponded to values on the fourth sensory dimension.

Each trial consisted of the presentation of an object on the sensory layer and a linguistic input. There were three possible linguistic inputs; what might be characterized as the questions *What color is it?*, *What size is it?*, and *What texture is it?* The first linguistic input was associated with ranges of variation on the first sensory dimension, the second with ranges of variation on the second sensory dimension, and the third with ranges of variation on the third sensory dimension. For each trial, a linguistic input was randomly selected and then an object was randomly generated such that each attribute term was the correct answer equally often. The network was trained on 15,000 randomly generated inputs and tested every 2500 inputs.

*2. Selective Attention Test*

We tested the network's ability to isolate attributes every 2500 trials by examining the patterns of activation on the perceptual layer for pairs of objects that were either same or different on the linguistically speicfied dimension. The idea is this: If the network has abstracted the property *red* from all other properties, then the pattern of activation on the perceptual layer should be the same when the network is asked "What color?" and given and a big, red, bumpy, rounded object *and* when it is asked "What color?" and given a little, red, smooth, angular object.

For the Selective Attention Test, we specifically examined two kinds of pairs: (1) Same-on-Relevant-Dimension pairs consisted of two inputs that were the same on the linguistically specified sensory dimension but different on the other three dimensions; and (2) Different-on-Relevant-Dimension pairs consisted of two inputs that were different on the linguistically specified dimension but the same on the other three. On each Selective Attention Test trial, each member of the pair was input and its resulting pattern of activation on the perceptual layer was stored. Then the second member of the pair was input and its resulting pattern of activation on the perceptual layer was stored. The dependent measure was the Euclidean distance between these two patterns of activation.

Prior to learning, the Same-on-Relevant Dimension items should yield *more dissimilar* patterns of activation on the hidden layer than the Different-on-Relevant Dimension items because the Same pairs are alike on one sensory dimension but different on three and thus are more wholistically different than are the Different pairs which are different on one sensory dimension but alike on three. If, however, in learning the attribute terms, the network learns to perceptually isolate and selectively attend to the linguistically specified dimension, then the patterns of activation for the Same-on-Relevant dimension items should become more similar, less distant, than the Different-on-Relevant dimension items.

This experiment (and the others that follow) was conducted ten times with the network starting learning each time with different initial and randomly determined connection weights. Each of the 10 runs also employed different randomly generated inputs. The results are reported as means over the 10 runs. We considered two definitions of a correct response: (1) the network was correct if the most highly activated output was correct or (2) the network was correct if the activation of the correct output unit was above a predetermined threshold. Both measures lead to the same pattern of results and conclusions. We report the results in all of the experiments in terms of the output with the highest activation.

## 3. Results and Discussion

Figure 3 shows the network's proportion correct labeling of attributes on the linguistically specified dimension as a function of training. By the 5000th input, the network was nearly always correct; given an object and a linguistic input that specified the relevant dimension, the network correctly labeled the appropriate attribute.

Figure 4 shows the results of the Selective Attention Test: The Euclidean distance between patterns of activation on the perceptual layer as a function of training for the Same-on-Relevant dimension pairs and the Different-on-Relevant dimensions pairs. At the beginning of training, the pattern of activations for the Different pairs were less distant, more similar, than the Same pairs which is to be expected because the Different items shared values on three sensory dimensions but the Same items shared a value on only one sensory dimension. With training, the distance between these Different pairs increases but the distance between the Same pairs does not decrease. That is, the network *did not* learn to perceptually isolate a common sensory property by learning to label it. This failure to isolate properties stands in marked contast to the high performance of the network in

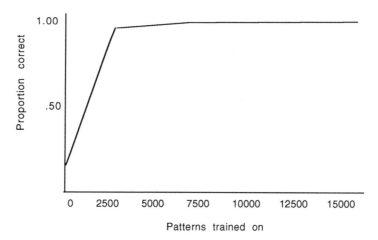

Fig. 3. Proportion correct responses in simulation 1 as a function of the number of training patterns.

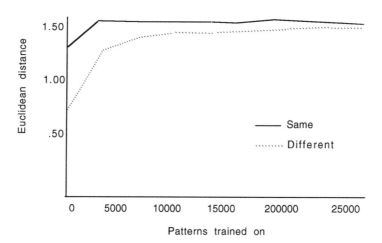

Fig. 4. The Euclidean distance between patterns of activation on the hidden later for two input objects that are the same on the queried dimension and different on all other dimensions (*solid line*) and for two input objects that are different on the queried dimension and the same on the other three (*dashed line*) as a function of training patterns.

learning to label attributes. The network learned to "call" blue objects *blue*, red objects *red*, big objects *big*, bumpy objects *bumpy*, and so on with accuracy but without learning to isolate the common sensory values that define these attribute categories.

The finding that correctly labeling attributes does not require the perceptual isolation of the attributes is not surprising in one sense. To succeed, the network only needs to find partitions of the hidden-layer activation space such that all instances of a dimensional term fall on one side of a boundary. The task does not demand that the network find an identical pattern of activation, an invariant, for all red things; even though there is one available in the sensory input.

However, the present results *are* surprising in the context of typical inferences in developmental psychology which take verbal behavior as a close indicator of underlying concepts and their constituent structure (e.g., Gelman & Coley, 1991; Keil, 1989). In this context, labeling red things *red* is prima facie evidence for "having the concept red." However, the present results show that "having the concept" need not mean having abstracted a common component. Notice that the behavior of the network does fit the behavior of children who use many dimensional terms correctly before they effectively attend selectively to the properties those terms name. The clear implication is that young children can correctly use a dimension word *before* they attend selectively to the property named by that word.

Although the network did not learn to isolate perceptually the attribute defining a lexical category, it did learn something about linguistic dimensions, forming robust word–word maps between linguistic inputs and outputs, and like young children it did so prior to learning to correctly label properties. Figure 5 shows the proportion of errors that were *within-dimension* errors. Given three dimensions each with three attribute categories, the proportion of within-dimension errors expected by chance is .25. As is apparent, these errors increase with training and after training occur more often than expected by chance. Again, this behavior is like that of young children who know the class of appropriate answers to a question before they correctly use individual dimensional terms.

In sum, the network learned to label properties without discovering the invariant "sensory" properties in the input. The network could succeed in this way because to be right it only had to find a set of connection weights that worked well enough. The results suggest that dimensional adjectives may be initially learned by children as broad multidimensional categories even when they correspond to "given" and separate sensory primitives.

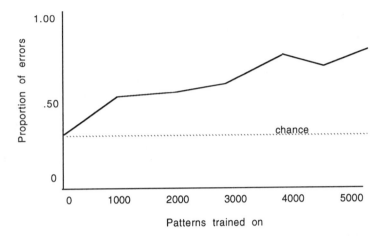

Fig. 5.  Proportion of errors that were within-dimension errors as a function training patterns in simulation 1.

## V.  Simulation 2: Learning to Selectively Attend

If perceived dimensions are not "givens" but must be discovered, and if they are not necessarily discovered by learning to label the attributes of objects, how are they learned? In this simulation, we ask if comparison of objects on a linguistically specified dimension results in the perceptual isolation of individual dimensions. That is, in this simulation, the network is asked to learn three sets of maps: word–word maps between linguistic inputs and outputs, property–word maps between input objects and linguistic outputs, and property–property maps between objects that are specified to be alike on a particular dimension. Learning this third relational map should teach the network to find common properties and to filter out irrelevant information from linguistically unspecified dimensions. The issue is how this training interacts with the learning of attribute categories.

We examined two training procedures. In the Joint-learning condition, we taught the network to label attributes and we also presented it with pairs of objects to compare on the linguistically specified dimension. Both kinds of training trials alternated from the start of training. In the Attributes-then-Comparison condition, we taught the network to label attributes as in simulation 1 and then after this first task was mastered we introduced the comparison task.

A.  METHOD

*1.  Stimuli*

The stimuli for learning to label attributes were identical to those used in simulation 1. The stimuli for comparison training were pairs of inputs. The two input patterns had identical values on the sensory dimension specified by the linguistic input and differed by at least 30% of the range on each of the other three dimensions. On each comparison training trial, pairs of inputs were randomly generated to meet these constraints. The stimuli for the Selective Attention Test were identical to those used in simulation 1.

*2.  Procedure*

Training to label attributes was conducted as in simulation 1. For each comparison training trial, a lexical dimension was first picked randomly to be the dimension specified by the linguistic input. Next, a pair of objects identical on the linguistically specified sensory dimension and different on the remaining three was generated. The first item in the pair was presented on the sensory layer, together with the appropriate linguistic input. The resulting pattern on the perceptual layer was then saved on the perceptual buffer. Next, the second object was presented on the sensory layer along with the appropriate linguistic input. The resulting (second) pattern on the perceptual layer was then compared to the (first) pattern on the buffer. The pattern on the buffer served as the target.

In the Joint-learning condition, comparison training was introduced along with training to label attributes from the start of training. The two tasks alternated during training.

For the Attributes-then-comparison condition, the network was trained in the attributes task alone for the first 5000 inputs. At 5000 inputs, comparison training was introduced and the two tasks alternated for the remainder of training.

In both training regimens, training continued until 15,000 patterns (7500 for each task) had been presented. Following every 2500 inputs, the network was tested in the Selective Attention Test also as in experiment 1.

*3.  Results and Discussion*

Figure 6 shows the network's performance labeling attributes in the Joint training condition, when the network learned to do both tasks from the start of training. As shown in the figure, the network learned the attribute names in this condition more slowly than in simulation 1 when it was trained only in the attribute labeling task. Learning to label attributes is clearly

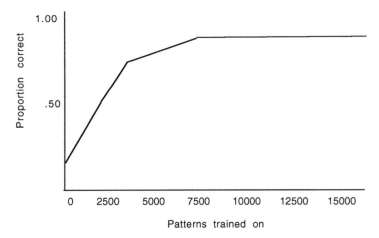

Fig. 6.   Proportion correct responses in the attribute labelling task under the Joint training regimen in simulation 2.

made more difficult by simulataneously learning to compare objects along the same lexical dimensions.

However, the results in the Selective Attention task, shown in Fig. 7, show that this joint training resulted in different knowledge about attributes

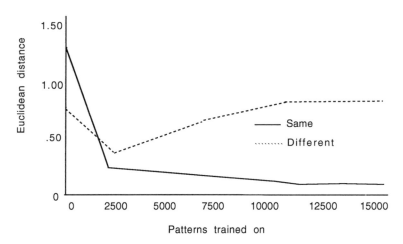

Fig. 7.   The Euclidean distance between patterns of activation on the hidden layer for pairs of inputs same on the queried dimension (*solid line*) or different on the queried dimension (*dashed line*) as a function of training patterns in the Joint training regimen of simulation 2.

than had the training in simulation 1. At the start of learning, the distance
(dissimilarity) of patterns of activation on the perceptual layer of Same-on-
Relevant dimension pairs is greater than Different-on-Relevant dimension
pairs. This is to be expected since Same pairs are alike only on the lexically
specified dimension but different on the remaining three, whereas Different
pairs are different on the lexically specified dimension but same on the
other three. However, briefly into Joint training, the pattern reverses so
that the network now internally represents objects that are alike on a
lexically specified dimension as being more alike than objects that differ
on the lexically specified dimension. The network has learned to isolate
the property common to objects labeled by the same term.

Figure 8 shows how well the network learned to label attributes when
it was first trained to name object properties and then given joint training
on both naming attributes and comparing objects. This training regimen is
clearly best for learning to label attributes; learning is rapid and largely
unaffected by the introduction of comparison training. Thus, although comparing objects on single dimensions slows learning to label attributes when
they are both taught from the beginning, the *addition* of this task does not
disrupt the labeling of already learned attribute names. This is intriguing
because what the network knows about attributes is different before and
after comparison training.

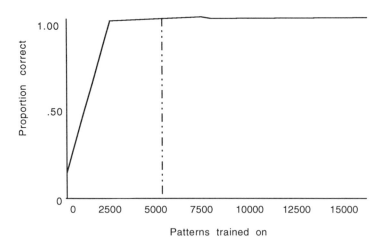

Patterns trained on

Fig. 8.   Proportion correct responses in the attribute labeling condition under the Incremental training regimen. The network receives categorization training only for the first 5000 trials
and then receives alternating categorization and comparison training for the remainder.

The results of the Selective Attention Test in the Attribute-then-Comparison condition are shown in Fig. 9. When the comparison task is introduced, the network quickly learns to selectively attend: patterns of activation for inputs that are the same on the lexically specified dimension become highly similar and patterns of activation for inputs that differ on the lexically specified dimension become very different. By 10,000 training patterns, performance in this condition on the Selective Attention Tasks equals that of the network on the Selective Attention Task in the Joint Training condition. Overall, this incremental learning schedule, by which the network learns to solve one task before starting on another, is superior to the one in which the network is faced with both tasks through out training. This fact and the fact that the addition of comparison training does not disrupt labeling object properties suggests that when learning attribute terms, the network learns attribute representations that *are in the right direction,* representations that are then refined by comparison training.

The results show that the network can learn to attend selectively and isolate sensory dimensions but that it needs explicit comparison training to do so. Learning to label attributes is not sufficient for the perceptual isolation of properties. Importantly, comparison training as realized in this network is not sufficient either. The perceptual isolation of attributes cannot be learned by learning property–property maps alone because the use of one input as a target for the other (i.e., the task of making the two patterns

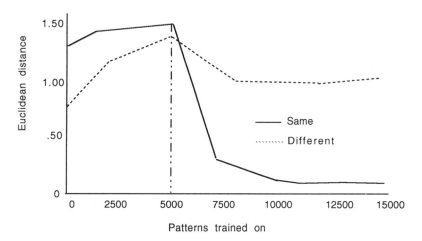

Fig. 9.   The Euclidean distance between patterns of activation on the hidden layer for pairs of inputs same on the queried dimension (*solid line*) or different on the queried dimension (*dashed line*) as a function of training patterns in the Incremental training regimen of simulation 2. Comparison training introduced after 5000 trails.

of activation on the comparison buffer and perceptual layer the same) drives *all* patterns of activation on these two layers to become alike. In a preliminary simulation in which we trained the network only in the comparison of objects, we found that after 2500 input patterns, the Euclidean distance between all inputs (whether the same or different on the relevant dimension) was lessn than .03. Thus, training to label attributes alone is insufficient *and* training in comparison alone is insufficient. Success requires the formation of multiple mappings through the same connection weights; training in word–property maps, word–word maps, and property–property maps. Apparently, learning attribute labels keeps the patterns of activations on the perceptual layer sufficiently different for lexically different attributes and comparison training along linguistically specified dimensions enables the network to isolate the common property.

In sum, the network learned to attend selectively to sensory dimensions by learning about linguistic dimensions; that is, by learning to name attributes and by finding what is alike about objects that are said to be the same on a nameable dimension. In the final simulation, we ask whether the network can learn to isolate attributes on dimensions that are not directly given in the sensory input.

## VI. Simulation 3: Creating A New Dimension

In the previous two experiments, the network was asked to discover sensory dimensions—to abstract what was common in the input description of individual objects. The network discovered sensory dimensions and learned to attend selectively to them by learning linguistic dimensions. In a sense, the network learned to "map" linguistic dimensions onto sensory dimensions. This was accomplished, however, not by gaining direct access to the sensory dimensions which are compressed at the perceptual level but by reconstructing them. Thus the question of this experiment: If the network can reconstruct sensory dimensions, can it also discover and perceptually isolate dimensions that are not simple sensory dimensions? This is important question because people appear to be able to learn new dimensions (Thibault & Schyns, 1995; Goldstone, 1995), and to talk about dimensions that do not directly correspond to the features and dimensions that are independent at early stages of sensory processing.

Accordingly, in this final simulation, we taught the network to label attributes and make comparisons on a dimension that did not correspond to any sensory dimension.

A.  METHOD

The network was the same as that used in simulations 1 and 2 except for two changes: (a) objects were specified along five sensory dimensions, and

(b) the linguistic input specified four linguistic dimensions. Each sensory dimension was organized as in simulations 1 and 2. The network was taught 12 attribute labels. Three labels referred to values on sensory dimension 1 and were associated with linguistic dimension 1; three attribute labels referred to values on sensory dimension 2 and were associated with linguistic dimension 2, and two attribute labels referred to values on sensory dimension 3 and were associated with linguistic dimension 3. We call the potentially isolatable dimensions that correspond to the sensory dimensions, Simple Dimensions. The range of values on each of these sensory dimensions named by each attribute term was 20% of the dimension. Thus, some portion of possible values on each dimension were not specifically labeled.

Four of the attribute labels, in contrast, were defined in terms of values on sensory dimensions 4 and 5 and were associated with a single linguistic dimension, linguistic dimension 5. Each of the attribute terms on this Complex Dimension was defined as a point along and near a linear relation between sensory dimensions 4 and 5. Specifically, values on the complex dimension were constrained as follows:

$$.8 < \text{sensory dimension 4} + \text{sensory dimension 5} < 1.0$$

and the four attributes were defined as ranges of values within these contraints. In the possible space of all visual inputs along the five sensory dimensions, this inequality defines a complex dimension with a rectangular shape. Each of the four complex attributes refers to a subregion that is 20% of the complex dimension. That is, there were boundary regions between attributes that were not labeled.

The training procedure was identical to that used in the Attributes-then-Comparison condition of simulation 2.

## 2. Results and Discussion

Figure 10 shows the performance of the network in the task of labeling attributes: the four dimensions as a function of training trials. The dotted vertical line indicates the point at which comparison training was introduced; that is, the point at which the network was asked to discover what the same about two objects that were labeled as same on a specific dimension. As is apparent, prior to the introduction of the comparison task, the network readily learned to label *all* the attributes—those on the Simple and those on the Complex dimension.

As is also apparent in Fig. 10, performance declines somewhat when the comparison training is introduced as when the network is asked to discover what is the same about two objects that are the *same on a dimension,* but as in Simulation 2, it returns to near perfect performance. Performance on

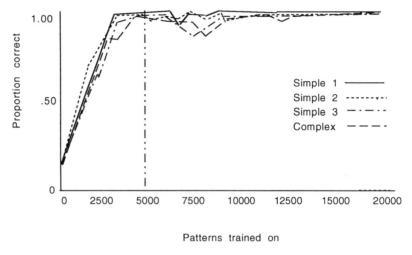

Patterns trained on

Fig. 10.   Proportion correct responses in the attribute labeling condition under the Incremental training regimen for the three Simple dimensions that correspond to sensory dimensions and for the Complex dimension. Comparison training was introduced after the first 5000 trials.

the complex dimension appears no different at this point than performance on the simple dimensions.

Figure 11 shows performance in the selective attention task for each dimension. The dependent measure is the distance between patterns of activation on the perceptual layer for visual inputs that are the same on the relevant dimension (and different on the others) or are different on the relevant dimension and the same on all others. Notice first the performance prior to the introduction of Comparison training. At this point, the network accurately labels attributes on all four dimensions. But for none of them does this correct labeling mean the perceptual isolation of the labeled attribute. *And,* for the complex dimension, the correct labeling occurs without a discretely localized representation of the dimension or its attributes *anywhere* in the network. This clearly shows how the outward behavior of a system may be a very poor guide to the internal processes that make that behavior.

However, the network did learn to attend selectively—to isolate what is common—given comparison training; and it did so for all four dimensions. Again, performance on the complex dimension is as good as performance on the best simple dimensions. The patterns of activation at the perceptual layer for objects that share a value on the relevant dimension are, at the end of training, considerably more similar than the patterns of activation for inputs that are different on the relevant dimension.

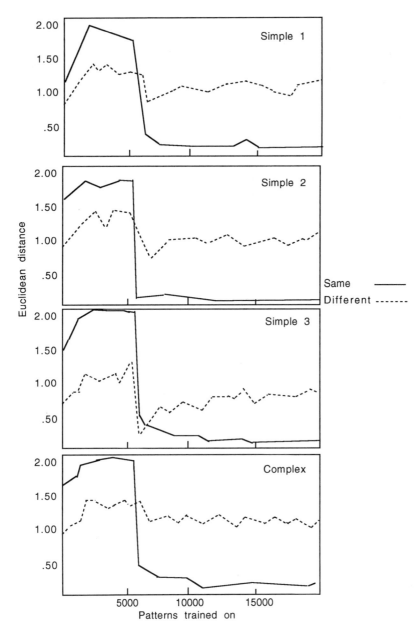

Fig. 11.  The Euclidean distance between patterns of activation on the hidden layer for pairs of inputs same on the queried dimension (*solid line*) or different on the queried dimension (*dashed line*) as a function of training patterns in the Incremental training regimen of simulation 3 for the three Simple and one Complex dimensions. Comparison training introduced after 5000 trials.

These results show that the network can learn to name attributes and attend selectively to a dimension that does not correspond to a single sensory dimensions as well as it can learn about sensory dimensions. Isolatable dimensions can be created that have no a priori existence in the system.

A final aspect of these results, like those in simulation 2, points again to how the outward behavior of a complex network need not reflect the same underlying processes. Prior to training in the explicit comparison task, the network outputs attributes labels accurately and often comparison training, the network still outputs attribute labels correctly, but the network's similar outward behavior in the two cases is based on radically different "representations." Moreover, the shift from one form of representation to another is only discernible in what are quite small and transient disruptions in the labeling of attributes. Further, in this experiment, the network learned to label attributes on simple and complex dimensions in comparable ways with nothing in its patterns of outputs to indicate that some attribute terms label values on the sensory "primitives," whereas others label values on complex learned dimensions.

## VII.  Developmental Implications

This chapter began with the developmental evidence on children's slow acquisition of dimensional terms and their difficulties in selective attention tasks. Our model provides new insights by showing how dimensions may exist at multiple noncorresponding levels, by showing how language learning involves learning a system of mappings between these levels, and by showing how jointly learning these mappings may create perceptual dimensions.

### A.  THE STARTING POINT IS WHOLISTIC PERCEPTION

The starting point for our developmental account is the wholistic compression of the sensory dimensions by the hidden layer, the layer we take as corresponding to subjective experience. The theoretical idea is that learning dimensional adjectives is hard because the system is structured to perceive objects as unitary wholes. This aspect of our model fits Markman's (1989) proposal about a "whole-object" bias in early word learning. She explains children's special difficulties in learning dimensional adjectives in terms of constraints on their initial hypotheses about possible word meanings. She proposed that young children first learning words assume that those words refer to individual whole objects rather than to the component properties of objects. This is a learning principle that promotes the acquisition of nouns because objects in the same nominal category are typically similar across many interrelated and correlated properties (e.g., Markman, 1989; Rosch & Mervis, 1975). Our network with its compression of sensory dimensions provides a mechanistic implementation of the whole-object assumption. In other works, we have shown that this network, like young children, is biased to learn noun meanings and that it learns nominal categories organized across many dimensions more rapidly than it learns dimensional-adjective categories (Gasser & Smith, in press).

What the present model adds to Markman's original idea is the further proposal that children must actually construct perceptual dimensions and that they do so through learning language. The developmental evidence has suggested this possibility to others (Bruner, 1957; Kendler, 1979; Gentner & Rattermann, 1991; Kotovsky & Gentner, 1996; Smith & Kemler, 1978; Smith, 1984; Smith, 1989). The present results demonstrate that such learning could occur.

Our network with its wholistic compression of sensory dimensions contrasts with a well-known model of dimensional learning in the adult literature—Kruschke's (1992) ALCOVE model. ALCOVE retains the separateness of distinct sensory dimensions across layers in the network by utilizing dimensionally distinct learning weights. ALCOVE thus instantiates the ideas depicted in Fig. 1: the same dimensions from the bottom of the system to the top. ALCOVE has not been applied to developmental phenomena but learning by this network fits well the pattern of adult learning in many simple categorization tasks (e.g., learning to classify a small set of instances into two mutually exclusive groups). In these tasks, ALCOVE, like adults, rapidly learns categories organized by one dimension. In brief, ALCOVE models well the end-state structure, how category learning works after separate dimensions are formed.

The question is whether ALCOVE can be made to fit the developmental data? One possible way is make changes in dimension weights as a function of training more sluggish such that the network continues to distribute attention across all dimensions longer through the learning process. Without actual simulations, it is difficult to know how much of the developmental evidence could be adequately captured by this approach. However, even if such an approach did work, ALCOVE would still offer no explanation of the noncorrespondence of the dimensions we talk about and those defined by sensory psychologists, no explanation of perceptual learning that creates new dimensions and properties, and no explanation of the variability in dimensional terms across languages.

## B. SEPARABLE DIMENSIONS AND SELECTIVE ATTENTION

The classic definition of a psychological dimension is context independency: judgments of one dimension should be independent of values on other dimension (e.g., Boring, 1933). Thus, Garner (1974) defined experientially separable dimensions as those that afforded (near) perfect selective attention to one dimension at time. This is the same benchmark we required of our network. This benchmark was achieved late in learning by the network and required more by way of training than merely learning categories well organized by one dimension. Dimensional separability by Garner's definitions also develops quite late in children (e.g., Smith & Kemler, 1978). Thus, again, the course of developments by the model mimics that observed in children.

One could argue, however, that the benchmark of perfect selective attention is too high. By this view, the network and children could be said to attend selectively to and "have" dimensions earlier; the only problem is that they selectively attend imperfectly. In order to label attribute categories, the network must have learned something about the attributes. It must have formed a partition of patterns of activation such that patterns turning on different outputs were on different sides of the partition. The problem is what evidence should count as indicating psychological dimensions. If the criteria for defining a dimension is independence from other dimensions, then imperfect selective attention would seem the product of partially created dimensions.

C.  DIFFERENT DIMENSIONS AT DIFFERENT LEVELS

A central claim of in our account is that dimensions exist at multiple levels: there are, initially, sensory dimensions that code the physical input and linguistic dimensions that organize dimensional adjectives. Perceptual dimensions are constructed, we propose, by learning multiple mappings between and within these levels. This idea of different dimensions at different levels helps explain some peculiarities in the developmental literature. The most important is the evidence purporting to show that infants can do what young children cannot: selectively attend to dimensions.

The evidence for selective attention to dimensions in infants derives from habituation studies (e.g., Cohen & Oakes, 1993; Fantz, 1963; Bornstein, 1985; Coldren & Colombo, 1994). In these studies, infants are shown repeated examples of objects that are alike on some dimension but vary on a second dimension. For example, as illustrated in Fig. 12, infants might be repeatedly shown red squares, red circles, and red triangles until looking at these objects declines. After habituation, the infant is presented with test trials. For example, infants might be shown an object that differed on the previously constant (relevant) dimension but which matches one of the exemplars on another (irrelevant) dimension: e.g., a green square. Or infants might be shown at this point an object that matches the exemplers on the

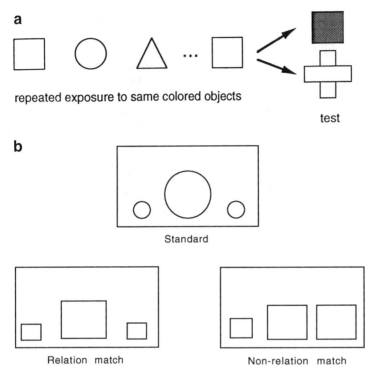

Fig. 12. (A) A series of possible stimuli in a habituation study. (B) Illustration of a possible stimulus set in Kotovsky and Gentner's experiment.

relevant dimension but differs from them on another dimension, e.g., a red cross. An increase in looking time to a test object suggests discrimination of that object from the habituation exemplars. The standard result is that infants look longer at test objects that differ on the relevant dimension (i.e., the green square in the example) than ones that differ on an irrelevant dimension (i.e., the red cross in the example). These results suggest selective attention to the relevant dimension (color) and the ignoring of irrelevant properties.

Two kinds of accounts have been offered of young children's difficulties in the face of infants successful selective attention. Several investigators (Smith, 1989; Aslin & Smith, 1988; Coldren & Colombo, 1994) take the data at face value and conclude that because infants can attend selectively to dimensions, then there must be a fixed and universal set of dimensions that structure perceptual experience. In this view, preschool children fail to attend selectively for other reasons. Noting the close relationship between the acquisition of dimensional language and successful selective attention. Coldren and Colombo went so far as to suggest that preschool children *lose* their ability to attend selectively because they are initially confused by dimensional language. This and the various other explanations of children's failure to attend selectively in terms of a failure to selectively attend are all unsatisfying in their circularity.

Kemler (1982), in contrast, argued that the infant data do not show what they seem to show. She correctly pointed out that the infant data do not conclusively demonstrate *perfect* selective attention to dimensions, which is the benchmark of dimensional separability in adults and the benchmark that young children fail to meet. Kemler argued that the same pattern of habituation-dishabituation could emerge given psychologically arbitrary (that is made-up) dimensions. Her point is that selective dishabituation does not guarantee preexisting internally represented dimensions. This idea is supported by our findings that the selective naming of red things *red* does not guarantee the abstraction of redness from other properties.

Our model also suggests a third account. Infants and preschool children's "dimensional" judgments may not conform because they do tap into dimensions at the same level. Habituation studies may measure sensory dimensions, whereas speeded classification and comparison tasks may measure perceptual dimensions. There may be no single sense of dimension that applies in all tasks and from the bottom to the top of the cognitive system.

Clearly, what is needed is a unified mechanistic account of selective habituation to dimensions in infancy, the learning of dimensional words, and the development of selective attention. These present simulations make a start in this direction.

### D.   DIMENSIONS ARE MADE THROUGH MULTIPLE MAPPINGS

The network learned mappings between questions asked about objects and classes of possible answers, it learned mappings between words and object properties, and it learned mappings between the internal representations of pairs of objects and a linguistic description of their relatedness. *All* of these mappings appear essential to the construction of perceptual dimensions, but none are sufficient. The task is not solvable without word–word maps from inputs to outputs. Without such maps, the network cannot know, given a big red smooth thing, whether it is to attend to red or smooth or big. Isolated perceptual dimensions cannot be formed from object-word maps. Rather, perceptual dimensions require comparison and explicit learning of property–property maps. Perceptual dimensions, however, cannot be formed by comparison alone. Gains from comparison must be bootstrapped on the prior learning of attributes categories.

This bootstrapping relation between comparison and category learning is reminiscent of Karmiloff-Smith's (1986) ideas about "re-representation." She proposed that earlier representations, often with the help of langauge, are compared to one another and re-represented in more abstract and context-free form. Our network offers one instantiation of how this might happen: The explicit comparison of two objects both called *red* encourages the re-presentation of redness as a discrete entity divorced from size or texture or other aspects of the whole object.

The importance of the comparison process has also been argued by Gentner and colleagues (Gentner & Rattermann, 1991; Kotovsky & Gentner, 1996). They also report relevant evidence. In one study, Kotovsky and Gentner examined children's ability to match patterns such as those shown in Fig. 12. Given the standard shown at the top, the child's task was to choose which of the bottom two patterns "was like" the top ones. This is a very hard task for preschool children. Kotovsky and Gentner found that children's performances were helped by teaching them labels for the relations. For example, the experimenter pointed to the matching endpoints and told the children that the exemplar won because it was "even." Children were trained on a set in which only the size varied and then successfully transfered to sets that demanded more difficult pattern matches. Kotovsky and Gentner concluded that repeated comparisons of objects said to be "even," enabled children to abstract the relevant relation.

### E.  LANGUAGE HELPS MAKE DIMENSIONS

In the simulations presented here, langauge is a strong force shaping perceptual dimensions. Is the implication, then, that language is necessary for the perceptual isolation of dimensions? Language is not logically necessary; the simulations show that. A learning task in which the inputs and outputs were not words but other contexts and other responses could accomplish the same set of mappings.

Experiments with nonhuman animals also suggest that the key is the system of mappings and not language per se. Many experiments in this literature demonstrate the acquisition and generalization of attribute categories—categories demanding the same response to objects alike in a particular way (e.g., Rescorla & Wagner, 1972; MacIntosh, 1965). There are fewer experiments that clearly demonstrate comparison training (see Premack, 1976, for a discussion). One comparison task, however, that has been widely used is matching-to-sample. In this task, the animal is presented with three objects and must find the two objects in a set of three that are the same. Experimentally, this task is accomplished by training the animal to select the two objects that are the same (or, alternatively, the one that is odd). The empirical question is whether the animal can learn to make the appropriate response over a diverse set of objects and then transfer that response to new instances. Such transfer implicates the learning of an abstract relation independent of the specific stimulus properties.

This task is like our explicit comparison task in that it asks the animal to find out what is the same about pairs of objects. And, it is a difficult one for many species, requiring many, many trials and even then transfer to new instances is not certain (e.g., Premack, 1978; Santiago & Wright, 1984). The very difficulty of this task supports our conclusion that explicit judgments of sameness require much more by way of internal representations than does mere categorization and response generalization. However, the fact that organisms without language *can* learn this matching-to-sample task suggests that language may not be *necessary* for the perceptual isolation and representation of abstract relations (see, especially, Oden, Thompson, & Premack, 1988).

Still, it may be that for children, language is the natural driving force behind the development of perceptual dimensions.

## VIII.   The Nontransparency of Mechanism

It is commonplace in psychological theorizing to impute to internal workings a "copy" of externally observed behavior (Smith & Thelen, 1993). Thus, sucking in infants is commonly explained by a sucking reflex, the alternate pattern of walking by a central pattern generator, categorization by represented categories, and syntax by an innate grammar. In each case, an abstract and sometimes truly elegant icon of the behavior to be explained is proposed to be the mechanism that produces the behavior. In cognitive psychology, this is particularly true when the behavior explained is verbal. Indeed, people's statements about their own cognitions have been argued to be the best windows on underlying category representation (Gelman & Coley, 1991; Keil, 1989). Moreover, one paradigm that has been used to study the relevant features for object categorization consists of *asking* people what the features are (e.g., Tversky, 1989; Rosch & Mervis, 1975; Malt, 1994; Rips, 1989). This, of course, is a far from foolproof method: The properties and features that people talk about could, in fact, have *no* localized internal representation as components. This point has also been empirically demonstrated by Schyns (1993). They showed that two groups of subjects could learn the very same three categories and perform equivalently in categorization tasks but have very different underlying representations. More specifically, the feature vocabularies defining contrasting categories varied qualitatively with the order in which the categories had been learned. Learning the same three categories in different order created qualitatively distinct feature vocabularies that affected subsequent learning and judgments. In brief, categorizations by the subjects in this experiment were misleading indicators of the perceptual representations. The structure of outwardly observable behavior does not map in simple ways to the structure of the underlying mechanisms that make that behavior.

The nontransparency of mechanism is also demonstrated in the present work by the emergent and distributed nature of dimensional knowledge. Consider what the network knew about dimensions at the end of simulations 2 and 3. It knew, for example, what is the same about all red things. It knew that red and blue are attributes of the same kind, a kind different from that of big. It knew that *red* and *blue* are both possible answers to the question *What color is that?* and that *big* is not. All this knowledge was manifest in the collective behavior of the network. However, none of these bits of knowledge are located in any one place in the network. Rather, the system of dimensional knowledge displayed by the network is the emergent result of multiple mappings that overlap and constrain each other.

## IX.  Conclusion

The idea of perceptual dimensions as the primitive atoms of experience has figured prominently in the study of cognition (Berlin & Kay, 1969; Heider & Oliver, 1972; Lakoff, 1987; Miller & Johnson-Laird, 1976). The reason is clear. If perceptual dimensions are fixed and universal, then perception is a bedrock on which language, knowledge, and truth can be built. If, in contrast, what is perceived and therefore what is knowable from one's own interactions with the world and, from the language one learns, then there is no single truth. What is knowable is relative. This is a conclusion we may have to accept. The dimensions that structure our conscious experience of the world are themselves the product of experience.

### ACKNOWLEDGMENTS

This research was supported by NIH grant HD28675 to Smith and by a Multidisciplinary Grant from Indiana University to Gasser and Smith. We thank Rob Goldstone, Doug Medin, Terry Regier, and Philippe Schyns for comments on a previous version.

### REFERENCES

Aslin, R. N., & Smith, L. B. (1988). Perceptual development. In M. R. Rosenweig & L. W. Porter (Eds.), *Annual Review of Psychology, 39,* 435–474.

Backscheider, G. A., & Shatz, M. (1993, April). Children's acquisition of the lexical domain of color. Twenty-ninth regional meeting of the Chicago Linguistics Society, Chicago.

Bates, E., Benigni, L., Bretherton, I., Camaioni, L., & Volterra, V. (1979). *The emergency of symbols.* New York: Academic Press.

Berlin, B. D., & Kay, P. (1969). *Basic color terms, their universality and evolution.* Berkeley, CA: University of California Press.

Binet, A. (1980). Perceptions d'enfants. *Revue Philosphique, 30,* 582–611.

Boring, E. G. (1933). *The physical dimension of consciousness.* New York: Century.

Boring, E. G. (1942). *Sensation and perception in the history of experimental psychology.* New York: Irvington Publishers.

Bornstein, M. H. (1985). Colour-name versus shape-name learning in young children. *Journal of Child Language, 12,* 387–393.

Bruner, J. S. (1957). *Ongoing beyond the information given.* Cambridge, MA: Harvard University Press.

Callahan, M. A. (1990). Parent's description of objects: Potential data for children's inferences about category principles. *Cognitive Development, 5,* 101–122.

Carey, S. (1978). The child as a word learner. In M. Haller, J. Brenan, & G. Miller (Eds.), *Linguistic theory and psychological reality.* Cambridge, MA: MIT Press.

Carey, S. (1982). Semantic development. The state of the art. In E. Wanner & L. R. Gleitman (Eds.), *Language acquisition: The state of the art,* New York: Cambridge University Press.

Carnap, R. (1967). *The logical structure of the world and pseudoproblems in philosophy.* Berkeley, CA: University of California Press. (Original work published in 1928).

Clark, E. V. (1973). What's in a word: On the child's acquisition of semantics in his first language. In T. E. Moore (Ed.), *Cognitive development and the acquisition of language.* New York: Academic Press.

Cohen, L. B., & Oakes, L. M. (1993). How infants perceive a simple causal event. *Developmental Psychology, 29,* 421–444.

Coldren, J. T., & Colombo, J. (1994). The nature and processes of proverbial learning: Implications from nine-month-old infants' discrimination problem solving. *Monographs of the Society for Research in Child Development, 59*(4), vii-75.

Cruse, D. A. (1977). A note on the learning of colour names. *Journal of Child Language. 4,* 305–311.

Donaldson, M., & Wales, R. J. (1970). On the acquisition of some relational terms. In J. R. Hayes (Ed.), *Cognition and the development of language* (pp. 235–268). New York: Wiley.

Dromi, E. (1987). *Early lexical development.* New York: Cambridge University Press.

Ehri, L. (1976). Comprehension and production of adjectives and seriation. *Journal of Child Language, 3,* 369–384.

Fantz, R. L. (1963). Pattern vision in newborn infants. *Science, 140,* 296–297.

Freyd, J. (1983). The mental representation of movement when static stimuli are viewed. *Perception & Psychophysics, 33,* 575–581.

Garner, W. R. (1974). *The processing of information and structure.* Potomac, MD: Erlbaum.

Gasser, M. S., & Smith, L. B. (in press). Learning nouns and adjectives: A connectionist account. *Language and Cognitive Processes.*

Gelman, S. A., & Coley, J. D. (1991). Language and categorization. The acquisition of natural kind terms. In S. A. Gelman & J. P. Byrnes (Eds.), *Perspectives on language and thought: Interrelations in development* (pp. 146–196). Cambridge, MA: Cambridge University Press.

Gentner, D., & Rattermann, M. J. (1991). Language and the career of similarity. In S. A. Gelman & J. P. Byrnes (Eds.), *Perspectives on thought and language: Interrelations in development.* Cambridge, MA: Cambridge University Press.

Gibson, J. J. (1966). *The senses considered as perceptual systems.* Boston: Houghton-Mifflin.

Goldstone, R. L. (1995). Effects of categorization on color perception. *Psychological Science, 6*(5), 298–304.

Halff, H. M., Ortony, A., & Anderson, R. C. (1976). A context-sensitive representation of word meanings. *Memory & Cognition, 4*(4), 378–383.

Harnad, S., Hanson, S. J., & Lubin, J. (1991, March). Categorical perception and the evolution of unsupervised learning in neural nets. AAAI Spring symposium on Symbol Gounding: Problem and Practice, Stanford, CA.

Heider, E. R., & Olivier, D. C. (1972). The structure of color space in naming and memory for two languages. *Cognitive Psychology, 3,* 337–354.

Hurvich, L. M., & Jameson, D. (1957). An opponent-process theory of color vision. *Psychological Review, 64,* 384–404.

Husaim, J., & Cohen, L. (1981). Infant learning of ill-defined categories. *Merrill-Palmer Quarterly, 27,* 443–456.

Jackson-Maldonado, D., Thal, D., Marchman, V., & Bates, E. (1993). Early lexical development in Spanish-speaking infants and toddlers. *Journal of Child Language, 20,* 523–549.

James, W. (1890/1950). *The principles of psychology, Vol. 1.* New York: Dover Publications.

Karmiloff-Smith, A. (1986). From metaprocesses to conscious access: Evidence from children's metalinguistic and repair data. *Cognition, 23,* 95–147.

Kay, P., & Kempton, W. (1984). What is the Sapir-Whorf hypothesis? *American Anthropologists, 86,* 65–79.

Keil, F., & Carroll, J. (1980). The child's acquisition of "tall": Implications for an alternative view of semantic development. *Papers and reports on child language development, 19,* 21–28.

Keil, F. C. (1989). *Concepts, kinds, and cognitive development.* Cambridge, MA: Cambridge University Press.

Kemler, G. G. (1982). The ability for dimensional analysis in preschool and retarded children: Evidence from comparison, conservation, and prediction tasks. *Journal of Experimental Child Psychology, 34,* 469–489.

Kendler, T. S. (1979). Cross-sectional research, longitudinal theory, and discriminative transfer ontogeny. *Human Development, 22,* 235–254.

Kotovsky, L., & Gentner, D. (1996). Progressive alignment: A mechanism for the development of relational similarity. *Child Development, 67,* 2797–2822.

Kruschke, J. K. (1992). ALCOVE: An exemplar-based connectionist model for category learning. *Psychological Review, 99,* 22–44.

Locke, J. (1964). *An essay concerning human understanding.* New York: World Publishing.

MacIntosh, N. J. (1965). Selective attention in animal discrimination learning. *Psychological Bulletin, 64,* 125–150.

Malt, B. C. (1994). Water is not $H_2O$. *Cognitive Psychology, 27,* 41–70.

Markman, E. M. (1989). *Categorization and naming in children: Problems of induction.* Cambridge, MA: MIT Press.

Marks, L. E., Hammeal, R. J. & Bornstein, M. H. (1987). Perceiving similarity and comprehending metaphor. *Monographs of the Society for Research in Child Development, 51,* (1, Serial No. 215).

Marks, L. E., Szczesiul, R., & Ohlott, P. J. (1986). On the cross-modal perception of intensity. *Journal of Experimental Psychology: Human Perception and Performance, 21,* 517–534.

Melara, R. D., & Mounts, J. R. W. (1994). Contextual influences on interactive processing: Effects of discriminability, quantity, and uncertainty. *Perception and Psychophysics, 56,* 73–90.

Mervis, C. B. (1987). Child-basic object categories and lexical development. In U. Neisser (Ed.), *Concepts and conceptual development: Ecological and intellectual factors in categorization.* Cambridge, England: Cambridge University Press.

Miller, G. A., & Johnson-Laird, P. N. (1976). *Language and perception.* Cambridge, MA: Harvard University Press.

Nelson, K. (1973). Structure and strategy in learning to talk. *Monographs of the Society for Research in Child Development, 38,* (1-2, serial no. 149).

Oden, D. L., Thompson, R. K., & Premack, D. (1988). Spontaneous transfer of matching by infant chimpanzees (*Pan troglodytes*). *Journal of Experimental Psychology: Animal Behavior Processes, 14,* 140–145.

Premack, D. (1976). *Intelligence in ape and man.* Hillsdale, NJ: Erlbaum.

Rescorla, R. A., & Wagner, A. R. (1972). A theory of Pavlovian conditioning: Variations in the effectiveness of reinforcement and non-reinforcement. In A. H. Black & W. F. Prokasy (Eds.), *Classical Conditioning (Vol II).* New York: Appleton-Century-Crofts.

Rice, M. (1980). *Cognition to language categories: Word, meaning and training.* Baltimore: University Park Press.

Rips, L. J. (1989). Similarly, typicality, and categorization. In S. Vosniadou & A. Ortony (Eds.), *Similarity and analogical reasoning* (pp. 21–59). Cambridge, England: Cambridge University Press.

Rosch, E., & Mervis, C. B. (1975). Family resemblances: Studies in the internal structure of categories. *Cognitive Psychology, 7,* 573–605.

Sandhofer, C. M., & Smith, L. B. (1996, November). *Learning a system of mappings: The acquisition of color terms.* Paper presented at the meeting of the Conference on Language Development, Boston, MA.

Sanocki, T. (1991). Intra- and interpattern relations in letter recognition. *Journal of Experimental Psychology: Human Perception and Performance.* 17(4), 924–941.

Sanocki, T. (1992). Effects of font- and letter-specific experience on the perceptual processing of letters. *American Journal of Psychology, 105*(3), 435–458.

Santiago, H. C., & Wright, A. A. (1984). Pigeon memory: *Same/different* concept learning, erial probe recognition acquisition, and probe delay effects recognition acquisition. *Journal of Experimental Psychology: Animal Behavior Processes, 10,* 498–512.

Schachter, P. (1986). Parts of speech systems. In T. Shopen (Ed.), *Language typology and syntactic description. Vol. 1. Clause structure.* Cambridge, MA: Cambridge University Press.

Schyns, P. (1993) Toward a theory of the development of primitives of representation in object categorization. Ph.D. Dissertation, Brown University.

Schyns, P. G., Goldstone, R. L., & Thibaut, J. P. (in press). *The development of features in object concepts. Brain and Behavioral Sciences*

Smith, L., & Sera, M. (1992). A developmental analysis of the polar structure of dimensions. *Cognitive Psychology, 24,* 99–142.

Smith, L. B., & Kemler, D. G. (1978). Levels of experienced dimensionality in children and adults. *Cognitive Psychology, 10,* 502–532.

Smith, L. B. (1984). Young children's understanding of attributes and dimensions: A comparison of conceptual and linguistic measures. *Child Development, 55,* 363–380.

Smith, L. B. (1993). The concept of same. *Advances in child development and behavior, 24,* 216–253.

Smith, L. B., & Evans, P. (1989). Similarly, identity, and dimensions: Perceptual classification in children and adults. In B. E. Shepp & S. Ballesteros (Eds.), *Object perception: Structure and process.* Hillsdale, NJ: Erlbaum.

Smith, L. B., & Thelen, E. (1993). Can dynamic systems theory be usefully applied in areas other than motor development? In L. B. Smith & E. Thelen (Eds.), *A dynamic systems approach to development: Applications* (pp. 151–170). Cambridge, MA: MIT Press.

Smith, L. B. (1989). From global similarities to kinds of similarities. The construction of dimensions in development. In S. Vosniadou & A. Ortony (Eds.), *Similarity and analogy*, (Pp. 146–178). Cambridge University Press

Snow, C. E. (1977). The development of conversation between mothers and babies. *Journal of Child Language, 4*, 1–22.

Stern, C., & Stern, W. (1924/1981). Die Kindersprache: einer psychologische und sprachtheoretische Untersuchung. Darmstadt: Wissenschaftliche Buchgesellschaft.

Thibaut, J-P., & Schyns, P. G. (1993). The development of feature spaces for similarity and categorization. *Psychologica Belgica, 35*, 167–185.

Tomasello, M., & Kruger, A. C. (1992). Joint attention on actions: Acquiring verbs in ostensive and non-ostensive contexts. *Journal of Child Language, 19*, 311–333.

Treisman, A., & Gelade, G. (1980). A feature integration theory of attention. *Cognitive Psychology, 12*, 93–136.

Tversky, B. (1989). Parts, partonomies, and taxonomies. *Developmental Pscyhology, 25*, 983–995.

Werner, H. (1957). The concept of development from a comparative and organismic point of view. In D. B. Harris (Ed.), *The concept of development* (pp. 125–148). Minneapolis, MN: University of Minnesota Press.

Wohlwill, J. (1962). From perception to inference: A dimension of cognitive development. *Monographs of the Society for Research in Child Development, 72*, 87–107.

Wood, D. J. (1980). Teaching the young child. Some relationships between social interaction, language, and thought. In D. R. Olson (Ed.), *The Social foundations of language and thought.* New York: Norton.

Woodward, A. L., Markman, E., & Fitzsimmons, C. M. (1994). Rapid word learning in 13- and 18-month-olds. *Developmental Psychology, 30*, 553–566.

# SELF-ORGANIZATION, PLASTICITY, AND LOW-LEVEL VISUAL PHENOMENA IN A LATERALLY CONNECTED MAP MODEL OF THE PRIMARY VISUAL CORTEX

*Risto Miikkulainen*
*James A. Bednar*
*Yoonsuck Choe*
*Joseph Sirosh*

## I. Introduction

The primary visual cortex, like many other regions of the neocortex, is a topographic map, organized so that adjacent neurons respond to adjacent regions of the visual field. In addition, neurons are responsive to particular features in the input, such as lines of a particular orientation or ocularity. All neurons in a vertical column in the cortex typically have the same feature preferences. Vertical groups of neurons with the same orientation preference are called orientation (OR) columns and vertical groups with the same eye preference are called ocular dominance (OD) columns. The feature preferences gradually vary across the surface of the cortex in characteristic spatial patterns that constitute the cortical maps.

Cortical maps are shaped by visual experience. Altering the visual environment can drastically change the organization of OD and OR columns (Hubel & Wiesel, 1962, 1968, 1974; Hubel, Wiesel, & LeVay, 1977). The animal is most susceptible during a critical period of early life, typically a few weeks. For example, if a kitten is raised with both eyes sutured shut, the

THE PSYCHOLOGY OF LEARNING
AND MOTIVATION, VOL. 36

cortex does not develop a normal organization, and OD and OR columns do not form. Even if the eye is opened after a few weeks, the animal remains blind, even though the eye and the lateral geniculate nucleus (LGN) are perfectly normal. Similarly, if kittens are raised in environments containing only vertical or horizontal contours, their ability to see other orientations suffers significantly. In the cortex, most cells develop preferences for these particular orientations, and do not respond well to the other orientations (Hirsch & Spinelli, 1970; Blakemore & Cooper, 1970; Blakemore & van Sluyters, 1975). Such experiments indicate that visual inputs are crucial to form a normal cortical organization, and suggest that the cortex tunes itself to the distribution of visual inputs.

The discovery by von der Malsburg (1973; see also Amari, 1980 and Grossberg, 1976) that simple computational rules could drive the development of oriented receptive fields from visual input, raised the hope that much of the structure and development of V1 could be understood in terms of very simple neuronal behavior. However, since then, substantial new discoveries have changed our understanding of the primary visual cortex. New evidence indicates that cells in V1 are coupled by highly specific long-range lateral connections (Gilbert, Hirsch, & Wiesel, 1990; Gilbert & Wiesel, 1983; Schwark & Jones, 1989). These connections are reciprocal and far more numerous than the afferents, and they are believed to have a substantial influence on cortical activity. They grow exuberantly after birth and reach their full extent in a short period. During subsequent development, they get automatically pruned into well-defined clusters. Pruning happens at the same time as the afferent connections organize into topographic maps (Callaway & Katz, 1990, 1991; Burkhalter, Bernardo, & Charles, 1993; Katz & Callaway, 1992; Luhmann, Martínez Millán, & Singer, 1986). The final clustered distribution corresponds closely to the distribution of afferent connections in the map. For example, in the mature visual cortex, lateral connections primarily run between areas with similar response properties, such as neurons with the same orientation or eye preference (Gilbert et al., 1990; Gilbert & Wiesel 1989; Löwel & Singer 1992).

Several observations indicate that the lateral connection structure is not defined genetically, but depends on the visual input: (1) When the primary visual cortex (of the cat) is deprived of visual input during early development, lateral connectivity remains crude and unrefined (Callaway & Katz, 1991). (2) The pattern of lateral connection clusters can be altered by changing the input to the developing cortex. The resulting patterns reflect correlations in the input (Löwel & Singer, 1992). (3) In the mouse somato-sensory barrel cortex, sensory deprivation (by sectioning the input nerve) causes drastic decreases in the extent and density of lateral connections (McCasland, Bernardo, Probst, & Woolsey, 1992). These observations suggest that the development of lateral connections, like that of afferent connections, depends on cortical activity driven by external input.

New discoveries have also changed the notion that the afferent structures and lateral connections are essentially static after a critical period of early development. Recent results show that the adult cortex can undergo significant, often reversible, reorganization in response to various sensory and cortical manipulations such as lesions in the receptive surface and the cortex (Gilbert, 1992; Kaas, 1991; Merzenich, Recanzone, Jenkins, & Grajski, 1990; Kapadia, Gilbert, & Westheimer, 1994; Pettet & Gilbert 1992).

Based on the above results, a new theory of the visual cortex has started to emerge. The cortex appears to be a continuously adapting structure in a dynamic equilibrium with both the external and intrinsic input. This equilibrium is maintained by cooperative and competitive lateral interactions within the cortex, mediated by lateral connections (Gilbert et al., 1990). The afferent and lateral connection patterns develop synergetically and simultaneously, based on the same underlying process. The primary function of the afferent and lateral structures is to form a sparse, redundancy-reduced encoding of the visual input (Barlow, 1972; Field, 1994). By integrating information over large portions of the cortex, lateral connections assist in grouping simple features into perceptual objects (Singer, Gray, Engel, König, Artola, & Bröcher, 1990; von der Malsburg & Singer, 1988), and may be responsible for low-level visual phenomena such as tilt illusions and aftereffects.

The exact mechanisms of such self-organization, plasticity, and function are still not completely understood. Computational models can play a fundamental role in this research. With the advent of massively parallel computers in the last 5 years, it has become possible to simulate large numbers of neural units and their connections. At the same time, neurobiological techniques for mapping the response properties and connectivity of neurons have become sophisticated enough to constrain and validate such models. This technological confluence provides a timely opportunity to test hypotheses about cortical mechanisms through large-scale computational experiments.

One of the most powerful computational abstractions of biological learning is the Hebb rule (Gustafsson & Wigström, 1988; Hebb, 1949), where synaptic efficacies are adjusted based on coincident pre- and postsynaptic activity. If two neurons are active at the same time, their connection is deemed useful and is strengthened. Hebbian learning is usually coupled with normalization so that the efficacies do not grow without bounds but only their relative strengths change (Miller, 1994b). A network of such units and connections may develop a globally ordered structure where units represent specific inputs, such as lines of different orientations. Such a process is called self-organization: There is no global supervisor directing the process, but learning is based on a local rule and driven by the input.

Several computational models have already shown how receptive fields and their global organization in the cortical network can develop through Hebbian self-organization of afferent synapses (Erwin, Obermayer, & Schulten, 1995; Goodhill, 1993; Kohonen, 1982; Miller, 1994a; Miller, Keller, & Stryker, 1989; Obermayer, Ritter, & Schulten, 1990b; von der Malsburg, 1973). Some of these models have also shown that aspects of cortical plasticity, such as remapping of cortical topography following peripheral lesions, can be explained with similar mechanisms (Obermayer, Ritter, & Schulten, 1990a; Ritter, Martinez, & Schulten, 1992). However, these models have not taken the lateral interactions between cells into account, or have assumed that they are preset and fixed and have a regular profile. Therefore, the simultaneous self-organization of lateral connections and afferent structures, and many aspects of cortical plasticity such as reorganization of the map in response to cortical lesions and reshaping of mature receptive fields in response to retinal lesions, cannot be explained by these models.

This article shows that Hebbian self-organization in a large recurrent network of simple neural elements can provide a unified account of self-organization, plasticity, and low-level function in the visual cortex. The model explains computationally (1) how the receptive fields develop selectivity to orientation, ocular dominance, and size, (2) how such receptive fields organize into intertwined columnar areas, (3) how the lateral connections develop synergetically with the afferent connections and follow their global organization, (4) how such structures are maintained in a dynamic equilibrium with the input, resulting in reorganization after retinal and cortical lesions, and (5) how fast adaptation of lateral connections can be responsible for functional phenomena such as tilt aftereffects and segmentation. The model also suggests a functional role for the lateral connections: During development, they learn the activity correlations between cortical neurons, and during visual processing, filter out these correlations from cortical activity to form a redundancy-reduced sparse coding of the visual input.

## II.  The Receptive Field LISSOM (RF-LISSOM) Model

Receptive Field Laterally Interconnected Synergetically Self-Organizing Map (RF-LISSOM; Sirosh, 1995; Sirosh & Miikkulainen, 1994, 1996, 1997; Sirosh, Miikkulainen, & Bednar, 1996; Fig. 1), was designed to give a computational account for the observed self-organization, plasticity, and

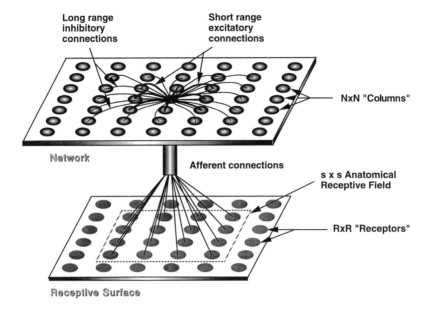

Fig. 1. The RF-LISSOM model. The lateral excitatory and lateral inhibitory connections of a single neuron in the network are shown, together with its afferent connections. The afferents form a local anatomical receptive field on the retina.

low-level functional phenomena in the primary visual cortex. The cortical architecture has been simplified to the minimum necessary configuration to account for the observed phenomena. Because the focus is on the two-dimensional organization of the cortex, each "neuron" in the model corresponds to a vertical column of cells through the six layers of the cortex. The transformations in the LGN are also bypassed for simplicity.

In RF-LISSOM the cortical network consists of a sheet of interconnected neurons. Through afferent connections, each neuron receives input from a receptive surface, or "retina." In addition, each neuron has reciprocal excitatory and inhibitory lateral connections with other neurons. Lateral excitatory connections are short range, connecting only close neighbors. Lateral inhibitory connections run for long distances, and may even implement close to full connectivity between neurons in the network. Such a lateral interaction profile is intended to establish local cooperation and global competition among the neurons, thereby making self-organization possible.

Neurons receive afferent connections from broad overlapping patches on the retina called anatomical receptive fields (RFs). The $N \times N$ network is projected on the retina of $R \times R$ receptors (for example the neuron in the top left corner of the network is projected to the top left of the retina, the center neuron to the center of the retina), and each neuron is assigned a square region of receptors of side $s$ centered on its projection as its RF. Typically $s$ is about half the side of the retina. Depending on the location of the neuron, its RF thereby consists of $\frac{1}{2}s \times \frac{1}{2}s$ (at the corners) to $s \times s$ (at the center) receptors.

Both afferent and lateral connections have positive synaptic weights. The weights are initially set to random values, and organized through an unsupervised learning process. At each training step, neurons start out with zero activity. An input activation pattern is introduced on the retina, and the activation propagates through the afferent connections to the cortical network. The initial response $\eta_{ij}$ of neuron $(i,j)$ is calculated as a weighted sum of the retinal activations:

$$\eta_{ij} = \sigma \left( \sum_{r_1,r_2} \xi_{r_1,r_2} \mu_{ij,r_1 r_2} \right), \tag{1}$$

where $\xi_{r_1,r_2}$ is the activation of a retinal receptor $(r_1,r_2)$ within the receptive field of the neuron, $\mu_{ij,r_1,r_2}$ is the corresponding afferent weight, and $\sigma$ is a piecewise linear approximation of the sigmoid activation function.

The response evolves over time through lateral interaction. At each time step, each cortical neuron combines the above afferent activation $\sum \xi \mu$ with its lateral excitation and inhibition:

$$\eta_{ij}(t) = \sigma \left( \sum_{r_1,r_2} \xi_{r_1,r_2} \mu_{ij,r_1 r_2} + \gamma_E \sum_{k,l} E_{ij,kl} \eta_{kl}(t - \Delta t) - \gamma_I \sum_{k,l} I_{ij,kl} \eta_{kl}(t - \Delta t) \right), \tag{2}$$

where $E_{ij,kl}$ is the excitatory lateral connection weight on the connection from neuron $(k,l)$ to neuron $(i,j)$, $I_{ij,kl}$ is the inhibitory connection weight, and $\eta_{kl}(t - \Delta t)$ is the activity of neuron $(k,l)$ during the previous time step. In other words, the retinal activity stays constant while the cortical response settles. The scaling factors $\gamma_E$ and $\gamma_I$ determine the strength of the lateral excitatory and inhibitory interactions. The activity pattern starts out diffuse and spread over a substantial part of the map, and converges iteratively into stable focused patches of activity, or activity bubbles.

The settling process determines the neighborhood around the initial response where the adaptation will occur. After the activity has settled, typically in a few iterations of equation 2, the connection weights of each active neuron are modified. Both afferent and lateral weights adapt according to the same mechanism: the Hebb rule, normalized so that the sum of the weights is constant:

$$w_{ij,mn}(t + 1) = \frac{w_{ij,mn}(t) + \alpha\eta_{ij}X_{mn}}{\sum_{mn}[w_{ij,mn}(t) + \alpha\eta_{ij}X_{mn}]}, \tag{3}$$

where $\eta_{ij}$ stands for the activity of the neuron $(i,j)$ in the settled activity bubble, $w_{ij,mn}$ is the afferent or the lateral connection weight ($\mu_{ij,r_1r_2}$, $E_{ij,kl}$, or $I_{ij,kl}$), $\alpha$ is the learning rate for each type of connection ($\alpha_A$ for afferent weights, $\alpha_E$ for excitatory, and $\alpha_I$ for inhibitory) and $X_{mn}$ is the presynaptic activity ($\xi_{r_1,r_2}$ for afferent, $\eta_{kl}$ for lateral). Afferent inputs, lateral excitatory inputs, and lateral inhibitory inputs are normalized separately.

As a result of this process, both inhibitory and excitatory lateral connections strengthen by correlated activity. At long distances, very few neurons have correlated activity and therefore most long-range connections eventually become weak. The weak connections are eliminated (i.e., pruned) periodically, modeling connection death during early development in animals (Burkhalter, Bernardo, & Charles, 1993; Dalva & Katz, 1994; Fisken, Garey, & Powell, 1975; Gilbert, 1992; Katz & Callaway, 1992; Löwel & Singer, 1992). Through the weight normalization, the remaining inhibition concentrates in a closer neighborhood of each neuron. The radius of the lateral excitatory interactions starts out large, but as self-organization progresses, it is decreased until it covers only the nearest neighbors. Such a decrease is necessary for global topographic order to develop and for the receptive fields to become well-tuned at the same time (for theoretical motivation for this process, see Kohonen, 1982, 1989, 1993; Obermayer et al., 1992; Sirosh & Miikkulainen, 1997, for neurobiological evidence, see Dalva & Katz, 1994; Hata, Tsumoto, Soto, Hagihara, & Tamura, 1993). Together the pruning of lateral connections and decreasing excitation range produce activity bubbles that are gradually more focused and local. As a result, weights change in smaller neighborhoods, and receptive fields become better tuned to local areas of the retina. Let us next turn to simulations that illustrate this process.

## III.  Self-Organization

In this section, three self-organizing experiments with the RF-LISSOM model are presented. The experiments show how the observed organization of feature detectors and lateral connections in the primary visual cortex could form based on activity-dependent self-organization, driven by the regularities in the input. In the first experiment, the input patterns consist of elongated Gaussian spots of light, and the model develops orientation maps. In the second experiment, a second retina is included in the model, and OD columns appear on the map. In the third experiment, Gaussian spots of different sizes are used as the input, resulting in size-selective columns. In all these cases, the lateral connectivity patterns are found to follow the receptive field properties, as has been observed in the cortex.

## A.  DEVELOPMENT OF OR COLUMNS AND LATERAL CONNECTIONS

In this experiment, the inputs to the network consisted of simple images of multiple elongated Gaussian spots on the retinal receptors. The activity $\xi_{r_1,r_2}$ of receptor $(r_1 \; r_2)$ inside a spot is given by

$$
\xi_{r_1,r_2} = exp\left(- \frac{((r_1 - x_i)cos(\alpha) - (r_2 - y_i)sin(\alpha))^2}{a^2} \right.
$$
$$
\left. - \frac{((r_1 - x_i)sin(\alpha) + (r_2 - y_i)cos(\alpha))^2}{b^2}\right),
$$
(4)

where $a^2$ and $b^2$ specify the length along the major and minor axes of the Gaussian, $\alpha$ specifies its orientation (chosen randomly from the uniform distribution in the range $0 \le \alpha < \pi$), and $(x_i, y_i) : 0 \le x_i, y_i < R$ specifies its center.

The model consisted of an array of $192 \times 192$ neurons, and a retina of $24 \times 24$ receptors. The anatomical receptive field of each neuron covered $11 \times 11$ receptors. The initial lateral excitation radius was 19 and was gradually decreased to 1. The lateral inhibitory radius of each neuron was 47, and weak inhibitory connections were pruned away at 30,000 iterations.[1] The network had approximately 400 million connections in total, and took 8 hr to simulate on 64 processors of the Cray T3D at the Pittsburgh Supercomputing Center.

---

[1] The lateral connections were pruned if their strength was less than 0.00025. The afferent weights were initially random (chosen from a uniform distribution). In this particular experiment, the lateral inhibitory connections were initially set to a Gaussian distribution with $\sigma = 100$, and the lateral excitatory connections to a Gaussian with $\sigma = 15$ to speed up learning; uniform random values can be used as well. The widths of the oriented Gaussian input spots were $a = 7.5$ and $b = 1.5$. The lateral excitation $\gamma_E$ and inhibition strength $\gamma_I$ were both 0.9. The learning rate $\alpha_A$ decreased from 0.007 to 0.0015, $\alpha_E$ from 0.002 to 0.001, and $\alpha_I$ was a constant 0.00025. The lower and upper thresholds of the sigmoid increased from 0.1 to 0.24 and from 0.65 to 0.82. Small variations of these parameters produce roughly equivalent results. Similar parameters were used in other experiments described in this article.

The self-organization of afferents results in a variety of oriented receptive fields similar to those found in the visual cortex (Fig. 2). Some are highly selective to inputs of a particular orientation, others unselective. The global organization of such receptive fields can be visualized by labeling each neuron by the preferred angle and degree of selectivity to inputs at that angle. The resulting orientation map (Fig. 3) is remarkably similar in structure to those observed in the primary visual cortex by recent imaging techniques (Blasdel, 1992; Blasdel & Salama 1986) and contains structures such as pinwheels, fractures and linear zones.[2] The results strongly suggest that Hebbian self-organization of afferent weights, based on recurrent lateral interactions, underlie the development of orientation maps in the cortex.

The lateral connection weights self-organize at the same time as the orientation map forms. Initially, the connections are spread over long distances and cover a substantial part of the network (Fig. 3A). As lateral weights self-organize, the connections between uncorrelated regions become weaker, and after pruning, only the strongest connections remain (Fig. 3B). The surviving connections of highly tuned cells, such as the one illustrated in Fig. 3B, link areas of similar orientation preference, and avoid neurons with the orthogonal orientation preference. Furthermore, the connection patterns are elongated along the direction that corresponds to the neuron's preferred stimulus orientation. This organization reflects the activity correlations caused by the elongated Gaussian input pattern: Such a stimulus activates primarily those neurons that are tuned to the same orientation as the stimulus, and located along its length. At locations such as fractures, where a cell is sandwiched between two orientation columns of very different orientation preference, the lateral connections are elongated along the two directions preferred by the two adjacent columns. Finally, the lateral connections of unselective cells, such as those at pinwheel centers, connect to all orientations around the cell. Thus the pattern of lateral connections of each neuron closely follows the global organization of receptive fields, and represents the long-term activity correlations over large areas of the network.

Some of these results have already been confirmed in very recent neurobiological experiments[3] (Fitzpatrick, Schofield, & Strote, 1994). In the iso-

---

[2] The similarity was measured by comparing Fourier transforms, autocorrelation functions, and correlation angle histograms of experimental and model maps. See (Erwin et al., 1995) for a discussion of these methods.

[3] Note that if the lateral connection patterns are observed on the cortex directly, it is very difficult to determine their orientation because of the log-polar mapping from the retina to the cortex. The cortical patterns would first have to be mapped back to the visual space. The model bypasses the log-polar transformation for simplicity, and the lateral connection patterns are directly observable.

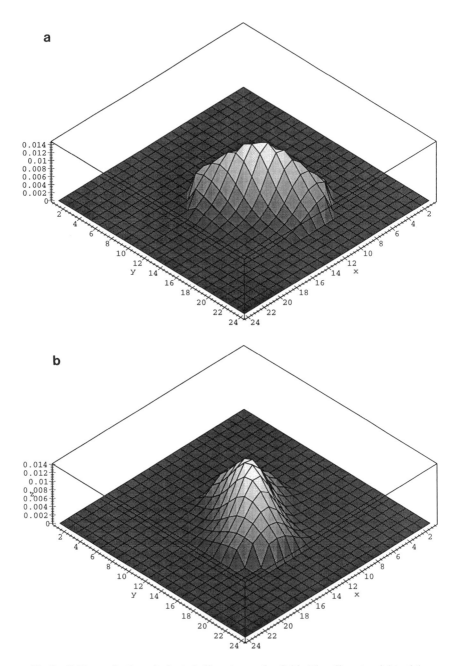

Fig. 2. Self-organization of oriented afferent receptive fields. The afferent weights of three neurons at different locations in the network are shown, plotted on the retinal surface. The first two are strongly oriented, whereas the third is unoriented and symmetric. (a) RF sharply tuned to 60°; (b) RF sharply tuned to 127.5°; (c) Unselective RF

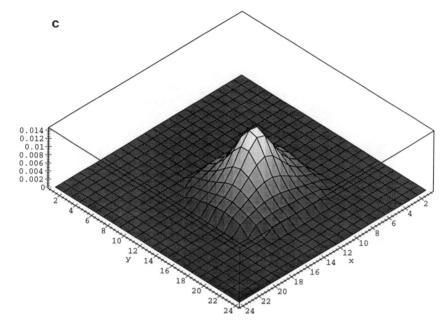

Fig. 2. *Continued*

orientation columns of the tree-shrew cortex, horizontal connections were found to be distributed anisotropically, extending farther and giving rise to more terminals along the preferred orientation of the neuron. Most of these terminals also connected to cells with the same orientation preference. The connection patterns at pinwheel centers and fractures have not been studied experimentally so far; our model predicts that they will have unselective and biaxial distributions, respectively.

## B. Self-organization of Ocular Dominance and Lateral Connection Patterns

In addition to responding to specific orientations, the neurons in the primary visual cortex are also selective to the eye from which the input originates. In the second experiment with RF-LISSOM self-organization, the development of eye selectivity, or ocular dominance (OD), was simulated. A second retina was added to the model and the afferent connections were set up exactly as for the first retina, with local receptive fields and topographically ordered RF centers. Multiple symmetric Gaussian spots were presented in each eye as input, where the activity inside each spot is given by

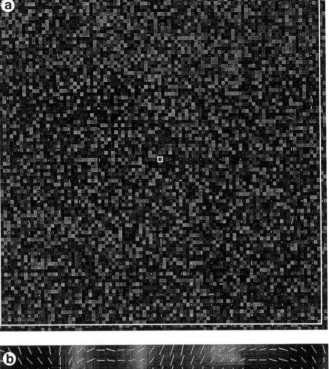

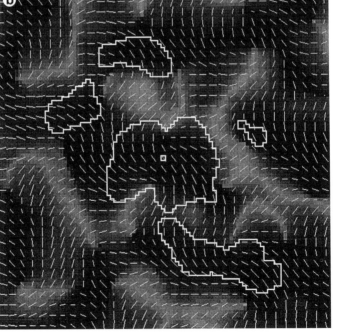

$$\xi_{r_1,r_2} = exp\left(- \frac{(r_1 - x_i)^2 + (r_2 - y_i)^2}{a^2}\right), \tag{5}$$

where $a^2$ specifies the width of the Gaussian, and the spot centers $(x_i,y_i): 0 \leq x_i,y_i < R$, were chosen randomly. Because of cooperation and competition between inputs from the two eyes, groups of neurons developed strong afferent connections to one eye or the other, resulting in patterns of OD in the network (cf. von der Malsburg, 1990; Miller et al., 1989).

The self-organization of the network was studied with varying between-eye correlations. At each input presentation, one spot is randomly placed at $(x_i,y_i)$ in the left retina, and a second spot within a radius of $c \times R$ of $(x_i,y_i)$ in the right retina. The parameter $c \in [0, 1]$ specifies the spatial correlations between spots in the two retinas, and can be adjusted to simulate different degrees of correlations between images in the two eyes.

---

Fig. 3.   Self-organization of the orientation map and lateral connections. Each neuron in this $100 \times 100$ central region of the map is shaded according to its orientation preference. Shades from dark to light represent changing orientation preference from 127.5 to 37.5° from the horizontal, and from light to dark preference from 37.5 to −52.5°, i.e., back to 127.5°. This gray-scale scheme was chosen so that the connections of the center neuron, which is tuned to 127.5° and identified by a small box in the figure, could be clearly plotted, and also so that the shading would be continuous through all angles (as is possible in color plots; see e.g., Sirosh, Miikkulainen, & Bednar, 1996). To disambiguate the shading, every third neuron in every third row is marked with a line that identifies the neuron's orientation preference. In addition, the length of the line indicates how selective the neuron is to its preferred orientation. The outlined areas indicate units from which the center unit has lateral connections. (a) Initially, the afferent weights of each neuron are random, and the receptive fields are randomly oriented and very unselective, as shown by the random shades and random and short lines (the line lengths were slightly magnified so that they could be seen at all). The lateral connections cover a wide area uniformly. (b) After several thousand input presentations, the receptive fields have organized into continuous and highly selective bands of orientation columns. The orientation preference patterns have all the significant features found in visuo-cortical maps: (1) *pinwheel centers,* around which orientation preference changes through 180° (e.g., the neuron eight lines from the left and four from the bottom), (2) *linear zones,* where orientation preference changes almost linearly (e.g., along the bottom at the lower left), and (3) *fractures,* where there is a discontinuous change of orientation preference (as in 7 lines from the left and 17 from the bottom). Most of the lateral connections have been pruned, and those that remain connect neurons with similar orientation preferences. The marked unit prefers 127.5°, and its connections come mostly from dark neurons. In the near vicinity, the lateral connections follow the twists and turns of the darkly shaded iso-orientation column, and avoid the lightly shaded columns representing the orthogonal preference. Further away, connections exist mostly along the 127.5° orientation, since these neurons tend to respond to the same input. All the long-range connections shown are inhibitory at this stage; there are excitatory connections only from the immediately neighboring units.

Multispot images can be generated by repeating the above step: the simulations below used two-spot images in each eye.

Figure 4 shows the final afferent receptive fields of two typical neurons in a simulation with $c = 1$. In this case, the inputs were uncorrelated, simulating perfect strabismus (i.e., the inputs from the two eyes cannot be matched to form a single percept). In the early stages of the simulation, some of the neurons randomly develop a preference for one eye or the other. Nearby neurons will tend to share the same preference because lateral excitation keeps neural activity partially correlated over short distances. As self-organization progresses, such preferences are amplified, and groups of neurons develop strong weights to one eye. Figure 4A shows the afferent weights of a typical monocular neuron.

The extent of activity correlations on the network determines the size of the monocular neuronal groups. Farther on the map, where the activations are anticorrelated due to lateral inhibition, neurons will develop eye preferences to the opposite eye. As a result, alternating OD patches develop over the map, as shown in Fig. 5.[4] In areas between OD patches, neurons will develop approximately equal strengths to both eyes and become binocular, like the one shown in Fig. 4B.

The lateral connection patterns closely follow the OD organization (Fig. 5). As neurons become better tuned to one eye or the other, activity correlations between regions tuned to the same eye become stronger, and correlations between opposite eye areas weaker. As a result, monocular neurons develop strong lateral connections to regions with the same eye preference, and weak connections to regions of opposite eye preference. The binocular neurons, on the other hand, are equally tuned to the two eyes, and have activity correlations with both OD regions. Their lateral connection weights are distributed more or less symmetrically around them and include neurons from both eye-preference columns.

The normal case (simulated with $c = 0.4$), looks otherwise similar to Fig. 5, but the OD stripes are narrower and there are more OD columns in the network. Most neurons are neither purely monocular nor purely binocular and few cells have extreme values of OD. Accordingly, the lateral connectivity in the network is only partially determined by OD. However, the lateral connections of the few strongly monocular neurons follow the OD patterns like in the strabismic case. In both cases, the spacing between the lateral connection clusters matches the stripe-width.

The patterns of lateral connections and OD shown above closely match observations in the primary visual cortex. Löwel and Singer (1992) observed

---

[4] For a thorough treatment of the mathematical principles underlying the development of ocular dominance columns, see (Goodhill, 1993; Miller et al., 1989; von der Malsburg & Singer, 1988).

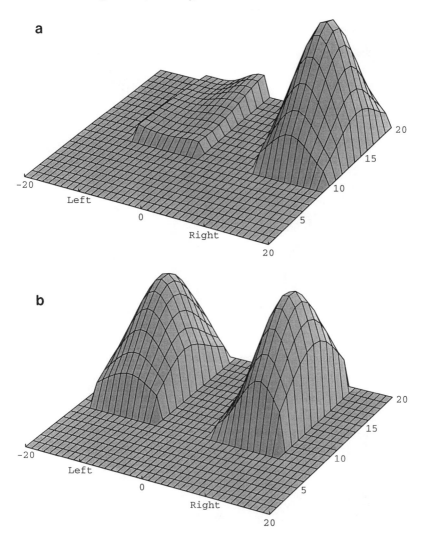

Fig. 4. Receptive fields with varying degrees of eye-preference. (a) The final afferent weights of a neuron at position (42, 39) in a 60 × 60 network. This particular neuron is monocular with strong connections to the right eye, and weak connections to the left. (b) The weights of a binocular neuron at position (38, 23). This neuron has approximately equal weights to both eyes.

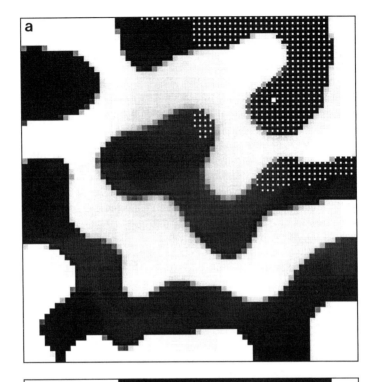

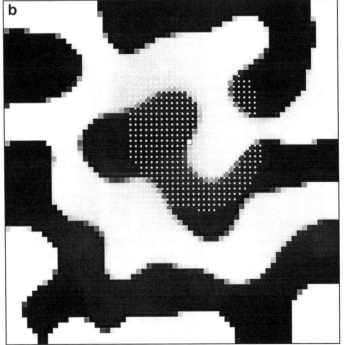

that when between-eye correlations were abolished in kittens by surgically induced strabismus, long-range lateral connections primarily linked areas of the same ocular dominance. However, binocular neurons, located between OD columns, retained connections to both eye regions. The OD stripes in the strabismics were broad and sharply defined (Löwel, 1994). In contrast, ocular dominance stripes in normal animals were narrow and less sharply defined, and lateral connection patterns overall were not significantly influenced by OD. The receptive field model reproduces these experimental results, and also predicts that the lateral connections of strongly monocular neurons would follow OD even in the normal case. The model therefore confirms that patterned lateral connections develop based on correlated neuronal activity and demonstrates that they can self-organize cooperatively with OD columns.

C.  DEVELOPMENT OF SIZE SELECTIVITY AND
     LATERAL CONNECTIONS

In their first recordings from the primary visual cortex of the cat, Hubel and Wiesel (1959, 1962) reported that cortical cells were more selective to the width of patterns than were retinal cells. They noted that cortical cells would give no response to a bar covering the whole receptive field, whereas in the retina and the LGN, cells would typically respond to such patterns. Subsequently, detailed studies by Campbell, Cooper, and Enroth-Cugell (1969), De Valois, Albrecht, and Thorell (1982) and others showed that cortical cells are narrowly tuned to the spatial frequency of inputs, and had typical bandpass responses, responding only to inputs in a specific frequency range. A continuum of spatial frequencies from low to high were represented in the cortex (Silverman, Grosof, De Valois, & Elfar, 1989), and

---

Fig. 5.  Ocular dominance and patterned long-range lateral connections. Each neuron is colored with a gray-scale value (*black → white*) that represents continuously changing eye preference from exclusive left through binocular to exclusive right. Most neurons are monocular, so white and black predominate. Small white dots indicate the strongest lateral input connections to the neuron marked with a big white dot. Only the long range inhibitory connections are shown. The excitatory connections link each neuron only to itself and to its eight nearest neighbors. (a) The lateral connections of a left monocular neuron predominantly link areas of the same ocular dominance. (b) The lateral connections of a binocular neuron come from both eye regions. In this simulation, the parameters were: network size $N = 64$; retinal size $R = 24$; afferent field size $s = 9$; sigmoid thresholds $\delta = 0.1$; $\beta = 0.65$; spot width $a = 5.0$; excitation radius $d = 1$; inhibition radius $= 31$; scaling factors $\gamma_E = 0.5$, $\gamma_I = 0.9$; learning rates $\alpha_A = \alpha_E = \alpha_I = 0.002$; number of training iterations $= 35,000$. The anatomical RF centers were slightly scattered around their topographically ordered positions (radius of scatter $= 0.5$), and all connections were initialized to random weights.

cells in each range of spatial frequency were organized into distinct spatial frequency columns (Tootell, Silverman, & De Valois, 1981; Tootell, Silverman, Hamilton, Switkes, & De Valois, 1988). In essence, cortical cells exhibited an organization of spatial frequency selectivity similar to OD and OR columns.

Modeling selectivity to spatial frequency would require much larger retinal and cortical networks than can currently be simulated. However, it is possible to test a special case of the hypothesis: whether selective receptive fields, columnar organization, and lateral connection patterns form when the size of the Gaussian light spot is the main dimension of variation in the input.

In the third RF-LISSOM self-organization experiment, therefore, inputs of a variety of sizes were presented to the network. The light spots were similar to those in the ocular dominance experiment (equation 5), except that the width $a$ was chosen uniformly randomly in the range [0.75,8.0]. The retinal activity vector was normalized to constant length, because without normalization, larger-sized spots would produce stronger activation. A total of 25,000 training steps were used, with the network and simulation parameters similar to those in the OR columns simulation (section III.A).

The self-organization of afferents results in smooth, hill-shaped RFs. A variety of RFs of different sizes are produced, some narrow and tuned to small stimuli, others large and most responsive to large stimuli (Fig. 6). Simultaneously with the RFs, each neuron's lateral connections evolve, and by the Hebbian mechanism, are distributed according to how well the neuron's activity correlates with the activities of the other neurons. Let us examine the nature of such activity correlations. The inputs vary in size from $a = 0.75$ to $a = 8.0$, and are normalized. Therefore, the smallest inputs produce very bright activity in a few receptors. They are also smaller than the size of each anatomical receptive field. Therefore, these inputs predominantly stimulate neurons with small receptive fields and having anatomical RFs in the same position as the spot. Such neurons will have strong activity correlations with other small receptive field neurons, but little correlation with neurons having broader receptive fields.[5] The global organization of size preferences and lateral connections can be visualized by labeling each neuron with a color that indicates the width of its RF, and plotting the patterns of lateral connections on top. As Fig. 7A shows, the RF organization has the form of connected, intertwined patches, similar to OD columns, and the lateral connections of neurons connect to regions of the same size preference.

---

[5] Note that even small spots produce quite widespread activity in the network, because each retinal receptor connects to a large number of cortical neurons.

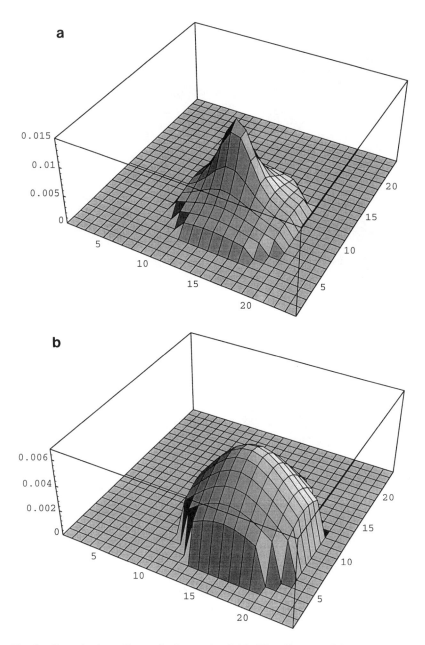

Fig. 6. Size-selective self-organized receptive fields. The afferent weights of neurons at two different locations in a $192 \times 192$ network are shown after self-organization. Initially the weights are random, but after self-organization, a smooth hill-shaped weight profile develops. Though the anatomical RFs are the same, the afferent weights are organized into a variety of sizes from narrow, highly peaked receptive fields to large and broad ones. (a) Small RF: neuron (78,109); (b) Large RF: neuron (69,124)

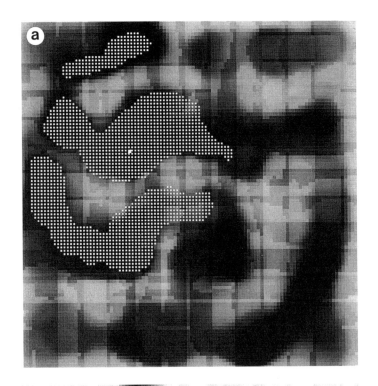

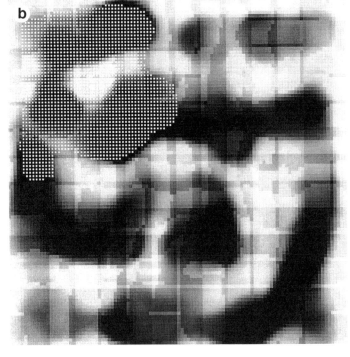

Neurons with larger receptive fields have a slightly different pattern of activity correlations. The larger spots are not localized within the anatomical RF as are the smaller inputs, but extend beyond it. They produce activity over a wider area in the network than the smaller, localized spots. As a result, the inputs that best stimulate larger RF neurons also cause activity in large parts of the network. Therefore, the activity correlations of such neurons are not as strongly determined by size as that of small RF neurons. Therefore, the lateral connections of neurons with larger RFs often link to smaller RF neurons also. In the cortex, neurobiologists have not yet studied how the patterns of lateral connections relate to either size or spatial frequency preferences.

The columnar organization does not develop in small networks. Simulations show that, for a given variance of the stimulus size, the ratio of neurons in the network to receptors in the retina (the magnification factor) has to be greater than a threshold value for a stable columnar organization to appear. Below the threshold, smooth RFs and an ordered topographic map develop, but all the RFs tend to have the same size, corresponding to the average width of the input stimulus. Above the threshold, symmetry breaking occurs, producing a variety of RF sizes for each location in the retina. Such symmetry breaking is similar to that of the Self-Organizing Map (Kohonen, 1982, 1989, 1995), where an input feature is represented in the network only if its variance is greater than a threshold proportional to the magnification factor (Obermayer et al., 1992).

It is not known whether the long-range lateral connections in the cortex are organized according to size or spatial-frequency selectivity. So far, the lateral connection patterns have only been studied in relation to the organization of OD and OR preference (Malach, Amir, Harel, Grinvald, 1993; Löwel & Singer, 1992; Gilbert & Wiesel, 1989). However, considerable psychophysical and neurobiological evidence indicates that selective lateral interactions exist between neurons tuned to different spatial frequencies (De Valois & Tootell, 1983; Bauman & Bonds, 1991). As in the RF-LISSOM model, these interactions are also known to be largely inhibitory (De Valois & Tootell, 1983; Vidyasagar & Mueller, 1994). The RF-LISSOM model

---

Fig. 7.    Size-selective columns and lateral connection patterns. Each neuron in the network is labeled with a gray-circle value (*black* → *white*) that represents continuously changing size preference from small values to large values. Small white dots indicate the lateral input connections to the neuron marked with the big white dot. The size preferences are organized systematically across the network into connected, intertwined patches, and the strongest lateral connections predominantly link areas of the same size selectivity. (a) Columns and lateral connections: Small RF; (b) columns and lateral connections: Large RF

is a first step toward modeling spatial-frequency selectivity, and suggests that the long-range lateral connections could be the anatomical substrate for inhibition between spatial-frequency channels. The model further predicts that the patterns of lateral connections in the cortex would be influenced not only by OD and OR preference, but also by selectivity to spatial frequency.

## IV.  Functional Role of the Self-Organized Maps and Lateral Connections

The results on self-organization of OD, OR, and size-selectivity maps and lateral connections suggest that a single Hebbian mechanism produces the receptive fields and lateral interactions in the primary visual cortex. If so, what could be the functional role of these self-organized structures in visual processing?

The information processing role of the afferent RFs is best seen by analogy with Self-Organizing Maps (Kohonen, 1982, 1989, 1995). The afferent connections self-organize in a similar fashion in both models. When presented with high-dimensional inputs, the self-organizing map selects the set of feature dimensions along which inputs vary the most and represents them along the dimensions of the map. For example, if the inputs lie mostly along the diagonal plane of a hypercube, the self-organized map (and hence the RFs) will spread out along this diagonal. If there is some input variance in the dimension perpendicular to this diagonal, receptive fields will be distributed along this direction as well, and the map will "fold" in that direction. If there are many such feature dimensions, a subset of them will be represented by the folds of the map in the order of their input variance (Obermayer et al., 1992).

The images in the visual world could be varying the most along the dimensions of ocular dominance, orientation preference, and spatial frequency, and if so, the self-organized RFs will represent these dimensions. During visual processing, the cortex then projects incoming visual inputs onto these dimensions. As shown by Field (1994), such a projection produces a *sparse coding* of the input, minimizing the number of active neurons and forming a more efficient representation, which is well suited for the detection of suspicious coincidences, associative memory and feature grouping (Barlow, 1972, 1985; Field, 1987, 1994). Projecting onto the dimensions of maximum variance also achieves minimal distortion and minimal spurious conjunctions of features.

What would the role then be for the lateral connections? Through Hebbian self-organization, the lateral connections learn correlations between the feature detectors in the network—the stronger the correlation between two cells, the larger the connection strength between them. However, these long-range connections are inhibitory. Therefore, the strongly correlated regions of the network inhibit each other—in other words, the lateral connections *decorrelate* (Barlow, 1972, 1989). Decorrelation is useful in producing efficient representations. If the connection between two cells is strong, then the response of one can be predicted to a large extent by knowing the response of the other. Therefore, the activity of the second cell is redundant, and a more efficient representation (in an information-theoretic sense) can be formed by eliminating the redundancy. Decorrelation filters out the learned redundancies and produces an efficient encoding of the visual input. Thus, the visual knowledge that lateral connections learn is used to filter out the already-known correlations between cortical cells, leaving only novel information to be passed on to higher levels of processing. The RF-LISSOM architecture demonstrates how decorrelation mechanisms could be implemented in the primary visual cortex.

To demonstrate sparse coding and decorrelation in RF-LISSOM, the representations in the orientation selectivity model of section III.A were analyzed in more detail. It was confirmed that (1) the network forms a sparse coding of the input, (2) the coding reduces redundancies, and (3) to get these effects, it is crucial that the lateral connections are self-organized.

Sparseness can be measured by the kurtosis (i.e., peakedness) of the network response. A small number of strongly responding neurons, that is, a sparse coding, will result in high kurtosis. In Fig. 8, the kurtosis measures of four different networks are compared: (1) a network without any lateral interactions at all (i.e., the initial response of the network), (2) a network with self-organized lateral weights, (3) one with fixed random lateral weights, and (4) one with lateral weights that have a fixed Gaussian profile (as assumed in some of the early self-organizing models). In each case, the amount of contrast in the input was varied: A constant pattern of several elongated Gaussian light spots was presented to the retina, and the height of the Gaussians was systematically increased.

The main observation is that the kurtosis of the self-organized lateral interactions is substantially higher than that of the other three networks. By Hebbian self-organization, the long-range lateral connections learn to encode correlations between the feature-selective units. Because the long-range connections are inhibitory, strongly correlated regions of the network inhibit each other. At the same time, the short-range lateral excitation locally amplifies the responses of active units. Together, the recurrent excitation and inhibition focuses the activity to the units best tuned to the features of the input stimulus, thereby producing high kurtosis, and a sparse coding of the input.

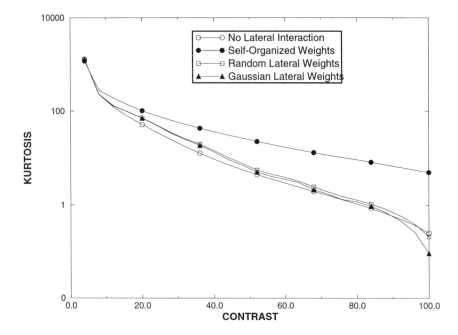

Fig. 8.  Sparse coding in the RF-LISSOM model. With self-organized lateral connections, the kurtosis (i.e., sparse coding) is significantly higher than with fixed lateral connections or without lateral connections at all. The difference is larger at higher intensities (measured by the intensity of the light spots, in percentage), suggesting that the self-organized lateral connections perform redundancy reduction on the response.

Second, the difference in kurtosis increases with contrast. As the light spots become more intense, there is more input activation to the network. More units will be activated, and kurtosis will decrease. This extra activity is mostly redundant, because the input pattern is still the same. The self-organized lateral connections are able to remove such redundant activation, and kurtosis decreases much slower than in the other cases. Third, such redundancy reduction occurs only when the lateral connections are self-organized. The kurtosis with fixed lateral weights decreases at the same rate as the kurtosis of the network without lateral weights.

In sum, the RF-LISSOM model suggests that the cortex performs two different computations during sensory processing: First, the inputs are projected onto the principal feature dimensions represented by the afferent receptive field structure. Then, the redundancies are filtered out by recurrent lateral interactions. The result is an efficient, redundancy-reduced sparse coding of the visual input which is then passed on to higher processing levels. This prediction can be verified experimentally by using information theory to analyze the optical images of cortical activity patterns produced in response to simple retinal images. If confirmed, it would constitute a major step in understanding the function of the observed primary visual cortex structures.

## V.  Plasticity of the Adult Visual Cortex

So far we have demonstrated how the laterally connected cortex could self-organize in response to the external input, and what the self-organized structures mean. The model can also be used to study dynamic phenomena in the adult cortex. The first experiment below shows how the network reorganizes after a retinal lesion, giving a computational explanation to the phenomenon of dynamic receptive fields. The second experiment shows how the network reorganizes in response to cortical lesions. These experiments suggest that the same processes that are responsible for the development of the cortex also operate in the adult cortex, maintaining it in a dynamic equilibrium with the input.

### A.  Reorganization After Retinal Lesions

Dynamic receptive fields are observed in response to temporary artificial scotomas in the retina. Such a lesion prevents part of the cortex from receiving input, producing a corresponding cortical scotoma. However, if the surround of the scotoma is stimulated for several minutes, and the scotoma is then removed, the receptive fields of the unstimulated neurons are found to have expanded (Pettet & Gilbert, 1992). The expansion is largest along the preferred orientation of each neuron. Psychophysical experiments further show that after removing the scotoma, a stimulus at the edge of the scotoma appears to have shifted toward the center (Kapadia et al., 1994). Prima facie, such a dynamic expansion of receptive fields, and the perceptual shift accompanying it, is incompatible with Hebbian self-organization (which is based on coincident activity), and has been difficult to explain.

The RF-LISSOM model suggests an explanation. Figure 9 shows how the orientation map of section III.A reorganizes when a retinal scotoma is introduced and inputs are presented in the surrounding area. The receptive fields of the central, unstimulated neurons remain in the same location as before. Neurons that have part of their receptive fields outside the scotoma are stimulated by the surrounding input, and by Hebbian adaptation, reorganize their afferent weights into the periphery of the scotoma. As a result,

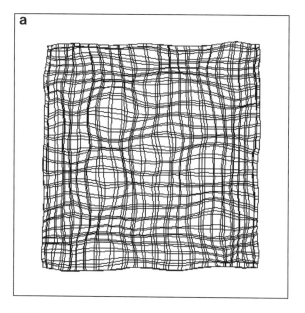

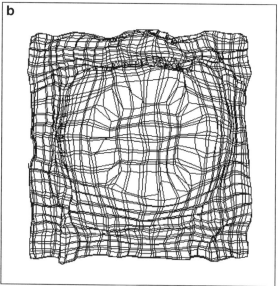

Fig. 9.  Reorganization of the topographic map after a retinal scotoma. The RF centers of every third neuron in the network are plotted in the retinal space, and the neighboring centers are connected by lines. (a) Before the scotoma, the centers are organized into a topographic map of the retina. (b) After the scotoma, neurons whose receptive fields were entirely covered by the scotoma remained unstimulated, and retained their old receptive

these neurons become insensitive to the central region. If the scotoma is now removed, and an input is presented in the scotoma region, only the previously unresponsive neurons respond vigorously to the new input; the surrounding ones do not. Therefore, there is considerably less lateral inhibition from the surrounding neurons to the central neurons, and responses that were previously suppressed by lateral inhibition are unmasked. Therefore, when the RF sizes of the central neurons are measured (based on network activity), they appear to have increased. The expansion is greatest along the preferred orientation because the strongest afferent weights lie in this direction (Fig. 2A,B), and any decrease of inhibition unmasks responses mainly in that direction.

Such a reorganization can account for the psychophysical experiments as well. The neurons whose receptive fields have moved outward now respond to inputs farther from the center than before. Therefore, an input at the edge of the retinal scotoma stimulates many neurons inside the cortical scotoma that previously would not have responded, and the response pattern is shifted inward, producing the perceptual shift. After the scotoma is removed and the normal stimulation reestablished, the reorganized RFs gradually return to the normal state (of Fig. 9A), and the shift disappears. The model thus shows how the same self-organizing processes and lateral interactions that sculpt the receptive fields during early development could, in the adult, maintain them in a continuously adapting, dynamic equilibrium with the visual environment.

## B.  REORGANIZATION AFTER CORTICAL LESIONS

To simulate effects of cortical lesions the RF-LISSOM network was first organized with symmetric Gaussian patterns such as those used in the OD simulation of section III.B. This resulted in regular Gaussian-shaped receptive fields, retinotopic global order, and a smooth "Mexican hat," or difference of Gaussians, lateral interaction profiles.

To study the effects of cortical lesions, a small set of neurons in the organized network were then made unresponsive to input. Three phases of reorganization were observed, like in the somatosensory cortex (Merzenich et al., 1990). Immediately after the lesion, the RFs of neurons in the perilesion zone enlarge. The lesion reduces the inhibition of the perilesion

---

Fig. 9 *Continued.*   fields. However, the surrounding neurons reorganized their afferent weights, and their receptive fields moved out into the periphery of the scotoma. Such reorganization produces dynamic expansions of receptive fields and an inward shift of the response at the edge of the scotoma.

neurons, and unmasks previously suppressed input activation. In effect, the perilesion neurons immediately take over representing part of the input to the lesioned region, and the apparent loss of receptive surface representation is smaller than expected based on the prelesion map (Fig. 10B).

The lesion disrupts the dynamic equilibrium of the network, and both lateral and afferent connections of the active neurons adapt to compensate for the lesion. Neurons close to the lesion boundary encounter a large imbalance of lateral interaction in their neighborhood, with no lateral activation from inside the lesion and normal activation from outside. As a result, the lateral connection weights to the lesioned area decrease to zero, and by Hebbian adaptation and normalization, all the lateral weights rapidly redistribute to the lesion's periphery. Neurons at the lesion boundary have the largest number of inhibitory connections from the lesioned zone; therefore, the reorganization of inhibition is especially pronounced at the boundary. As a result, in the second phase the lateral inhibition very rapidly becomes strong outside the lesion, and the previously unmasked activity is partly suppressed (Fig. 10C). This produces an apparent outward shift of perilesion receptive fields.

Even after the lateral connections reorganize, the remaining unmasked input activation causes an imbalance in the network. Such activation forces the afferent weights to reorganize and respond better to inputs that were previously stimulating the lesioned zone. Gradually, the representation of the receptive surface within the lesion zone is taken over by the neurons around it (Fig. 11), and the cortical lesion is partly compensated for (Fig. 10D). The RF-LISSOM model predicts that for full compensation to occur the lesion must be small enough so that neurons across the lesion are connected with excitatory connections. In that case they can act as neighbors on the map and the gap (such as that in Fig. 11B) can be closed.

The results with the RF-LISSOM model suggest two techniques to accelerate recovery following surgery in the sensory cortices. Normally, the

---

Fig. 10. Changing response patterns after a cortical lesion. The activity of neurons across the network are shown for the same input before the lesion and at several stages after it. The lesioned area is seen as a white square with no activity, and the black dot inside the square indicates the maximally responding neuron before the lesion. Immediately after the lesion, the activity spreads out to neurons that were previously inactive and therefore the functional loss appears less severe than expected. As lateral connections reorganize, the unmasked activity decreases because of increased lateral inhibition. Several thousand adaptation steps after the lesion, afferent weights of the perilesion neurons have spread out into the area previously represented by the lesioned neurons (Fig. 11B). Though lateral inhibition is still stronger in the perilesion area, the input activation after reorganization overcomes the inhibition, and neurons at the boundary of the lesion become more responsive to inputs previously stimulating lesioned neurons. (a) Activity before lesion; (b) immediately after; (c) after 500 iterations; (d) after complete reorganization

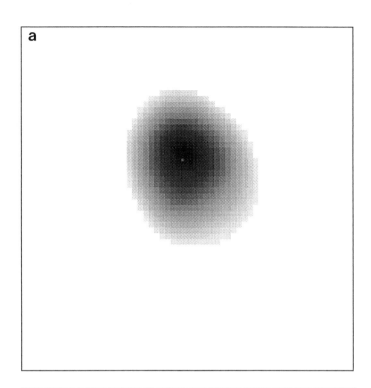

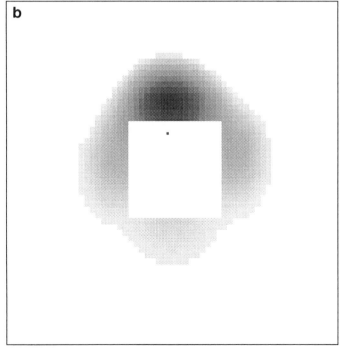

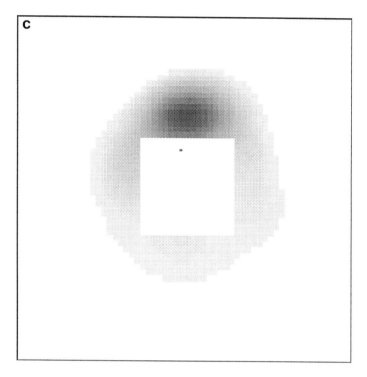

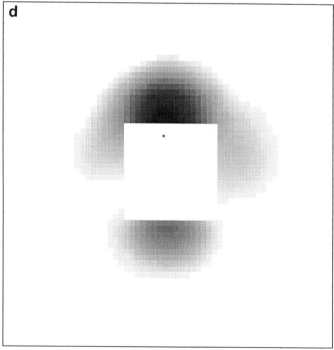

Fig. 10. *Continued*

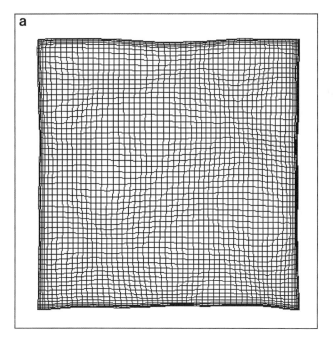

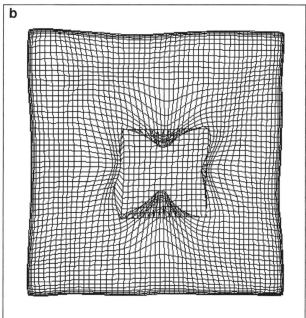

Fig. 11. Reorganization of receptive fields after a cortical lesion. Initially the centers of the Gaussian receptive fields are regularly and uniformly distributed over the retinal area. After lesion, the receptive fields of neurons near the periphery of the lesion move toward the center, partly compensating for the loss of function. (a) Map before lesion; (b) reorganized map

recovery time after cortical surgery would include an initial period of regression due to the reorganization of inhibition, and gradual and slow compensation afterward. The first phase of regression could be ameliorated if a transient blocker of inhibitory neurotransmitters were applied locally around the surgical area. Neurons around the surgical area would then fire intensively because of reduced inhibition, and afferent connections would adapt rapidly to compensate for the lesion. Though the inhibition would strengthen when the blockade goes away, the pace of recovery would have been hastened. Secondly, the topographic map could be shifted (as in Fig. 11) even before surgery. This preshifting could be achieved by intensive and repetitive stimulation of the area expected to lose sensation and by sensory deprivation of its surroundings. The receptive fields would then have to move less to reach the final state, and the recovery would be faster.

The model shows that receptive fields are maintained dynamically by excitatory and inhibitory interactions within the cortex. The combined effect of afferent input, lateral excitation, and lateral inhibition determine the responses of neurons. When the balance of excitation and inhibition is perturbed, neuronal response patterns change dynamically, and receptive fields appear to expand or decrease in size rapidly. If the perturbations are transient, they produce only transient changes in synaptic weight patterns and the topographic map does not shift much. However, if the perturbation persists for long, synaptic weight changes accumulate, and the topographic map reorganizes substantially. Such receptive field dynamics have been recently observed in the visual cortex (Pettet & Gilbert, 1992). RF-LISSOM provides a computational explanation of why such dynamics occur, and illustrates the primary role of lateral interactions in cortical plasticity.

## VI.  Modeling Low-Level Visual Functions

The lateral connections in the visual cortex are believed to be mediating several low-level visual phenomena such as tilt illusions, tilt aftereffects, segmentation and binding (Tolhurst & Thompson, 1975; von der Malsburg & Singer, 1988; Singer et al., 1990). In this section, two experiments are presented that rely on adaptation of connections after the network has self-organized. In the first one, tilt aftereffects are shown to result from increased inhibition between neurons responsive to similar orientations. In the second, after extending the RF-LISSOM architecture with a more realistic spiking model of the neuron, fast adaptation of lateral connections is shown to establish synchronization between neurons representing the same input object, forming a basis for binding and segmentation.

## A. TILT AFTEREFFECTS

The tilt aftereffect (TAE; Gibson & Radner, 1937) is an intriguing visual phenomenon that has long been studied as an indication of the underlying mechanisms of the visual system. After staring at a pattern of tilted lines or gratings, subsequent lines appear to have a slight tilt in the opposite direction. Figure 12 demonstrates the effect. The effect resembles an afterimage from staring at a bright light, but it changes in orientation perception rather than color or brightness perception.

Several explanations have been proposed for the TAE over the years. Gibson and Radner (1937) hypothesized that the TAE results from perceptual normalization, where the subjective vertical and horizontal norms are modified by visual experience. This theory does not explain why the effect occurs also for vertical and horizontal adaptation angles. Köhler and Wallach (1944) postulated that activation of cortical sensory areas results in local electrical fields that spread electrotonically to nearby areas. Activated areas experience satiation, which results in displacement of subsequent perceptions to unsatiated areas. Such electrotonic mechanisms have not been found, and a more modern version of that theory was devised based on feature-detector fatigue: if neurons with orientation preferences close to the adaptation figure become fatigued as a result of activation, a different set of neurons will be activated for the test figure, accounting for the perceptual shift (Coltheart, 1971; Sutherland, 1961). This theory has also been discounted because such fatigue mechanisms have not been found, and cell firing has been shown neither necessary nor sufficient for adaptation (Vidyasagar, 1990).

The prevailing theory for these effects attributes them to lateral interactions between orientation-specific feature-detectors in the primary visual cortex (Tolhurst & Thompson, 1975). The lateral inhibitory connection strengths between activated neurons are believed to increase temporarily

Fig. 12.   Tilt aftereffect patterns. Fixate on the circle inside the square at the left or the right for at least 30 sec, moving the eye slightly inside the circle to avoid developing strong afterimages. Now fixate on the line or square at the center; they should appear tilted in the direction opposite to the previous pattern. (Adapted from Campbell & Maffei, 1971).

while an input pattern is inspected, causing changes in the perception of subsequent orientations. This occurs because the detectors are broadly tuned, and detectors for neighboring orientations also adapt somewhat. When a subsequent line of a slightly different orientation is presented, the most strongly responding units are now the ones with orientation preferences further from the adapting line, resulting in a change in the perceived angle.

Although the inhibition theory was proposed in the 1970s (in a slightly different form), it is computationally very expensive to simulate and has not been tested in a detailed model of cortical function. RF-LISSOM is such a model, and it is computationally feasible to test it on the orientation network of section III.A. The results suggest that tilt aftereffects are not flaws in an otherwise well-designed system, but an unavoidable result of a self-organizing process that aims at producing an efficient, sparse encoding of the input through decorrelation.

To compare with results from human subjects, the tilt aftereffect was measured in the orientation map model as a function of the angular separation of the inducing and test figures. For adaptation on the inducing stimulus, the $x$ and $y$ coordinates of the center of a vertical Gaussian on the retina were fixed at the center of the retina. The learning rates $\alpha_I$, $\alpha_A$, and $\alpha_E$ were all set to 0.000005. All other parameters remained as in the self-organization of the orientation map.

To obtain a quantitative estimate of the aftereffect in the model, the perceived orientation in the model was measured as an activity-weighted sum of the preadaptation orientation preference of all active units. Perceived orientation was computed separately for each possible orientation of a test Gaussian at the center of the retina, both before and after adaptation. For a given angular separation of the adaptation stimulus and the test stimulus, the computed magnitude of the tilt aftereffect is the difference between the initial perceived angle and the one perceived after adaptation.

Figure 13 plots these differences after adapting to a vertical training line. For comparison, the figure also shows results from the most detailed recent data available for the tilt aftereffect in human foveal vision (Mitchell & Muir, 1976). The results from the model are clearly consistent with those seen in human observers.

In the model, the amount of aftereffect increases with adaptation as connection weights gradually change. The S-shape of the curve in Fig. 13 results from the redistribution of inhibitory weights to connections linking active neurons. Because the most active neurons are those encoding vertical orientations, the response to vertical and nearly vertical lines decreases dramatically. This causes the *direct effect* of angle expansion at these angles (0–35°), just as predicted by the lateral inhibition theory of tilt aftereffects.

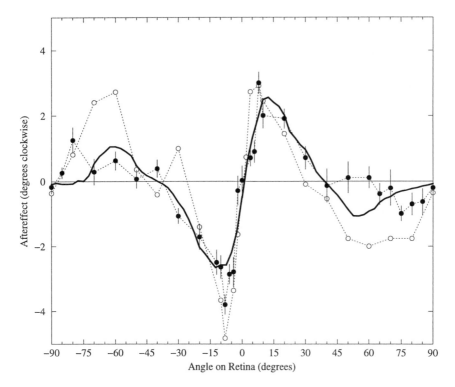

Fig. 13.   Tilt aftereffect vs retinal angle. The heavy line shows the magnitude of the tilt aftereffect in the RF-LISSOM model for each orientation after adapting to a vertical training line for 128 iterations. Positive values denote a clockwise change in the perceived orientation of the test line, and negative counterclockwise. The filled circles represent the average tilt aftereffect for a single human subject (DEM) from Mitchell and Muir (1976) over 10 trials; this subject had the most complete data of the four in the study. For each angle in each trial, the subject was trained for 3 min on a sinusoidal grating of a given angle, and then the effect was measured on a horizontal grating. Error bars indicate ±1 standard error of measurement from that study. The unfilled circles show the tilt aftereffect under similar conditions for subject DWM from that study; this subject showed the largest indirect effect of the four from the study.

At the same time as the lateral inhibitory connections increase between active neurons, they must decrease between those neurons and inactive ones (i.e., those encoding distant orientations). This happens because the inhibitory weights are normalized to a constant sum in the model. The result is an *increase* in the response to lines from 45–90°, or the *indirect effect.* Of the detectors activated for a test line in this range, those with preference closer to vertical are more active due to the reduction of inhibitory connections to them, whereas those encoding nearly orthogonal preference are unchanged. The perceived orientation thus shifts toward the adaptation orientation. This result is a straightforward consequence of the lateral inhibition theory when the fact of limited synaptic resources is taken into account (cf. Purves, 1988), which idea is a major contribution of the RF-LISSOM model.

The current results provide strong computational support for the theory that plastic lateral interactions are responsible for the tilt aftereffect as well as the initial self-organization of the orientation detectors. Through similar mechanisms, the model should also be able to explain simultaneous tilt illusions between overlapping or nearby stimuli [as proposed by Carpenter & Blakemore (1973)]. However, the simple method of computing the perceived orientation as a weighted average of activated units requires that the stimuli be spatially sufficiently separated so that their responses do not overlap. With the single-spot training inputs used for this version of the orientation map, connections do not develop over areas large enough to permit such separations, and thus the magnitude of the effect cannot be measured for the simultaneous case using this technique. To overcome this difficulty, it will be necessary to train the system with inputs that have longer-range correlations between similar orientations, such as sinusoidal gratings (representing objects with parallel lines). A version of the RF-LISSOM model trained on such patterns should be able to account for tilt illusions as well as tilt aftereffects. Although such experiments require even larger cortex and retina size, they should become practical in the near future.

In addition, many similar phenomena such as aftereffects of curvature, motion, spatial frequency, size, position, and color have been documented in humans (Barlow, 1990). Since specific detectors for most of these features have been found, RF-LISSOM is expected to be able to account for them by the same process of decorrelation mediated by self-organizing lateral connections.

B.  SEGMENTATION AND BINDING

The RF-LISSOM model suggests that lateral connections play a central role in self-organization and in function of the visual cortex by establishing competitive and cooperative interactions between feature detectors. They may also mediate function at lower level by modulating the spiking behavior of neuronal groups. This way they could cause synchronization and desynchronization of spiking activity, thus mediating feature binding and segmentation. Such synchronization of neuronal activity emerges in the visual cortex of the cat when light bars of various length are presented (Gray & Singer 1987; Eckhorn, Bauer, Jordan, Kruse, Munk, & Reitboeck, 1988; Gray, König, Engel, & Singer, 1989). Several models have been proposed to explain this phenomenon (von der Malsburg, 1987; von der Malsburg & Buhmann, 1992; Eckhorn et al., 1990; Reitboeck, Stoecker, & Hahn, 1993; Wang, 1996). The model of Reitboeck et al. is particularly interesting because of its sophisticated model of the neuron: The synapses are leaky integrators that sum incoming signals over time with exponential decay. A network of such neurons can segment multiple objects in a scene by synchronizing neuronal activity. Spikes of neurons representing the same object are synchronized, and those of neurons representing different objects are desynchronized.

The leaky integrator model of the spiking neuron can be integrated with the RF-LISSOM model of self-organization to model segmentation and binding. This extension of RF-LISSOM is called Spiking Laterally Interconnected Synergetically Self-Organizing Map (SLISSOM). SLISSOM forms a topological map from an initially random network through synergetic self-organization as before, and generates synchronized and desynchronized neuronal activity that can be used for segmenting multiple objects in the scene.

Each connection in SLISSOM is a leaky integrator that performs decayed summation of incoming spikes, thereby establishing not only spatial summation, but also temporal summation of activity (Fig. 14). Each new spike is added to the sum of the previous ones, and the sum is exponentially decayed over time. The current sums are multiplied by the connection weight and added together[6] to form the net input to the neuron. The spike generator compares the net input to a threshold and decides whether to fire a spike. The threshold is a sum of two factors: the base threshold $\theta$ and the decayed sum of past spikes, formed by a similar leaky integrator as in the input synapses. Active spiking therefore increases the effective threshold, making further spiking less likely and keeping the activation of the system within a reasonable range.

Each connection has a queue that stores previous spikes. In calculating the postsynaptic potential, the latest spike has the value of 1.0 and older ones are decayed by $\dfrac{1}{e^{\lambda_q}}$, where $\lambda_q$ is the decay parameter, as they are shifted through the queue. The inhibitory feedback loop in the spike generator (Fig. 14) is a similar queue that receives spikes from the spike generator itself, with decay $\dfrac{1}{e^{\lambda_s}}$.

---

[6] This differs from Eckhorn et al. (1990) and Reitboeck et al. (1993) who *multiplied* the weighted sums from afferent connections and those from lateral connections. Multiplying exerts better modulation on the neuronal activity, but disturbs self-organization by rapid fluctuation. In our experiments, modulation turned out to be possible with *additive* neurons as well.

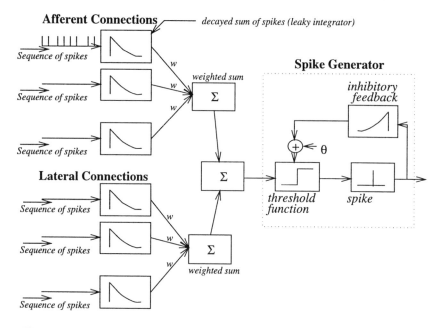

Fig. 14.   The leaky integrator neuron in SLISSOM. Leaky integrators at each synapse perform decayed summation of incoming spikes. The spike generator compares the weighted sum of the integrator outputs to a dynamic threshold, firing a spike if the sum is greater. Each spike increases the threshold, with exponential decay.

The input to the network consists of squares of fixed size ($3 \times 3$ in the experiments reported below), activated at random locations on the retina. Spikes are generated at the active retinal neurons and sent through the afferent connections to the cortical neurons. The net input $s_{ij}$ to the spike generator of the cortical neuron at location $(i, j)$ at time $t$ is calculated by summing the afferent and excitatory lateral contributions and subtracting the inhibitory lateral contributions:

$$s_{ij}(t) = \gamma_A \sum_{r_1, r_2} \xi_{r_1, r_2} \mu_{ij, r_1 r_2} + \gamma_E \sum_{k,l} E_{ij,kl} \eta_{kl}(t - 1) - \gamma_I \sum_{k,l} I_{ij,kl}, \ \eta_{kl}(t - 1) \quad (6)$$

where $\gamma_A$, $\gamma_E$, and $\gamma_I$ are the scaling factors for the afferent, excitatory, and inhibitory contributions, $\xi_{r_1, r_2}$ is the decayed sum of the incoming queue from the retinal neuron at $(r_1, r_2)$, $\mu_{ij, r_1 r_2}$ is the corresponding afferent connection weight, $\eta_{kl}(t - 1)$ is the decayed sum of the incoming queue from the map neuron at $(k, l)$ at time $t - 1$, and $E_{ij,kl}$ is the corresponding excitatory and $I_{ij,kl}$ the inhibitory lateral connection weight. The spike generator fires a spike if $s_{ij} > \theta + \phi_{ij}$, where $\theta$ is the base threshold and $\phi_{ij}$ the output of the spike generator's leaky integrator.

Through equation 6, SLISSOM goes through a similar setting process as the RF-LISSOM network. The input is kept constant and the cortical neurons are allowed to exchange spikes. After a while, the neurons reach a stable rate of firing, and this rate is used to modify the weights. Both the afferent and the lateral weights are modified according to the Hebbian principle:

$$w_{ij,mn}(t) = \frac{w_{ij,mn}(t - 1) + \alpha V_{ij}X_{mn}}{N}, \tag{7}$$

where $w_{ij,mn}(t)$ is the connection weight between neurons $(i, j)$ and $(m, n)$, $w_{ij,mn}(t - 1)$ is the previous weight, $\alpha$ is the learning rate ($\alpha_A$ for afferent, $\alpha_E$ for excitatory, and $\alpha_I$ for inhibitory connections), $V_{ij}$ and $X_{mn}$ are the average spiking rates of the neurons, and $N$ is the normalization factor, $\Sigma_{mn}[w_{ij,mn}(t - 1) + \alpha V_{ij}X_{mn}]^2$ for afferent connections and $\Sigma_{mn}[w_{ij,mn}(t - 1) + \alpha V_{ij}X_{mn}]$ for lateral connections (cf. Sirosh & Miikkulainen, 1994).

The SLISSOM experiment consists of two parts: self-organization and object segmentation. During self-organization, single objects are shown to the network, and the lateral and afferent connection weights are adapted to form a topological map of the input space. After the network has stabilized, multiple objects are presented to the retina and the network segments the objects by temporally alternating the activity on the map.

The retina and the cortex both consisted of $11 \times 11$ units. Each neuron was fully connected to the retina. The afferent weights were initialized to be most sensitive to a $3 \times 3$ area on the retina, centered right below each neuron, and then 65% noise was added to their values. The lateral connection weights were randomly initialized. Inhibitory connections covered the whole map, and excitatory connections linked to a square area centered at each neuron, with initial radius of 8, gradually decreasing to 1. At the same time, the lateral inhibitory learning rate $\alpha_I$ gradually increased from 0.001 to 0.1. Slow adaptation in the beginning captures long-term correlations within the inputs, which is necessary for self-organization. Fast adaptation toward the end facilitates quick modulation of the activity necessary for segmentation.

During self-organization, single $3 \times 3$ square objects were presented to the network. The retinal neurons representing objects were spiking at each time step, and the settling consisted of 15 cycles of cortical activity update (equation 6). After settling, connection weights were modified according to equation 7. Each such presentation was counted as an iteration. After 5500 iterations, both the afferent and the lateral weights stabilized into smooth profiles. Afferent weights formed smooth Gaussian receptive fields most sensitive to input from the retinal neuron right below the map neuron, and the lateral weights formed smooth Mexican-hat profiles. Figure 15 shows the global organization of the map during the process. The final map (Fig. 15B) closely resembles the ideal map of the input space (Fig. 15C).

Once the SLISSOM network had formed smooth and concentrated receptive fields and lateral interaction profiles, segmentation experiments were conducted on it. Several input objects (again, 3 × 3 squares) were presented to the retina at the same time, separated by at least 3 rows or columns of receptors. The objects constantly spiked on the retina for several

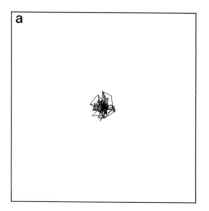

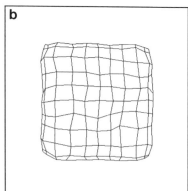
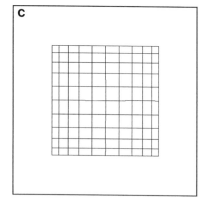

Fig. 15.   Self-Organization of the SLISSOM Map. (a) The afferent weights are initially randomized and their centers of gravity are about the same. (b) After 5500 iterations, the network forms a well-formed mapping of the input space, comparable to (c), the ideal grid where each node represents a Gaussian receptive field located directly below the map unit.

hundred time steps, and the spike activity at the cortical layer was recorded. For each object, a separate 5 × 5 area on the map responded and the other areas remained silent. Segmentation is evident in the total number of spikes per time step (i.e., the multi-unit activity, or MUA; Fig. 16). The spikes within the same area are synchronized, and spikes across the different areas desynchronized. This result is very robust and works for different locations on the retina and for different numbers of objects.

Several studies have shown that fast adaptation of synaptic efficacy may mediate feature binding through temporal coding (von der Malsburg, 1987; Wang, 1996). Similarly in the experiments with SLISSOM, rapid adaptation of lateral weights was found crucial for oscillatory behavior. On the other hand, self-organization requires slow adaptation so that long-term correlations can be learned. If the weights are initially random and change rapidly, they will fluctuate too much and an ill-formed map will result. One way to deal with this problem is to start out with a slow learning rate and gradually make learning faster. Such a change does not disturb the self-organization since the activity on the map becomes more consistent and predictable as the training goes on, and the need for keeping track of the long-term correlations disappears. The parameter $\alpha_l$ was increased to 0.1 at iteration 3500, allowing segmentation to occur, but that did not disrupt the already well-formed map (Fig. 15).

The MUAs show some overlap even when the input is successfully segmented (Fig. 16). This is due to the slightly overlapping receptive fields in the model. Gray et al. (1989) observed that in the cat visual cortex, strong phase-locking occurred when the receptive fields were clearly separate. Apparently when they overlap slightly, phase locking becomes less well-defined at the edges. The overlap is unavoidable in the current small SLISSOM network, but could be reduced in larger-scale simulations. Simulations on a more detailed self-organized model of the visual cortex with orientation columns and patterned lateral connections might also account for perceptual phenomena such as Gestalt effects. For example, principles such as proximity, smoothness, and continuity of contours can be seen as regularities among image features. They would be encoded as correlations in the lateral connections, and could aid in determining object boundaries.

## VII.  Discussion and Future Work

The RF-LISSOM model is based on three fundamental assumptions: First, vertical columns form the basic computational units in the visual cortex, and it is possible to approximate cortical function by modeling the two-dimensional layout of such columns instead of having to model each individ-

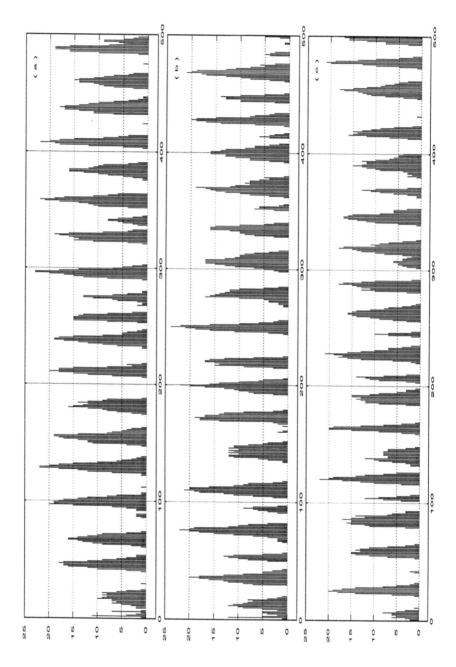

ual neuron separately. Since neurons in such columns are known to have similar response properties (Hubel & Wiesel, 1959, 1965), this is a reasonable abstraction that makes computational modeling tractable.

Second, the lateral interactions between such columns are primarily excitatory in the short range and inhibitory in the long range. This assumption is more controversial since about 80% of the long-range connections are known to have excitatory synapses in the cortex (Gilbert et al., 1990). However, the connections in RF-LISSOM are intended to model the overall excitation/inhibition between columns, not the individual synapses. The long-range excitatory connections could link to inhibitory cells in simple local circuits, and the overall effect could be inhibitory. Optical imaging and electrophysiological studies indeed suggest that there is substantially more inhibition in the cortex than predicted by the synapse types (Grinvald, Lieke, Frostig, & Hildesheim, 1994; Hata et al., 1993; Hirsch & Gilbert, 1991). The nature of long-range interactions remains controversial at this point. The RF-LISSOM model makes the computational prediction that the overall effect of long-range interactions on the column is inhibitory; otherwise self-organization does not occur in the model.

Third, the input patterns are sufficiently sparse so that distinct feature detectors may develop. As the number of spots in the images are increased, the organization of the map gradually degrades. When there is more overlap in the input more complex and random visual features are created, and the network attempts to represent these features as well. At first this seems incompatible with the dense nature of natural input images. However, there are two ways how such sparse input patterns might actually be realistic: (1) It is possible that much of the self-organization occurs prenatally based on traveling activity waves in the retina, such as those observed in the ferret and in the cat (Meister, Wong, Baylor, & Shatz, 1991; Wong, Meister, & Shatz, 1993). Such waves appear to have the necessary sparse structure. (2) Although the natural images may be dense originally, after the edge-enhancement mechanisms in the retina, they also have a sparse structure, with linear features at the local level (Wandell, 1995). If retinal preprocessing mechanisms are added, it is likely that the RF-LISSOM network can develop realistic orientation, OD, and size maps from natural images.

The main difference between RF-LISSOM and other recent models of cortical self-organization (Amari, 1980; Bienenstock, Cooper, & Munro,

Fig. 16.   The multi-unit activities of areas responding to three different objects. The total number of spikes per time step in each of the three $5 \times 5$ areas are plotted over 500 time steps. Although initially there is simultaneous activity in all areas, they quickly desynchronize and activation rotates from one area to another.

1982; Durbin & Mitchison 1990; Erwin et al., 1995; Goodhill, 1993; Gross-berg, 1976; Kohonen, 1982; Linsker, 1990; Miller, 1994a; Miller et al., 1989; Obermayer et al., 1992; Ritter et al., 1992; Shouval, 1995; Stryker et al., 1990; Tanaka, 1993; Willshaw & von der Malsburg, 1976) is that in RF-LISSOM, the lateral connections between feature detectors are explicitly modeled. Therefore, the model can explain how not only the observed afferent structures but also the lateral connectivity patterns emerge as a result of self-organization. Several testable predictions can be made based on the model, such as the connectivity at the pinwheel centers and fractures. The explicit lateral connections also make it possible to test the decorrela-tion hypothesis, possible plasticity mechanisms, and the inhibitory theory of tilt aftereffects computationally.

The tilt aftereffect and segmentation and binding in RF-LISSOM are modeled using the same adaptation processes as the self-organization. How-ever, these processes operate in different time scales, and most likely would have to be based on two different processes in the cortex. The mechanisms underlying perceptual phenomena may be a short time-scale, temporary version of the self-organizing processes that capture longer-term correla-tions. These fast weights could act as a small additive or multiplicative term on a relatively static long-term weight. Each inhibitory weight $w$ could be represented as $w_o + \Delta\omega$, where the $w_o$ portion would be comparatively static, keeping its value indefinitely in darkness and changing with a long time constant. The $\Delta\omega$ term, on the other hand, would adapt and decay very quickly, presumably to represent the short-term correlations between image elements. The tilt aftereffect and the segmentation and binding phenomena would be a result of such short-term adaptation.

Future work on RF-LISSOM models focuses on three areas: scaling the model up to more realistic scales, extending the functional simulations, and modeling self-organization of hierarchical representations. The models presented in this article were simplified in two ways: (1) there were separate models for each experiment (although with very similar networks and pa-rameters), and (2) simple light spots were used as inputs instead of realistic images. This way it was possible to study each individual aspect separately, and show how cortical structure and function depends on the structure of the inputs. With complex natural images, it would have been difficult to perform such an analysis and identify the crucial parameters that are respon-sible for each effect. In the future, this work should be extended to more complex inputs, to study the combined organization of various features in the cortex. One problem is that more computational power will be needed for such simulations than is currently available. When more features have to be represented on the map at the same time, the maps need to be larger. Perhaps $512 \times 512$ units are needed for simultaneous orientation, ocular dominance, and size preferences to develop. The requirement will grow perhaps fourfold if gratings such as those used in tilt illusions in humans are to be used on the organized network. The leaky integrator model of the neuron in turn doubles or triples the resource requirements. This is beyond the current computational resources, but could be available in the next few years. It may also be possible to approximate such large networks with smaller ones and address issues in processing realistic input with realistic-size networks sooner.

The second main direction of future work consists of extending the functional simulations on the organized model. In addition to tilt aftereffects, other figural aftereffects and also simultaneous tilt illusions can be modeled, as outlined in section VI.A. Binding and segmentation can be studied with more complex images, with multiple, differently shaped, and moving objects. Because the lateral connections in RF-LISSOM store long-range activity correlations, it may be possible to model perceptual grouping, or Gestalt, effects such as continuity of contours, proximity, and smoothness.

The time course of the organization of representations could be matched with developmental data on young animals. The network develops coarse representations of average inputs at first and gradually makes the map more accurate. For example, when it becomes computationally feasible to form maps of spatial frequency selectivity, it should be possible to model early perceptual development, where infants first are aware of only low spatial frequencies, but develop sensitivity to higher frequencies during the first few months.

Fahle, Edelman, and Poggio (1995) and Weiss, Edelman, and Fahle (1993) found that performance in hyperacuity tasks, such as deciding whether two lines of same orientation are separated by a small perpendicular offset, improves with practice even without feedback. The effect is specific to position and orientation, but transfers between eyes to some degree. Shiu and Pashler (1992) reported similar results for orientation discrimination tasks, although they found that the effect also depends on cognitive factors. The RF-LISSOM model should be able to account for such psychophysical learning phenomena. The active feature detectors and lateral connections between them would adapt, resulting in representation and discrimination of smaller differences. Hyperacuity and discrimination phenomena might also form a good testbed for extensions of RF-LISSOM that include feedback from higher cortical levels.

Third, the RF-LISSOM model could be extended to learning of hierarchical visual representations to discover increasingly complex structures in the input. Other self-organizing algorithms such as the self-organizing map (Kohonen, 1982, 1989, 1995) do not directly lend themselves to such hierarchical networks. A higher-level map will pick up essentially the same features of the input as the lower-level map, and represent the same level of information. However, the lateral interactions in RF-LISSOM eliminate redundant activity, and the map encodes the input in terms of unique feature detectors. A higher-level RF-LISSOM network would learn the correlations between the first level of feature detectors, and thereby form more complex detectors. Thus, by combining self-organization and decorrelation in one algorithm, a mechanism is obtained that can be applied in multiple stages to extract increasingly complex structures from the input. Therefore, LISSOM networks can possibly be cascaded in multiple levels to model the hierarchical representations in the visual cortex.

Large-scale computational models like RF-LISSOM are likely to play a significant role in future research on the structure and function of the visual cortex, because only computational models can be rigorous enough and detailed enough to verify ideas about how the visual cortex operates. At the current rate of technological progress, computers will be powerful enough to simulate the visual cortex at realistic details within a decade or two. Such models should provide a fundamental understanding of higher brain function and perception, and suggest novel algorithms for pattern recognition, computer vision, and sensory processing.

## VIII.  Conclusion

The RF-LISSOM model demonstrates how a variety of phenomena in the visual cortex can be explained by local cooperation and global competition whose specific form is learned from correlations in the input. Both the feature detectors and the lateral interactions self-organize simultaneously and synergetically based on a single Hebbian learning mechanism, resulting in patterns of selectivity and lateral connectivity some of which have already been observed in the visual cortex, and others that constitute testable predictions of the model. Such self-organization stores long-range activity correlations between units into the lateral connections, and during visual processing, this information is used to eliminate redundancies and to form an efficient sparse coding of the input. Many aspects of cortical plasticity can be explained by the model, such as reorganization after retinal lesions and that after cortical lesions, and the model suggests ways to hasten recovery from such lesions. The simulated reorganizations are reversible, and demonstrate how a topographic map can be maintained in a dynamic equilibrium with extrinsic and intrinsic inputs.

The model demonstrates that not only cortical structure, but also many of its functional characteristics could be emergent properties driven by activity-dependent self-organization. Tilt aftereffects in the model result from the same decorrelating process that is responsible for the initial development of the orientation map. Combined with the leaky integrator model of the spiking neuron, adaptation in RF-LISSOM can also account for segmentation by synchronization. These results suggests that both the development and function of the primary visual cortex could eventually be understood computationally based on Hebbian adaptation of laterally interconnected leaky integrator neurons.

## Acknowledgments

Thanks to Rob Goldstone, Philippe Schyns, and Jim Tanaka for insightful comments on an earlier draft of this chapter. This research was supported in part by National Science Foundation under grant #IRI-9309273. Computing time for the simulations was provided by the Pittsburgh Supercomputing Center under grants IRI930005P and IRI940004P, and by a High Performance Computer Time Grant from the University of Texas at Austin. Various LISSOM software, visualizations, and papers are available at http://www.cs.utexas.edu/users/nn.

## References

Amari, S.-I. (1980). Topographic organization of nerve fields. *Bulletin of Mathematical Biology,* *42,* 339–364.

Barlow, H. B. (1972). Single units and sensation: A neuron doctrine for perceptual psychology? *Perception, 1,* 371–394.

Barlow, H. B. (1985). The twelfth Bartlett memorial lecture: The role of single neuron in the psychology of perception. *Quarterly Journal of Experimental Psychology, 37A,* 121–145.

Barlow, H. B. (1989). Unsupervised learning. *Neural Computation, 1,* 295–311.

Barlow, H. B. (1990). A theory about the functional role and synaptic mechanism of visual aftereffects. In C. Blakemore (Ed.), *Vision: Coding and Efficiency* (pp. 363–375). New York: Cambridge University Press.

Bauman, L., & Bonds, A. (1991). Inhibitory refinement of spatial frequency selectivity in single cells of the cat striate cortex. *Vision Research, 31*(6), 933–944.

Bienenstock, E. L., Cooper, L. N., & Munro, P. W. (1982). Theory for the development of neuron selectivity: Orientation specificity and binocular interaction in visual cortex. *Journal of Neuroscience, 2,* 32–48.

Blakemore, C., & Cooper, G. F. (1970). Development of the brain depends on the visual environment. *Nature, 228,* 477–478.

Blakemore, C., & van Sluyters, R. C. (1975). Innate and environmental factors in the development of the kitten's visual cortex. *Journal of Physiology (London), 248,* 663–716.

Blasdel, G. G. (1992). Orientation selectivity, preference, and continuity in monkey striate cortex. *The Journal of Neuroscience, 12,* 3139–3161.

Blasdel, G. G., & Salama, G. (1986). Voltage-sensitive dyes reveal a modular organization in monkey striate cortex. *Nature, 321,* 579–585.

Burkhalter, A., Bernardo, K. L., & Charles V. (1993). Development of local circuits in human visual cortex. *Journal of Neuroscience, 13,* 1916–1931.

Callaway, E. M., & Katz, L. C. (1990). Emergence and refinement of clustered horizontal connections in cat striate cortex. *Journal of Neuroscience, 10,* 1134–1153.

Callaway, E. M., & Katz, L. C. (1991). Effects of binocular deprivation on the development of clustered horizontal connections in cat striate cortex. *Proceedings of the National Academy of Sciences, USA, 88,* 745–749.

Campbell, R., Cooper, G., & Enroth-Cugell, C. (1969). The spatial selectivity of the visual cells of the cat. *Journal of Physiology (London), 203,* 223–235.

Campbell, F. W., & Maffei, L. (1971). The tilt aftereffect: A fresh look. *Vision Research, 11,* 833–840.

Carpenter, R. H. S., & Blakemore, C. (1973). Interactions between orientations in human vision. *Experimental Brain Research, 18,* 287–303.

Coltheart, M. (1971). Visual feature-analyzers and aftereffects of tilt and curvature. *Psychological Review, 78,* 114–121.

Dalva, M. B., & Katz, L. C. (1994). Rearrangements of synaptic connections in visual cortex revealed by laser photostimulation. *Science, 265,* 255–258.

De Valois, K. K., & Tootell, R. B. H. (1983). Spatial-frequency-specific inhibition in cat striate cortex cells. *Journal of Physiology (London), 336,* 359–376.

De Valois, R. L., Albrecht, D. G., & Thorell, L. G. (1982). Spatial frequency selectivity of cells in macaque visual cortex. *Vision Research, 22,* 545–559.

Durbin, R., & Mitchison, G. (1990). A dimension reduction framework for understanding cortical maps. *Nature, 343,* 644–647.

Eckhorn, R., Bauer, R., Jordan, W., Kruse, M., Munk, W., & Reitboeck, H. J. (1988). Coherent oscillations: A mechanism of feature linking in the visual cortex? *Biological Cybernetics, 60,* 121–130.

Eckhorn, R., Reitboeck, H. J., Arndt, M., & Dicke, P. (1990). Feature linking via synchronization among distributed assemblies: Simulations of results from cat visual cortex. *Neural Computation, 2,* 293–307.

Erwin, E., Obermayer, K., & Schulten, K. (1995). Models of orientation and ocular dominance columns in the visual cortex: A critical comparison. *Neural Computation, 7,* 425–468.

Fahle, M., Edelman, S., & Poggio, T. (1995). Fast perceptual learning in hyperacuity. *Vision Research, 35,* 3003–3013.

Field, D. J. (1987). Relations between the statistics of natural images and the response properties of cortical cells. *Journal of the Optical Society of America, 4,* 2379–2394.

Field, D. J. (1994). What is the goal of sensory coding? *Neural Computation, 6,* 559–601.

Fisken, R. A., Garey, L. J., & Powell, T. P. S. (1975). The intrinsic, association and commissural connections of area 17 of the visual cortex. *Philosophical Transactions of the Royal Society of London Series B, 272,* 487.

Fitzpatrick, D., Schofield, B. R., & Strote, J. (1994). Spatial organization and connections of iso-orientation domains in the tree shrew striate cortex. In *Society for Neuroscience Abstracts, 20,* 837.

Gibson, J. J., & Radner, M. (1937). Adaptation, after-effect and contrast in the perception of tilted lines. *Journal of Experimental Psychology, 20,* 453–467.

Gilbert, C. D. (1992). Horizontal integration and cortical dynamics. *Neuron, 9,* 1–13.

Gilbert, C. D., Hirsch, J. A., & Wiesel, T. N. (1990). Lateral interactions in visual cortex. In *Cold Spring Harbor Symposia on Quantitative Biology, Volume LV,* 663–677. Cold Spring Harbor Laboratory Press, Cold Spring Harbor, NY.

Gilbert, C. D., & Wiesel, T. N. (1983). Clustered intrinsic connections in cat visual cortex. *Journal of Neuroscience, 3,* 1116–1133.

Gilbert, C. D., & Wiesel, T. N. (1989). Columnar specificity of intrinsic horizontal and cortico-cortical connections in cat visual cortex. *Journal of Neuroscience, 9,* 2432–2442.

Goodhill, G. (1993). Topography and ocular dominance: A model exploring positive correlations. *Biological Cybernetics, 69,* 109–118.

Gray, C. M., König, P., Engel, A., & Singer, W. (1989). Oscillatory responses in cat visual cortex exhibit inter-columnar synchronization which reflects global stimulus properties. *Nature, 338,* 334–337.

Gray, C. M., & Singer, W. (1987). Stimulus specific neuronal oscillations in the cat visual cortex: A cortical functional unit. In *Society for Neuroscience Abstracts, 13,* 404.

Grinvald, A., Lieke, E. E., Frostig, R. D., & Hildesheim, R. (1994). Cortical point-spread function and long-range lateral interactions revealed by real-time optical imaging of macaque monkey primary visual cortex. *Journal of Neuroscience, 14,* 2545–2568.

Grossberg, S. (1976). On the development of feature detectors in the visual cortex with applications to learning and reaction-diffusion systems. *Biological Cybernetics, 21,* 145–159.

Gustafsson, B., & Wigström, H. (1988). Physiological mechanisms underlying long-term potentiation. *Trends in Neurosciences, 11,* 156–162.

Hata, Y., Tsumoto, T., Sato, H., Hagihara, K., & Tamura, H. (1993). Development of local horizontal interactions in cat visual cortex studied by cross-correlation analysis. *Journal of Neurophysiology, 69,* 40–56.

Hebb, D. O. (1949). The organization of behavior: A neuropsychological theory. New York: Wiley.

Hirsch, H., & Spinelli, D. (1970). Visual experience modifies distribution of horizontally and vertically oriented receptive fields in cats. *Science, 168,* 869–871.

Hirsch, J. A., & Gilbert, C. D. (1991). Synaptic physiology of horizontal connections in the cat's visual cortex. *The Journal of Neuroscience, 11,* 1800–1809.

Hubel, D. H., & Wiesel, T. N. (1959). Receptive fields of single neurons in the cat's striate cortex. *Journal of Physiology, 148,* 574–591.

Hubel, D. H., & Wiesel, T. N. (1962). Receptive fields, binocular interaction and functional architecture in the cat's visual cortex. *Journal of Physiology (London), 160,* 106–154.

Hubel, D. H., & Wiesel, T. N. (1965). Receptive fields and functional architecture in two nonstriate visual areas (18 and 19) of the cat. *Journal of Neurophysiology, 28,* 229–289.

Hubel, D. H., & Wiesel, T. N. (1968). Receptive fields and functional architecture of monkey striate cortex. *Journal of Physiology, 195,* 215–243.

Hubel, D. H., & Wiesel, T. N. (1974). Sequence regularity and geometry of orientation columns in the monkey striate cortex. *Journal of Comparative Neurology, 158,* 267–294.

Hubel, D. H., Wiesel, T. N., & LeVay, S. (1977). Plasticity of ocular dominance columns in monkey striate cortex. *Philosophical Transactions of the Royal Society of London [Biology], 278,* 377–409.

Kaas, J. H. (1991). Plasticity of sensory and motor maps in adult animals. *Annual Review of Neuroscience, 14,* 137–167.

Kapadia, M. K., Gilbert, C. D., & Westheimer, G. (1994). A quantitative measure for short-term cortical plasticity in human vision. *Journal of Neuroscience, 14,* 451–457.

Katz, L. C., & Callaway, E. M. (1992). Development of local circuits in mammalian visual cortex. *Annual Review of Neuroscience, 15,* 31–56.

Kohonen, T. (1982). Self-organized formation of topologically correct feature maps. *Biological Cybernetics, 43,* 59–69.

Kohonen, T. (1989). *Self-organization and associative memory.* 3rd ed. New York: Springer.

Kohonen, T. (1993). Physiological interpretation of the self-organizing map algorithm. *Neural Networks, 6,* 895–905.

Kohonen, T. (1995). *Self-organizing maps.* New York: Springer.

Köhler, W., & Wallach, H. (1944). Figural after-effects; an investigation of visual processes. *Proceedings of the American Philosophical Society, 88,* 269–357.

Linsker, R. (1990). Perceptual neural organizations: Some approaches based on network models and information theory. *Annual Review of Neuroscience, 13,* 257–281.

Löwel, S. (1994). Ocular dominance column development: Strabismus changes the spacing of adjacent columns in cat visual cortex. *Journal of Neuroscience, 14,* 7451–7468.

Löwel, S., & Singer, W. (1992). Selection of intrinsic horizontal connections in the visual cortex by correlated neuronal activity. *Science, 255,* 209–212.

Luhmann, H. J., Martínez Millán, L., & Singer, W. (1986). Development of horizontal intrinsic connections in cat striate cortex. *Experimental Brain Research, 63,* 443–448.

Malach, R., Amir, Y., Harel, M., & Grinvald, A. (1993). Relationship between intrinsic connections and functional architecture revealed by optical imaging and in vivo targeted biocytin injections in the primate striate cortex. *Proceedings of the National Academy of Sciences, USA, 90,* 10469–10473.

McCasland, J. S., Bernardo, K. L., Probst, K. L., & Woolsey, T. A. (1992). Cortical Local circuit axons do not mature after early deafferentation. *Proceedings of the National Academy of Sciences, USA, 89,* 1832–1836.

Meister, M., Wong, R., Baylor, D., & C. J. Shatz (1991). Synchronous bursts of action-potentials in the ganglion cells of the developing mammalian retina. *Science, 252,* 939–943.

Merzenich, M. M., Recanzone, G. H., Jenkins, W. M., & Grajski, K. A. (1990). Adaptive mechanisms in cortical networks underlying cortical contributions to learning and nonde-clarative memory. In *Cold Spring Harbor Symposia on Quantitative Biology, Vol. LV,* 873–887. Cold Spring Harbor Laboratory Press, Cold Spring Harbor, NY.

Miller, K. D. (1994a). A model for the development of simple cell receptive fields and the ordered arrangement of orientation columns through activity-dependent competition between on- and off-center inputs. *Journal of Neuroscience, 14,* 409–441.

Miller, K. D. (1994b). The role of constrains in Hebbian learning. *Neural Computation, 6,* 98–124.

Miller, K. D., Keller, J. B., & Stryker, M. P. (1989). Ocular dominance column development: Analysis and simulation. *Science, 245,* 605–615.

Mitchell, D. E., & Muir, D. W. (1976). Does the tilt aftereffect occur in the oblique meridian? *Vision Research, 16,* 609–613.

Obermayer, K., Blasdel, G. G., & Schulten, K. J. (1992). Statistical-mechanical analysis of self-organization and pattern formation during the development of visual maps. *Physical Review A, 45,* 7568–7589.

Obermayer, K., Ritter, H. J., & Schulten, K. J. (1990a). Large-scale simulation of a self-organizing neural network. In *Proceedings of the International Conference on Parallel Processing in Neural Systems and Computers (ICNC).* New York: Elsevier.

Obermayer, K., Ritter, H. J., & Schulten, K. J. (1990b). A principle for the formation of the spatial structure of cortical feature maps. *Proceedings of the National Academy of Sciences, USA, 87,* 8345–8349.

Pettet, M. W., & Gilbert, C. D. (1992). Dynamic changes in receptive-field size in cat primary visual cortex. *Proceedings of the National Academy of Sciences, USA, 89,* 8366–8370.

Purves, D. (1988). *Body and brain: A trophic theory of neural connections.* Cambridge, MA: Harvard University Press.

Reitboeck, H., Stoecker, M., & Hahn, C. (1993). Object separation in dynamic neural networks. In *Proceedings of the IEEE International Conference on Neural Networks* (San Francisco, CA), *2,* 638–641.

Ritter, H. J., Martinetz, T., & Schulten, K. J. (1992). *Neural computation and self-organizing maps: An introduction.* Reading, MA: Addison-Wesley.

Schwark, H. D., & Jones, E. G. (1989). The distribution of intrinsic cortical axons in area 3b of cat primary somatosensory cortex. *Experimental Brain Research, 78,* 501–513.

Shiu, L.-P., & Pashler, H. (1992). Improvement in line orientation discrimination is retinally local but dependent on cognitive set. *Perception and Psychophysics, 52,* 582–588.

Shouval, H. (1995). *Formation and organization of receptive fields, with an input environment composed of natural scenes.* PhD thesis, Department of Physics, Brown University.

Silverman, M. S., Grosof, D. H., De Valois, R. L., & Elifar, S. D. (1989). Spatial frequency organization in primate striate cortex. *Proceedings of the National Academy of Sciences, USA, 86,* 711–715.

Singer, W., Gray, C., Engel, A., König, P., Artola, A., & Bröcher, S. (1990). Formation of cortical cell assemblies. In *Cold Spring Harbor Symposia on Quantitative Biology, Vol. LV,* 939–952. Cold Spring Harbor Laboratory Press, Cold Spring Harbor, NY.

Sirosh, J. (1995). *A self-organizing neural network model of the primary visual cortex.* PhD thesis, Department of Computer Sciences, The University of Texas at Austin.

Sirosh, J., & Miikkulainen, R. (1994). Cooperative self-organization of afferent and lateral connections in cortical maps. *Biological Cybernetics, 71,* 66–78.

Sirosh, J., & Miikkulainen, R. (1996). Self-organization and functional role of lateral connections and multisize receptive fields in the primary visual cortex. *Neural Processing Letters, 3,* 39–48.

Sirosh, J., & Miikkulainen, R. (1997). Topographic receptive fields and patterned lateral interaction in a self-organizing model of the primary visual cortex. *Neural Computation, 9,* 577–594.

Sirosh, J., Miikkulainen, R., & Bednar, J. A. (1996). Self-organization of orientation maps, lateral connections, and dynamic receptive fields in the primary visual cortex. In J. Sirosh, R. Miikkulainen, & Y. Choe (eds.), *Lateral Interactions in the Cortex: Structure and Function.* Austin, TX: The UTCS Neural Networks Research Group. Electronic book, ISBN 0-9647060-0-8, http://www.cs.utexas.edu/users/nn/web-pubs/htmlbook96.

Stryker, M., Chapman, B., Miller, K., & Zahs, K. (1990). Experimental and theoretical studies of the organization of afferents to single orientation columns in visual cortex. In *Cold Spring Harbor Symposia in Quantitative Biology,* vol. LV, 515–527. Cold Spring Harbor Laboratory Press, Cold Spring Harbor, NY.

Sutherland, N. S. (1961). Figural after-effects and apparent size. *Quarterly Journal of Psychology, 13,* 222–228.

Tanaka, K. (1993). Neuronal mechanisms of object recognition. *Science, 262,* 685–688.

Tolhurst, D. J., & Thompson, P. G. (1975). Orientation illusions and aftereffects: Inhibition between channels. *Vision Research, 15,* 967–972.

Tootell, R. B., Silverman, M. S., & De Valois, R. L. (1981). Spatial frequency claims in primary visual cortex. *Science, 214,* 813–815.

Tootell, R. B., Silverman, M. S., Hamilton, S. L., Switkes, E., & De Valois, R. L. (1988). Functional anatomy of macaque striate cortex. V. Spatial frequency. *Journal of Neuroscience, 8,* 1610–1624.

Vidyasagar, T. R. (1990). Pattern adaptation in cat visual cortex is a co-operative phenomenon. *Neuroscience, 36,* 175–179.

Vidyasagar, T. R., & Mueller, A. (1994). Function of GABA inhibition in specifying spatial frequency and orientation selectivities in cat striate cortex. *Experimental Brain Research, 98,* 31–38.

von der Malsburg, C. (1973). Self-organization of orientation-sensitive cells in the striate cortex. *Kybernetik, 15,* 85–100.

von der Malsburg, C. (1987). Synaptic plasticity as basis of brain organization. In J.-P. Changeux & M. Konishi (Eds.), *The neural and molecular bases of learning* (pp. 411–432). New York: Wiley.

von der Malsburg, C. (1990). Network self-organization. In S. F. Zornetzer, J. L. Davis, & C. Lau (Eds.), *An introduction to neural and electronic networks* (Chapter 22, pp. 421–432). New York: Academic Press.

von der Malsburg, C., & Buhmann, J. (1992). Sensory segmentation with coupled neural oscillators. *Biological Cybernetics, 67,* 233–242.

von der Malsburg, C., & Singer, W. (1988). Principles of cortical network organization. In P. Rakic & W. Singer (Eds.), *Neurobiology of neocortex* (pp. 69–99). New York: Wiley.

Wandell, B. A. (1995). *Foundations of vision.* Sunderland, MA: Sinauer Associates.

Wang, D. (1996). Synchronous oscillations based on lateral connections. In J. Sirosh, R. Miikkulainen, & Y. Choe (Eds.), *Lateral interactions in the cortex: Structure and function.* Austin, TX: The UTCS Neural Networks Research Group. Electronic book, ISBN 0-9647060-0-8, http://www.cs.utexas.edu/users/nn/web-pubs/htmlbook96.

Weiss, Y., Edelman, S., & Fahle, M. (1993). Models of perceptual learning in vernier hyperactivity. *Neural Computation, 5,* 695–718.

Willshaw, D. J., & von der Malsburg, C. (1976). How patterned neural connections can be set up by self-organization. *Proceedings of the Royal Society of London, B, 194,* 431–445.

Wong, R., Meister, M., & Shatz, C. (1993). Transient period of correlated bursting activity during development of the mammalian retina. *Neuron, 11*(5), 923–938.

# PERCEPTUAL LEARNING FROM
# CROSS-MODAL FEEDBACK

*Virginia R. de Sa and Dana H. Ballard*

## I. Introduction

Ultimately we must understand how humans and animals are able to learn the complicated tasks they do. An important component of that learning process is the learning of how to form useful categories from sensory data. Thus the focus of this chapter is that of learning to classify—learning to recognize that particular patterns belong to the same class which is different from the set of classes that represent other patterns. That such learning can be difficult is illustrated by a commonly used two-dimensional vowel dataset taken from Peterson and Barney (1952),[1] shown in Fig. 1. The data represent different utterances of the common vowels of English. As you can easily see, the distributions from different classes overlap making error-free classification impossible and simple clustering nonoptimal.

Learning algorithms for classification have been the subject of study in the field of pattern recognition since the 1950s. Such algorithms attempt to find decision boundaries that best divide the distributions of exemplars from different classes. More recently such learning algorithms have been cast in the form of networks. These algorithms are termed "neural networks" since their primitives are models for biological neurons. One advantage of casting the algorithms in this form is that they can be more directly related to biological neural processing and development.

[1] The original dataset contains more dimensions (formant frequencies) but the two-dimensional version is commonly used for benchmarking algorithms.

THE PSYCHOLOGY OF LEARNING
AND MOTIVATION, VOL. 36

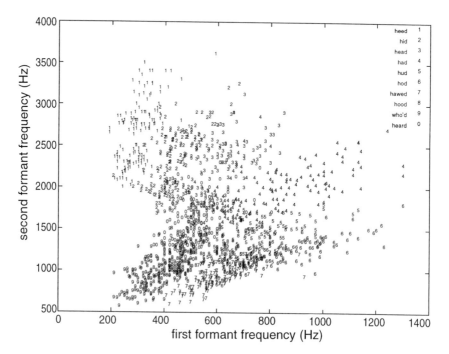

Fig. 1.   The Peterson-Barney vowel dataset. Each number (0-9) represents a different
vowel class. Each plotted number corresponds to the formants measured from one instance
of the uttered vowel plotted in terms of the first two formant frequencies (F1 and F2).

Such algorithms usually work by adjusting the connection strengths between model neurons (or units) and for that reason are termed *connectionist
algorithms*. There have been many examples of applications of connectionist
algorithms that are able to provide insight into the computational processes
in the brain. The technique used in (Lehky & Sejnowski, 1988; Zipser &
Anderson, 1988) is to train a back-propagation (Werbos, 1974; Rumelhart,
Hinton, & Williams, 1986) network with many examples of hypothesized
inputs and desired outputs and then observe the resulting receptive field
structure (as determined by the pattern of connectivity from the input
neurons). The logic behind this work is that if a network constructed to
do a task using abstract neuronal elements results in receptive fields similar
to those observed in the brain, it is possible that the brain is performing a
similar computation. While this argument has led to many computational
insights, the advances in understanding the brain are somewhat diminished
in the use of a biologically implausible learning algorithm that cannot
address the question of how the particular computational network might

develop in the brain. The two major drawbacks with back-propagation as a model of neural learning are (1), the necessity of the target output with each input pattern, and (2), the requirement of the back-propagation of the error measures to neurons in the hidden layers (those that are neither inputs nor outputs). The first problem of requiring desired outputs to learn cognitive tasks is not unique to back-propagation or connectionist modeling in general. Many cognitive models assume that the answer is somehow magically available to the learner during learning. These algorithms are called *supervised* algorithms and are tantamount to assuming that the desired mapping to be learned has already been learned by some entity whose output is available to the output of the training model!

Many models of the development of the early areas of the visual system (e.g., Linsker, 1986a–c; Miller, Keller, & Stryker, 1989; Obermayer, Ritter, & Schulten, 1990; Obermayer, Ritter, & Schulten, 1992) use more biologically plausible learning rules. These models provide a mechanism for the development of the orientation columns, ocular dominance columns, and even the particular patterns of interaction observed. The learning algorithm in these models depends only on the correlations between input patterns, and maps very well to neurophysiological ideas about the rules governing neural plasticity. The correspondence between the biologically motivated network models of the first visual cortical area (V1) and the known anatomy and physiology of monkey and cat V1 are extremely striking. However, they have been limited to modeling only this and earlier stages of processing and do not address the particular cognitive task in which an area may be participating. It seems that in order to learn high-level cognitive tasks, some indication of the desired outputs are needed during training. In other words,

. . . purely unsupervised learning based strictly on statistics, does not lead to conceptualization. This is due to the implicit assumption that every distinguishable input state potentially carries a different message. In conceptualizing, on the other hand, different input states which carry the same useful message are grouped together. This grouping requires some further knowledge that distinguishes signal from noise, or provides a measure of closeness on the signal space (Kohonen, 1984), or provides active supervision as in perceptual learning (Redlich, 1993, p. 302).

This raises the question: Is there some way to model high level cognitive tasks using more biologically plausible learning algorithms? This chapter attempts to address this question for the particular task of object recognition or classification. The major idea is that, while it is implausible that the neuronal output label is available, it is true that the environment is providing extra information not currently considered in most unsupervised algorithms (algorithms that do not provide the target signal). We argue that the world provides much more information at a global level than is available to any one sensory modality and that this information can be used to learn classifications within each modality. We use this to address the problem of required supervision in developing the *Minimizing-Disagreement* algorithm. The model is based on gross cortical anatomy and achieves powerful classification results using biologically plausible computations without requiring the correct output signal.

We begin by clarifying the inherent weakness of unsupervised algorithms for classification and discuss various versions of adding supervision to the basic competitive algorithm.

### A.  UNSUPERVISED LEARNING

A general way of representing sensory inputs is in terms of $n$-dimensional points, or vectors, groups of which can be summarized with prototypes or *codebook vectors* (because their purpose is to recode the input). A simple classification border between two such codebook vectors representing different classes is the $(n - 1)$-dimensional hyperplane midway between them. With several codebook vectors per class and several classes, nonlinear boundaries may be devised by taking the border from the *Voronoi* tessellation of these prototype points. Each codebook vector is assigned a class label and patterns are classified as belonging to the class of the closest codebook vector. These classifiers are often termed piecewise-linear classifiers for the shapes of their classification borders.

In learning algorithms, classification borders are moved indirectly by moving the codebook vectors. Competitive learning (Grossberg, 1976a,b; Kohonen, 1982; Rumelhart & Zipser, 1986) is an unsupervised, biologically plausible (Coultrip, Granger, & Lynch, 1992; Miikkulainen, 1991) way of achieving this for easily separable data clusters. In competitive learning, different neurons become responsive to different input patterns. If there are more patterns than output neurons within a competing group, then similar patterns (where similarity is defined in terms of closeness in the input space) will map to the same competitive neuron. In this way competitive learning algorithms learn to group similar inputs without a supervisory signal.

### B.  SUPERVISED LEARNING

The natural grouping produced by competitive learning is a disadvantage in many classification tasks that require the mapping of dissimilar inputs to similar outputs. In order to achieve classification based on a task-dependent semantic similarity as opposed to similarity of the inputs, it is necessary to provide more information. A common form of additional information is the label of the correct class for each input pattern, which is provided during a training phase.

One simple use of the labels is to use them to determine the cluster to which each datapoint belongs. In Fig. 2 we term this approach Supervised Competitive learning. A more powerful use of the labels is to monitor the number of misclassified patterns and minimize that number. Kohonen's (1990) LVQ2.1 algorithm is designed to find optimal borders in this way (though see de Sa & Ballard, 1993; Diamantini & Spalvieri, 1995). The

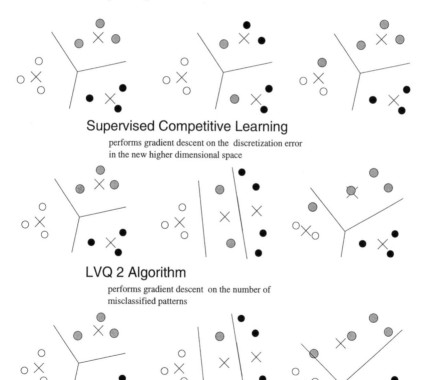

Fig. 2.   Performance of the different algorithms on three different classification problems. The three different colored circles (white, gray, and black) represent three different classes of patterns. Only the LVQ2 algorithm is able to separate the three classes appropriately. See the text for more description.

idea is to move the codebook vectors so that the border between them moves toward the crossing point of the distributions. The distributions are sampled near the currently estimated border in order to decide which way to move the border.

The LVQ2.1 learning rule moves weight vectors only when exactly one of the two closest weight vectors is from the correct class. Then, as long as the pattern falls within a "window" around the current border, the weight vector from the correct class is moved toward the pattern and the one from the other class is moved away.

It can be described informally as:

> If the pattern is near a current border, move the codebook vector of the same class toward the pattern and that of the other class away.

or more rigorously,

$$\vec{w}_i(t + 1) = \vec{w}_i(t) - \varepsilon(t)(\vec{\xi}(t) - \vec{w}_i(t))$$

$$\vec{w}_j(t + 1) = \vec{w}_j(t) + \varepsilon(t)(\vec{\xi}(t) - \vec{w}_j(t))$$

where $\vec{w}_i$ and $\vec{w}_j$ are the two closest codebook vectors and $\vec{\xi}$ belongs to $C_j$ but not $C_i$ and $\vec{\xi}$ falls in the "window" between $\vec{w}_i$ and $\vec{w}_j$. The resulting border movement increases the chances of an incorrectly classified pattern being correctly classified on a subsequent trial.

## C. SUMMARY

To summarize, the standard unsupervised algorithm classifies only based on input similarity. It is oblivious to the particular labels associated with each different task. For the three pattern distributions given at the top of Fig. 2, each classification task has the same input patterns (just with different labels) and so it classifies them all the same way. This only results in a correct separation for the first problem. By adding supervision to the standard competitive learning algorithm we can provide it with task-specific information to allow it to classify the problems in Fig. 2 differently. For appropriately separated classes, the simple algorithm of competitive learning in the augmented input space (with a dimension for each class) can provide appropriate boundaries. The algorithm is still limited, however, as it is not designed for optimal placement of the boundaries. For optimal classification with arbitrary class separation (and overlapping classes) the LVQ2.1 algorithm is best as it actually takes into account the current performance in order to improve it. These kinds of algorithms show that information about misclassifications can greatly increase the classification abilities of a piecewise-linear classifier. The power of the supervised approach lies in the fact that it directly minimizes its final error measure (on the training set). The positions of the codebook vectors are placed not to approximate the probability distributions but to decrease the number of misclassifications.

## II. Cross-Modal Information

The power of supervised algorithms in handling difficult classification tasks makes them an attraction, but unfortunately, when modeling human category learning, one must deal with the fact that there is no omniscient homunculus (or pretrained network) correctly labeling all the incoming sensory patterns. The algorithm employed by the brain does not have the correct answer always available, cannot measure its classification errors while learning, and hence cannot directly minimize them.

One solution is to use the *cross-modal structure* between signals from two or more modalities to help develop a piecewise-linear classifier within each modality. This takes advantage of the structure available in natural environments that results in sensations to different sensory modalities (and submodalities) that are correlated. For example, hearing "mooing" and seeing cows tend to occur together. So, although the sight of a cow does not come with an internal homuncular "cow" label it often co-occurs with an instance of a "moo."

These correlations have been noted before and are often used for justification in supervised cognitive models. Thus providing a "cow" label with cow images (in a model learning to recognize animals) may be justified with the statement that "an infant is told 'cow' when shown a cow." The major point of disagreement of this model from the supervised cognitive models stems from the observation that the spoken word "cow" is not a useful teaching signal until the auditory system has started to correctly parse and group speech signals. This is immediately apparent to those who have tried to build a machine speech recognition system or even observed sound spectrograms of spoken words. Similarly, as computer vision researchers are well aware, the cow picture is not a useful teaching signal for the "cow" acoustic signal until the visual system has started to appropriately group visual images. Thus although the world provides extra information in cross-modal structure it is *not* in the form of the correct neuronal target output.

If it were possible to use a multimodal feature space that combined visual and auditory signals, the class distributions would be more distant and more readily separable. Thus if $X$ is the feature space for vision and $Y$ is the feature space for audition, then $X \times Y$ should be more separable. This suggests that unsupervised clustering, or density estimation in this joint visual-auditory space would be helpful. However, simple clustering in the combined feature space, means that full-featured patterns would be needed to access the correct category (in other words, a full auditory-visual feature vector would always be needed). More suitable density estimation techniques that are capable of handling missing features rapidly become infeasible in high dimensions due to the large number of parameters. Thus the desire is to use the greater structure in the multimodal feature space while still processing in the lower dimensional spaces.

The key is to process the "moo" sound to obtain a self-supervised label for the network processing the visual image of the cow and vice-versa. This idea is schematized in Fig. 3. In lieu of correct labels each network receives the output of the other network. Again, this is fundamentally different than running two separate supervised learning systems—the networks actually develop together. Initially they do not provide very good labels for each other but the algorithm allows the networks to develop into better classifiers together. Because the networks help each other we refer to this kind of algorithm as *self-supervised*.

This general strategy was introduced in the IMAX algorithm (Becker & Hinton, 1992). The Minimizing-Disagreement (M-D) algorithm differs in that it was specifically designed to perform multi-class categorization with all communication occurring through natural and neurophysiologically plausible one-way connections. Phillips, Kay, and Smyth (1995) have recently developed a plausible implementation of IMAX for the binary classification case. Our algorithm uses reentrant feedback to allow multimodality information to influence the development of unimodal systems as in (Reeke,

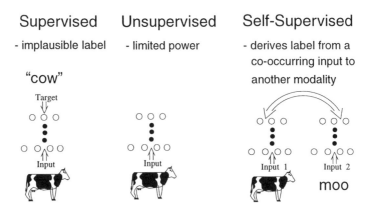

Fig. 3.   The idea behind the self-supervised algorithm.

Sporns, & Edelman, 1990; Edelman, Reeke, Gall, Tononi, & Williams, 1992); however, we concentrate solely on classification, but attack real classification tasks with overlapping input patterns. The fact that both networks are learning makes this approach significantly harder than approaches where one modality trains another (Munro, 1988; Carpenter, Grossberg, & Reynolds, 1991; Tan, 1995) or others that combine two already trained networks (Yuhas, Goldstein, & Sejnowski, 1988; Stork, Wolff, & Levine, 1992).

To start we give some of the biological motivation behind the idea of using the cross-modality structure.

## A. PSYCHOPHYSICS

The coincidence between auditory and visual events is pervasive throughout our experience. From just after birth, babies are able to turn crudely toward sounds. Over time we develop a rather precise auditory-visual spatial map. This enables us to be able to pick up correlations between auditory and visual sensations. For example, with sound localization we are able to notice that mooing comes from cows.

Another example of information picked up in this way is the ability to read lips. Anyone who has conversed in a noisy environment, is aware of the improved speech recognition achieved when the speaker's face (particularly the lips) is visible. [This has also been demonstrated in more controlled experimental conditions (Sumby, & Pollack, 1954).] The visual signal from the motion of the lips, jaw, and tongue help the auditory system understand the speech.

This ability to recognize relationships between lip movements and emitted sound develops early. By four and a half months of age infants are able to recognize that particular lip motions go with particular sounds. Kuhl and Meltzoff (1984) showed that infants looked significantly longer at the matching face when presented with the sound /a/ or /i/. Their preference was specific to the actual speech information as they did not show this effect when the speech signals were replaced with tones that followed the duration, amplitude envelope and onset/offset timing of the original speech sounds (Kuhl & Meltzoff, 1984).

The effect of lip movement on speech recognition is even more prominent when the stimuli are experimentally manipulated so that the visual and acoustic signals are discordant. In the experiments of (McGurk & MacDonald, 1976; MacDonald & McGurk, 1978) subjects are presented with acoustic stimuli of various consonant-vowel pairs and simultaneously shown images of faces speaking a different consonant with the vowel. Thus for example when presented acoustically with a /ba/ syllable and visually with a face speaking /ga/, 98% of adult subjects hear /da/ (McGurk & MacDonald, 1976). The result is very striking and not subject to conscious control. It shows that visual and auditory stimuli are able to interact to produce a unified percept, different from the stimuli actually given to either modality. Furthermore, it seems that the ability of visual signals to influence acoustic classification is at least partially learned. Preschool and school children show significantly less of the effect than do adults (McGurk & MacDonald, 1976).

Another example of experienced auditory-visual correlations affecting an auditory perception is given as an anecdote in Howells (1944). Howells reports that a driver who was familiar with an intersection that made a concurrent whistle sound as the lights changed for stop and go, failed to notice when the whistle was later disabled.

> On the next trip to the crossing, in spite of counter suggestions recently received, the driver reported a distinct hallucination of the whistle (Howells, 1944, p. 89).

In another anecdotal example where the frequencies of the whistles were different for lights changing to the stop or go signal. Howells reports

> Few drivers noticed that there was a difference in the tones, or even that a whistle sounded at all, until the wires controlling the whistles were accidentally crossed by a repairman, so the usual combinations of color and tone were reversed. The result was general confusion and a collision at the crossing (Howells, 1944 p. 90).

Under more controlled conditions, Howells (1944) trained subjects with tones followed by colored screens. On 95% of the trials, the color-tone pairing was consistent and on the other 5% of trials it was reversed. After an initial period, half the presentations were at full saturation and the other half much paler. Subjects showed increasing errors (on the pale screens preceded by the inconsistent tone) with training. Subjects tested with white stimuli after conditioning reported always the color associated with the co-occurring sound and subjects instructed to produce a white color in the presence of the high or low tone were offset in the direction opposite to that imposed during training.

A similar example of auditory events influencing visual perception is demonstrated in a cross-modal experiment in (Durgin, 1995; Durgin & Proffitt, 1996). The experiment involved repeated brief presentations of random dot patterns in two rectangular areas of a screen. On each presentation, one of the two areas received 25 dots/deg$^2$ and the other 2 dots/deg$^2$. The visual presentations were paired with auditory tone stimuli such that the pitch of the tone was perfectly correlated with the side of the denser dot pattern. After 180 flashed presentations, a staircase procedure was used to determine the perceived density equivalence (for test patterns with dot densities between the two trained densities) between the two areas when presented with each of the two tones. The experiment showed that there was a significant effect of the tone on the perceived density relationship between the patterns in the two areas. The simultaneous presentation of the tone associated with a denser texture in one area during training, lead to an impression of greater dot density in that area during testing. To match a constant density, the difference between the density required in the presence of the high pitch and that with a low pitch was 10% (Durgin, 1995).

Hefferline and Perera (1963) have shown that correlated proprioceptive (an invisibly small thumb twitch detected electromyographically) and auditory events (tone) can lead to a subject later reporting that he "still heard it (the tone)" to subsequent proprioceptive events in the absence of the tone.

Zellner and Kautz (1990) have also shown that color can affect odor perception. In their experiments, colored solutions were perceived as having a more intense odor.

> Even after being told the solutions were of equal concentrations, they [subjects] insisted that the solutions were not the same intensity (Zellner & Kautz, 1990, p. 396).

It is clear that the co-occurrence of multisensory signals can assist or interfere with processing. There is also evidence that after experience with cross-modal correlations, a unimodal discrimination can be affected by a stimulus to the other modality. We would like to go one step farther and hypothesize that this multimodality integration is important not only for improved recognition but is useful for the development of recognition features in both individual modalities. Along these lines, there is some evidence that exposure to auditory-visual co-occurrences is important for normal attentional development. Quittner and colleagues (Quittner, Smith, Osberger, Mitchell & Katz, 1994) report that deaf children show reduced *visual* attention (in a nonauditory task) than hearing children. The authors conclude that though auditory information is not used in their tested task the development of focused visual attention is helped by auditory experience (presumably coincident with visual experience).

## B.  NEUROBIOLOGY

The previous section examined results showing that information from different sensory modalities is combined in determining our perception. Often, the combination is not subject to conscious control. It is as if the results are not simply being combined at a high-level output stage but are able to influence each other in the individual processing stages. This is corroborated by neurophysiological studies which have found responses of cortical cells in primary sensory areas that respond to features from other sensory modalities. For example, Spinelli, Starr, and Barrett (1968) found sound frequency specificity in cells in primary *visual* cortex of the cat and Fishman and Michael (1973) found that these bimodal cells tend to be clustered together. As support for the unified percept observed in psychophysical studies, the stimuli are able to affect the same cell. In fact acoustic responses in a single cell could be inhibited by inhibitory visual stimuli (Morrell, 1972). More recently, Maunsell and colleagues (Haenny, Maunsell, & Schiller, 1989; Maunsell, Sclar, Nealey, & DePriest, 1991) have shown responses in visual neurons in Area V4 to oriented tactile stimuli that the animal has been trained to match to subsequently presented oriented visual gratings.

Sams and colleagues (Sams, Aulanko, Hämääinen, Hari, Lounasmaa, Lu, & Simola, 1991) have also shown effects of visual input on auditory processing in humans. Using magnetoencephalographic (MEG) recordings, they showed that although a visual signal by itself did not result in a response over the auditory cortical area, different visual signals changed the response to the auditory signal. They again used the McGurk effect stimuli. Subjects were trained with a higher percentage of either agreeing or disagreeing stimuli. Significantly different neuromagnetic measurements were made to the frequent and infrequent stimuli. As no similar differences occurred when two different light stimuli occurred with the sounds, they argue that this shows that the visual information from the face is reaching the auditory cortex.

The neurophysiological and psychophysical evidence must be reconciled with the fact that anatomically the information from the different sensory modalities goes to spatially separate, segregated cortical areas. Retinal input goes to occipital cortex whereas auditory input goes to auditory cortex in the temporal lobe. Even within the auditory and visual cortex there are many different areas which seem to be specialized to processing different parts of the signal. For instance, color processing seems to be mostly separate from motion processing (Merigan & Maunsell, 1993; Desimone & Ungerleider, 1989). There is a significant restriction on the amount of cross-modality interaction that can occur. This is thought to be due to restrictions on connectivity; it is not physically possible to have all neurons connected to all other neurons (or even any significant fraction). Therefore input from each modality and submodality must be processed separately, at least in the early stages, with little cross-talk.

As there are no direct afferent (feed-forward) connections from one input modality to another, the information from other modalities could either be coming bottom-up from shared subcortical structures such as the superior colliculus or alternatively top-down from the multi-sensory integration areas such as entorhinal cortex and other limbic polymodal areas. This idea has been suggested before (e.g., Rolls, 1989) and seems to be supported by the evidence from visual cortex. As stated by Spinelli et al. (1968)

non-visual stimuli affect the activity of ganglion cells only minutely (Spinelli, Pribram, & Weingarten, 1965; Spinelli & Weingarten, 1966; Spinelli, 1967); they affect that of the geniculate cells to a greater extent (Meulders, Colle, & Biosacq-Schepens, 1965) and very markedly affect cortical cells (Murata, Cramer, & Bach-y-Rita, 1965). Even more interaction appears to be present in prestriate cortex (Buser & Borenstein, 1959) (p. 82).

Thus we know from psychophysical studies that information from different modalities is combined and information from one modality can assist or interfere with classification in another. The physiological evidence supports this finding in showing that input to other modalities can influence processing in another sensory pathway. This combined with the anatomical evidence that shows no direct input from one modality's transducers to another pathway, suggests that this information is coming top-down through feedback pathways from multi-sensory areas. Furthermore we suggest that this integration may not just affect the properties of developed systems but play an important role in the learning process itself. Just as lip-reading is a learned classification ability, correlations between inputs to different sensory modalities may affect other classification learning in the individual modalities. This section will investigate the power that this kind of integration might provide to learning classifiers in the individual modalities.

## C. Using Cross-Modality Information for Self-Supervised Learning

Following the anatomical evidence presented earlier and acting under the assumption that it is infeasible to have neurons receiving input from the sensory transducers of all the senses, we propose an architecture such as that schematized in Fig. 3 in which each modality has its own processing stream (or classification network) but access to each other's output at a high level. This information can reach the lower levels within each processing stream through feedback within the stream.

One way to make use of the cross-modality structure in a network like this is to cluster the codebook vectors in their individual spaces, but use the joint structure to learn to label co-occurring codebook vectors with the same label. After clustering in the input space, the activity patterns in the resulting hidden unit (codebook) activation space (the space of dimensionality equal to the sum of the number of codebook vectors in each space) can be clustered. For example using Competitive learning on the second layer of weights in a network such as that in Fig. 4 will tend to cluster the codebook vectors. Each codebook vector is given the label of the output

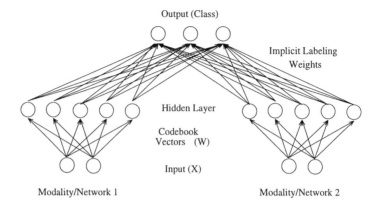

Output (Class)

Implicit Labeling
Weights

Hidden Layer

Codebook
Vectors   (W)

Input (X)

Modality/Network 1

Modality/Network 2

Fig. 4. Network for learning the labels of the codebook vectors. The weight vectors of the hidden layer neurons represent the codebook vectors while the weight vectors of the connections from the hidden layer neurons to the output neurons represent the output class that each codebook vector currently represents. In this example there are three output classes and two modalities each of which as two-dimensional input patterns and five cookbook vectors.

neuron in whose cluster it belongs (the neuron to which it projects most strongly); thus these weights can be considered implicit labeling weights.

The above use of cross-modality structure is useful and we will use it to initialize our algorithm (calling it the initial labeling algorithm); however, a more powerful use of the extra information is for better placement of the codebook vectors themselves. The insight in this algorithm is that we can make use of the joint cross-modal information without directly connecting all codebook vectors to each other and without requiring implausible communication.

The true classification goal of minimizing the number of misclassified patterns is explicitly supervised in that in order to monitor the number of misclassified patterns, one must be aware of the real class labels. For an unsupervised error function, we propose the *Disagreement Error*—the number of patterns classified differently by the two networks. The motivation behind this goal is that, in the absence of an external label, the output of the other network can take the role of the label. Each network will provide a "label" for the other network to aim for. The two modalities, representing different but co-occurring information from the same source, teach each other by finding a local minimum in their output disagreement.

We will explain the computational motivation for the learning rules with a simple one-dimensional example. Consider the 2-class example in Fig. 5. Each class has a particular probability distribution for the sensation received by each modality. If modality 1 experiences a sensation from its pattern A

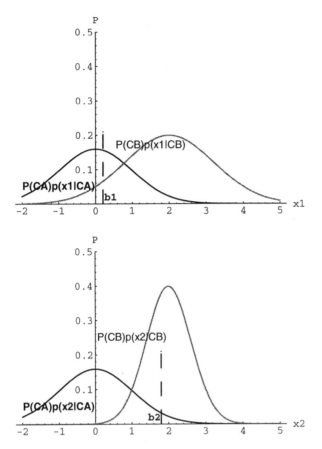

Fig. 5.   An example world as sensed by two different modalities. If modality 1 receives a pattern from its Class A distribution, modality 2 receives a pattern from its own class A distribution (and the same for Class B). Without receiving information about which class the patterns came from, they must try to determine appropriate placement of the boundaries $b_1$ and $b_2$. $P(C_i)$ is the prior probability of Class $i$ and $p(x_j|C_i)$ is the conditional density of Class $i$ for modality $j$.

distribution, modality 2 experiences a sensation from its own pattern A distribution. That is, the world presents patterns from the two-dimensional joint distribution shown in Fig. 6 but each modality can only sample its one-dimensional marginal distribution (the sum of the curves in the subfigures in Fig. 5, shown along the sides in Fig. 6). If $b_1$ is the midpoint between codebook vectors of different classes in modality 1 and $b_2$ is the same for modality 2, we can write the Disagreement Error, $E(b_1,b_2)$, in terms of these class borders (or thresholds). If the codebook vectors are such that

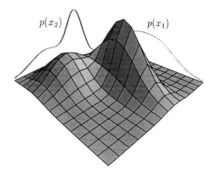

Fig. 6. The joint distribution for the example in Fig. 5. The higher dimensional joint distribution has greater structure and is used to guide the placement of borders in the individual modalities. The figure shows an example where the two variables are conditionally independent but this is not required (although as mentioned later it helps significantly).

the codebook vector for Class A is to the left of that for Class B in both modalities, the Disagreement Error is written as:

$$E(b_1,b_2) = Pr\{x_1 < b_1 \ \& \ x_2 > b_1\} + Pr\{x_1 > b_1 \ \& \ x_2 < b_2\} \tag{1}$$

$$= \int_{-\infty}^{b_1} \int_{b_2}^{\infty} f(x_1,x_2)dx_1dx_2 + \int_{b_1}^{\infty} \int_{-\infty}^{b_2} f(x_1,x_2)dx_1dx_2 \tag{2}$$

where $f(x_1,x_2)$ is the joint probability density for the two modalities. We stress again that this energy function does not depend on the class information but does make use of the joint density of all inputs and thus contains more information than that in the distributions of the individual modalities.

Applying stochastic gradient descent (Robbins & Monro, 1951; Wassel & Sklansky, 1972; Sklansky & Wassel, 1981; de Sa, 1994a,b; Diamantini & Spalvieri, 1995) to this error function gives a simple "on-line" rule for updating the position of both networks' classification borders

> If the pattern received by a modality is close to a current border, move the codebook vector of the class *that is output by the other modality* towards the pattern, and that of the other class away.

This rule moves the borders to increase the local proportion assigned to the class output by the other modality.

Similarly one can derive a generalization of this rule for multidimensional space that moves borders through moving codebook vectors. The M-D algorithm applies this rule after each presentation of multimodal stimuli; it is

1. Initialize codebook vectors (randomly from data vectors or by unsupervised clustering)

2. Initialize labels of codebook vectors using the labeling algorithm

3. Repeat for each presentation of input patterns $X_1(n)$ and $X_2(n)$ to their respective modalities

   • Find the two nearest codebook vectors in each modality to their respective input patterns

   • Find the hypothesized output class in each modality (as given by the label of the closest codebook vector)

   • For each modality update the weights according to the following rules (Only the rules for modality 1 are given)

   Updates are performed only if the current pattern $X_1(n)$ falls within c(n) of the border between two codebook vectors of different classes (one of them agreeing with the output from the other modality). In this case

   $$\vec{w}_{1_i} (n) = \vec{w}_{1_i} (n-1) + \epsilon(n) \frac{(X_1(n) - \vec{w}_{1_i} (n-1))}{||X_1(n) - \vec{w}_{1_i} (n-1)||}$$

   $$\vec{w}_{1_j} (n) = \vec{w}_{1_j} (n-1) - \epsilon(n) \frac{(X_1(n) - \vec{w}_{1_j} (n-1))}{||X_1(n) - \vec{w}_{1_j} (n-1)||}$$

   where $\vec{w}_{1_i}$ is the codebook vector with the same label, and $\vec{w}_{1_j}$ is the codebook vector with another label.

   • Update the labeling weights

Fig. 7. The Minimizing-Disagreement (M-D) algorithm—a self-supervised piecewise-linear classifier.

summarized in Fig. 7.[2] We will often refer to step 2 of the algorithm as the initial labeling stage and step 3 as the M-D stage. Weights are only updated if the current patterns falls near the middle between two codebook vectors of different classes. (The specification of this "window" and the decrease in learning step size are as in Kohonen's 1990 supervised algorithm.)

[2] The rule shown was derived from generalizing the one-dimensional rule and is slightly simpler than the rule derived from differentiating in the multidimensional space (as in Diamantini & Spalvieri, 1995). As it is simpler and in our hands has performed as well as the multidimensionally derived rule, it was used in the simulations.

To minimize disagreement with respect to the labels (last point of step 3 in Fig. 7), the implicit labeling weights of the winning codebook vector unit in one modality are moved toward the label of the co-occurring codebook vector in the other modality. In order to avoid the undesirable solution where both networks always output the same class, we use weight normalization of the "implicit labeling weights" from the hidden units to the output units in Fig. 4. In a biologically plausible implementation of the algorithm, the codebook vectors can be informed of the output class of the other network by using feedback weights from the output to codebook vector units. [These weights can be appropriately learned using Hebbian (Hebb, 1949) learning (de Sa & Ballard, in preparation).] The close codebook vectors with augmented activation are moved toward the input pattern and close ones that are not augmented with feedback activity are moved away. This type of learning rule is compatible with experimentally observed neural plasticity in visual cortical cells (Artola, Bröcher, & Singer, 1990).

Intuitively we can understand that this update rule minimizes the disagreement as follows. If Network 2 outputs Class A then Network 1 increases its future probability of saying Class A by moving its Class A codebook vector toward the pattern and the one from the other class away. If Network 2 outputs Class B then Network 1 increases its future probability of saying Class B similarly.

One might note that the global minima of the M-D Energy are all codebook positions for which all patterns are classified as the same output. However, with small enough overlap in the joint space, a local minimum exists between the two class centers. An initial border determined by most simple clustering algorithms would start within the basin of attraction of this minimum. We can show (de Sa & Ballard, in preparation) that an appropriate local minimum exists beyond the case where clusters could be separated given the individual modalities alone, but just short of what could be achieved if one could look for clusters in the joint space. The algorithm is able to extract most of the greater structure in the higher dimensional joint distribution without requiring the extra parameters for modeling in this large space. We could add additional terms to ensure this [analogous to the individual entropy terms $H(Y_1)$, $H(Y_2)$ in the IMAX (Becker & Hinton, 1992) algorithm]. However, for the datasets we have encountered this is not necessary and in fact with the vowel dataset in the next section, yielded slightly worse performance (probably because the addition of the terms changes the position of the local minimum—it is no longer minimizing the disagreement). However, it is possible that for problems with more overlap between classes (where an appropriate local minimum might not exist), terms like this might help if the current algorithm does not perform well.

In summary, instead of minimizing the misclassifications (which cannot be done without a measure of the misclassifications provided by the labels), the M-D algorithm minimizes the disagreement between the outputs of the two networks. This makes the algorithm fundamentally different from supervised algorithms. Before both networks have developed, they are providing bad label estimates—they must develop together. The next section reviews some experimental results that show that the networks are able to assist each other and significantly improve their classification abilities over their initial configuration. *We test the performance of each modality separately. The purpose of the algorithm is not to develop a method of combining sources of information for discrimination, but to develop a method of combining information for better development of the individual modules themselves.*

## III.  Artificial Modality Experiments

In order to compare performance between the M-D algorithm and unimodal supervised and unsupervised algorithms it is important that the difficulty in both modalities of the M-D problem be the same as that of the unimodal problem. This is because the M-D algorithm's performance within a modality depends not only on the difficulty of the pattern classification within that modality but also on that of the other "labeling" modality; it is this modality that is providing a better or worse teaching signal.[3] For this reason, we ran a set of experiments that applied the M-D algorithm to two networks both simultaneously learning to classify the same dataset. Thus in this case *the two "modalities" are artificial and represent two independent sources drawing from the same input distributions.* Each source is the input to one modality. Accuracy was measured for each "modality" separately (on the training set). It is important to note that we are not combining the outputs of the two modalities as in methods that reduce variance by averaging over different networks (see, e.g., Breiman, 1996). The purpose of combining the two instances of the dataset is to learn appropriate classifiers for an individual dataset. The results described below are also tabulated in Table 1 and displayed in Fig. 14.

The dataset chosen was the Peterson and Barney (1952) vowel formant dataset which consists of the formant frequencies[4] of 10 vowels spoken in

---

[3] This also addresses the criticism that it is just the "easier" modality supervising the other modality.

[4] Formant frequencies are peak frequencies in the acoustic signal and reflect resonances of the vocal tract. These resonant frequencies are characteristic of different configurations of the vocal tract and are useful features for vowel recognition.

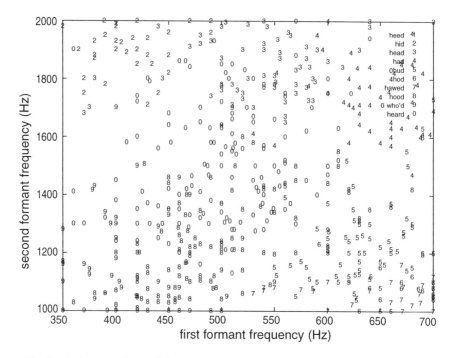

Fig. 8. A close-up of part of the Peterson-Barney vowel dataset. Note the large amount of overlap between the pattern classes in this central area.

a /hVd/ context (e.g., /had/, /hid/, . . .). We employed a version, used by and obtained from Steven Nowlan, consisting of the frequencies of the first and second formants of vowels spoken by 75 speakers (32 males, 28 females, 15 children).[5] (See Figs. 1 and 8). We stress again that each modality receives an independently chosen two-dimensional vowel from the chosen class. The purpose in these experiments was not to study vowel recognition but to better understand and examine the M-D algorithm in an easily visualizable (two-dimensional) dataset.

In the first experiment, the classes were paired so that the modalities received patterns from the same vowel class. If modality 1 received a pattern from the /a/ vowel class, modality 2 received an independently chosen pattern from the same (/a/) vowel class and likewise for all the vowel classes (i.e., $p(x_1|C_j)$-$p(x_2|C_j)$ for all $j$).

---

[5] Each speaker repeated each vowel twice except three speakers that were each missing one vowel. The raw data were linearly transformed to have zero mean and fall within the range $[-3,3]$ in both components.

## A. BETTER BORDER PLACEMENT

After the initial labeling algorithm stage (the second step in Fig. 7), the accuracy was 60 ± 5% reflecting the fact that the initial random placement of the codebook vectors does not induce a good classifier. After application of the M-D stage (the third step in Fig. 7) the accuracy was 75 ± 4%. At this point the codebook vectors are much better suited to defining appropriate classification boundaries.

The improvement in border placement can be seen by observing the arrangement of misclassified patterns after each stage. Figures 9 and 10 show the misclassified patterns after the initial labeling and M-D stage of the algorithm. These results are averaged over 20 runs in one modality. The results for the other modality are similar. The size of the diamonds corresponds to the fraction of classifiers from the 20 runs that misclassified the pattern. For both stages of the algorithm there are several patterns that are surrounded by many patterns of the same class and are always classified correctly as well as many patterns that are surrounded by patterns

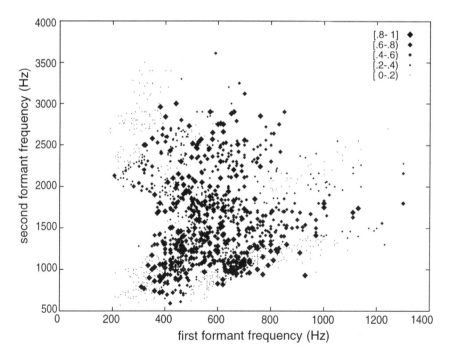

Fig. 9. Performance of initial labeling algorithm on the Peterson-Barney dataset. The size of the diamonds corresponds to the fraction of classifiers that misclassified the pattern.

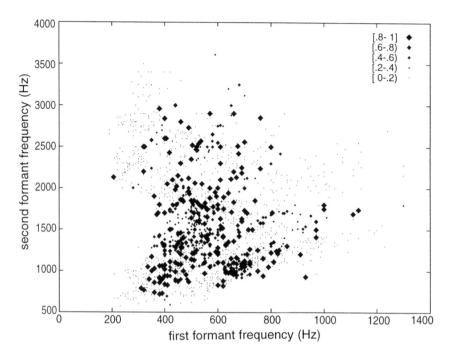

Fig. 10.   Performance after M-D algorithm on the Peterson-Barney dataset. The size of
the diamonds corresponds to the fraction of classifiers that misclassified the pattern.

from other classes that are always misclassified. However, after the M-D
stage many of the patterns between the two extremes, especially those at
the edges of the class distributions, are classified more reliably (correctly
by more of the classifiers). This shows as a decrease in diamond size from
Fig. 9 to Fig. 10.

   This difference between the two figures is made explicit in Fig. 11 where
the size of the diamonds corresponds to the difference in percentage of
classifiers that correctly classified the pattern. Filled diamonds represent
positive differences or better classification after the complete M-D algorithm and open diamonds better classification after only the initial labeling.
The improvements from the M-D stage are in the border regions between
classes indicating that minimizing the disagreement tends to find better
border placements.

### B.   CYCLING HELPS

The final performance figures were positively correlated with the performance after the label initialization step, which in turn was positively corre-

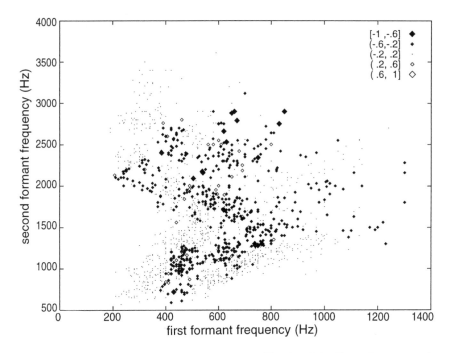

Fig. 11.   Improvement from running the M-D stage. The size of the diamonds corresponds to the difference in percentage of classifiers that correctly classified the pattern. Filled diamonds represent better classification after the M-D algorithm and open diamonds better classification after only the initial labeling.

lated with (and bounded by) the best performance possible with the randomly chosen initial codebook vectors (as measured independently with optimal labels). This suggested that improved methods of choosing the initial codebook vector positions and/or labels might result in improved final performance. Thus, we tried using the final codebook vectors from a run of the M-D algorithm as the initial codebook vectors for another run (replacing the first step in Fig. 7). This results in improved performance (73 ± 4% after step 2 and 76 ± 4% after step 3). Figure 12 shows performance after the initial labeling, first application of the M-D algorithm, and second application of the M-D algorithm for 30 different trials. This cycling of steps 2 and 3 was repeated several more times with no further significant increase in performance (see Table 1).

   The improvement can be seen in the difference plot in Fig. 13. Again the size of the diamonds corresponds to the difference in performance. The main area of improvement is in the crowded and very overlapped middle area.

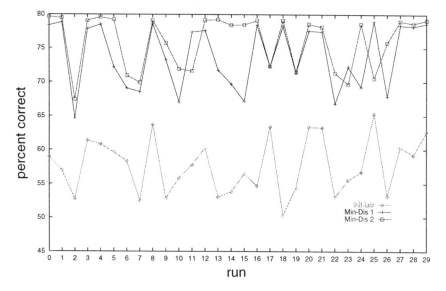

Fig. 12. The performance (for 30 different initial configurations). Performance was measured after: initial labeling (init-lab), one application of the M-D algorithm (Min-Dis 1), and two applications of the M-D algorithm (Min-Dis 2).

## C. Improvement When the Confusable Classes Are Different in the Two Modalities

One feature of cross-modality information is that classes that are easily confusable in one modality may be well separated in another. This is evident in lip-reading. For example, consonants /b/ and /p/ which differ only in voicing (the presence of vocal cord vibration) are easily acoustically distinguished even in the presence of noise (Miller & Nicely, 1955). Visually,

### TABLE I

Tabulation of Performance Figures (Mean Percent Correct and Sample Standard Deviation over 30 Trials and 2 Modalities)

|                       | 1-2(IL)  | 1-3(M-D) | 2-2     | 2-3(M-D2) | 3-3     | 4-3     | 5-3     |
|-----------------------|----------|----------|---------|-----------|---------|---------|---------|
| Same-paired vowels    | 60 ± 5   | 75 ± 4   | 73 ± 4  | 76 ± 4    | 76 ± 4  | 76 ± 4  | 76 ± 4  |
| Random pairing        | 60 ± 4   | 77 ± 3   | 77 ± 3  | 79 ± 2    | 79 ± 2  | 79 ± 2  | 79 ± 2  |

*Note*: The heading $i - j$ refers to performance measured after the $j^{th}$ step during the $i^{th}$ iteration. Step 1 is not repeated during the multiiteration runs.)

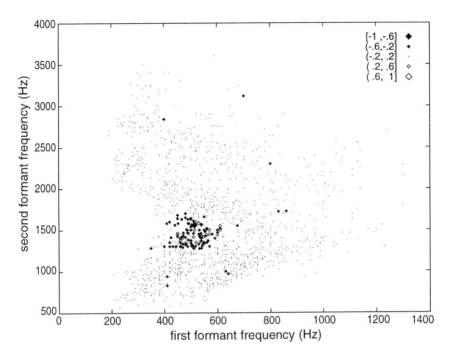

Fig. 13.    Difference in performance after one or two iterations of the M-D algorithm. The size of the diamonds corresponds to the difference in percentage of classifiers that correctly classified the pattern. Filled diamonds represent better classification after the two iteration algorithm and open diamonds better classification after the first iteration.

however, they are indistinguishable. On the other hand /b/ and /d/, which differ in their place of articulation, are visually distinct but more acoustically confusable in the presence of noise. This difference in confusable classes between the modalities should lead to improved performance with the M-D algorithm. As the "labeling" signal for separating the overlapping classes is likely determined between two nonoverlapping distributions in the other modality, it will tend to be more reliable.

To explore this, more tests were conducted with random pairing of the vowels between the modalities for each run. Vowel patterns from one class to one network were paired with vowel patterns from another class to the other network. This pairing of classes was chosen randomly before the experiments but kept consistent for each experiment. For example, presentation of patterns of /a/ vowels to one modality would be paired with presentation of patterns of /i/ vowels to the other. That is $p(x_1|C_j) = p(x_2|C_{\alpha j})$ for a random permutation $\alpha_1, \alpha_2 \ldots \alpha_{10}$. For the labeling stage the performance was as before (60 ± 4%) as the difficulty within each modality has not changed. However after the M-D algorithm the results were better as expected. After one and two iterations of the algorithm, 77 ± 3% and 79 ± 2% were classified correctly.

## D.  COMPARISON TO OTHER ALGORITHMS

The algorithm performs better than a hybrid unsupervised-supervised algorithm—Kohonen feature mapping algorithm (with 30 codebook vectors) followed by optimal labeling of the codebook vectors—which achieved 72%. [In fact if the same optimal labeling algorithm is applied to the codebook vectors resulting from the M-D algorithm, an average performance of 76% and 78% (for applying after one or two iterations, respectively) results]. Performance is not as good as that of the related fully supervised LVQ2.1 algorithm, which achieved an average performance of 80%, but is comparable to the performance of (supervised) back-propagation (with 25–200 hidden layer neurons) which obtained average performances of 73.4–78.5% (Nowlan, 1991). Nowlan's more complicated mixture model (supervised) achieved an average performance of 86.1%. These results are all shown in Fig. 14.

Figure 15 shows a comparison between the results from the two-stage M-D algorithm (with same-vowel pairs) and the results from using the supervised LVQ2.1 algorithm. Again the size of the diamonds reflects the

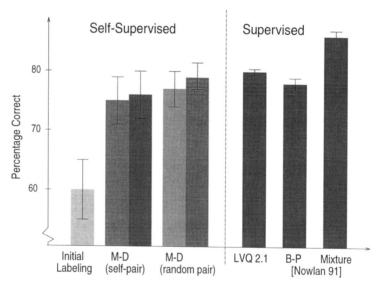

Fig. 14.   Results from different algorithms on the Peterson-Barney Vowel Dataset. The double bars for the M-D algorithms represent results from one iteration and two iterations. The error bars represent 1 standard deviation.

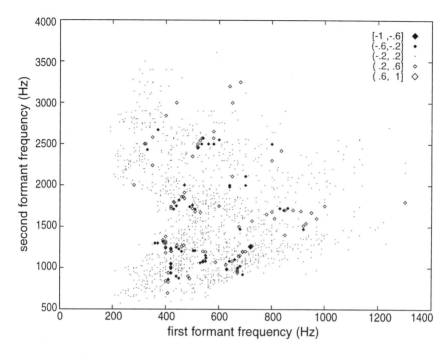

Fig. 15.  Difference in performance between the supervised and M-D algorithm. The size of the diamonds corresponds to the difference in percentage of classifiers that correctly classified the pattern. Filled diamonds represent better classification with the M-D algorithm (with two iterations) and open diamonds better classification with the supervised algorithm.

magnitude of the difference in performance and the color reflects the sign. The larger number of open diamonds reflects the slight superiority of the supervised algorithm. More strikingly though, this plot emphasizes the borders between the regions. The two algorithms differ so slightly in the resulting classifiers that the only patterns classified differently are right at the borders. The two algorithms tend to pick slightly different borders resulting in some border patterns being better classified by one algorithm and others by the other.

## IV.   Cross-Modal Experiments

### A.  DATA COLLECTION

Data were collected using an 8mm camcorder from 5 male English speakers as they spoke 26 iterations of /ba/ /va/ /da/ /ga/ /wa/.[6] Each set of 10 utter-

---

[6] A few speakers spoke more iterations.

ances (twice through the set) was preceded by a clap using a clapboard arrangement similar to that used in commercial movie production for matching the visual and auditory signals. The camera recorded 30 frames a second and was roughly positioned to view the tip of the nose through chin of the speaker. The audio was recorded through a directional microphone positioned approximately 12 cm from the speaker's mouth.

The acoustic data were transferred to a Sparc LX and low-pass filtered. Utterances were detected using threshold crossings of the smoothed time-domain waveform (using the ESPS software from Entropic Research Laboratory, Inc.). As some of the consonantal information is low amplitude (before the threshold crossing), each utterance was taken from 50 msec before the automatically detected utterance start to 50 msec after. These utterances were then encoded using a 24 channel mel code[7] over 20 msec windows overlapped by 10 msec. This is a coarse short time frequency encoding, which crudely approximates peripheral auditory processing. The final auditory code is a (24*9 = 216) dimension vector for each utterance.

The visual data were processed using software designed and written by Ramprasad Polana (1994). Visual frames were digitized as $64 \times 64$ 8 bit gray-level images using the Datacube MaxVideo system. The video and auditory tracks were aligned using the clapboard arrangement and visual detection of the clap was performed manually which allowed alignment to within 1 video frame (1/30 sec). (For an example of a video sequence showing a clap frame see Fig. 16.) The frame of the clap was matched to the time of the acoustically detected clap allowing the automatic segmentation obtained from the acoustic signal to be used to segment the video. Segments were taken as six frames before the acoustically determined utterance onset and four after. Example segments of the five different classes are shown in Figs. 17–21. The normal flow was computed using differential techniques between successive frames. Each pair of frames was then averaged resulting in 5 frames of motion over the $64 \times 64$ pixel grid. The frames were then divided into 25 equal areas ($5 \times 5$) and the motion magnitudes within each frame were averaged within each area. This gave a final visual feature vector of dimension (5 frames * 25 acres) = 125.

## B. Results

The data for one speaker were unusable due to a problem with the video-tape. The training set was made up of each of the other speakers' first 20 cycles through the utterances (minus a few cycles that could not be used due to lost frames during digitization). The test set was made up of the

---

[7] A frequency transform in which the frequency bands have linear space below 1000 Hz and logarithmic above 1000 Hz.

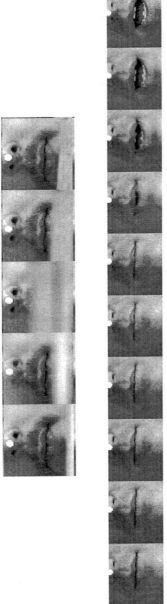

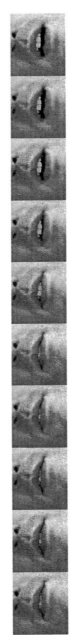

Fig. 16.   Example frames showing the clap detection. The clap is in the center frame.

Fig. 17.   Example /ba/ utterance.

Fig. 18.   Example /va/ utterance.

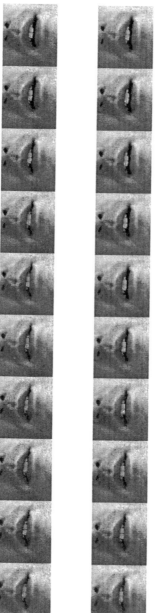

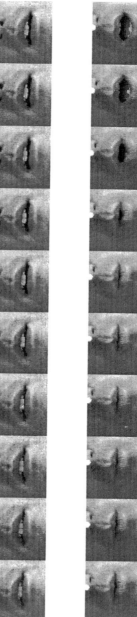

Fig. 19.   Example /da/ utterance.

Fig. 20.   Example /ga/ utterance.

Fig. 21.   Example /wa/ utterance.

next six cycles.[8] For all experiments 30 codebook vectors were used in the auditory pattern space and 60 in the visual pattern space. As the auditory signal contains more reliable information, the relative contributions from the auditory and visual networks during the labeling algorithm were weighted (1.5 to 1) in favor of the auditory choice.

We first benchmarked the dataset by running the supervised LVQ2.1 algorithm. Using 30 codebook vectors for the auditory patterns we achieved an accuracy of 99% on the training set and 93% on the test set. Using 60 codebook vectors for the visual patterns the performance was 83% on the training set and 60% on the test set. We also ran the unsupervised-supervised algorithm of Kohonen feature mapping followed by optimal labeling of the codebook-vectors. This gave accuracies of 84% and 55% on the two training sets.

Ideally we would like to test the M-D algorithm by presenting to the auditory and visual networks the pairs of patterns that occurred together. However, to get a good covering of the spaces, many utterances need to be collected. Due to the time involved in the current method of synchronizing the audio and video (they are processed separately and synchronized manually through the visual clap detection) it was decided to run preliminary experiments that artificially expand the dataset using the technique employed with the vowel dataset. This technique makes the assumption that within an utterance class the exact auditory and visual patterns are independent and thus each auditory pattern can be paired with each visual pattern from the same class (not just the one with which it actually co-occurred). For example, an individual acoustic pattern from a /ba/ utterance is randomly paired with a visual sample from a randomly chosen /ba/ utterance.

For these experiments, the M-D algorithm was applied to codebook vectors resulting from the unsupervised Kohonen learning algorithm instead of randomly initialized ones in the respective spaces.[9] The initial labeling algorithm on the codebook vectors resulting from the Kohonen learning algorithm resulted in 72% on the training set and 68% on the test set for the auditory network and 48% (training) and 36% (test) for the visual network. The M-D stage was able to greatly increase the classification performance from this initial state to 97% and 92% for the auditory network and 82% and 58% for the visual network. The performance results are summarized in Fig. 22.

While the previous results were encouraging, it was important to demonstrate the algorithm in the fully unsupervised way, making no assumptions

---

[8] For some speakers there were a few extra cycles that were also included.

[9] Initial experiments suggested that this might provide better results but later tests indicated there was not much difference.

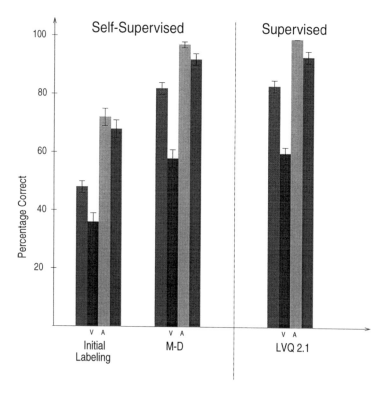

Fig. 22. Results on the preliminary cross-modal dataset. The two leftmost bars in each set of four give the performance of the visual network and the rightmost bars show the auditory network's performance. Within the two bars for each modality, the lighter and leftmost bar represents performance on the training set. The darker, rightmost bars give results on the test set. The error bars represent 1 standard deviation.

about the independence between the modalities, and using only the cross-modality information sampled from the environment. In order to accurately sample the space, we restricted the problem to that of a single speaker. This speaker repeated 120 cycles of /ba/, /va/, /da/, /ga/, and /wa/. The first 100 cycles (minus two that lost frames during the digitization) were used as the training set and the last 20 were used as the test set. Again for this cross-modal dataset the M-D algorithm was applied using the results of the Kohonen learning algorithm as the initial codebook vector positions. The algorithm achieved accuracies of 92% (train), 92% (test) on the auditory data and 91% (train), and 78% (test) on the visual data. For comparison the supervised LVQ2.1 algorithm, as well as the M-D algorithm using full-pairings as before, were also run on this dataset. The supervised results were 99% (aud-train), 95% (aud-test) and 96% (vis-train), and 82% (vis-test). The M-D algorithm using the artificial increased pairing resulted in 98% (aud-train), 95% (aud-test) and 95% (vis-train), 80% (vis-test). These results are displayed in Fig. 23).

The results demonstrate that for one speaker, the natural lip-sound co-occurrences were enough to give performance within 7 percent of the supervised results on the training set and within 4 percent of the supervised results on the test set. More data collection is needed to determine if the fully unsupervised algorithm would work on the multi-speaker problem.

## V. What Makes A Modality?

Often, as in the previous example, input data for a classification task arise from separate sources (e.g., visual and auditory sources for speech). Al-

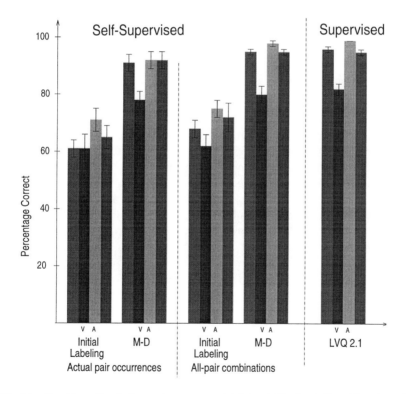

Fig. 23.    Results on the single-speaker cross-modal dataset. The two leftmost bars in each set of four give the performance of the visual network and the rightmost bars show the auditory network's performance. Within the two bars for each modality, the lighter and leftmost bar represents performance on the training set. The darker, rightmost bars give results on the test set. The error bars represent 1 standard deviation.

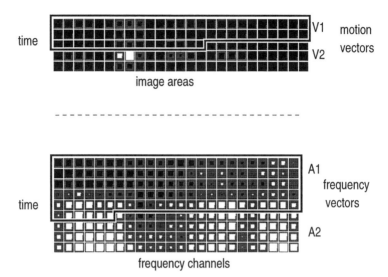

Fig. 24.   Dividing up the auditory and visual data. For the mixed-modality experiments the auditory and visual data are divided into two parts. V1 refers to the first 65 dimensions of the visual feature vector and A1 refers to the first 126 dimensions of the auditory feature vector as shown.

though these inputs from multiple sources can be considered as one long input vector for training, we have seen that having separate modalities for processing different sets of input dimensions allows the subnetworks to teach each other and avoids density modeling in high dimensional spaces. In this section we investigate the importance of, and requirements for, properly choosing the input subsets (or "modalities").

Consider splitting the auditory and visual data to produce two "submodalities" consisting of part visual or part auditory data. The data are divided as shown in Fig. 24. These new sets of dimensions (or submodalities) A1, A2, V1, and V2 can be combined in various ways to make up "pseudo-modalities." In this section, all performance figures are calculated by dividing the data 10 times into a training, validation, and test set.[10]

In order to not bias performance toward one division due to the learning parameters, a variety of reasonable parameter ranges were tried. For the supervised algorithms, the best parameters were discovered using the validation data and then trained with these parameters on the combined training and validation sets. For the M-D experiments the networks were trained

---

[10] Due to the performance averaging across the 10 divisions, the test set for some divisions appears in the training and validation sets for others. This might tend to inflate the performance results but we don't believe it would bias them toward any particular division.

## TABLE II

TABLE OF SUPERVISED PERFORMANCE FOR
THE SUBMODALITIES

| Pseudomodality | Supervised performance |
|----------------|------------------------|
| A1 | 89 ± 2 |
| A2 | 91 ± 2 |
| V1 | 83 ± 2 |
| V2 | 77 ± 3 |

*Note*: The numbers give the percentage correct performance on the test sets (and standard deviation across the 10 dataset divisions).

on the combined training and validation sets; classification performance on this set was averaged across all 10 divisions to find the best parameters.[11] The performance with the best parameters is reported on the test sets. As with the earlier cross-modal experiments, the same parameters were used for both modalities. It is possible that all the networks would benefit from different parameters on each side; however, we don't believe that this would change the general trend of our results.

First consider the submodality A1, being trained by A2 or V1 or V2. Which of the other submodalities when trained using the M-D algorithm with A1 will lead to the best subsequent A1 classifier? One could try to discover how much potential is in the various subsets by comparing the performance of supervised algorithms on each one. These results for A1, A2, V1, and V2 are reported in Table 2.

Given that A2 seems to have more potential than either set of the visual dimensions, one might think that A2 would be the best "co-modality" for training A1. The actual results however are surprising. The performance of A1 when trained with A2, V1, and V2 are shown in Table 3. V1 and A2 are equally good co-modalities for A1. The results for training A2 are even more surprising. V1 is a better co-modality than A1, and V2 and A1 are equivalent.

This relative improvement of the visual submodalities as co-modality for the auditory submodalities stems from the benefit of having uncorrelated dimensions in the other modality. If the relationships between the various dimensions does not differ much between classes (i.e., if the conditional

[11] We realize that using the classification metric to pick the learning parameters is not the best for evaluating unsupervised learning algorithms (though one can make evolutionary arguments for this), but it allowed us to quickly compare the relative capabilities of the different divisions. Also as our intent was to compare the relative benefits of divisions, we did not use the improved double iteration technique.

TABLE III

TABLE OF PERFORMANCE FIGURES FOR A1 AND A2 WHEN TRAINED BY THE
OTHER SUBMODALITIES

| Trained by | A1 | A2 | V1 | V2 |
|---|---|---|---|---|
| Performance of A1 | N/A | 69 ± 5 | 69 ± 3 | 63 ± 3 |
| Performance of A2 | 74 ± 5 | N/A | 80 ± 4 | 74 ± 5 |

*Note*: The numbers give the percentage correct performance on the test sets (and standard deviation across the 10 dataset divisions).

correlational structure is the same as the correlational structure across the whole dataset), then the clusters in the joint space are not as obvious. A simple demonstration of this is shown in Fig. 25. It is shown that as the conditional dependence between the two dimensions is increased, the bi-

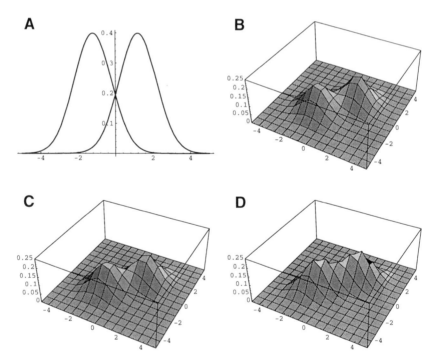

Fig. 25.    The effect of correlated dimensions. (A) Example distributions for two classes in one modality. (B) Joint distribution for two modalities as in (A) with no cross-modal correlation within the class. (C) Joint distribution for two modalities as in (A) with stronger class-modal correlations. (D) Joint distribution for the two modalities as in (A) with even stronger correlations.

modal shape in the joint distribution is less obvious. This means that the joint structure is less able to help the individual modalities to find the appropriate borders. For the M-D algorithm, the best co-modalities are those that have a lot of separation between the different classes *and* are conditionally uncorrelated (or even better have opposite correlational structure within the class than between classes) with the first modality. The auditory features for similar frequencies and time are correlated with each other, as are sets of similar spatio-temporal visual features; the auditory and visual features are reasonably uncorrelated allowing them to help significantly in the M-D architecture.

Now, let's compare the performance of the various pseudo-modalities trained with the M-D algorithm. The results are shown in Figure 26; they are arrayed in a graphical form to display many numbers at once. By comparing the numbers in the middle of the quadrants with those in the right corners we can measure the teaching ability of a M-D network given that division of modalities. The numbers below each big square give the numerical average of the M-D trained performances of each of the modalities represented by that division. This also gives a rough idea of the utility

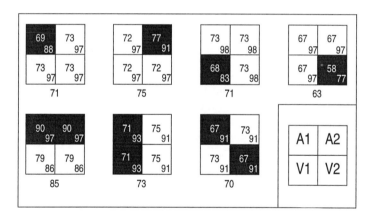

Fig. 26. The pseudo-modality results. All numbers represent the percentage of correct classifications on the test sets. Each large square represents the results from one division of modalities. Each quadrant represents one of the data subsets A1, A2, V1, and V2 as shown in the key in the lower right. All quadrants colored the same color within a square were in the same modality for training. The number in the middle of the quadrant gives the results of the pseudo-modality of that color after M-D training using the other colored quadrants as the other modality. The numbers in the lower right corner of each quadrant give the corresponding supervised performance for a network given all the quadrants of the same color (in that square). The standard deviations (across the 10 runs) vary from ±4 to ±7 for the M-D runs and ±1 to ±3 for the supervised runs.

of the particular modality division. Also, looking in one quadrant across all the squares (network architectures), one can look at the best distribution for teaching that particular quadrant. So, for example, if the goal was to have an A1 classifier at the end, and the other dimensions A2, V1, V2 were available to distribute, looking at the numbers in the A1 quadrants gives the combination of these dimensions that would be the best for the performance of the modality that includes A1.

The results reveal that the best division is to keep the auditory dimensions together, and separate from the visual dimensions. Also observe that the A1 dimensions are best helped with the M-D algorithm by training with A2 and using V1 and V2 as the teaching modality. This may not be that surprising as the A2 dimensions are very informative (as measured by their supervised performance) and by adding them to the A1 side, they are available during testing. What may be more surprising is that for V1 the best combination is to have V2 on its side and A1 and A2 on the *other* side. Again this results from the relative suitabilities of the input division. There is an increased benefit obtained by having the teaching network's input conditionally *uncorrelated* with those of its pair (uncorrelated within a class). (Note that another totally correlated input would provide very little new information.)

Finally we note that though the M-D algorithm was described as an algorithm to minimize the disagreement between the output of two sensory modalities it can be viewed more generally (keeping in mind the advantage of independence between the modalities). Ideally the algorithm could be applied hierarchically with lower levels minimizing disagreement between submodalities such as color and form. For example as the lighting changes, the color of an object may change while its form may stay relatively constant. On the other hand, while moving around the form will change but the color will stay relatively constant. The M-D algorithm could also be applied hierarchically in a spatial sense. Low-level processing could minimize disagreement between small areas while high-level processing would be minimizing disagreement over larger areas.

The algorithm can also be generalized to apply to patterns near in time. The two networks would represent delayed versions of the same input stream. The signal to the other "modality" could be a temporally close sample from the same modality. As sensations change slowly over time, the network could learn to classify objects by minimizing the disagreements between outputs for input patterns received close in time. This approach is more powerful than that of (Foldiak, 1991) as signals close in time need not be mapped to the *same* codebook vector but the closest codebook vector of the *same class*.

## VI. Concluding Remarks

### A. Summary

Many problems are better classified when the labels of the data points are available during training and classifiers can be further improved if the network attempts to minimize the number of misclassifications. We showed how to approach the performance of the minimizing misclassifications classifier without requiring labeled input patterns. The labels were replaced by an assumption that the world present patterns to different modalities in such a way that patterns from Modality 1's Class A occur with patterns from Modality 2's class A distribution. By iterating the algorithm, the labeling algorithm is able to take advantage of the better codebook vector placement and produce better results allowing the M-D algorithm to perform even better. With this two iteration algorithm the performance on the benchmark dataset was within 5% of the analogous supervised algorithm. The results were better when the confusable classes were different for the two modalities as they could provide better labeling where it was needed most. In this case the performance was within 2% of the supervised algorithm. The experiments on the visual-auditory speech data showed that the algorithm works on higher dimensional "real" patterns and the single-speaker experiments demonstrated the ability of the algorithm to work with cooccurrences present in natural cross-modal signals. The experiments with the pseudo-modalities indicate that performance with the M-D algorithm is much better when the modalities are divided with correlated dimensions kept together and those that are independent (given the class label) separated (as for example in the visual/auditory separation).

### B. Discussion

The work is shaped by the belief that to some extent, and particularly at higher levels, perceptual learning is shaped by the tasks for which it will be needed. In other words, the perceptual development of features is not an unsupervised bottom-up process but involves top-down feedback about the utility of the current features. This idea is also expressed in (Goldstone & Schyns, 1994) and is implicit in the work of Becker and Hinton (1992; Becker, 1993).

From a biological viewpoint, this work offers an explanation for why cells in one sensory area also respond to inputs to another sensory modality. We have shown that without connecting neurons to all sensory input we can still take advantage of the greater structure available in the higher dimensional total space of inputs. This occurs through integrating the modalities at a higher level and using feedback connections. The work provides an explanation for the ubiquitous back-projections in cortex whose purpose is not yet well understood. We suggest that these back-projections are important for the organization of the incoming sensory stimuli during learning.

It has long been argued that the reliable relationships between the sensations to different modalities may be an important source of "teaching" information; in this chapter we have embodied the argument in a powerful working model. We have developed an abstract algorithm for making use of the cross-modal information, examined its properties mathematically and demonstrated its performance empirically on real data.

### ACKNOWLEDGMENTS

This chapter was largely excerpted from de Sa, 1994b. In preparing this chapter, the first author was supported by postdoctoral fellowships from the Sloan Foundation and from the Natural Sciences and Engineering Research Council of Canada (NSERC). We would like to thank Robert Goldstone, Philippe Schyns, and an anonymous reviewer for comments on an earlier version of this chapter.

### REFERENCES

Artola, A., Bröcher, S., & Singer, W. (1990, September). Different voltage-dependent thresholds for inducing long-term depression and long-term potentiation in slices of rat visual cortex. *Nature, 347,* 69–72.

Becker, S. (1993). Learning to categorize objects using temporal coherence. In C. Giles, S. J. Hanson, & J. Cowan (Eds.), *Advances in neural information processing systems 5* (pp. 361–368). Morgan Kaufmann.

Becker, S., & Hinton, G. E. (1992, January). A self-organizing neural network that discovers surfaces in random-dot stereograms. *Nature, 355,* 161–163.

Breiman, L. (1996). Bagging predictors. *Machine Learning, 24*(2), 123–140.

Buser, P., & Borenstein, P. (1959). Responses somesthesiques, visuel et auditives, recuellies, au niveau du cortex "associatif" infrasylvien chez le chat curarise non anesthesie. *Electroencephalography of Clinical Neurophysiology, 11* 285–304.

Carpenter, G. A., Grossberg, S., & Reynolds, J. H. (1991). Artmap: Supervised real-time learning and classification of nonstationary data by a self-organizing neural network. *Neural Networks, 4,* 565–588.

Coultrip, R., Granger, R., & Lynch, G. (1992). A cortical model of winner-take-all competition via lateral inhibition. *Neural Networks, 5,* 47–54.

de Sa, V. R., & Ballard, D. (1993). A note on learning vector quantization. In C. L. Giles, S. J. Hanson, & J. D. Cowan (Eds.), *Advances in neural information processing systems 5* (pp. 220–227). Morgan Kaufmann.

de Sa, V. R. (1994a). Minimizing disagreement for self-supervised classification. In M. Mozer, P. Smolensky, D. Touretzky, J. Elman, & A. Weigend (Eds.), *Proceedings of the 1993 Connectionist Models Summer School* (pp. 300–307). Hillsdale, NJ: Erlbaum.

de Sa, V. R., (1994b). *Unsupervised classification learning from cross-modal environmental structure.* Unpublished doctoral dissertation, Department of Computer Science, University of Rochester, Rochester, NY. Also available as TR 536 (November 1994).

Desimone, R., & Ungerleider, L. G. (1989). Neural mechanisms of visual processing in monkeys. In F. Boller & J. Grafman (Eds.), *Handbook of neuropsychology* (Vol. 2). New York: Elsevier Science Publishers B. V.

Diamantini, C., & Spalvieri, A. (1995, November). Pattern classification by the bayes machine. *Electronics Letters, 31*(24), 2086–2088.

Durgin, F. H. (1995). *Contingent aftereffects of texture density: Perceptual learning and contingency.* Unpublished doctoral dissertation, Department of Psychology, University of Virginia, Charlottesville, VA.

Durgin, F. H., & Proffitt, D. R. (1996). Visual learning in the perception of texture: Simple and contingent aftereffects of texture density. *Spatial Vision, 9*(4), 423–474.

Edelman, G. M., Reeke, G. N., Jr., Gall, W. E., Tononi, G., & Williams, D. (1992, August). Synthetic neural modeling applied to a real-world artifact. *Proceedings of the National Academy of Sciences USA, 89,* 7267–7271.

Fishman, M. C., & Michael, C. R. (1973). Integration of auditory information in the cat's visual cortex. *Vision Research, 13,* 1415–1419.

Földiák, P. (1991). Learning invariance from transformation sequences. *Neural Computation, 3*(2), 194–200.

Goldstone, R., & Schyns, P. (1994). Learning new features of representation. In *Proceedings of the 16th Annual Meeting of the Cognitive Science Society* (pp. 974–978). Hillsdale, NJ: Erlbaum.

Grossberg, S. (1976a). Adaptive pattern classification and universal recoding: I. Parallel development and coding of neural feature detectors. *Biological Cybernetics, 23,* 121–134.

Grossberg, S. (1976b). Adaptive pattern classification and universal recoding: II. Feedback, expectation, olfaction, illusions. *Biological Cybernetics, 23,* 187–202.

Haenny, P., Maunsell, J., & Schiller, P. (1989). State dependent activity in monkey visual cortex II. retinal and extraretinal factors in V4. *Experimental Brain Research, 69*(2), 245–259.

Hebb, D. O. (1949). *The organization of behavior.* New York: Wiley.

Hefferline, R. F., & Perera, T. B. (1963, march). Proprioceptive discrimination of a covert operant without its observation by the subject. *Science, 139,* 834–835.

Howells, T. (1944). The experimental development of color-tone synesthesia. *Journal of Experimental Psychology, 34*(2), 87–103.

Kohonen, T. (1982). Self-organized formation of topologically correct feature maps. *Biological Cybernetics, 43,* 59–69.

Kohonen, T. (1990). Improved versions of learning vector quantization. In *IJCNN International Joint Conference on Neural Networks* (Vol. 1, pp. I-545–I-550). Piscataway, NJ: IEEE.

Kuhl, P. K., & Meltzoff, A. N. (1984). The intermodal representation of speech in infants. *Infant Behavior and Development, 7,* 361–381.

Lehky, S., & Sejnowski, T. (1988). Network model of shape-from-shading: Neural function arises from both receptive and projective fields. *Nature, 333,* 452–454.

Linsker, R. (1986a, November). From basic network principles to neural architecture: Emergence of orientation-selective cells. *Proceedings of the National Academy of Sciences USA, 83,* 8390–8394.

Linsker, R. (1986b, November). From basic network principles to neural architecture: Emergence of orientation columns. *Proceedings of the National Academy of Sciences USA, 83,* 8779–8783.

Linsker, R. (1986c, October). From basic network principles to neural architecture: Emergence of spatial-opponent cells. *Proceedings of the National Academy of Sciences USA, 83,* 7508–7512.

MacDonald, J., & McGurk, H. (1978). Visual influences on speech perception processes. *Perception & Psychophysics, 24*(3), 253–257.

Maunsell, J., Sclar, G., Nealey, T., & DePriest, D. (1991). Extraretinal representations in area V4 of macaque monkey. *Visual Neuroscience, 7*(6), 561–573.

McGurk, H., & MacDonald, J. (1976, December). Hearing lips and seeing voices. *Nature, 264*, 746–748.

Merigan, W. H., & Maunsell, J. H. R. (1993). How parallel are the primate visual pathways? In *Annual Review of Neuroscience* (Vol. 16, pp. 369–402). Palo Alto, CA: Annual Reviews Inc.

Meulders, M., Colle, J., & Biosacq-Schepens, N. (1965). Macro and microelectrode studies of somatic responses in the lateral geniculate body. In *Proceedings, XXIII International Congress of Physiological Sciences* (p. 364) New York: Excerpta Medica Foundation.

Miikkulainen, R. (1991). Self-organizing process based on lateral inhibition and synaptic resource redistribution. In T. Kohonen, K. Makisära, O. Simula, & J. Kangas (Eds.), *Artificial neural networks* (pp. 415–420). New York: Elsevier.

Miller, G. A., & Nicely, P. E. (1955, March). An analysis of perceptual confusions among some english consonants. *The Journal of the Acoustical Society of America, 27*(2), 338–352.

Miller, K. D., Keller, J. B., & Stryker, M. P. (1989, August). Ocular dominance column development: Analysis and simulation. *Science, 245*, 605–615.

Morrell, F. (1972, July). Visual system's view of acoustic space. *Nature, 238*, 44–46.

Munro, P. (1988, January). *Self-supervised Learning of Concepts by Single Units and "Weakly Local" Representations,* Report. No. LIS003/IS88003, School of Libary and Information Science, University of Pittsburgh, Pittsburgh, PA.

Murata, K., Cramer, H., & Bach-y-Rita, P. (1965). Neuronal convergence of noxious, acoustic and visual stimuli in the visual cortex of the cat. *Journal of Neurophysiology, 28*, 1233–1239.

Nowlan, S. J. (1991). *Soft competitive adaptation: Neural network learning algorithms based on fitting statistical mixtures.* Unpublished doctoral dissertation, School of Computer Science, Carnegie Mellon University. Pittsburgh, PA.

Obermayer, K., Ritter, H., & Schulten, K. (1990, November). A principle for the formation of the spatial structure of cortical feature maps. *Proceedings of the National Academy of Sciences, USA, 87*, 8345–8349.

Obermayer, K., Schulten, K., & Blasdel, G. (1992). A comparison between a neural network model for the formation of brain maps and experimental data. In J. E. Moody, S. J. Hanson, & R. P. Lippmann (Eds.), *Advances in Neural Information Processing Systems 4* (pp. 83–90). Morgan Kaufmann.

Peterson, G., & Barney, H. (1952). Control methods used in a study of vowels. *The Journal of the Acoustical Society of America, 24*, 175–184.

Phillips, W., Kay, J., & Smyth, D. (1995). The discovery of structure by multi-stream networks of local processors with contextual guidance. *Network: Computation in Neural Systems, 6*, 225–246.

Polana R. (1994). *Temporal texture and activity recognition.* Unpublished doctoral dissertation, Department of Computer Science, University of Rochester, Rochester, NY.

Quittner, A., Smith, L., Osberger, M., Mitchell, T., & Katz, D. (1994). The impact of audition on the development of visual attention. *Psychological Science, 5*(6), 347–353.

Redlich, A. N. (1993). Redundancy reduction as a strategy for unsupervised learning. *Neural Computation, 5*, 289–304.

Reeke, G. N., Jr., Sporns, O., Edelman, G. M. (1990). Synthetic neural modeling: The "Darwin" series of recognition automata. *Proceedings of the IEEE, 78*, 1498–1530.

Robbins, H., & Monro, S. (1951). A stochastic approximation method. *Annals of Mathematical Statistics, 22*, 400–407.

Rolls, E. (1989). The representation and storage of information in neuronal networks in the primate cerebral cortex and hippocampus. In R. Durbin, C. Miall, & G. Mitchison (Eds.), *The Computing Neuron*. Reading, MA: Addison-Wesley.

Rumelhart, D. E., Hinton, G. E., & Williams, R. J. (1986). Learning representations by back-propagating errors. *Nature, 323*, 533–536.

Rumelhart, D. E., & Zipser, D. (1986). Feature discovery by competitive learning. In D. E. Rumelhart, J. L. McClelland, & the PDP Research Group (Eds.), *Parallel distributed processing: Explorations in the microstructure of cognition* (Vol. 1, pp. 151–193). Cambridge, MA: MIT Press.

Sams, M., Aulanko, R., Hämääinen, M., Hari, R., Lounasmaa, O. V., Lu, S.-T., & Simola, J. (1991). Seeing speech: visual information from lip movements modifies activity in the human auditory cortex. *Neuroscience Letters, 127*, 141–145.

Sklansky, J., & Wassel, G. N. (1981). *Pattern classifiers and trainable machines*. New York: Springer-Verlag.

Spinelli, D. (1967). Receptive field organization of ganglion cells in the cat's retina. *Experimental Neurology, 19*, 291–315.

Spinelli, D., Pribram, K., & Weingarten, M. (1965). Centrifugal optic nerve responses evoked by auditory and somatic stimulation. *Experimental Neurology, 12*, 303–319.

Spinelli, D., Starr, A., & Barrett, T. W. (1968). Auditory specificity in unit recordings from cat's visual cortex. *Experimental Neurology, 22*, 75–84.

Spinelli, D., & Weingarten, M. (1966). Afferent and efferent activity in single units of the cat's optic nerve. *Experimental Neurology, 15*, 347–362.

Stork, D. G., Wolff, G., & Levine, E. (1992). Neural network lipreading system for improved speech recognition. In *IJCNN International Joint Conference on Neural Networks* (Vol. 2, pp. II-286–II-295) Piscataway, NJ: IEEE.

Sumby, W., & Pollack, I. (1954, March). Visual contribution to speech intelligibility in noise. *Journal of the Acoustical Society of America, 26*(2), 212–215.

Tan, A.-H. (1995). Adaptive resonance associative map. *Neural Networks, 8*(3), 437–446.

Wassel, G. N., & Sklansky, J. (1972). Training a one-dimensional classifier to minimize the probability of error. *IEEE Transactions on Systems, Man, and Cybernetics, SMC-2*(4), 533–541.

Werbos, P. (1974). *Beyond regression: New tools for prediction and analysis in the behavioral sciences*. Unpublished doctoral dissertation, Harvard University, Cambridge, MA.

Yuhas, B., Goldstein, M. H., Jr., & Sejnowski, T. (1988). Neural network models of sensory integration for improved vowel recognition. *Proceedings of the IEEE, 78*(10), 1658–1668.

Zellner, D. A., & Kautz, M. A. (1990). Color affects perceived odor intensity. *Journal of Experimental Psychology: Human Perception and Performance, 16*(2), 391–397.

Zipser, D., & Andersen, R. (1988). A back-propagation programmed network that simulates response properties of a subset of posterior parietal neurons. *Nature, 331*, 679–684.

# LEARNING AS EXTRACTION OF LOW-DIMENSIONAL REPRESENTATIONS

*Shimon Edelman*
*Nathan Intrator*

## I. Introduction

It is widely assumed that the sophisticated behavior of biological cognitive systems is due to their ability to learn from the environment, and, furthermore, that a direct consequence of learning is the formation of an internal representation of information pertinent to the task. Because learned representations can be employed in shaping the behavior in similar, and thus potentially related situations in the future, representation is a central concept in the study of learning, as it is in other fields of cognitive science.

The very universality of the idea of representation, which makes it equally useful in connectionist and in symbolic accounts of cognition, may suggest that a general theory of representation is likely to be a multifaceted, loosely coupled collection of domain-specific subtheories. We contend, however, that it is possible to identify certain core properties that any representation of the world must possess to be able to support efficient learning and learning-related behavior. Specifically, we believe that representations aimed at capturing similarity—itself the basis for generalization in learning (Shepard, 1987)—must be *low-dimensional.*

The link between the issues of similarity and of low-dimensional representations (LDRs) becomes apparent when one considers problems that arise in visual psychophysics. By definition, such problems involve a relationship between the physical characteristics of a stimulus and the perceptual event it evokes. Now, in many situations, a natural framework for a physical description of various relationships—among them similarities—between the different possible stimuli is a low-dimensional metric space. In those cases, it is reasonable to expect that the representational system reflects the dimensional structure, the topology, and maybe even the metrics, of the stimulus space. The remainder of this section examines the extent to which this expectation is fulfilled in a typical perceptual task (namely, color perception), and discusses the computational implications of these findings.

## A. A CASE STUDY: COLOR SPACES

A paradigmatic perceptual task the understanding of which requires dealing with issues of dimensionality is the perception of color. Consider the problem of computing the reflectance of a surface patch from measurements performed on its retinal image. The central feature of this problem is that the expected solution (i.e., the reflectance function of the surface) resides, in principle, in an infinite-dimensional space, because a potentially different (in the worst case, random) value of reflectance may have to be specified for each of the infinite number of wavelengths of the incident light (D'Zmura & Iverson, 1996). Furthermore, the spectral content of the illumination (which is confounded with the reflectance function multiplicatively, and which must be discounted to allow the computation of the reflectance) is also potentially infinite-dimensional, for the same reason.

In human vision, the recovery of surface reflectance in the face of possible variations in the illumination is known as color constancy. Computationally, the achievement of color constancy is difficult enough because of the need to pry apart two multiplicatively combined functions: reflectance and illumination. The infinite dimensionality of these functions seems to suggest that no set of measurements (short of an infinite and therefore an infeasible one) would suffice to support the recovery of surface reflectance. Nevertheless, human vision exhibits color constancy under a wide range of conditions (Beck, 1972), despite the small dimensionality of the neural color coding space (De Valois & De Valois, 1978); moreover, the dimensionality of the psychological (perceived) color space is also small (Boynton, 1978). In fact, both these color spaces are two-dimensional.[1]

### 1. Low-dimensional Physiological Color Space

In human vision, there are three kinds of different retinal cone types (R, G, B; in addition, there are the rods, whose spectral selectivity resembles

[1] An additional dimension in both cases is that of luminance. It should be noted that color constancy requires simultaneous processing of more than one spatial location, so that the effective dimensionality of the input to the constancy mechanism is slightly higher than two.

that of the R cones). The hue information contained in the cone responses is further transformed on its way to the brain by combining these into two channels: $R - G$ and $B - Y$, where $Y$ denotes $R + G$. The question arises, therefore, how is it possible to recover the potentially infinite-dimensional spectral quantities using this measurement mechanism.[2]

The solution to this paradox is made possible by the finite (in fact, low) dimensionality of the space of the *actual* surface reflectances. This observation has been quantified by Cohen (1964), who showed that more than 99% of the variance in the set of Munsell chip reflectance functions could be accounted for using just three basis functions (corresponding roughly to variations in intensity and in color-opponent $R - G$ and $B - Y$ channels). The space of illuminations likely to be encountered in nature appears to be equally low-dimensional: A principal component analysis of 622 measurements of daylight illumination (carried out at different times of day) showed that more than 99% of the variance can be accounted for by as few as three principal components ( Judd, MacAdam, & Wyszecki, 1964).

The findings of Cohen (1964) and of Judd et al. (1964) help one understand why a small number of independent color-selective channels suffice to represent internally most of the richness of the world of color.[3] The reason is simple: the internal representation space can be low-dimensional, because the distal space happens to be low-dimensional.

## 2.   Low-dimensional Psychological Color Space

In the preceding section we have seen that the physiological coding space for color is low-dimensional, and that its dimensionality matches that of the universe of stimuli it is geared to respond to. It should not be surprising, therefore, that the representation space fed by the color coding system is equally low-dimensional. Note, however, that the question of the dimensionality of the perceived color space belongs to psychology, not physiology. The only means for its resolution lies, therefore, in processing the responses of observers to color stimuli.

---

[2] There are several dedicated color channels (as well as a luminance channel) *for each location* in the central visual field, so that the dimensionality of the measurement system is much higher; moreover, the number of dimensions per unit solid angle varies with retinal eccentricity, being the highest around the fovea. In the present discussion, however, we are only concerned with the applicability of this system to the estimation of color, not with its spatial resolution.

[3] All of it, for all we know; any pair of colors that are metameric with respect to our color vision are indistinguishable for us. Note that metamery (or like representations for unlike stimuli) may also occur when the illumination conditions are radically different from those which our visual system has evolved to tolerate (try to distinguish between US 1 cent and 10 cent coins under an orange sodium street lamp).

A data processing tool that proved to be exceptionally useful in the characterization of internal representation spaces, including that of color, is *multidimensional scaling* (MDS). This technique is derived from the observation that the knowledge of distances among several points constrains the possible locations of the points (relative to each other) to a sufficient degree as to allow the recovery of the locations (i.e., the coordinates of the points) by a numerical procedure (Young & Householder, 1938). Assuming that the perceived similarities (that is, inverse distances, or proximities) among stimuli such as colors determine the responses made to those stimuli, one can process the responses by MDS, and examine the dimensionality of the resulting configuration of the points and the relative locations of the points. The assumption of the orderly relationship between the measured proximities and those derived from the resulting configuration is verified in the process, by the success of the MDS procedure, as manifested in the low stress (which is the cumulative residual discrepancy between those two quantities, computed over all the points). In the processing of color perception data, the configuration derived by MDS is invariably found to be approximately circular (placing violet close to red), and to reside in two dimensions, one of which corresponds to the hue, and the other to the saturation of the color (Shepard, 1962; Boynton, 1978).

## B.  IMPLICATIONS

The exploration of the metric and the dimensional structure of psychological spaces has been boosted by the improvement of the metric scaling techniques and by the development of nonmetric multidimensional scaling in the early 1960s (Shepard, 1966; Kruskal, 1964). By 1980, a general pattern was emerging from a large variety of perceptual scaling experiments: The subject's performance in tasks involving similarity judgment or perception can be accounted for to a substantial degree by postulating that the perceived similarity directly reflects the metric structure of an underlying perceptual space, in which the various stimuli are represented as points (Shepard, 1980).[4]

This pattern has not escaped the attention of theoretical psychologists. In a paper which appeared on the tri-centennial anniversary of the publication of Newton's *Philosophiae Naturalis Principia Mathematica,* and was motivated by a quest for psychological laws that would match those of mechanics, Shepard (1987) proposed a law of generalization that tied the

---

[4] The metric model of the system of internal representations is not always directly applicable, as shown by asymmetry and lack of transitivity of similarity judgments that can be obtained under a range of conditions (Tversky, 1977). A recent proposal for a reconciliation of the feature contrast theory derived from these results with the metric perceptual scaling theory is described in (Edelman, Cutzu, & Duvdevani-Bar, 1996).

likelihood of two stimuli evoking the same response to the proximity of the stimuli in a psychological representation space—the same space that so persistently turned out to be low-dimensional in the experiments surveyed in (Shepard, 1980).

The significance of Shepard's insight is twofold. First, the introduction of the notion of a psychological space puts novel stimuli on an equal footing with familiar ones: A point corresponding to a novel stimulus is always located somewhere in the representation space; all one has to do is characterize its location with respect to the familiar points. The great importance of generalization stems from the fact that the visual system literally never encounters the same stimulus twice: there are always variations in the viewing conditions such as illumination; objects look different from different viewpoints; articulated and flexible objects change their shape. Mere memory for past stimuli, faithful and extensive as it may be, is, therefore, a poor guide for behavior. In contrast, a suitable representation space can help the system concentrate on the relevant features of the stimulus, which, presumably, remain invariant.[5] In such a space, proximity is a reliable guide for generalization. Shepard's (1987) work shows that the validity of proximity as the basis for generalization is universal, and can be derived from first principles.

The second reason behind the importance of having a common space for the representation of a range of perceptual qualities in any given task has to do with the low dimensionality of such a space. This point became gradually clear only recently, with the emergence of formal approaches to the quantification of complexity of learning problems. Whereas in some perceptual tasks (such as color vision) low dimensionality of the representation stems naturally from the corresponding low dimensionality of the stimulus space, in other tasks (notably, in object shape recognition) the situation is less clear, although there are some indications that a useful common low-dimensional parameterization of diverse shapes can be achieved (see Fig. 1).

In the case of object recognition, it is tempting to argue that one should use the multidimensional signal as is, because the shape information that the visual system needs it certainly present there: "The photoreceptors are [. . .] necessarily capable of coding, by their population response, any conceivable stimulus. Why are subsequent populations needed?" (Desimone & Ungerleider, 1989, p. 268).[6] We now know that this approach to representation is untenable, as far as *learning* to recognize objects from

---

[5] The issue of invariant feature spaces is beyond the scope of the present discussion, which focuses on dimensionality.

[6] Desimone and Ungerleider meant this question to be rhetorical; representations of visual stimuli in the higher cortical areas are clearly different from those at the retinal level.

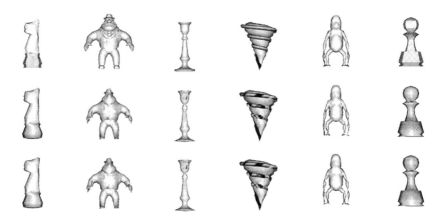

Fig. 1. *Top.* Images of several three-dimensional objects. *Middle.* Images of the same objects, parameterized with 15625 parameters and re-rendered. The parameterization was defined by computing the occupancy indices for each voxel in a 25 × 25 × 25 subdivision of the volume of each object. *Bottom.* Images rendered from the representations of the objects in a common five-dimensional parameter space, obtained from the high-dimensional voxel-based space using principal component analysis. (Data courtesy of S. Duvdevani-Bar.) If the parameterization is carried out in this manner, it will depend on the choice of objects, because the latter determines the set of basis functions that span the object space. If universal basis functions for shape, such as deformation modes, are used, the parameterization will be universal too (although its dimensionality is likely to be somewhat higher). In any case, the possibility of such parameterization indicates that a low-dimensional distal shape space may provide a basis for shape representation that is just as powerful as the low-dimensional spaces of naturally occurring illumination and reflectance spectra, discussed in section I.A.

examples is concerned. The reason for this is related to the notion of the *curse of dimensionality:* the number of examples necessary for reliable generalization grows exponentially with the number of dimensions (Bellman, 1961; Stone, 1982). Learnability thus necessitates dimensionality reduction.

## C.  DIMENSIONALITY REDUCTION

Although empirical evidence for the low dimensionality of the psychological representation spaces has been accumulating steadily for some decades now, there is still a widespread tendency in psychology to overlook the computational problem presented by the derivation of low-dimensional representations from perceptual data. The main reason behind this state of affairs is the mistaken assumption that the raw data available to the cognitive system reside in an immediately accessible low-dimensional space. For example, textbooks typically describe visual perception as the extraction of information from the *two-dimensional* retinal image, completely ignoring the fact that the immediate successor of the retinal space in the processing hierarchy is, in primates, a million-dimensional space spanned by the activities of the individual axons in the optic nerve (cf. the discussion on the dimensionality of space in Poincaré, 1913).

Obviously, the million numbers available at any given moment at the point of entry to the visual system must be somehow combined together if the dimensionality of the signal is to be reduced. How is this reduction to be done? The visual needs of a simple organism—think of a sea snail equipped with a few dozens of photoreceptors—may be satisfied, e.g., by computing the mean and the standard deviation of the activities of the photoreceptors. Such an approach to LDR extraction would result in a two-dimensional representation making explicit the ambient luminance in the creature's environment and something like the contrast of the optical stimulus—signals possibly related to the presence and the size of other creatures in the vicinity of the observer.

Obtaining a greater amount of visual information from the environment calls for a more advanced approach to dimensionality reduction. Consider, for example, a system intent on learning to discriminate between images of two human faces, under varying viewpoint and illumination. Under the present formalism, an image of a face is presented initially as a point in the high-dimensional space corresponding to the photoreceptors in the fovea (or the pixels, in a computer vision system). To learn to attribute a point to its proper class, itself represented by a cluster of points in the high-dimensional pixel space, a system must be able to distinguish between two kinds of movements in this space: (1) those precipitated by changes in the viewing conditions, and (2) those that correspond to changes in the identity of the face. These changes span two manifolds in the million-dimensional space of pixels. While each of these manifolds may be of a much lower dimensionality, they are likely to be very difficult to find, because they are embedded in so many dimensions. Thus, the problem of the extraction of the relevant dimensions may, as it were, be difficult or easy, but it is quite obvious that this problem is not trivial.

The choice of an approach to the reduction of dimensionality to a manageable level clearly depends on the computational reasons for having an initially high-dimensional measurement space. One such reason is the need for the highest possible resolution in the input space. For example, in shape discrimination, high spatial resolution may be required for distinguishing objects that belong to the same category. Note that even when a family of objects can be given a common low-dimensional description, the features involved in such a description (that is, the dimensions of an appropriate representation space) are unknown a priori to the observer. Furthermore, the relevant features may change from one task to another even when the collection of objects under consideration is fixed. Thus, a visual system would do well if it insures itself against the possibility of losing an important dimension by making as many measurements as possible. This increases the likelihood that any dimension of variation in the stimulus will have a nonzero projection on at least some of the dimensions of the measurement space. Finally, another reason for having a high-dimensional measurement space at the front end of a perceptual system is the need for sparse feature sets; the importance for learning of having just a few features active for any give object is discussed in (Barlow, 1959, 1990, 1994); see also (Young & Yamane, 1992; Field, 1994; Rolls & Tovee, 1995).

### D.  Intermediate Conclusions

The conclusions of the above introductory survey of the issue of dimensionality in perceptual representation and learning constitute a curious mixture of opposites: Even if the task at hand can be given a low-dimensional parameterization, a visual system has no direct access to the distal parameter space, and must, therefore, resort to massively redundant measurements, which carry with them the curse of dimensionality. In the rest of this chapter, we argue that the hope of exploiting the intrinsic low-dimensional structure of problems of vision is, nevertheless, well-founded. In section II, we review a number of relevant computational approaches to dimensionality reduction. Section III then presents, in some detail, two empirical studies that support our view of LDR extraction. Finally, section IV recapitulates the central message of our approach, and suggests possible directions in which it can be extended.

## II.  Some Computational Approaches to Dimensionality Reduction

The full importance of the characterization of the psychological spaces as metric (or, at least, topological) and low-dimensional cannot be realized in the absence of the proper mathematical apparatus. Fortunately, the recent developments in mathematical statistics and in computational learning theory supplied some useful tools; some of these will be surveyed in this section. The different approaches to dimensionality reduction are to be judged, within the present framework, by the following features:

1. *Biological relevance.* Procedures for dimensionality reduction are mostly of interest to us insofar as they can serve as models for this function in biological information processing systems.

2. *The ability to deal with high-dimensional spaces.* The approaches described in the literature are tested, typically, on the reduction of dimensionality by a factor of 3–10. In comparison, the problem of dimensionality reduction that arises in biological perceptual systems involves spaces whose dimensionality runs in the tens of thousands, if not millions.

3. *Data- and task-dependence.* Those approaches that define the low-dimensional space relative to or in terms of a given data set (rather than in absolute terms) are of special interest, because the relevant structures change from one task to another.

4. *Fidelity.* Of particular value are those methods that reflect as closely as possible the layout of some intrinsic low-dimensional pattern formed by the data points, despite their embedding in the high-dimensional measurement space.

In the remainder of this section, we survey a number of approaches that address some of the above concerns; two additional promising methods are discussed in section III, in connection with some psychophysical and computational experiments in dimensionality reduction.

## A. Vector Quantization and Clustering

Clustering methods, which have a long history in pattern recognition (Duda & Hart, 1973), can serve to reduce dimensionality if each data point (vector) is quantized—represented by the label of the cluster to which it is attributed. Network versions of clustering algorithms frequently involve familiar learning rules, such as the Hebbian rule of synaptic modification (Moody & Darken, 1989). The basic idea behind these methods is two-phase iterative optimization. Given the required or expected number of clusters, the algorithm first adjusts the means of the candidate clusters so as to reflect the cluster membership of each observation. Second, cluster memberships are updated based on the new means.

Many variations on this approach are possible. A statistically relevant formal framework here is that of fitting the data with a mixture of Gaussians, for which the estimation of the parameters is guided by the maximum likelihood principle ( Jacobs, Jordan, Nowlan, & Hinton, 1991). In general, clustering techniques tend to be very sensitive to the dimensionality of the data, leading to large quantization distortions and to problems associated with local minima of the optimization criterion; to alleviate these problems, recently proposed global vector quantization methods use optimization by simulated annealing (Rose, Gurewitz, & Fox, 1992). Another potential problem with vector quantization is its reliance on the raw (measurement-space) distances between data points, which, in many cases, are inappropriate.[7] In principle, this problem may be approached by incorporating knowledge about the task into the definition of the distance function (Baxter, 1995), although the practical value of this approach is as yet unclear.

## B. DISCRIMINANT ANALYSIS

Given a number of independent features (dimensions) relative to which data are described, discriminant analysis (Fisher, 1936) creates a linear combination of these which yields the largest mean differences between the desired classes (clusters). In other words, discriminant analysis seeks those projections that minimize intra-class variance while maximizing inter-class variance. If the dependent (class) variable is a dichotomy, there is one discriminant function; if there are $k$ levels of the dependent variable, up to $k - 1$ discriminant functions can be extracted, and the useful projections can be retained. Successive discriminant functions are orthogonal to one another, like principal components (discussed below), but they are not the same as principal components, because they are constructed to maximize the differences between the values of the dependent variable. Recently, it has been observed that the classical formulation of discriminant analysis is not accurate when the dimensionality is close to the number of training patterns used to calculate the discriminating directions; an added variability due to the high dimensionality should be taken into account (Buckheit and Donoho, 1995). As far as network implementation is concerned, linear discrimination is efficiently learned by a single-layer Perceptron (Rosenblatt, 1958). Some recent nonlinear extensions of discriminant analysis are discussed in (Hastie, Tibshironi, & Buja, 1994).

## C. PRINICIPAL COMPONENTS AND MAXIMUM INFORMATION PRESERVATION

In the reduction of dimensionality by principal component analysis (PCA), data are projected onto the leading eigenvectors of their covariance matrix, corresponding to the directions of maximum variance. Numerous network-based approaches to PCA have been proposed (Sejnowski, 1977; Oja, 1982; Linsker, 1986; Kammen & Yuille, 1988; Miller, Keller, & Stryker, 1989; Sanger, 1989). Linear reconstruction of the original data from principal component projections is optimal in the mean square error sense. This approach is thus optimal when the goal is to reconstruct accurately the inputs, and is also optimal for the maximum information preservation (mutual information maximization), if the data are normally distributed. PCA

---

[7] For example, in the pixel space, the distance between two images of the same face taken under different illuminations is likely to be larger than the distance between images of two different faces, taken under similar illuminations (Moses, Adini, & Ullman, 1994).

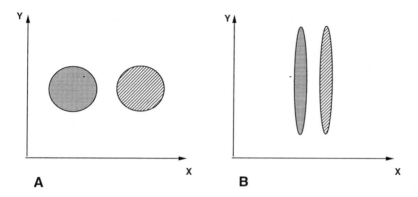

Fig. 2. Principal components find useful structure in data (A) and fail when the variance of each cluster is different in each direction (B).

is not optimal when the goal is classification, as illustrated by the simple example in Fig. 2 (see also Duda & Hart, 1973, p. 212). This figure presents two sets of points, each belonging to a different class. The goal is to simplify the representation with a minimal loss in information, which, in this case, amounts to finding a one-dimensional projection that captures the class structure exhibited in the data.

Clearly, the structure in the data is conveyed by projecting the data onto the $x$ direction. This direction also maximizes the projection variance for Fig. 2A, but not for Fig. 2B. Similarly, minimizing the reconstruction error is achieved by projecting onto the $x$ direction for Fig. 2A and by projecting onto the $y$ direction for Fig. 2B. Here, therefore, is a simple example in which the goal of cluster information preservation contradicts that of finding the principal component of the data.[8] This suggests that information preservation is to be preferred over PCA for pattern recognition applications (these two criteria coincide for the normal data distribution).

## D. Projection Pursuit

Following the realization that information preservation may be very different from the extraction of principal components, and that projection onto the principal component directions may not be useful in the case of non-Gaussian distribution, it becomes relevant to ask: What can count as an interesting structure (important information) in a high-dimensional non-Gaussian data distribution?

[8] One may wonder why principal components miss the important structure in the data, while another projection does not. The answer lies in the fact that principal components are concerned with first and second order moments of the data; when there is important information in higher-order moments, it cannot be revealed by PCA.

One possible answer here is provided by the Projection Pursuit (PP) methods (Huber, 1985). These seek features emphasizing the non-Gaussian nature of the data, which may be exhibited by (semi) linear projections. The relevance to neural network theory is clear, since the activity of a neuron is widely believed to be a semilinear function of the projection of the inputs onto the vector of synaptic weights. Diaconis and Freedman (1984) have shown that for most high-dimensional clouds (of points), most low-dimensional projections are approximately Gaussian. This finding suggests that important information in the data is conveyed in those directions whose single-dimensional projected distribution is far from Gaussian. Polynomial moments are good candidates for measuring deviation from Gaussian distribution; for example, skewness and kurtosis which are functions of the first four moments of the distribution, are frequently used in this connection.

Intrator (1990) has shown that a BCM[9] neuron can find structure in the data that exhibits deviation from normality in the form of multimodality in the projected distributions. Because clusters cannot be found directly in the data due to its sparsity (recall the curse of dimensionality), this type of deviation, which is measured by the first three moments of the distribution, is particularly useful for finding clusters in high-dimensional data, and is thus useful for classification or recognition tasks. Applications of this method are described in (Intrator, 1993; Intrator, Reisfeld, & Yeshurun, 1996).

E.  INDEPENDENT COMPONENT ANALYSIS

Independent component analysis (ICA) (Comon, 1994; Bell & Sejnowski, 1995) attempts to find an affine transformation of the input data so that in the new coordinate system, the different dimensions are statistically independent. This is a stronger constraint compared with principal component analysis, which only requires that the different dimensions be uncorrelated. In other words, ICA seeks a factorizing transformation so that the joint probability density function becomes a product of unidimensional densities, by minimizing the mutual information between the different dimensions. This actually leads to a minimization of higher order correlations, in addition to the second-order correlation of the PCA. It is yet unclear whether this formulation is appropriate for dimensionality reduction, although an attempt to extend the formulation to a dimensionality reduction method was recently presented (Amari, Cichocki, & Yang, 1996).

[9] BCM stands for Bienenstock, Cooper, and Munro (1982), who formulated a learning rule designed to model early visual cortical plasticity. The current version of this rule, its mathematical properties, statistical motivation and network extensions are discussed in (Intrator & Cooper, 1992).

## F.  Topology-Preserving Dimensionality Reduction

We now turn to the discussion of topology-preserving methods; these can be especially useful for representing data for which an a priori pattern of similarities is given, and which are known to reside in an intrinsically low-dimensional space (embedded in a high-dimensional measurement space).[10] Intuitively, such data may be thought of as a set of points drawn on a sheet of rubber, which is then crumpled into a (high-dimensional) ball. The objective of a dimensionality reducing mapping is to unfold the sheet and make its low-dimensional structure explicit. If the sheet is not torn in the process, the mapping is topology preserving; if, moreover, the rubber is not stretched or compressed, the mapping preserves the metric structure of the original space, and, hence, the original configuration of points.

The requirement that the mapping be of the latter kind (i.e., an isometry) is very restrictive: if it is to hold globally, the mapping must be linear. For local approximate isometry, any smooth and regular mapping is sufficient.[11] Moreover, near linearity and smoothness are also *necessary* for topology preservation. This is good news, as far as the learnability of the mapping is concerned: A smooth mapping implies a small number of parameters to be learned. This, in turn, reduces the likelihood of overfitting and poor generalization, which plague learning algorithms in high-dimensional spaces.

The oldest nonlinear method for topology-preserving dimensionality re-duction is multidimensional scaling, already mentioned in section I.A.2. MDS has been originally developed in psychometrics, as a method for the recovery of the coordinates of a set of points from measurements of the pairwise distances between those points. MDS can serve to reduce dimen-sionality if the points are embedded into a space of fewer dimensions than the original space in which interpoint distances were measured. The main problem with MDS, if it is considered as a method for massive dimensional-ity reduction rather than as a tool for exploration of experimental data in applied sciences (Shepard, 1980; Siedlecki, Siedlecki, & Sklansky, 1988), is its poor scaling with dimensionality (Intrator & Edelman, 1997).

In the context of learning, a number of methods for topology-preserving dimensionality reduction have been derived from the idea of a self-supervised auto-associative network (Elman & Zipser, 1988; DeMers & Cottrell, 1993; Demartines & Hérault, 1996). Because these methods are unsupervised, they extract representations that are not orthogonal to the

---

[10] A good simple example is, again, color: there is a natural pattern of similarities that must be observed (e.g., pink should be presented as closer to red than to green), and the objective color spaces are low-dimensional, as we have seen in section I.A.

[11] A discussion of such *quasiconformal* mappings in the context of shape representation can be found in (Edelman & Duvdevani-Bar, 1997).

irrelevant dimensions of the input space. An interesting approach that combines supervised feature extraction with topology preservation was proposed in (Koontz & Fukunaga, 1972), whose dimensionality reduction algorithms explicitly optimize a joint measure of class separation and (input-space) distance preservation (see also Webb, 1995). This approach, which resembles MDS, suffers from the same poor scaling with the dimensionality.

A recent technique that combines PCA and clustering (Kambhatla & Leen, 1994) attempts to first cluster the input space and then perform bottleneck dimensionality reduction in different regions separately. In this way, they attempt to overcome the drawback of PCA, namely, its ability to find only linear structure. However, the clustering part of this method is sensitive to the dimensionality.

## G. HYBRID DIMENSIONALITY REDUCTION

Because of the potential benefits of bringing all possible kinds of information to bear on the problem of dimensionality reduction, numerous attempts have been made to combine unsupervised with supervised learning for that purpose (Yamac, 1969; Gutfinger & Sklansky, 1991; Bridle & MacKay, 1992). Typically, these approaches use a hybrid learning rule to train a network, which then develops a reduced-dimensionality representation of the data at its hidden layer. In this context, it is possible to impose prior knowledge onto the network by minimizing the effective number of its parameters using weight sharing, in which a single weight is shared among many connections in the network (Waibel, Hanazawa, Hinton, Shikano & Lang, 1989; Le Cun, Boser, & Denker, 1989). An extension of this idea is the "soft" weight sharing, which favors irregularities in the weight distribution in the form of multimodality (Nowlan & Hinton, 1992). This penalty has been shown to improve generalization results obtained by hard weight elimination, under which a weight whose value becomes smaller than a predefined threshold is set to zero. Both these methods make an explicit assumption about the structure of the weight space, but disregard the structure of the input space.

As described in the context of projection pursuit regression (Intrator, 1993), a penalty term may be added to the cost function minimized by error back-propagation, for the purpose of measuring directly the goodness of the projections[12] (see Fig. 3). This emphasizes the choice of the "right" prior, as a means to improve the bias/variance tradeoff (Geman, Bienenstock, & Doursat, 1992). Penalty terms derived from projection pursuit constraints tend to be more biased toward the specific problem at hand, and therefore may yield improved generalization for instances of that problem.

[12] The essence of Exploratory Projection Pursuit (Friedman, 1987) is to seek projections so that the projected distribution is far from Gaussian.

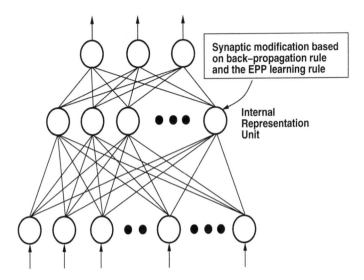

Fig. 3.  A hybrid neural network for dimensionality reduction, which combines exploratory projection pursuit and standard backpropagation learning rules; see section II.G. The low-dimensional representation is formed at the hidden layer of the network.

## III. Examples

The multiplicity of the available approaches to dimensionality reduction prompts one to ask which of them constitutes the best model of the shape processing subsystem in human vision, or, for that matter, whether the framework of dimensionality reduction is at all relevant to shape processing. Unlike the objective color spaces (the spectra of surface reflectances, and of daylight illumination), which, as we noted above, have been known for quite some time to be low-dimensional (Cohen, 1964; Judd et al., 1964), spaces of naturally occurring shapes still await characterization.[13]

Even though it is as yet unknown whether or not classes of natural objects can be considered as residing in inherently low-dimensional spaces, it is possible to find out whether the human visual system is geared to take advantage of low dimensionality, if the latter is forced on a set of artificially constructed stimuli. An early study involving such stimuli (closed contours, parameterized by two orthogonal variables), conducted by Shepard and Cermak (1973), showed that human subjects judge shape similarity as if they represent the shapes as points in a two-dimensional space, whose

[13] An exception here is the space of human head shapes (Atick, Griffin, & Redlich, 1996); see also section III.B.

placement is correct in the sense of being isomorphic (with respect to shape similarity) to the original parameter space used to generate the shapes.

## A. VERIDICAL PERCEPTION OF LOW-DIMENSIONAL SIMILARITY PATTERNS AMONG THREE-DIMENSIONAL SHAPES

A recent systematic study of shape similarity perception that we describe next confirmed the ability of the human visual system to attune itself to the proper low-dimensional contrasts among shapes, despite the embedding of these contrasts in high-dimensional measurement and in intermediate representation spaces (Edelman, 1995a; Cutzu & Edelman, 1996).

### 1. The Psychophysical Experiments

The experiments by Cutzu and Edelman (1996) involved animal-like solid objects, generated and rendered using computer graphics software. The shape of each object was defined by a point in a common 70-dimensional parameter space (the *shape space*). The planar (two-dimensional) and regular shape-space configurations formed by the stimuli in each experiment (see Fig. 4, left, for an example) were chosen to facilitate the comparison

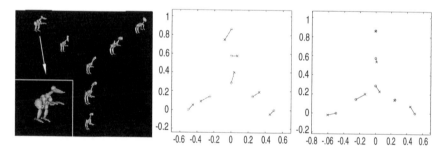

Fig. 4. *Left.* STAR, one of the four shape-space configurations used in the experiments of (Cutzu and Edelman, 1996) (see section III.A). The inset shows one of the shapes, at about one third of its actual screen size, as seen by the subjects in a typical experiment. *Middle.* The 7-point configuration (corresponding to the seven members of the STAR pattern), recovered by multidimensional scaling from subject data, then Procrustes-transformed (i.e., scaled, rotated, translated, and possibly reflected) to align with the true configuration (by "true" configuration we mean the one constructed in a parameter space chosen arbitrarily in advance of the experiments. For a discussion of the issue of different possible parameterizations, see Edelman & Duvdevani-Bar (1997)). The circles mark the true shape-space locations of the seven objects; the x's – the locations determined by MDS; lines connect corresponding points. The total length of the lines if the Procrustes distance between the two configurations; Monte Carlo analysis indicated that this distance was significantly below that obtained by chance, in all the experiments. *Right.* The configuration recovered by MDS from the response data of a computational model of shape perception, described in section III.A. Here too, the similarity between the recovered and the true configurations was highly significant.

between the (distal) shape space and the (proximal) representation space, recovered from the subject's response data using multidimensional scaling. The psychophysical data were gathered using three different methods for estimating perceived similarity. In the pairs of pairs comparison experiments, the subjects differentially rated pairwise similarity when confronted with two pairs of objects, each revolving in a separate window on a computer screen. In the long-term memory variant of this method, the subjects were first trained to associate a label with each object, then carried out the pairs of pairs comparison task from memory, prompted by the object labels rather than by the objects themselves. In the delayed match-to-sample experiments, pairs of static views of the same object or of different objects were consecutively and briefly flashed on the screen; the subject had to decide whether or not the two views were of the same object under different orientations, or of different objects. The response time and error rate data from each experiment were entered into proximity tables, as described in (Cutzu & Edelman, 1996), and were submitted to MDS.

In all the experiments, the parameter-space configurations according to which the stimuli had been arranged (such as the STAR configuration in Fig. 4, left) were easily recognizable in the MDS plots. Procrustes analysis (Borg & Lingoes, 1987) indicated that the similarity between the MDS-derived and the objective configurations was significantly above chance, as estimated by bootstrap (Efron & Tibshirani, 1993). Notably, the parameter-space configurations of the stimuli were also recovered in the long-term memory experiments, in which the subjects could not rely on immediate percepts or short-term memory representations of the stimuli (cf. Shepard & Chipman, 1970).

## 2. A Computational Model: Chorus of Prototypes

By virtue of the algorithmic definition of the MDS procedure, the two-dimensional shape space recovered from the subject data closely reflects the subjects' internal representation space.[14] The low dimensionality of the latter space indicates, therefore, that the faithful perception of similarities among the stimuli by the subjects was accompanied by a massive dimensionality reduction, which, moreover, preserved the topographic layout of an original low-dimensional space throughout the shape processing pathway.

To elucidate the possible computational basis for this feat of the human visual system, the shape perception experiments were replicated with two computer models. In the first model, designed to illustrate the behavior of a raw image-based measure of similarity, object views were convolved with

[14] Provided that the MDS stress is small (Kruskal & Wish, 1978), as it was in the above experiments.

an array of overlapping Gaussian receptive fields. The proximity table for each parameter-space configuration was constructed by computing the Euclidean distances between the views, encoded by the activities of the receptive fields. In the MDS-derived view-wise configurations, views of different objects were grouped together by object orientation, not by object identity. Thus, a simple image-based representation (which may be considered roughly analogous to an initial stage of processing in the primate visual system, such as the primary visual area V1), could not reproduce the results observed with human subjects.

The second model, which we call the Chorus of Prototypes (Edelman, 1995b), corresponded to a higher stage of object processing, in which nearly viewpoint-invariant representations of familiar object classes are available; a rough analogy is to the inferotemporal visual area IT (Young & Yamane, 1992; Logothetis, Pauls, & Poggio, 1995). Such a representation of a three-dimensional object can be relatively easily formed, given several views of the object (Ullman & Basri, 1991), e.g., by training a radial basis function (RBF) network to interpolate a characteristic function for the object in the space of all views of all objects (Poggio & Edelman, 1990). In the simulations, an RBF network was trained to recognize each of a number of reference objects (in the STAR configuration, illustrated in Fig. 4, the three corner objects were used as reference). At the RBF level, the (dis)similarity between two stimuli was defined as the Euclidean distance between the vectors of outputs they evoked in the RBF modules trained on the reference objects. Unlike in the case of the simple image-based similarity measure realized by the first model, the MDS-derived configurations obtained with this model showed significant resemblance to the true parameter-space configurations (Fig. 4, right).

The nature of dimensionality reduction performed by the Chorus scheme can be characterized by viewing its action as interpolation: intuitively, one would expect the proximal representation of the distal (objective) shape space to be a (hyper) surface that passes through the data points and behaves reasonably in between. Now, different tasks carry with them different notions of reasonable behavior. Consider first the least specific level in a hierarchy of recognition tasks: deciding whether the input is the image of some (familiar) object. For this purpose, it would suffice to represent the proximal shape space as a scalar field over the image space, which would express for each image its degree of "objecthood" (that is, the degree to which it is likely to correspond to some familiar object class). Some of the relevant quantities here are the activity of the strongest-responding prototype module, and the total activity of the modules (cf. Nosofsky, 1988). Note that it is possible to characterize a superordinate-level category of the input image, and not merely decide whether it is likely to be the image of a familiar object, by determining the identities of the prototype modules that respond above some threshold (i.e., if say, the "cat," the "sheep," and the "cow" modules are the only ones that respond, the stimulus is probably a four-legged animal; see Edelman et al., 1996).

At the basic and the subordinate category levels, one is interested in the location of the input *within* the shape space, which, therefore, can no longer be considered a scalar. Parametric interpolation is not possible in this case, as the intrinsic dimensionality of the shape space is not given a priori. Now, the prototype response field induced by the reference-object modules constitutes a nonparametrically interpolated vector-valued representation of the shape space, in the following sense: changing the shape ("morphing") one object into another, corresponding to a movement of the point in the shape space, makes the vector of reference-module responses rotate smoothly between the point corresponding to the two objects.

The multiple-classifier Chorus scheme for dimensionality reduction possesses a number of useful properties, which extend beyond the list of requirements stated at the beginning of section II (namely, biological relevance, the ability to deal with high-dimensional inputs, data-dependence, and fidelity). Of particular interest in the context of categorization is the possibility to use Chorus as the basis for the construction of a versatile and flexible model of perceived similarity; if the saliency of individual classifiers in distinguishing between various stimuli is kept track of and is taken into consideration depending on the task at hand, then similarity between stimuli in the representation space can be made asymmetrical and non-transitive, in accordance with Tversky's (1977) general contrast model (Edelman et al., 1996).

Surprisingly, Chorus shares its most valuable feature—the ability to make explicit, with a minimal distortion, the low-dimensional pattern formed by a collection of stimuli that reside in an extremely high-dimensional measurement space—with an entire class of other methods. Specifically, any method that (1) realizes a smooth mapping between a distal low-dimensional problem space (e.g., a shape space) and an internal representation space; (2) can be taught to assign a proper label to each distal stimulus; and (3) can be made to ignore irrelevant dimensions of variation in the data (e.g., downplay variation in viewpoint relative to variation in shape), is likely to support a faithful low-dimensional representation of all members of the category from which its training data are chosen (Edelman & Duvdevani-Bar, 1997). Support for this observation is provided by the results cited in the next section, where faithful low-dimensional representation of a space of human head shapes emerges following training on a classification task unrelated to similarity preservation, in an architecture that is unrelated to that of the multiple-classifier scheme described above.

B.  LOW-DIMENSIONAL REPRESENTATION AS A SUBSTRATE FOR THE
    TRANSFER OF LEARNING

Our next case study, taken from (Intrator & Edelman, 1997), is intended
to demonstrate (1) that a low-dimensional representation is an efficient
means for supporting the development of versatile categorization performance through learning, and (2) that topographically faithful representations can emerge through a process of learning, even when the latter is
guided by considerations other than the preservation of topography.[15]

   The study that we summarize below addressed the problem of learning
to recognize visual objects from examples, whose solution requires the
ability to find meaningful patterns in series of images, or, in other words,
in spaces of very high dimensionality. As in the cases we discussed above,
dimensionality reduction in this task is greatly assisted by the realization
that a low-dimensional solution, in fact, exists. In particular, the space of
images of a given object is a smooth, low-dimensional subspace of the space
of images of all objects (Ullman & Basri, 1991; Jacobs, 1996).

   The mere knowledge of the existence of a low-dimensional solution does
not automatically provide a method for computing that solution. To do
that, the learning system must be biased toward solutions that possess the
desirable properties—a task that is highly nontrivial in a high-dimensional
space, because of the curse of dimensionality. The method for dimensionality reduction described in (Intrator & Edelman, 1997) effectively biases
the learning system by combining multiple constraints via an extensive use
of class labels. The use of multiple class labels steers the resulting low-
dimensional representation to become invariant to those directions of variation in the input space that are irrelevant to classification; this is done
merely by making class labels independent of these directions. In this
section, we describe the outcome of a computational experiment involving
images of human faces, which indicates that the low-dimensional representation extracted by this method leads to improved generalization in the
learned tasks, and is likely to preserve the topology of the original space.

### 1.  The Extraction of a Low-Dimensional Representation

As in the "bottleneck" approaches to dimensionality reduction (Cottrell,
Munser, & Zipster, 1987; Leen & Kambhatla, 1994), Intrator and Edelman
(1996) forced a classifer (which, for the purpose of the present discussion,
may remain a black box) to learn a set of class labels for input objects,
while constraining the dimensionality of the representation used by the
classifier. Unlike in the standard methods, however, the classifier had to

---

[15] In this section, we are concerned with the formation of task-dependent representations that
possess useful properties such as topography preservation; the integration of these into a coherent
global representation space will be treated elsewhere (Intrator & Edelman, in preparation).

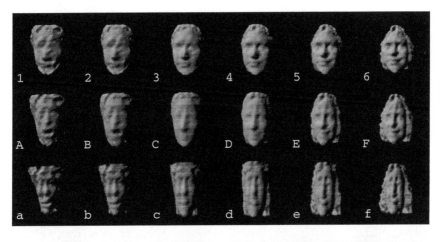

Fig. 5. Some of the images from the FACES data set (see section III.B). *Top.* The 18 heads obtained by placing $3 \times 6$ grid in the space of the two leading principal components of the original nine heads. *Bottom.* The 7 views of the rightmost head in the top row above; the views differ by 3° steps of rotation in depth, summing up to a total difference of 18°. Prior to classification, the images, originally of size $400 \times 400$, were reduced to $49 \times 16 = 784$ dimensions by cropping the background and by correlation with a bank of filters (the exact spatial profile of these filters turned out to be unimportant; Gaussian filters did just as well as opponent center-surround ones).

produce only the labels, rather than reconstruct the input patterns. This approach, therefore, constitutes a compromise between completely unsupervised and totally supervised methods in that it uses a label that individuates a given data item, but does not require information regarding the relationship between the different items, let alone the complete reconstruction of the data as in the bottleneck autoencoder systems.

The ability of this method to discover simple structure embedded in a high-dimensional measurement space was demonstrated on a face data set, in which the extraction of the LDR (low-dimensional representation) requires a highly nonlinear transformation on the measurement space.[16] At the basis of this data set lies a two-dimensional parametric representation space, in which 18 classes of faces are placed on a regular $3 \times 6$ grid; an

[16] Intrator and Edelman (1997) applied their method also to another data set, consisting of parameterized fractal images.

additional parametric dimension, orthogonal to the first two, models the within-class variation (see Fig. 5). To impose a distinctive low-dimensional structure on the set of faces, we followed the simple approach of common parameterization by principal component analysis (PCA). This was done by starting with a set of nine three-dimensional laser scans of human heads, and by embedding the $3 \times 6$ grid in the two-dimensional space spanned by the two leading "eigenheads" obtained from the data by PCA. Each of the 18 heads derived by PCA from the original scanned head data was piped through a graphics program, which rendered the head from seven viewpoints, obtained by stepping the (simulated) camera in $3°$ rotation steps around the midsagittal axis.

## 2. Results

The application of the label-based method led to a good recovery of the relevant low-dimensional description of the FACES data set (see Fig. 6). The performance of this method in recovering the row/column parametric

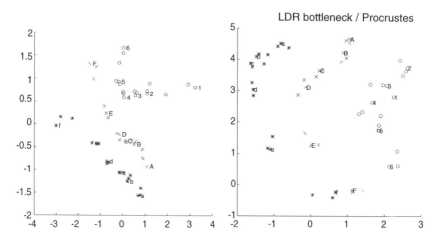

Fig. 6. FACES data set, dimensionality reduction by a bottleneck multilayer perceptron (MLP); the plots show the locations of the $18 \times 3$ test stimuli in the space spanned by the activities of the units residing in a hidden layer (18 faces times 3 test orientations per face). *Left.* Results obtained with a 3-layer MLP with 13 units in the middle hidden layer, trained for 20,000 epochs on the 18-way classification task. The low-dimensional representation proved to be a good substrate for solving classification tasks on which the system has not been trained: the error rate on a random nonlinear dichotomy involving the 18 classes was 0.02, compared to 0.07 obtained by a system trained specifically on that dichotomy, but using the raw multidimensional representation; see Intrator & Edelman (1997) for details. *Right.* Results for a 5-layer bottleneck MLP with 2 hidden units in the middle hidden layer, trained on the 18-way classification task. The test dichotomy error rate was 0.1, compared to 0.29 on the raw data.

structure of the 18 classes seems to be especially amazing. Thus, combining multiple constraints via an extensive use of class labels is an effective way to impose bias on a learning system whose goal is to find a good LDR.[17] In particular, the use of multiple class labels helps to steer the system to become *invariant* to those directions of variation in the input space that play no role in the classification tasks. This is done merely by using class labels that are invariant to these directions.

## 3.  Implications

An important feature of the LDR computed by this method is the preserva-tion of the topology of the "true" parametric space underlying the data, which is especially relevant in the context of human cognition. As we have seen in section III,A, a low-dimensional pattern built into complex two-dimensional shapes (by arranging these shapes in a conspicuous configura-tion in an underlying parameter space) is recovered by the visual system of subjects required to judge similarities between the shapes (Shepard & Cermak, 1973; Cortese & Dyre, 1996; Edelman, 1995a; Cutzu & Edelman, 1996). These findings show that the human visual system is capable of recovering the proper low-dimensional representation of the stimuli from a several thousand-dimensional measurement space (dictated by the num-ber of pixels taken by this object representation), while preserving the topology of the original space (and in many cases the exact relative place-ment of the stimuli in that space). The comparable capabilities of the two computational models of LDR extraction (the one described in section III.A, and the other outlined in the present section) suggest that topography-preserving dimensionality reduction may be less elusive than previously thought, and, in fact, may be a generic property of systems that realize a broad class of mappings between the world and their internal representation space,[18] as proposed in (Edelman & Duvdevani-Bar, 1997).

## IV.  Summary and Conclusions

To paraphrase the title of E. Wigner's (1960) paper, the unreasonable effectiveness of living representational systems may seem to suggest, at first, that there must be something special about such systems that allows

[17] A series of control experiments with a 5-layer nonlinear bottleneck autoencoder (Kamb-hatla & Leen, 1994) showed that self-supervised dimensionality reduction cannot recover a good LDR in the present case, illustrating the importance of guidance provided by the class labels.

[18] Namely, mappings that are smooth, regular, and that project out the irrelevant dimensions, while preserving the relevant ones at least to some minimal extent.

them to harbor representations of the world. It seems to be more likely, however, that the phenomenon of representation may be yet another natural category, which developed under evolutionary pressure in response to certain traits of the world with which the system interacts (cf. Millikan, 1984). No doubt, some of the relevant properties of the world contribute more than others in any given case of successful representation. We propose that over and above those diverse properties there is a unifying principle: various aspects of the world are represented successfully insofar as they can be expressed in a low-dimensional space.

Specifically, we suggest that the possibility of effective representation stems from the low-dimensional nature of the real-world classification tasks: an intelligent system would do well merely by reflecting the low-dimensional distal space internally. This undertaking, however, is not as straightforward as it sounds. Because the relevant dimensions of the distal stimulus variation are neither known in advance nor immediately available internally, the preceptual front end to any sophisticated representational system must start with a high-dimensional measurement stage, whose task is mainly to assure that none of the relevant dimensions of stimulus variation are lost in the process of encoding. The ultimate performance of the system depends, therefore, on its capability to reduce the dimensionality of the measurement space back to an acceptable level, which would be on par with that of the original, presumably low-dimensional, distal stimulus space.

## ACKNOWLEDGMENTS

Thanks to Peter Dayan and Josh Tenenbaum for useful suggestions, and to Rob Goldstone and Julian Hochberg for comments on an early version of this paper. Shimon Edelman is an incumbent of the Sir Charles Clore Career Development Chair at the Weizmann Institute of Science.

## REFERENCES

Amari, S., Cichocki, A., & Yang, H. H. (1996). A new learning algorithm for blind signal separation. In G. Tesauro, D. Touretzky, & T. Leen (Eds.), *Advances in neural information processing systems* (Vol. 8). Cambridge, MA: MIT Press.

Atick, J. J., Griffin, P. A., & Redlich, A. N. (1996). The vocabulary of shape: Principal shapes for probing perception and neural response. *Network, 7,* 1–5.

Barlow, H. B. (1959). Sensory mechanisms, the reduction of redundancy, and intelligence. In *The mechanisation of thought processes* (pp. 535–539). H.M.S.O., London.

Barlow, H. B. (1990). Conditions for versatile learning, Helmholtz's unconscious inference, and the task of perception. *Vision Research, 30,* 1561–1571.

Barlow, H. B. (1994). What is the computational goal of the neocortex? In C. Koch & J. L. Davis (Eds.), *Large-scale neuronal theories of the brain* (Chap. 1, pp. 1–22). Cambridge, MA: MIT Press.

Baxter, J. (1995). The canonical metric for vector quantization. NeuroCOLT NC-TR-95-047, University of London.

Beck, J. (1972). *Surface color perception.* Ithaca, NY: Cornell University Press.

Bell, A. J., & Sejnowski, T. J. (1995). An information-maximisation approach to blind separation and blind deconvolution. *Neural Computation, 7*(6), 1129–1159.

Bellman, R. E. (1961). *Adaptive control processes.* Princeton, NJ: Princeton University Press.

Bienenstock, E., Cooper, L., & Munro, P. W. (1982). Theory for the development of neural selectivity: orientation specificity and binocular interaction in visual cortex. *Journal of Neuroscience, 2,* 32–48.

Borg, I., & Lingoes, J. (1987). *Multidimensional similarity structure analysis.* Berlin: Springer.

Boynton, R. M. (1978). Color, hue, and wavelength. In E. C. Carterette & M. P. Friedman (Eds.), *Handbook of perception* (Vol. V, pp. 301–347). New York, Academic Press.

Bridle, J. S., & MacKay, D. J. C. (1992). Unsupervised classifiers, mutual information and 'Phantom Targets'. In J. Moody, S. Hanson, & R. Lippmann (Eds.), *Advances in neural information processing systems,* (Vol. 4, pp. 1096–1101). San Mateo, CA: Morgan Kaufmann.

Buckheit, J., & Donoho, D. L. (1995). Improved linear discrimination using time-frequency dictionaries. Stanford university technical report.

Cohen, J. (1964). Dependency of the spectral reflectance curves of the Munsell color chips. *Psychonomic Sciences, 1,* 369–370.

Comon, P. (1994). Independent component analysis, a new concept? *Signal Processing, 36,* 287–314.

Cortese, J. M., & Dyre, B. P. (1996). Perceptual similarity of shapes generated from Fourier Descriptors. *Journal of Experimental Psychology: Human Perception and Performance, 22,* 133–143.

Cottrell, G. W., Munro, P., & Zipser, D. (1987). Learning internal representations from grayscale images: An example of extensional programming. In *Ninth Annual Conference of the Cognnitive Science Society* (pp. 462–473). Hillsdale, NJ: Erlbaum.

Cutzu, F., & Edelman, S. (1996). Faithful representation of similarities among three-dimensional shapes in human vision. *Proceedings of the National Academy of Science, 93,* 12046–12050.

Demartines, P., & Hérault, J. (1996). Curvilinear component analysis: a self-organizing neural network for non linear mapping of data sets. Submitted to IEEE Transaction on Neural Networks.

DeMers, D., & Cottrell, G. (1993). Nonlinear dimensionality reduction. In S. J. Hanson, J. D. Cowan, & C. L. Giles (Eds.), *Advances in neural information processing systems* (Vol. 5, pp. 580–587). San Mateo, CA: Morgan Kaufmann.

Desimone, R., & Ungerleider, L. (1989). Neural mechanisms of visual processing in monkeys. In F. Boler & J. Grafman (Eds.), *Handbook of neuropsychology* (Vol. 2, pp. 267–299). Amsterdam, Elsevier.

De Valois, R. L., & De Valois, K. K. (1978). Neural coding of color. In E. C. Carterette, & M. P. Friedman (Eds.), *Handbook of perception* (Vol. V, pp. 117–166). New York: Academic Press.

Diaconis, P., & Freedman, D. (1984). Asymptotics of graphical projection pursuit. *Annals of Statistics, 12,* 793–815.

Duda, R. O., & Hart, P. E. (1973). *Pattern classification and scene analysis.* New York: Wiley.

D'Zmura, M., & Iverson, G. (1996). A formal approach to color constancy: the recovery of surface and light source spectral properties using bilinear models. In C. Dowling, F. Roberts, & P. Theuns (Eds.), *Recent progress in mathematical psychology.* Hillsdale, NJ: Erlbaum.

Edelman, S. (1995a). Representation of similarity in 3D object discrimination. *Neural Computation, 7,* 407–422.

Edelman, S. (1995b). Representation, similarity, and the chorus of prototypes. *Minds and Machines, 5,* 45–68.

Edelman, S., Cutzu, F., & Duvdevani-Bar, S. (1996). Similarity to reference shapes as a basis for shape representation. In G. W. Cottrell (Ed.), *Proceedings of 18th Annual Conf. of the Cognitive Science Society,* pp. 260–265, San Diego, CA.

Edelman, S., & Duvdevani-Bar, S. (1997). Similarity, connectionism, and the problem of representation in vision. *Neural Computation, 9,* 701–720.

Efron, B., & Tibshirani, R. (1993). *An introduction to the bootstrap.* London: Chapman and Hall.

Elman, J. L., & Zipser, D. (1988). Learning the hidden structure of speech. *Journal of the Acoustical Society of America, 83,* 1615–1626.

Field, D. J. (1994). What is the goal of sensory coding? *Neural Computation, 6,* 559–601.

Fisher, R. A. (1936). The use of multiple measurements in taxonomic problems. *Annals of Eugenics, 7,* 179–188.

Friedman, J. H. (1987). Exploratory projection pursuit. *Journal of the American Statistical Association, 82,* 249–266.

Geman, S., Bienenstock, E., & Doursat, R. (1992). Neural networks and the bias-variance dilemma. *Neural Computation, 4,* 1–58.

Gutfinger, D., & Sklansky, J. (1991). Robust classifiers by mixed adaptation. *IEEE Transactions on Pattern Analysis and Machine Intelligence, 13,* 552–567.

Hastie, T., Tibshirani, R., & Buja, A. (1994). Flexible discriminant analysis by optimal scoring. *Journal of the American Statistical Association, 89,* 1255–1270.

Huber, P. J. (1985). Projection pursuit (with discussion). *The Annals of Statistics, 13,* 435–475.

Intrator, N. (1990). A neural network for feature extraction. In D. S. Touretzky & R. P. Lippmann (Eds.), *Advances in neural information processing systems* (Vol. 2, pp. 719–726). San Mateo, CA: Morgan Kaufmann.

Intrator, N. (1993). Combining exploratory projection pursuit and projection pursuit regression with application to neural networks. *Neural Computation, 5*(3), 443–455.

Intrator, N., & Cooper, L. N. (1992). Objective function formulation of the BCM theory of visual cortical plasticity: Statistical connections, stability conditions. *Neural Networks, 5,* 3–17.

Intrator, N., & Edelman, S. (1997). Learning low dimensional representations of visual objects with extensive use of prior knowledge. *Network,* in press.

Intrator, N., Reisfeld, D., & Yeshurun, Y. (1996). Face recognition using a hybrid supervised/unsupervised neural network. *Pattern Recognition Letters, 17,* 67–76.

Jacobs, D. W. (1996). The space requirements of indexing under perspective projections. *IEEE Transactions on Pattern Analysis and Machine Intelligence, 18,* 330–333.

Jacobs, R. A., Jordan, M. I., Nowlan, S. J., & Hinton, G. E. (1991). Adaptive mixtures of local experts. *Neural Computation, 3*(1);79–87.

Judd, D. B., MacAdam, D. L., & Wyszecki, G. (1964). Spectral distribution of typical daylight as a function of correlated color temperature. *Journal of the Optical Society of America, 54,* 1031–1040.

Kambhatla, N., & Leen, T. K. (1994). Fast non-linear dimension reduction. In J. D. Cowan, G. Tesauro, & J. Alspector (Eds.), *Advances in neural information processing systems,* (Vol. 6). San Mateo, CA: Morgan Kaufmann.

Kammen, D., & Yuille, A. (1988). Spontaneous symmetry-breaking energy functions and the emergence of orientation selective cortical cells. *Biological Cybernetics, 59,* 23–31.

Koontz, W. L. G., & Fukunaga, K. (1972). A nonlinear feature extraction algorithm using distance information. *IEEE Trans. Comput., 21,* 56–63.

Kruskal, J. B. (1964). Multidimensional scaling by optimizing goodness of fit to a nonmetric hypothesis. *Psychometrika, 29*(1), 1–27.

Kruskal, J. B. and Wish, M. (1978). *Multidimensional scaling.* Beverly Hills, CA: Sage Publications.

Le Cun, Y., Boser, B., Denker, J., Henderson, D., Howard, R., Hubbard, W., & Jackel, L. (1989). Backpropagation applied to handwritten zip code recognition. *Neural Computation, 1,* 541–551.

Leen, T. K., & Kambhatla, N. (1994). Fast non-linear dimension reduction. In J. D. Cowan, G. Tesauro, & J. Alspector (Eds.), *Advances in neural information processing systems* (Vol. 6). San Francisco, CA: Morgan Kauffman.

Linsker, R. (1986). From basic network principles to neural architecture. *Proceedings of the National Academy of Sciences, USA, 83,* 7508–7512, 8390–8394, 8779–8783.

Logothetis, N. K., Pauls, J., & Poggio, T. (1995). Shape recognition in the inferior temporal cortex of monkeys. *Current Biology, 5,* 552–563.

Miller, K. D., Keller, J., & Stryker, M. P. (1989). Ocular dominance column development: Analysis and simulation. *Science, 240,* 605–615.

Millikan, R. (1984). *Language, thought, and other biological categories.* Cambridge, MA: MIT Press.

Moody, J., & Darken, C. (1989). Fast learning in networks of locally tuned processing units. *Neural Computations, 1,* 281–289.

Moses, Y., Adini, Y., & Ullman, S. (1994). Face recognition: the problem of compensating for illumination changes. In J.-O. Eklundh (Ed.), *Proc. ECCV-94,* pp. 286–296. Springer-Verlag.

Nosofsky, R. M. (1988). Exemplar-based accounts of relations between classification, recognition, and typicality. *Journal of Experimental Psychology: Learning, Memory and Cognition, 14,* 700–708.

Nowlan, S. J., & Hinton, G. E. (1992). Simplifying neural networks by soft weight-sharing. *Neural Computation, 4,* 473–493.

Oja, E. (1982). A simplified neuron model as a principal component analyzer. *Journal of Mathematical Biology, 15,* 267–273.

Poggio, T., & Edelman, S. (1990). A network that learns to recognize three-dimensional objects. *Nature, 343,* 263–266.

Poincaré, H. (1913/1963). *Mathematics and science: Last essays.* New York: Dover. Translated by J. W. Bolduc.

Rolls, E. T., & Tovee, M. J. (1995). Sparseness of the neuronal representation of stimuli in the primate temporal visual cortex. *Journal of Neurophysiology, 73,* 713–726.

Rose, K., Gurewitz, E., & Fox, C. (1992). Vector quantization by deterministic annealing. *IEEE Transactions on Information Theory, 38,* 1249–1257.

Rosenblatt, F. (1958). The perceptron: A probabilistic model for information storage and organization in the brain. *Psych. Rev.,* 65:386–407. [Reprinted in *Neurocomputing* (MIT Press, 1988).]

Sanger, T. (1989). Optimal unsupervised learning in feedforward neural networks. AI Lab TR 1086, MIT.

Sejnowski, T. J. (1977). Storing covariance with nonlinearly interacting neurons. *Journal of Mathematical Biology, 4,* 303–321.

Shepard, R. N. (1962). The analysis of proximities: Multidimensional scaling with unknown distance function. part i. *Psychometrika, 27*(2), 125–140.

Shepard, R. N. (1966). Metric structures in ordinal data. *Journal of Mathematical Psychology*, *3*, 287–315.

Shepard, R. N. (1980). Multidimensional scaling, tree-fitting, and clustering. *Science*, *210*, 390–397.

Shepard, R. N. (1987). Toward a universal law of generalization for psychological science. *Science*, *237*, 1317–1323.

Shepard, R. N., & Cermak, G. W. (1973). Perceptual-cognitive explorations of a toroidal set of free-form stimuli. *Cognitive Psychology*, *4*, 351–377.

Shepard, R. N., & Chipman, S. (1970). Second-order isomorphism of internal representations: Shapes of states. *Cognitive Psychology*, *1*, 1–17.

Siedlecki, W., Siedlecka, K., & Sklansky, J. (1988). An overview of mapping techniques for exploratory pattern analysis. *Pattern Recognition*, *21*, 411–429.

Stone, C. J. (1982). Optimal global rates of convergence for nonparametric regression. *Annals of statistics*, *10*, 1040–1053.

Tverksy, A. (1977). Features of similarity. *Psychological Review*, *84*, 327–352.

Ullman, S., & Basri, R. (1991). Recognition by linear combinations of models. *IEEE Transactions on Pattern Analysis and Machine Intelligence*, *13*, 992–1005.

Waibel, A., Hanazawa, T., Hinton, G., Shikano, K., & Lang, K. (1989). Phoneme recognition using time-delay neural networks. *IEEE Transactions on ASSP*, *37*, 328–339.

Webb, A. R. (19959). Multidimensional-scaling by iterative majorization using radial basis functions. *Pattern Recognition*, *28*, 753–759.

Wigner, E. P. (1960). The unreasonable effectiveness of mathematics in the natural sciences. *Comm. Pure Appl. Math.*, *XIII*, 1–14.

Yamac, M. (1969). Can we do better by combining "supervised" and "nonsupervised" machine learning for pattern analysis. Ph.D. dissertation, Brown University.

Young, G., & Householder, A. S. (1938). Discussion of a set of points in terms of their mutual distances. *Psychometrika*, *3*, 19–22.

Young, M. P., & Yamane, S. (1992). Sparse population coding of faces in the inferotemporal cortex. *Science*, *256*, 1327–1331.

# INDEX

# CONTENTS OF RECENT VOLUMES

389

ISBN 0-12-543336-0

90051